What Others Are Saying about This Book . . .

Love and tenderness are palpable in a sensitive recount of this amazing historical memoir. This is NOT a one time read. A literary prism, relevant to the boardroom as it is to a book club or fireside/poolside read. Truly an inspirational legacy reminding us in the words of Proust that: "the voyage of discovery lies not in finding new landscapes, but in having new eyes."

—Diane Bruno, CISION MEDIA

An exciting and thoughtful book, part memoir, part history, part family saga, that reveals the triumphs and tragedies behind the many faces of Maybelline.

—Mark A. Clements, author, *Lorelei*

We are especially fascinated to slip vicariously into the lives of the rich and privileged yet cheer for the underdog who overcomes obstacles to astound doubters with his success. We are enthralled with the historical sweep of events whose repercussions live on to the present—all elements of this amazing story, which reads like a juicy novel but is a memoir distilled from nine hundred pages of family accounts from the 1920s to the present.

—Steve Hudis, producer, IMPACT Motion Pictures

Superb! An exciting tale that gives an insider's view into the genesis of a corporate giant. A wild ride, an enticing saga.

—Alan Andrews Ragland, son of Maybelline legend "Rags" Ragland

Spanning four generations, *The Maybelline Story* traces the founding of one of the true great family enterprises that spawned the billion-dollar cosmetic industry and reveals the glamour—and seedy underside—of sudden fortune and unrestrained vanity on the family dynasty behind it. Wow to seeing this on screen!

—Nina Siemaszko, actress, *The West Wing*

A richly told story of a forty-year, white-hot love triangle that fans the flames of a major worldwide conglomerate.

—Neil Shulman, MD, associate producer, *Doc Hollywood*

A truly inspirational story chronicling the journey and unwaivering faith of the family behind the rise of an iconic brand.

Brigitte Lamblot, Publisher, VIE Magazine

Even if you come away from reading this book thinking that the family dynasty created in the founding of Maybelline was a bit over the top, "over the top" was what was expected from the generation that brought it about. This story may read like a novel, but it is, alas, a true one!

—Nancy Williams Fesler, great niece of Tom Lyle Williams

We loved this!

—Holly Siegel, beauty editor, *NYLON* Magazine

This book has value beyond its capacity to glimpse history and even beyond its sheer joy to entertain. This exciting book provides insight into the nature of money, and inherent issues in building a dynasty.

—Kolie Crutcher III, CEO and publisher, *Get Money* magazine

Tom Lyle, my great-uncle—and the godfather of our family—made us all rich, in more ways than one! But it is hard for us to separate Maybelline from our family, because it was a family affair, literally. This is a story I lived and a family I love.

—William Preston Williams III

An interesting—and astonishing—account of the making of a mega-giant [Maybelline] and a cast of characters you won't believe! Entertaining and insightful.

—Charmaine Hammond, author, *On Toby's Terms*

Exciting stuff! A captivating story that uncovers the intriguing past behind one of America's most well-known cosmetic companies.

—Michele Marcotte, features editor, *The Daily Sentinel*

As an immigrant who escaped the tyranny of Communist Romania, I survived my ordeal because of the devotion and values learned at the knees of my parents. In this story, the values learned focused on the world of artifice . . . also learned at the knees of their parents . . . but oh what a different legacy. A jolting story.

—Aura Imbarus, author, *Out of the Transylvania Night*

A rich and colorful story. I guarantee you won't be able to put this book down! I only hope it goes to the big screen, and you can bet I'd like to play Evelyn!

—Marla Martenson, actress, author, *Diary of a Beverly Hills Matchmaker*

A most amazing story.

—John St. Augustine, author, *Living an Uncommon Life:*
Essential Lessons from 21 Extraordinary People

THE *Maybelline* STORY

and the Spirited Family Dynasty Behind It

SHARRIE WILLIAMS with BETTIE B. YOUNGS

BETTIE YOUNGS BOOKS

Health Communications, Florida • HarperCollins, Australia
Thomas Allen, Canada • PGUK, England • Phambili, South Africa
CK International, Korea • Swindon Book, Hong Kong
Times/Pansing, Singapore, Malaysia, Thailand • PT Gramedia, Indonesia
Ceil, Lebanon • Southern Publisher, New Zealand
Almaya, UAE • Micronesia Media, Guam • Mohammed Books, Trinidad

Disclaimer: This is a true story, and the characters and events
are real. However, in some cases, the names, descriptions, and
locations have been changed, and some events have been altered,
combined, or condensed for storytelling purposes, but the overall
chronology is an accurate depiction of the author's experience.

On the cover: Mildred Davis (the very first Hollywood
starlet used in a Maybelline ad), Evelyn Boecher Williams,
and screen star Betty Grable.

Cover design by Mark A. Clements and Jane Hagaman
Photo of Sharrie Williams by Vicki Lynn Gaines of Vicki Lynn Photography
Photograph of Bettie Youngs by Martin Mann Photography

BETTIE YOUNGS BOOKS PUBLISHING CO.
www.BettieYoungsBooks.com

If you are unable to order this book from your local bookseller,
you may order directly from the publisher.

Library of Congress Control Number: 2010930785

ISBN: 978-0-9843081-1-8
10 9 8 7 6 5 4 3 2 1
Printed on acid-free paper

Dedication

To the beloved
Pauline Elna MacDonald-Williams

January 17, 1924 – August 22, 2010

Contents

Part 1

An Idea Is Born (1912–1926)

Part 2

The Eyes Have It

The Start of Something Big (1927–1936)

Part 3

The Third Front (1937–1949)

Part 4
Fantasy vs. Reality (1950–1969)

Part 5
Miss Maybelline Reborn (1970–1979)

Foreword

I think that every girl I ever dated as a teenager had one of those pink and green tubes of Maybelline Great Lash mascara stashed in her purse. I know this because the contents of all those purses regularly spilled out of school lockers, from behind bleachers, out from under the seats of cars. If the purse's owner wasn't scrambling to hide her other feminine products, then she was diving for the mascara, because that was clearly the key to her enchanting doe-eyed beauty.

As I've grown older, gotten married, divorced, and begun dating all over again, I've seen the contents of many beautiful women's cosmetic bags. And there has always been a Maybelline product inside.

I recognize things like this because I'm a brand man myself. At an early age, I discovered the power of perception—specifically, the perception of value, which can be even more important than price itself. For example, the Tiffany brand is indomitable because one need only see the powder blue box and white satin ribbon to think that whatever is inside is premium—simply because it comes from Tiffany.

So I was delighted when I was asked to read *The Maybelline Story* and learned about the origins and growth of this modest company into the best-known eye beauty brand around the world. And what a story it is!

From humble beginnings in rural Kentucky to gangster-ridden Prohibition Chicago to Hollywood in the 1930s and '40s, and eventually to the whole world, this is a classic tale of a makeshift product that developed from one woman's innovative need to fix something else, and her brother's prescient understanding that she was onto something BIG!

In 1915, Mabel Williams singed her eyelashes and brows while cooking. Horrified that she no longer looked feminine, she concocted a mixture and applied it to her remaining lashes and brows, giving them some added sparkle and sheen. One of her brothers, Tom Lyle Williams, noticed the successful effect.

But he also noticed something more profound: a woman's eyes were her calling card. They could say many things: "Come look at me." "Coax me out of my bashfulness." "Yes, I'm flirting." "I'm interested in you." He appreciated beauty in all women, and their beauty spoke to him straight through their eyes. Tom Lyle wanted to reproduce his sister's formula to see whether women everywhere would pay a little to "glamour themselves."

All Tom Lyle needed was $500 and a rudimentary chemistry set to give his idea a real try. But amassing $500 in 1915 wasn't easy. So when his brother Noel agreed to loan him the money, he promised to repay him in full. Little did any of them realize then the astonishing return that Noel would receive on his investment.

For more than a half century, Maybelline operated as a private company owned by the Williams family. What Tom Lyle started as a small mail-order business eventually became an internationally recognized brand, acquired eighty-two years later by French conglomerate L'Oreal for over $700 million. I can tell you, it's one thing to recognize a winning product discovered by accident, and quite another to turn it into an empire that, for decades, transcended all competition and remains an icon to this day.

Unusual for such an enormously successful businessman, the unlikely legend Tom Lyle Williams kept a low personal profile and let his creativity speak through his work. And how creative he was: he was first to enlist movie stars to promote his products; his was one of the first companies to promote corporate social responsibility by supporting war bonds; first to take advantage of advertising on broadcast television; first to employ market research; and first to truly understand the buying power of women.

Surely such a creative man must have had a muse—and indeed he did. Although he named the company for his sister, his muse was actually his sister-in-law Evelyn. She was gorgeous, driven, and smart—in fact, often too smart for her own good.

The drama of the Maybelline story, as with many such sagas, lies in the intersection between the business of the Maybelline Company and the foibles of the family who ran it. Secrets existed, lies were told, and façades masqueraded as truth—often to protect the family from itself and always to protect Maybelline above all else.

Edison made light bulbs. Ford manufactured cars. Here's another great American rags-to-riches story. This time, the name is Williams. You won't forget it.

—Michael Levine, Founder,
Levine Communications and author, *Guerrilla P.R. 2.0*

Preface

Let me introduce myself. I am Alan "Rags" Ragland, son of another Rags Ragland—the marketing genius who played such a pivotal role in the expansion of a little company called Maybelline. It gives me great pleasure to reflect personally on this amazing success story.

Around 1930, during the first phase of the Great Depression, my father was the Midwestern sales manager of a commercial magazine largely directed at women. As part of his job, he made headquarters calls to key people, including Tom Lyle Williams, the proprietor of the Maybelline Company. At this time, Maybelline sold primarily via direct mail—but my father would help change that.

Many business people have marketing skills but lack imagination. Conversely, many creative, artistic people have imagination but lack business skills. My father, a jazz musician who worked his way to a business degree by playing clarinet and alto sax in the band of the legendary Bix Beiderbecke, had both. In fact, in time, Tom Lyle would come to call Dad "my bandleader."

Like Tom Lyle, my dad could readily see the exponential potential of Maybelline, if only the company had a sales and marketing strategist. "Put me in charge of sales, Mr. Williams," he told Tom Lyle, "and I will double your business in six months. If I don't, you can fire me."

The rest, as they say, is history.

With my father running the marketing department—in fact, for years he *was* the marketing department—Maybelline's sales soared. Together Tom Lyle and Rags set out to capture an ever greater marketplace. They created the Maybelline Eye Fashion Center, with its rotating rack displaying more than 130 Maybelline items and colors, and sold Maybelline eye products into chain drugstores and grocery stores. Innovative mavericks, these men! With Rags focused on marketing and Tom Lyle in charge of advertising, Maybelline's sales just kept climbing.

Then, in the early 1950s, Tom Lyle announced to Dad that he was going to move full-time from Chicago to the West Coast, where he would continue to handle consumer advertising while being able to "worry in comfort." Tom Lyle was a perfectionist and prone to worry and stress. Even after he moved to Los Angeles, he and Dad would talk on the phone for one or two hours each business day. What a team! They had such synergy.

Tom Lyle was a savvy and brilliant businessman. From the company's inception until its sale in 1968, he and a couple of associates handled the bulk of Maybelline's print and television advertising, inventing new and cutting-edge techniques still used to this day.

On a personal level, Tom Lyle was a profoundly generous and thoughtful human being, even after his little family-owned company became the most successful cosmetics company on the planet. He changed the lives of thousands of people with his charitable donations and his support of family members and friends. My father's compensation was set at 1 percent of Maybelline's gross sales—*gross* sales, not net—resulting in remuneration so enormous that the Internal Revenue Service investigated both him and Maybelline.

But for my father, being a part of the Maybelline story was not just about money. Dad truly loved his work. He also loved Tom Lyle. So did I. I fondly remember the elegant Tom Lyle, as handsome as any movie star, coming over to our home. I remember being a guest at his beautiful home on Airole Way in Bel Air. I remember him playing the piano at family gatherings and parties. I felt comfortable in his company because Tom Lyle, like my own father, was a classic, self-made man—a boy from small-town America who, through determination, great ideas, and plain old hard work, created an astonishingly successful company called Maybelline.

Enjoy this enticing story, an insider's view into the genesis of a corporate giant.

—Alan Andrews Ragland

Prologue
Smoke and Fire

At around one-thirty in the afternoon on March 2, 1978, two men stepped out of a stand of swamp pines on a six-acre estate on Lake Hamilton in Hot Springs, Arkansas. Each man carried a five-gallon tin of gasoline.

They walked to a paved driveway and approached a huge, ornate iron gate, scrolled with the words Maybelline Manor. The gate stood open as they knew it would be. They walked through, and soon a beautiful house appeared across a wide swath of lawn. It was a sprawling structure with a couple of taller, peaked sections crowning it. On the ground floor of one of these sections was the front entrance, but the men avoided that. They walked around the house to the rear, beneath a sky swarming with clouds as black as India Ink. Thunder and lightning boomed and quivered across the lake.

Awkward with their burdens, the men approached the unlocked back door. They slipped inside, into an expansive living room with a ceiling that seemed to go up forever. To one side, a hallway crowded with framed photographs led to a closed door. The rich heiress would be on the far side of that door, in a sound stupor, after her big night the evening before. The men went efficiently about their business. There was the thing with the doorknob, the thing with the wigs, and of course the thing with the gasoline. As they worked their way back toward the rear door, one of the men devoted extra attention to the hallway with all the pictures: the portraits and group photos of generations of rich, handsome folks staring down at him in their expensive clothes. Men, women, children, a newborn or two. The beautiful people.

The two men trailed long fuses out the back door, into a blustery spring wind that smelled of lake water and the oncoming rain. The rain, if it arrived at all, would be too late.

The fuses lit just fine.

The men were climbing into their motorboat, which had been moored just beyond the stand of swamp pines, when the sound of three small explosions came to them through the trees. The pops didn't bother them, of course; nor would they bother anyone else. This was Arkansas; people hunted here even in March. Guns going off were heard all the time.

Their boat was halfway across the lake when the first feather of smoke rose into the wind behind it.

Part 1

An Idea Is Born
(1912–1926)

One
Inventing Tom
Lyle Williams

"Many a wreck is hid under a good paint job," my grandmother, "Miss Maybelline," always told me. That and she loved, and often repeated, Dorothy Lamour's line, "Glamour is just sex that got civilized." And so the Maybelline story begins, as it should, with illusion: the illusion of perpetual, larger-than-life beauty. As a fifteen-year-old, my great-uncle Tom Lyle Williams loved movies in a way that was different from that of most people his age. I imagine him poised over the film projector in the back of the nickelodeon where he worked after school for six dollars a week, watching a silent movie flickering in the darkness while a pianist bangs out ragtime melodies in time with the action on the screen. The year is 1911, and even a small farming town like Morganfield, bordering the coalfields of western Kentucky, provides enough business to keep a movie theater thriving.

But for Tom Lyle, as everyone calls him, working in the nickelodeon is not merely a job. He does not just project the films, and he does not just watch them. He is absorbed by them. Through them he can slip into realities utterly unlike Morganfield's, and the people who dwell there. Mary Pickford in *In the Sultan's Garden,* so ethereal with her blonde curls and lambent eyes, so captivating in her every expression and gesture . . . it's a jolt to look from her to the audience of farmers and their wives, all weary faces and drab clothing.

This is the mystery that holds Tom Lyle spellbound in the darkness: what makes the performers flickering on the screen so much more attractive and fascinating than ordinary people? Even his sisters Mabel and Eva, whom he loves dearly, are so plain in comparison to Mary Pickford. And can any man Tom Lyle has ever seen in person compare in handsomeness to the sleek, square-chinned Wallace Reid or the dapper Dell Henderson? What is their secret, these stars, these larger-than-life miracles? Are they born special, or is it something they learn? And if it is something they learn, can Tom Lyle Williams of Morganfield, Kentucky, acquire that knowledge too?

One day Unk Ile, as I came to call him, would tell me how he studied the film stars: how they stood, how their gazes caught and held the audience's, how they moved their bodies. He noted the clothing they wore and the way they combed their hair, searching for the key that would unlock their secrets.

His neighbors in Morganfield had already pegged him as a hopeless dreamer, a lad who would never amount to anything. And such a shame. Did he not come from one of the better local families? Was his father not both a gentleman farmer and the town sheriff, a tough, no-nonsense fellow more likely to toss a person in jail than discuss the interplay of light and shadow on the silver screen?

And yet it was the art and artifice behind beauty that would one day tear our clan away from its deep Kentucky roots and sweep us into a new world of glamour and fortune. It was the desire to possess this magical power and all that went with it that eventually seduced us all, as surely as if we had been sitting with Unk Ile in the nickelodeon back in 1911.

To this day, I personally identify with Unk Ile more than I do with his younger brother, Preston—my own grandfather. For one thing, Preston died before I was born, but that is not the main reason. I relate to my great-uncle's thoughtful, sensitive nature—which by all accounts was the antithesis of my grandfather's mercurial misbehaviors. Both men were handsome, but again in different ways—one sunlight, one moonlight. My great-grandmother said that of all the children, her fourth, Tom Lyle—with his head of curly blond hair, his twinkling brown eyes, his provocative personality—was the most beautiful.

Dreamer or not, Tom Lyle loved, respected, and wanted to please his parents. It wasn't always easy. Thomas Jefferson "TJ" Williams and his wife, Susan, assumed Tom Lyle would one day become a gentleman farmer like his father and grandfathers, although other acceptable career options included professor or priest. But when Tom Lyle looked in the mirror, he saw none of these things. He saw a boy who didn't match the man living inside his skin. At age fifteen, he had less muscular definition than his thirteen-year-old brother, Preston, and no facial hair at all. No wonder nobody took him seriously. How could he expect to win the heart of Bennie Gibbs, the only girl in Morganfield as lovely as the actresses on the silver screen? She seemed to like him, holding his gaze a moment longer than necessary when she came into the nickelodeon or when they bumped into each other in town, but that wasn't enough. He needed more. He needed her to know he was special, too. For inspiration, he headed straight for the family Bible, which he slid aside in favor of what was always kept beneath it: the *Sears, Roebuck and Co.* catalogue.

For Tom Lyle, the catalogue offered sojourns into the sophisticated existence he craved, an overview of the desires, habits, and customs of people far more worldly than his neighbors—or himself. The catalogue so fascinated him that he had taught himself to read, at age four, by poring over its product descriptions.

But that wasn't all. The greatest thing about the catalogue was that through the magic of mail order, a small-town boy like Tom Lyle had access to the same products as the most stylish city dweller. He turned to the well-thumbed page advertising motorcycles. He had practically memorized the information by now, but he went over it again. The black Pierce four-cylinder had an appealing aura of menace, but was far too expensive for a nickelodeon operator. The Pope one-cylinder was much cheaper, but it seemed so ordinary. Then there was the Indian two-cylinder: candy-apple red, with the sexy curves of a woman—and inexpensive enough to save for.

Although Tom Lyle was every bit the dreamer townsfolk thought him to be, he also possessed the pragmatism of any hard-bitten farmer. He calculated that he would need two months to save what he needed using his nickelodeon salary alone—too long to suit him. So he supplemented that income with earnings from a business he had started at the age of nine: selling baseball cards. Although he was a fan of the sport and loved the pictures, player information—and advertising copy—on the cards, he mostly viewed his collection as an investment. At age ten he had begun selling off his most prized cards, then used the profits to buy more highly collectible cards and sold those. By his teenage years he had expanded his business to include the trading cards found in cigarette packages, which featured photos of portions of scantily clad women that could be pieced together to form a pinup. He charged the highest prices for a pretty face or an exposed ankle.

Another quality Tom Lyle possessed in volume was determination. In only six weeks, he had amassed the formidable sum of forty dollars. He placed his order for the Indian, and only then admitted the deed to his parents. They scowled and lectured, but did not forbid him to have the motorcycle.

When the Indian finally arrived, gleaming and beautiful, Tom Lyle was ready. He had already purchased goggles and leather gloves, and borrowed a red-fringed scarf. He brushed his initials onto the cycle's rear fender out in the barn, then climbed onto the saddle. When he kick-started the engine, he stopped being an ordinary small-town boy. On the instant he transformed into a dashing, irresistible hero like those he saw flickering across the movie screen each night.

Chickens squawked and feathers flew as he took the bike for a few turns around the barnyard. Then, with his whole family watching and the red scarf fluttering around his neck, he struck out on the road that ran along the Ohio River. His destination: the home of thirteen-year-old Bennie Gibbs, with her flawless skin and sparkling eyes.

Tom Lyle knew he cut an impressive figure as he sped past Morganfield's red brick courthouse, the library, and the town square with its big American flag flying high. He roared along at a breathtaking thirty-five miles per hour, then accelerated to forty, passing fields of tobacco and hay, fruit orchards and pastures, feeling the glory of the ride down to his toes. In a mere twenty minutes, he covered the twelve miles to Millburn where Bennie lived.

Mrs. Gibbs wouldn't allow her daughter to get on "that contraption," so Tom Lyle parked the cycle and he and Bennie wandered away on foot, holding hands as they strolled past the rosebushes and the massive cottonwood trees. When they kissed for the first time, it was almost an accident.

The afternoon slipped blissfully past, until Tom Lyle noticed the position of the sun. "Oh, gosh, I have to get home! I can't be late for dinner."

"Not even a minute?" Bennie asked.

"Not even a second." He began hauling her back toward her house by the hand. "My father's very strict about the family eating together. I don't want to get thrown in jail."

"*Jail?*"

"Don't forget, Dad's the Morganfield sheriff."

"But *jail*? His own son?"

Tom Lyle laughed. "My brother Preston's already been there twice—once for running away into the woods, and another time for not doing his chores."

"But that's *terrible!*"

"Not for Preston. He just sat around reading dime novels and ignoring Dad's lectures. But I've got a motorcycle to worry about—my folks are already upset I bought it."

They had reached the Gibbs house. "When will I see you again?" Bennie asked Tom Lyle as he released her hand.

"Soon, if I make it home in time for dinner. Pray for me!" And he leaped on the motorcycle and kicked the engine alive.

"Take the old Cummings road!" Bennie yelled through a cloud of blue smoke. "It's shorter!"

In his rearview mirror, Tom Lyle saw her waving her hankie and blowing him a kiss.

He urged the bike to nearly fifty miles per hour down the tree-lined dirt road, and made good time until he spotted a muddy little gulch cutting across the path ahead. Decision time. He could turn around and find another route, or he could stop and try to muscle the heavy bike across the gap, both at the cost of valuable time.

He opened the throttle as wide as it would go and, as the ditch yawned in front of him, shifted his weight back. He felt the bike sail miraculously free of the ground—and crashed.

When he raised his head from the dust, coughing and groaning, he saw the Indian lying across the road in a battered, mud-smeared heap. He himself had suffered only a few scrapes and bruises, but the bike would not start. He managed to half-walk, half-drag it the remaining distance home, crestfallen, hurting, muddy, and worst of all, late.

TJ Williams was sitting on the porch, a toothpick in his mouth, when Tom Lyle limped into view, pushing the battered, muddy remains of his brand-new motorcycle. Once TJ ascertained that his son was in one piece, he exploded. "Goddamn it, Tommy Lyle! Your mother's scared half to death! You *will* get rid of that infernal piss-ant death trap."

"Yes, sir," Tom Lyle said.

But first he fixed it. Impelled by the same determination that would serve him well throughout his life, he locked himself in the barn with the machine, took it apart, cleaned it, straightened what needed to be straightened, and put it all back together.

When he rolled the resurrected motorcycle out of the barn, his parents gaped.

"That thing still run?" TJ asked.

"Yes, sir, it does. I mean to sell it."

TJ circled the bike, running his hands over the paint, then slapped Tom Lyle on the shoulder. "Well, I guess you've earned the right to keep it if you want."

Susan shot her husband an alarmed look. "You mean he can keep it *if . . .*"

"*If* you give us your word you won't pull any more damn-fool stunts on it," TJ said.

"You have my word," Tom Lyle said.

That was another thing about Tom Lyle: he was a man of his word. For another year, he rode the bike, a rolling trophy of his persistence. But it did nothing to enhance his image in Morganfield. Townsfolk gossiped that he had been a show-off ever since he was five and hung up posters billing himself as "Tommy Lyle, the Great Actor-Bat" to advertise the first of many shows he and his little sister, Eva, performed. Instead of praising his energy and gumption, people wrote him off as a dreamer. All the noisy motorbike did was add new pejoratives to the list: flashy, flighty, vain.

Tom Lyle ignored the talk as best he could, but vowed he would show them all someday.

In fact, he was thinking about the future more and more nowadays, as he fell deeper in love with Bennie Gibbs. He bought her trinkets and carved their initials in the big oak tree by the one-room schoolhouse. They began stealing away to meet in secluded places. This was wonderful, but as usual, Tom Lyle wanted more.

Two days before Christmas, the day Bennie turned fourteen, he took her for a cherry cola at the new soda fountain in town, where he presented her with his latest purchase from the Sears catalogue: a ring featuring a ruby in a setting of fourteen karat gold. "This is just the beginning," he assured her as he slid the ring on her finger. "I've got three hundred dollars in savings, and I'm going to turn it into a fortune. I promise."

Bennie stared in awe at the ring. "I believe you, Tom Lyle, but..." She hesitated. Her parents' opinion of her boyfriend wasn't much better than that of most people in town. "But *how?*"

"Like this." He whipped out a pamphlet. "If I go to Florida and grow vegetables in the winter, I can ship them up north for a huge profit."

She frowned at the pamphlet. Tom Lyle clutched her hands. "One of these days I'm going to be able to support you, Bennie. You understand what I'm saying?"

She looked back at the ring, and gripped his fingers hard and smiled into his eyes. "I love you, Tom Lyle."

Although what happened next was never discussed in detail by anyone, including Unk Ile, I can visualize it. Three weeks later, on Tom Lyle's sixteenth birthday, I imagine him and Bennie sneaking off to an abandoned log cabin or barn. Whatever the exact setting, one thing is certain: on that day, fourteen-year-old Bennie Gibbs gave Tom Lyle the most wonderful present he had ever received.

And several months later, she gave him something else—a piece of news delivered through tears and sobbing: she was pregnant. "I'm so scared, Tommy Lyle. My daddy is a real strict Baptist. He'll just kill me."

Tom Lyle the dreamer, bursting with love and pride, did not share her fear. Of course Mr. Gibbs would be upset—a daughter pregnant at fourteen by a sixteen-year-old Catholic boy! But for the sake of his grandchild, surely he would come around. "Bennie," Tom Lyle said, "don't worry. I'll take care of you and our baby, no matter what."

For practical advice he turned to his big brother, Noel, always so steady and dependable. Noel's answer was simple: "You must do the right thing by her, Tommy Lyle."

This was exactly what Tom Lyle wanted to hear. Without speaking to Bennie's parents, he asked Bennie to be his wife, and they hopped on the Indian and rode off.

I picture that April day as lovely and sunny. I imagine their euphoria as they reached the ferry that took them across the Ohio River, brown and swollen with spring rains, to Old Shawneetown in Illinois. Bennie knew there was a justice of the peace there because her own mother had gotten married in the historic trading town. It was also far enough away from Morganfield that nobody would know who they were, or how young.

In a three-minute ceremony, the same judge, now eighty-two, who had heard the vows of her parents, pronounced Tom Lyle and Bennie husband and wife.

The marriage didn't last much longer than the ceremony. When the newly-weds returned to Morganfield, the first place they went was Bennie's house, to tell her parents about their elopement.

Instead of offering congratulations, Mr. Gibbs snatched up a broomstick. "How dare you marry my daughter without my consent?" he roared, jabbing the young man out of the house. "Do you actually think I'd allow my Bennie to marry a heathen Catholic? Get off my property and don't ever come back!"

The marriage was quickly annulled, but the other issue was not so easily erased. As Bennie's swelling belly became more obvious, she was sent off to live with her aunt in Ohio in hopes of keeping her condition a secret. Such hopes proved futile. Soon everyone in Morganfield knew what had happened between Bennie Gibbs and Tom Lyle—and sure enough, scandal ensued. Whenever Tom Lyle entered Morganfield, he encountered cold silence or head-shaking contempt.

He couldn't believe his situation. How had all his good intentions and studied charm led to such disastrous results? When newspaper headlines blared *TITANIC SINKS,* he half wished he had been aboard the doomed vessel.

Since he no longer made the long trips on his motorcycle to see Bennie, he felt little joy in riding it, and decided to put it up for sale. After several weeks without an offer, he realized that nobody in Morganfield could afford the fifty dollars he was asking—or else nobody wanted the bike because it was *his.*

One day at the barber shop, glumly paging through a copy of *Popular Mechanics,* he came to the classified ads, and had an idea—an idea no one had ever tried before, as far as he knew. Rushing home, he penned a fifteen-word "motorcycle for sale" ad and sent it to the magazine, along with a dollar fifty to pay for it.

After that he checked the mailbox on a daily basis, certain his brainstorm would pay off in no time.

Nothing.

One evening, after he had sat through dinner stewing about the lack of response to his ad, he became aware of how silent the table had become, and looked up to see TJ and Susan ushering the other children out of the room. When his parents came back and took their seats, TJ—who, as both sheriff and the county Tax Collector had lost an eye in a shootout over property rights some years earlier—popped out the replacement glass eye, polished it on his sleeve, and put it back in said, "This scandal about Bennie and the baby is hurting the rest of our family, Tom Lyle."

Tom Lyle hung his head. "I know, Papa. I'm sorry."

TJ sounded weary rather than angry. "Our people came over on the Mayflower. My granddaddy Josiah was a magistrate while he farmed these five hundred acres. We've got a tradition to uphold."

Tom Lyle realized his mother had the Bible on her lap, opened to her family tree. Tears trembled in her eyes. "Tom Lyle, I can't hold my head up in town anymore. I hear whispers wherever I go. We all do."

He glanced back and forth between his parents. "What are you saying?"

TJ leaned forward. "Son, we think it's best if you leave home. Leave Morganfield. Your brother Noel got himself a good job up in Chicago; you could go up there and stay with him, find your way up there."

The rest of the lecture was a blur. The injustice of being exiled filled Tom Lyle with shame, despair, and rage unlike anything he had ever felt before. Hadn't he done the honorable thing, marrying Bennie with every intention of supporting her and their child? Was it his fault her parents had stripped him of that honor? Was it his fault people liked to wag their tongues?

He rose to his feet. "If you want me to leave, I'll leave."

Then something happened that would change the course of my great uncle's life: his advertisement for the Indian got a response. And not just one, but a dozen over the course of a few days, each envelope contained a money order for fifty dollars. A dozen orders! Of course he would have to return all but one, but the incredible fact remained: he could have sold twelve motorcycles with that single ad.

He dug out the pamphlet about Florida produce that he had shown Bennie and lost himself in its vivid portrayal of profits to be made. Photos showed crowds of bundled-up Northerners waiting in line at the market for so-called "late" vegetables grown in the Deep South. His parents wanted him to leave? Fine. But forget Chicago and some dreary railroad job like his brother's—he'd go to Florida and get rich.

Anger and resentment solidified into resolve. Counting his savings and the income from the bike, he had enough stake money to make a success of himself. Then he would win his Bennie back and be the husband and father he knew he could be.

The kind of father who would never send his son away in shame.

At the far end of his first solo train trip, Tom Lyle stepped into the Florida heat and promptly used all his savings to purchase a vegetable tract outside Orlando. He persuaded a local fifteen-year-old boy to help him cultivate his first crop, and for several months he worked hard at farming—the one thing he had been certain he did not want to do. But it would be worth it. When he returned to Morganfield in glory, that would show the Gibbs family that he was a worthy son-in-law—and everyone else that he was not a ne'er-do-well dreamer.

The crops were growing beautifully when he received a letter from Ohio announcing that Cecil Anderson Williams had been born to Bennie Gibbs on September 9, 1912. Tom Lyle was delighted to see that despite her father's objections, Bennie had put "Williams" on the baby's birth certificate.

A month later, when the frosts set in up north, he and his assistant harvested their crop. That was when Tom Lyle discovered that the cost of shipping produce up north was prohibitively high. He couldn't pay for shipping and still make a profit.

He lost everything.

Returning penniless to Morganfield took all the emotional reserves he could muster, but his parents seemed to think his banishment had done its job. His father discussed plans for Tom Lyle to help run the farm and possibly even become a deputy sheriff in a few years.

Tom Lyle wasn't too keen on either idea—except that it meant he could be near Bennie and their son. That made it worth considering.

He had finally met Cecil for the first time, through a bit of romantic subterfuge that defeated his ban from the Gibbs farm. A friend of his named Lucy arranged for Bennie to come over to visit for a day. Bennie didn't know that Tom Lyle was also on his way, walking three miles through the rain carrying a bunch of flowers. When he knocked on his friend's door, Lucy opened it—and there behind her was beautiful Bennie, rocking and breast-feeding their baby in the parlor.

Tom Lyle dropped to his knees in front of her. "You look like a goddess."

Bennie sobbed as she swaddled the baby and held him out to his father.

Surely the love manifested in their child would bind them together forever.

Two

A Thousand Dimes a Day

I once saw an old family portrait that included a young, expressive face I didn't recognize. "Who's that?" I asked my great-aunt Mabel, Tom Lyle's older sister. "Our Pearl," she said, and I realized I was looking at Unk Ile's oldest brother, the beloved firstborn, who had died of pneumonia at age nineteen.

That tragedy had hung over the Williams family for many joyless years, and Tom Lyle hated the idea of causing his parents still more pain. He had brought disgrace on not one but two families, yet he refused to give up his dream of regaining his wife and son. The thing was, he could never do that by staying in Morganfield as a farmer or a deputy under the disapproving gaze of so many eyes.

So he turned his thoughts north, toward Chicago, where his twenty three-year-old brother, Noel, worked as a bookkeeper for the Illinois Central Railroad. The idea of moving there, which had sounded like exile a year earlier, now appealed to him. For one thing, in the big city he would be just another young man, rather than an object of gossip. For another, where better than a fast-growing metropolis to fulfill his dream of owning his own business?

After scraping together a few dollars for a train ticket, he sent a message by wire: *Dear Noel, arriving Oct 20. Hope you have room on the floor for me.*

Ironically, TJ and Susan were now opposed to him leaving Morganfield, but Tom Lyle begged until they gave in. He promised his mother that if things didn't work out, he would return and perhaps become a priest.

So it was that Tom Lyle Williams made the long trip to the shore of Lake Michigan, riding the train along with hordes of other rural Americans hoping to find better-paying jobs in the face of fierce competition.

The mammoth train station in Chicago connected people, livestock, and products from coast to coast and border to border, and was so overwhelming that Tom Lyle almost melted with relief when Noel met him at the platform. They walked fifteen blocks to an old boarding house situated between the West Side and the rough South Side. The brothers had to cross from one sidewalk to the other to avoid the beggars, drunks, con artists, and hookers who loitered in alleys or worked the streets. As Tom Lyle looked around in astonishment, Noel explained that by that year of 1912, the population of Chicago had ballooned to almost 1.7 million, with new apartment buildings and boarding houses springing up all over.

"But you'll be sharing my room for now, little brother," he said.

Noel's boarding house skirted a slum of overcrowded tenement buildings, flagged with ragged gray laundry, cluttered with refuse, and rife with the stink of inadequate sewage disposal.

"Did you hear Teddy Roosevelt got shot a few days ago?" Noel said as they started up a narrow staircase. "That happened not too far from here."

"Is it true his glasses saved his life?"

"The bullet hit the case in his pocket, and didn't go very far into his chest. Roosevelt went ahead and finished his speech before he let them take him the hospital. Now there's a real man!"

Finally they reached the fifth floor, and Noel opened the door to his dollar-fifty-a-week accommodations. "It's not much; in fact it's the cheapest room in the house. Toilet down the hall. Baths cost twenty-five cents at a bathhouse down the block."

"It's fine," Tom Lyle said. He dropped his satchel on the floor he would be sleeping on. It was an improvement on the dirt floor of his tool shed in Florida.

The next day he looked through the jobs section of the newspaper and circled a single item:

MONTGOMERY WARD AND COMPANY
order-filler, $8.00 a week

Another auspicious decision.

I like to think Montgomery Ward hired Unk Ile because he impressed somebody there with his familiarity with mail-order catalogues. In any case, it was the ideal job for the man who had been taught to read by Sears and Roebuck. Founder Aaron Montgomery Ward had launched the revolutionary idea of a mail-order catalogue with a single page in 1872. Forty years later, when Tom Lyle hired on, the Ward catalogue had thickened to 540 pages. Sometimes referred to as the "Wish Book," it set Tom Lyle's mind spinning around the idea of creating his own mail-order business. He studied the language of the product descriptions as avidly as if he had to pass a test on them.

Soon he was able to send Bennie and the baby two of the eight dollars he earned each week. The rest he saved, even walking the three miles to and from Montgomery Ward each day to avoid a ten-cent trolley fare. He often skipped meals, and he refused to buy an overcoat despite Chicago's knife-sharp winter winds.

Noel shook his head. "You look like a rake."

"Noel, I plan to start my own mail-order business, and that takes money. I'm willing to go without until I achieve my goal. I did it before."

"And look where it got you. This time you won't even have a pile of vegetables to eat if things go wrong. Seriously, Tom Lyle, you have to learn to be more practical."

"I'd rather be rich," Tom Lyle said.

When the holidays arrived, Noel went back to Morganfield to visit his sweetheart, Frances, but Tom Lyle chose to remain in Chicago. He wasn't ready to face the townspeople down there. Not yet.

One day, as he hung around the advertising department at Montgomery Ward, he met a young man named Emery Shaver, who wrote ad copy part time while studying literature at the University of Chicago. His ultimate goal, he said, was to become a playwright. Tom Lyle found him fascinating: charming, intelligent, and self-assured—a born salesman, the kind of man who could talk a shell off a turtle's back. Barely twenty, Emery was dapper in style and dress, and spoke with the warm, smooth tones Tom Lyle had always imagined film stars must have in real life. Moreover, he shared Tom Lyle's driving ambition and belief that hard work would lead to success.

Tom Lyle shared his own plans with his new friend. "Sounds wonderful," Emery said. "Do you have a typewriter?"

"A typewriter?"

"How else are you going to write your own mail-order catalogue?"

"Good question," Tom Lyle said, almost as amused at his own naiveté as Emery was. He promptly invested part of his savings in a secondhand typewriter and taught himself how to use it. Then, after negotiating wholesale prices, he attempted to sell imported fifty-cent safety razors, risqué postcards, and other novelty items through individual advertisements placed in various publications.

For the next two years he experimented with buying and selling all kinds of inexpensive things, but none of them caught on.

"Well, Tommy Lyle, like I always told you, it was a crackpot scheme anyway," Noel said. He was sick of having their tiny floor space crowded with the junk Tom Lyle called "inventory." "Please don't waste any more of your hard-earned money on these frivolous ideas. Take a job with the railroad. Start at the bottom and work your way up. The railroad business is booming and will only get better."

But Tom Lyle refused to give up on his dream. By now he had located a wholesale company that sold easily-mailed novelties: comic pictures, postcards, and trick items like sneezing powder and itching powder. He purchased samples of twenty different items and had a pamphlet-sized catalogue printed. Then he wrote a one-inch ad:

Fascinating pictures, post cards, tricks, novelties, etc.
Send dime for samples and catalogue.

This time he gambled all his savings—as well as some of Noel's—to place the ad in a mail-order magazine called *The Household Guest*.

"You're insane," Noel said. "And so am I for backing you up. I have the feeling I'm going to regret this."

For the next five days, Tom Lyle lived to check the mail—and then, on the sixth day, a dozen letters arrived at the boarding house, each containing a silver dime.

"I don't believe it," Noel said. But he was smiling.

In thirty days, Tom Lyle received enough dimes to repeat the advertisement and still make a fifty-dollar profit. He promptly placed the same ad in other mail-order publications, and the influx of dimes increased. Within a couple of weeks he received almost two thousand letters—and two thousand dimes. Some customers also ordered additional items from the small catalogue he sent out with every filled order.

Tom Lyle felt thrilled; perhaps he had finally found his niche in the world. He placed still more ads. The flow of income kept increasing.

He and Noel moved from the cheapest room in the house to two-bunk accommodations.

In 1914, at the age of eighteen and having been in Chicago for two years, Tom Lyle Williams was a serious businessman, making real money. He gave his notice to Montgomery Ward and asked Emery Shaver to join him in his new novelty-catalogue business. Emery agreed and, in celebration of leaving "the Ward," suggested they go to Weeghman Park and watch the opening game of the Chicago Federal League baseball team, the Chicago Whales. Tom Lyle, who had taken almost no time off since arriving in Chicago, was delighted by the invitation and eager to see some of the athletes he had admired on trading cards.

Emery picked him up at the boarding house in what he described as his father's new car, a Packard.

"Whew!" Tom Lyle admired the hood ornament. "What's your dad do for a living?"

"Real estate investment. He always has the best car in Chicago."

"I'm not used to such luxury." Tom Lyle climbed into the passenger seat and inhaled the new leather smell. "But I'd sure love to *get* used to it."

Three

A Secret
from the Harem

In 1915, Tom Lyle wired his sister Mabel to come to Chicago and help him run his budding business. This was no longer the surprising request it would have once been. Women were beginning to defy their traditional roles, taking jobs outside the home, holding suffragist rallies, flying airplanes across the English Channel, redefining themselves in every way.

Plus, Tom Lyle suspected Mabel wanted out of the family home almost as much as he had.

He was right, although her reasons were very different from what his had been. In truth, Mabel was a bit plain and not getting younger; she feared she would become an old maid if she stayed any longer in Morganfield, where she had already met all the potential husbands.

In August, she moved to Chicago and began helping fill orders, which by then were coming in at the rate of a thousand a day—so fast that Tom Lyle had already hired five additional girls to handle the money and ship out postcards and novelties.

Mabel calculated that one thousand dimes a day came to $36,500 a year—the equivalent to well over half a million dollars today—and suggested to her brothers that they move out of the boarding house to an apartment where she could cook for them as well as fulfill her other duties. Tom Lyle, always frugal, preferred to stay where they were a little longer so he could put every dime he made back into advertising. Mabel agreed to the delay on two conditions: "I'd like have a room of my own, and I'd like to make you some of Mama's home cooking on a real stove once in a while."

The owner of the boarding house, Mrs. O'Brien, granted Mabel access to the stove, provided she help prepare supper for the other boarders on Sunday afternoons after church. Mabel was happy to oblige, but asked another favor in return: to ride with Mrs. O'Brien to the Old St. Patrick's Catholic Church each Sunday.

After a couple of weeks, Mabel, always the virtuous sister, had her two brothers in church on their knees thanking God for their blessings. In Morganfield, the Williamses may have been ostracized for being Catholic, but in Chicago they fit right in.

Mabel also had an unexpected passion. Although she would leave the room when Noel and Tom Lyle discussed politics and world events, such as the ongoing Turkish massacre of the Armenians or the sinking of the Lusitania by a German U-boat, she was quick to discuss Lillian Gish and her latest film, *Birth of a Nation*. In order to keep up to date on the latest dish on Hollywood personalities, she regularly read the lurid gossip magazines of the time.

Ironically, it was Mabel's enthusiasm for this hobby that set the stage for the next big change.

One morning, Mabel was making cake frosting by melting sugar in a pan on the stove. As she leaned over to stir it, a flame shot up into her face, singeing away her eyebrows and eyelashes. She chipped ice from the ice block and pressed it to her burning forehead until the pain abated, then stared dejectedly at her reflection in the looking glass. The finely-shaped brows and dark eyelashes that had given definition to the unrefined lines of her face were gone. She looked like an unfinished mannequin. How long would it take the hairs to grow back? What if they never did?

"Well," she said to the mirror, "your life is ruined. No man will want you now. Mother will be so happy to know you'll soon be entering a convent."

But Mabel was as plucky and clever as any of the Williams clan. That evening, when Tom Lyle looked in on her to say goodnight, he grimaced at the scorched smell in her room. Then he looked closer. His sister sat in front of her vanity, burning a piece of cork with a match. As Tom Lyle watched, she collected the ash in the palm of her left hand.

"What're you doing, Sis?"

"It's a harem secret," she said, scooping a bit of petroleum jelly out of a jar with the tip of her right index finger and stirring it into the ash. "I read about it in *Photoplay* magazine." Using the fingertip, she carefully dabbed sooty goo onto her sparse brows and the stubs of her eyelashes. "Vaseline is good for everything. It soothes burns and will help my eyebrows and lashes grow back faster. Meanwhile, the ash and a little coal dust make what hairs are left show up better. See?"

She turned to face her brother. Tom Lyle's mouth fell open. The charcoal eyebrows and lashes next to his sister's porcelain skin made for a dramatic and lovely contrast. With no more than a blob of Vaseline, some incinerated cork and a bit of coal dust, Mabel had not only resurrected her appearance, she had *improved* it.

"Your eyes are beautiful," he said. "They make you look like Gloria Swanson or . . . Lillian Gish!"

Why hadn't he realized this before? The magic key to the beauty of Hollywood goddesses was not their figures or their wardrobes or their smiles. It was their eyes.

The next morning, Tom Lyle set out to learn what sort of eye-enhancing products already existed in the marketplace. His interest was not casual. He knew that he could sell only so much sneezing powder before interest trailed off; in fact, orders of his novelties were already thinning. He needed a new product to market, and the transformation of Mabel from plain sister to glamorous woman had fired his imagination.

But he quickly discovered that women were just beginning to accept wearing cosmetics of any kind, after shunning them during the prim Victorian era. Creams and powders were fairly common, but products to enhance the beauty of eyes?

"Oh, noooo! No, indeed," said the woman selling beauty products at Marshall Fields and Co. "We don't sell that sort of thing."

"I don't mean to be rude," Tom Lyle said, "but why not?"

"Because no proper woman would ask for them."

Tom Lyle had his doubts about that, but thanked her and moved on. He discovered the existence of a crude colored wax that was heated and stuck on the lashes to create a beaded effect, but this product was used only on stage. In one store, a woman behind the beauty counter whispered that she knew someone who made a "decoction" from ground walnut hulls, based on a recipe from the charmingly named book, *Homely Girls,* by Sarah Jane Pierce.

In short, Tom Lyle confirmed that the market for eye beauty products was wide open. The problem was that no such products existed, unless you counted secret concoctions bubbling on stovetops across America.

Lying in bed at night, he envisioned a mail-order advertisement featuring a photo of Mabel with her alluring new eyes, alongside a bold slogan like *A magic potion for more beautiful eyes* or *Making any man want you*. He hadn't quite found the right angle yet, but he would. He was inspired. His sister had made herself beautiful through artifice. She would be the muse of his company's new product line—because if plain Mabel could do it, any woman could.

He was ready to start shipping this new product immediately, if only it existed. The fact that it didn't exist was only a minor obstacle.

He would just have to create the product himself.

Ablaze with his vision, Tom Lyle skipped a day of regular work to experiment with Mabel's initial smudgy concoction. His friend Carl had a chemistry set, and, surrounded by dozens of test tubes and Petri dishes, Tom Lyle crouched for hours in Carl's dank, uncomfortable basement, mixing and testing different versions of what he quickly dubbed the "eye dye." The best mixture included Vaseline and a little cottonseed oil, which congealed quickly when mixed with any sort of powder, such as something from the chemistry set called "carbon black." A drop of safflower oil provided sheen.

At last he had a product—or so he thought, until Mabel dabbed it on her lashes, and it ran straight down into her eyes, with painful results.

Frustrated yet more determined than ever, Tom Lyle decided to take the train to Detroit to visit a wholesale drug manufacturing company called Park-Davis. Noel and Emery went with him and watched as Tom Lyle described to a chemist what he wanted: a fine, pure product that would be beneficial for eyebrows and eyelashes.

Several weeks later, the chemist submitted to Tom Lyle a sample of refined white petroleum mixed with several fine oils and a touch of perfume—a cosmetic meant primarily to stimulate hair follicles to grow, without irritating the eyes. There was no dark coloration in this substance, but Tom Lyle noticed that it did add a distinct sheen to the little hairs, helping to brighten the eyes and make them sparkle.

He placed an order for ten pounds.

The production facilities for repackaging this new product into individual-sized containers consisted of a teapot on the boarding house stove. The three members of the Chicago Williamses melted batches of raw material in the pot and poured it into small aluminum containers, which they labeled "Lash-Brow-Ine," a combination of syllables from "eyelash," "eyebrow," and "Vaseline."

Tom Lyle finally had a product to sell, and a name for it. Now all he needed was the funding to launch his new venture. Unfortunately, his own funds were tied up in unsold novelty inventory, not to mention ongoing payroll for Emery,

Mabel, and the mail-order workers, as well as living expenses and support payments to Bennie.

He asked Noel to lend him five hundred dollars, but his brother shook his head. "Sorry, little brother, but I've been saving for five years to marry Frances. I can't risk that now."

"I understand," Tom Lyle said. And he did.

But of course he had no intention of giving up on Lash-Brow-Ine.

At Thanksgiving that year, the Williams family homestead in Kentucky welcomed a slightly expanded contingent from Chicago: not only Noel, Mabel, and Tom Lyle, but Tom Lyle's charming new friend, Emery. The meal proceeded around conversation about life in Chicago, what various relatives were doing, the latest news from the ongoing war in Europe—anything but business. Although TJ and Susan were impressed with how far their wayward middle son had come in only a couple of years, business was simply never discussed at the Williams table.

It was only after dinner that the matter of funding for Tom Lyle's prospective new enterprise arose.

Noel exchanged a glance with his fiancée, Frances, and held her hand. "I wish I could help you out, Tommy Lyle, but we're ready to get married now. We don't want to put it off forever."

Frances looked troubled. "I know a woman whose husband divorced her for wearing makeup. Aren't you encouraging women to look like music-hall performers or...." She lowered her voice. ". . . prostitutes?"

Tom Lyle smiled. "Is that what you would call Mabel?"

"Goodness, no! I heard that story about the fire and all, and I understand why she did what she did, but that's different."

"Is it?" Tom Lyle slipped a small glass bottle out of his pocket and held it up so everyone could see the label: *Mascaro.* "Men use this stuff to dye their sideburns and mustaches, and no one objects. So why shouldn't women do the same with their eyebrows and lashes? Can't everyone use a little help sometimes?" He leaned toward Frances. "What do you think of Lillian Gish?"

"Oh, she's very beautiful. But Tom Lyle, she's a movie star."

"Exactly. A movie star. How much of her beauty is her own, and how much comes from lighting and makeup? What if I told you every woman could have a bit of that beauty in her own life? Is that so wrong?"

Again his hand dipped into a pocket, this time producing a small round tin labeled Lash-Brow-Ine. "Try this, Frances. It's the new product we want to take to market."

"Oh, I don't know. . . "

"I'll try it!" cried Eva, the youngest of the clan. She had just turned fourteen, and though her mother forbade it, hid a movie magazine or two under her mattress.

"Certainly not," said TJ.

Mabel took Frances by the hand. "I'll help you put it on, Frances. I'm wearing some right now."

"I thought your eyes looked awfully nice." Frances glanced at Noel.

He sighed. "Sweetheart, when Tom Lyle gets his teeth set in something, he doesn't let it go. Better get this over with."

Frances disappeared upstairs with the Williams sisters.

While they were gone, Tom Lyle asked his father how things were going in Morganfield. He had lost his interest in strutting around the little town to demonstrate how far he had come, although he still resented being barred from visiting Bennie and Cecil at her parents' home.

TJ shrugged. "Susan and I are thinking about selling the farm."

"What?" Tom Lyle didn't have to point out that the five hundred acres represented everything his father valued: continuity, legacy, family.

"Times are changing," TJ said. "Farming's getting mechanized, turning into a different kind of business. Prices are falling. I have a bad feeling about the way things are going around here."

Across the table, Tom Lyle's younger brother, Preston, squirmed and scowled. "I can hunt and fish for food if we need it."

"Grand idea," TJ said without looking at him. "But—"

He broke off as giggling at the top of the stairs announced the return of the sisters and Frances. As they came down the steps, Frances blushing, Noel had to smile. It was true; although his fiancée insisted she had dabbed on only a little Lash-Brow-Ine, the sheen from the jelly really did make her eyes sparkle in a remarkable way.

"Doesn't she look beautiful?" Eva cried. "I want to try it!"

"Eva!" TJ said.

"Take the money, Tom Lyle," Frances said. "I don't think we'll have to delay our wedding by a single minute."

Noel laughed. "See? I told you." He turned to Tom Lyle. "Okay, little brother, count us in. If anyone can make this work, it's you."

At only nineteen years of age, Tom Lyle already had the ideal experience and setup for developing his new product. His knowledge of inventory management proved useful in ordering raw ingredients and product containers. His mail-order team was already in place, and his eye for advertising assured product appeal and visibility.

They added Mabel's picture to the little tin, and used Noel and Frances's wedding money to purchase a trademark on a company name: Maybell Laboratories, chosen in honor of Mabel and her "secret of the harem" self-treatment.

Tom Lyle and Emery designed a one-and-a-half inch ad, and placed it in *Photoplay* magazine. The ad featured an illustration of an alluring eye along with the fateful words:

BEAUTIFY YOUR LASHES WITH LASH-BROW-INE
SEND 25 CENTS

As soon as the issue appeared on newsstands, quarters started pouring into the company's coffers. Thousands of quarters. In fact, returns from the first ad made such a substantial profit that Tom Lyle branched out with ads in *Pictorial Review, Delineator, the Police Gazette,* and the *Saturday Evening Post.* Together, he and Emery worked out additional copy that included the line, "Your lashes will grow longer and fuller."

They didn't realize that this claim crossed an unseen line—ignorance that would later have dire consequences.

Each day Tom Lyle and Noel made several trips to the train station, hauling heavy mailbags by wheelbarrow because the post office would no longer tote the commercial volume of weighty bags. Soon the brothers and Mabel moved out of the boarding house and into a little office and work space over a three bedroom apartment on the South Side of Chicago, at a cost of fifteen dollars a month. Although the accommodations improved, they continued to do almost all the work—taking orders, filling boxes, mailing packages—themselves.

It was time to bring in the rest of family.

Noel and Frances were married on November 16, 1916. The Kentucky farm sold shortly thereafter, and the rest of the family moved up to Chicago, where everyone pitched in to help with Tom Lyle's burgeoning business. Noel, his $500 investment more than repaid, quit his job with the railroad and devoted himself to the new company full-time. Mabel had already secured her place managing the mail-order workers. Eva enjoyed removing the coins stuck to postcards, stuffing packages, and shipping orders to customers. TJ, who had also served as a tax collector back in Morganfield, took over some of the bookkeeping duties.

Only Preston resisted, claiming to hate the city, hate the warehouse, hate the work.

And there was a lot of work. After nearly four years in Chicago, Tom Lyle had created a mail-order business likely to produce a gross volume of $300,000 in the coming year. As TJ had said, times were changing—but in this case, in a good way. The movie stars in *Photoplay* made vanity appealing to the demure Gibson Girl, who was beginning to gain her own sense of style. Fashionable clothing had arrived in America with Coco Chanel's designs for the everyday woman. And now the importance of enhancing the eyes was becoming recognized as well.

At last Tom Lyle felt financially secure enough to buy a car that would more than rival one that Emery's father might own. In those days, anyone with enough money could go to the factory and design a one-of-a-kind car made to order, and that was what he and Noel did. They took the train to Detroit and visited the Paige automobile factory, builders of "the most beautiful car in America." There, Tom Lyle designed a convertible with a sleek fish-tail back end to set it apart from the run-of-the-mill, square-ended cars seen on the road every day. His preference for elegant, personalized cars would prove to be one area where Tom Lyle, in most ways a very frugal man, chose to indulge himself throughout his life.

By now, he could afford it. Beauty was becoming big business, and he was one of the first people to capitalize on it. He created a document called *The Maybell Booklet, The Woman Beautiful,* containing hints on the art of becoming more attractive—and, of course, a list of Maybell preparations that would aid in that art.

The options expanded as new, scientifically developed products rolled out of the Park Davis lab: Maybell Lily of the Valley face powder; Maybell Beauty Cream; Odor-Ine Toilet Lotion, an early antiperspirant and deodorant whose ad read: *Every woman of refinement should always have a bottle of "ODOR-INE" on her dressing table.*

But Lash-Brow-Ine remained the heart of the product line. Women wrote letters endorsing it as a "splendid preparation for stimulating and promoting the growth of eye lashes and eye brows." Even men jumped on the bandwagon, using Lash-Brow-Ine in an attempt to stimulate hair growth on their balding heads.

And therein lay a problem: at that time, hair growth could not be stimulated by any known means. But people believed it could be, and Tom Lyle and Emery did not hesitate to capitalize on the public perception that Lash-Brow-Ine had this magical property. To bolster the claim, they advertised endorsements from the likes of Professor Allyn of the famous McClure-Westfield Laboratories. Those were the Wild West days of advertising, when embellishing the truth to catch the public's eye was standard practice, especially in a brand-new arena of business like so-called "purchased beauty."

But then the Bureau of Chemistry (precursor of the FDA) announced a crackdown on exactly these kinds of unsupported advertising promises—and identified Lash-Brow-Ine as one of the snake-oil products under investigation.

The effect was immediate and profound: the public stopped buying Lash-Brow-Ine. Tom Lyle was caught unprepared. He had never before manufactured a product of his own, and wasn't aware of the power Washington wielded. Now all his working capital was tied up in raw ingredients and inventory for a product no one wanted, and his usual advertising approaches were useless, if not illegal. To his shock, he found himself in the same situation he had been in down in Florida: surrounded by a product he couldn't sell.

He was broke.

Four
The Little Red Box

At the age of twenty, Tom Lyle had already experienced spectacular financial ups and downs, yet his unshakable tenacity and faith in himself remained intact. Broke or not, he intended to rebuild his business.

He and Noel surveyed their warehouse with its thousands of containers of unsold inventory. Oddly, considering the extent of the catastrophe, Noel's mind seemed to be elsewhere. When Tom Lyle asked him about this, Noel said, "Have you seen the papers this morning? The death toll at Verdun in France is likely to reach half a million. You know what that means?"

"It will be harder to get raw materials."

"I'm serious, Tommy Lyle. The US will have to get involved over there. We'll be at war soon."

"I'm sure you're right." Tom Lyle began to pack up the little tins of Lash-Brow-Ine. "But the *Wall Street Journal* says trade is at an all-time high."

Noel also began boxing up tins. "War has always stimulated business—but what percentage of that trade is for cosmetics? That's the question. Maybe there's some other product line you could go into."

"I've been trying to think of a way to turn Lash-Brow-Ine into something else people would . . . " Tom Lyle stopped and eyed his brother. "A product line *I* could go into? Not *we?*"

"Well, someone's got to bring in a steady income around here. The farm is gone, and Frances depends on me."

"But, Noel, I can't run this business without you."

"Going back to the railroad would be temporary. I do believe in you, Tommy Lyle, you know that—but eye cosmetics are new, and you're trying to create demand for a product that many people still see as crossing the line into loose morals."

"Those attitudes are changing. Especially with women. And now that they have jobs and spending money of their own, nothing's going to stop them from wanting to be more beautiful. Not even a war."

"Now you sound like Emery."

"That's because we've been researching this. Before the American Revolution, Colonial women used white powder, rouge, and lipstick. It was only after the Revolution that an unpainted face became the sign of a good Republican."

"Great, but right now there's a priest in Boston ranting about the 'pandemonium of powder, the riot of rouge.' That's what we're up against, Tom Lyle."

Tom Lyle shook his head. "Women are done being plain and submissive. The era when makeup was used only by performers and prostitutes has passed. The age of cosmetics has begun."

"You're absolutely sure of that?"

"I'd better be. I'm gambling the whole family's future on it."

And gamble he did. Not only did he start over, he expanded. Before the Bureau of Chemistery crackdown, he had received letters from women happy with their Lash-Brow-Ine but wanting more products. They asked, "Why don't you put out something to darken eyelashes and eyebrows and make them show up more?"

That reminded him of the burnt cork and coal dust Mabel had mixed with petroleum jelly to re-create her singed brows. Surely there was a way to do the same thing, only easier and better.

Once again Tom Lyle, Emery and Noel traveled to Park-Davis Chemicals, where they plunged into a whirlwind of work. With a chemist they mixed and tested different solutions of oils, gels, and powders, along with henna, carbon black, and other dyes, until they created a cake of material with a more natural black hue than Mabel's burnt cork and coal dust. To apply it, all a woman had to do was rub a tiny brush back and forth across the cake, then stroke it onto her eyelashes. The result: thicker, darker, more striking lashes. This simply had to be bankable.

After this new eye cosmetic passed all tests of quality, purity, and safety with high marks, Tom Lyle applied for official approval from the Bureau of Chemistry.

While awaiting the results, he and Noel discussed the crucial matter of what to name their new product. They didn't want to use the discredited Lash-Brow-Ine brand anymore, but Tom Lyle longed for some sense of continuity. Also, it would be useful if the new name made reference to the company name, which would still appear on all packaging.

The two men said it at the same time: *"Maybelline."*

With the new name came the need for new packaging. The actual cake of lash makeup would have the Maybelline logo embossed on it; they agreed on that—but what about the box? Tom Lyle loved the color red, so that was chosen for the background. Emery added text in gold lettering:

Maybelline eyelash and eyebrow beautifier . . .
Harmless, Tearless, Waterproof
Will not smart the eyes

Despite his worries about finances, Noel had chosen to stay on with the company, and now he raised a new concern: "With these new ingredients and packaging, the retail price will have to triple if we aim to make a profit."

Even Tom Lyle was taken aback. He was certain he still had a market of women willing to pay twenty-five cents for eyelash enhancer—but *seventy-five* cents?

Like an omen, two positive things happened at the same time: approval from the Bureau of Chemistry came through, and Rory Kirkland, the salesman from Post Keys Gardner who placed their ads, made a savvy offer. He was so certain the company would bounce back that he had persuaded the agency to front the cost of the next Maybelline ads until they got back on their feet.

Tom Lyle made the leap.

NOW YOU CAN BEAUTIFY YOUR EYE-LASHES AND
EYEBROWS INSTANTLY WITH—MAYBELLINE.
ORDER BY MAIL—75 cents postpaid.

Shortly after appearing in a movie magazine, this ad eliminated all fear that Maybelline had become too expensive. Orders began arriving at the rate of more than one hundred a day, seventy-five cents enclosed in each. As before, Tom Lyle promptly turned the income around and used it to place ads in more magazines. Soon he was receiving more than a thousand orders a day, and not just from individuals—drugstores, wholesale houses, and retail stores were requesting three or four boxes of Maybelline at a time.

The team ran larger ads, changing the copy from *mail order only* to *obtainable at your cosmetic's dealer.* Steadily, clearly, the voices of women calling for Maybelline reflected itself in the influx of money orders, bills, and coins stuck to postcards with chewing gum and glue.

As the money poured in, Tom Lyle sent generous payments to Bennie, but put every other dime he made directly into advertising, cosmetics research, and a nascent form of market analysis meant to find out what women wanted so he could tailor ads to those desires.

He repeated his ads in Photoplay, Pictorial Review, and the Saturday Evening Post, and also branched into magazines geared specifically toward women: Ladies' Home Journal, McCall's, Woman's Home Companion, and Good Housekeeping.

It was Emery who came up with the next groundbreaking idea: rather than using an illustration of a woman in the next *Photoplay* ad, they would use a photograph of a real model. The tagline was simplicity itself:

ANY WOMAN CAN HAVE BEAUTIFUL EYES

Orders rolled in faster than ever before.

That same year, Lucky Strike Tobacco Company launched a massive campaign to lure more people into smoking, using the healthy-sounding slogan "It's toasted!" and placing their cigarettes strategically in stores of the first self-serve grocery store chain, Piggly Wiggly.

Watching the success of this approach, Tom Lyle sought more and more means to make Maybelline just as irresistible. The company also released its eye enhancers in a waterproof liquid form that year.

The money gushed in.

Only one member of the family remained unimpressed with Maybelline's success. Born on January 17, 1899, William Preston Williams was blessed with chiseled features and boyish charm, attributes that would open doors for him his entire life. Yet he was miserable in Chicago. He was depressed by the sale of farmland that had been in the family for a hundred years, and blamed Tom Lyle for its loss. If not for his big brother, most of the family—Preston included—would still be in Morganfield, close to the woods and fields. A country boy through and through, Preston felt out of place in the big city. Where were the live trout and garden-fresh vegetables? Where could he do a little target practice or go horseback riding or hiking or camping? Independent and not just a little wild, Preston was qualified by his athletic body and rebellious nature for a life of adventure, not a career in women's cosmetics. He felt he had nothing to contribute to the company. Both charming and brooding, he had always been trouble, and trouble he would remain.

His father put it succinctly: "Preston is rebellious for the sake of being rebellious." And for years TJ had tried to break his youngest son in the time-honored style of his generation: with the flat of a belt. This invariably backfired, the way locking the boy in the Morganfield jail had failed. Not only had Preston relaxed in the cell reading dime novels about life as a cowboy, he had done so in comfort. His mother, terrified that her youngest son might sicken and die like Pearl, had sent his sisters with blankets and hot food for him.

Preston was now eighteen years old, but he refused to grow up. He still talked like a boy of ten or twelve. He wanted to be cattle herder out West. He wanted to be an explorer and discover treasure in a far-off land. But in the end, where he was most likely to be found was relaxing on the Chicago River with a fishing pole or out on the town drinking beer.

He was an angry drunk, confiding in anyone who cared to listen that Tom Lyle had always been the undeserving golden child of the family and that he, Preston, should have been allowed to pursue his dreams back in Kentucky, not be trapped in a warehouse "like a rat."

In early April 1917, he was finally offered a way to find all the adventure he sought. When word got out that Germany had been plotting to persuade Mexico to attack the United States, Americans were finally jolted from their wartime neutrality. Congress declared war on Germany.

Preston saw his chance. When every man between the ages of eighteen to thirty-one was ordered to register with the Selective Service, he enlisted in the navy without a second's hesitation. He had no problem leaving behind a family that dithered over eyelashes and little red boxes of black goo. It was time for bold action, and Preston Williams intended to take part.

Susan begged him not to go. "For me, Preston," she pled. "Stay for your mother."

But he would not. Mabel and Eva didn't even try to persuade him; they knew it was futile to argue with their ornery brother. As for TJ, he just stood with his arms folded and glowered—an act he put on for Susan's sake—while deep inside he was pleased to see his youngest son at last acting like a man.

Tom Lyle, keeping a secret of his own, simply shook Preston's hand and told him he would surely make the family proud.

Five

The Return of a
Different Man

While war might be devastating for families, it is often great for business, just as the *Wall Street Journal* had pointed out. During World War I, much of this business came from an unprecedented source: women. As more and more fighting men were needed Over There, the army and navy air corps began allowing women to join the military as administrators and recruiters. With their men away at war, homebound women also pitched in, swelling the domestic workforce dramatically. Tom Lyle encouraged their efforts with his latest slogan: *"Patriotism through Beauty!"*

Whether this made sense or not, women listened—and Maybelline sales doubled.

In Europe, Preston was trained to engage in the now-legendary aerial dog fighting as a tail gunner in a DH-1, an experimental two-seat British fighter plane nicknamed the "flying stick in the sky." If Susan Williams had been told the life expectancy of aircrews in those days, her heart might have stopped instantly.

Sure enough, not long after Preston assumed his new duties, his plane was shot down low over the Atlantic Ocean. The pilot managed to nurse the smoking

DH-1 almost to the water's surface before it exploded in flames and cartwheeled into the frigid waves. My grandfather, although stunned and scorched, swam toward the blazing wreckage and tried to reach the pilot, but the heat blasted him away. Alternately burning and freezing, he clutched at pieces of shattered aircraft as they sank, hissing smoke and vapor.

For the rest of his life, my grandfather needed little encouragement to retell the story of how, as one piece of wreckage sank into the ocean, he struggled to grab another. But soon the entire plane was gone, taking the pilot with it, and Preston spent what seemed like eons of misery in the icy waters, kicking to relieve the numbness in his legs, fighting desperately against fatigue and hypothermia. Finally, as he was on the brink of giving up, a passing navy ship spotted him and pulled him from the water.

He was hospitalized for exposure, shell shock, and trauma. But far worse than his physical suffering was his mental anguish over being unable to save his pilot. That part of the story he forever refused to talk about.

When Preston returned to Chicago in July 1918, he had changed. Nightmares of fire and death haunted his sleep and woke him in a cold sweat. His stomach constantly ached; he startled easily and never sat or slept without facing the door. The family grew accustomed to his screams in the middle of the night, but in their traditional stiff-upper-lip fashion, chose not to broach the subject in daylight. I think they believed that if they ignored the problem, it would go away on its own.

But it didn't. As time went on, Preston grew increasingly subdued, depressed, withdrawn, anxious. To silence his survivor's guilt, he drank more heavily than ever and smoked cigarettes in an endless chain. Then, drunk and belligerent, he would reminisce about life on the farm in Morganfield, a time he recalled as being simply uncomplicated.

Tom Lyle tried to help the best way he knew how, by offering Preston a position with the company. Preston responded with a sneer. "Why do you think I'd care about selling face paint? I was out fighting for my country while all you had to worry about was the shine on your fancy car."

Tom Lyle said nothing, even though Preston was living in Tom Lyle's apartment and enjoying the rich lifestyle provided by Maybell Laboratories—including driving around in Tom Lyle's "fancy car," the silver Paige.

Then came an evening that would live forever in family lore: Tom Lyle came home after work to find Preston drunk, crying, and fumbling with family photos on the floor.

Tom Lyle bent over his brother. "Preston, how about we go have some dinner and…"

The next thing he knew he was reeling backward, Preston's fist receding from his face.

"Coward!" Preston shouted. "You act so high and mighty, but you never fought for your country. *I* fought! I fought for freedom! What did you do? Tell me! What did you ever do?" He tried to stand, stumbled, sat down again. Covered his face with his hands. "But they all love you. They all love you better."

A moment later, a piece of paper landed on the floor in front of Preston: Tom Lyle's enlistment card. Preston lifted his blurry gaze from the paper to his brother's swollen, angry face.

"I tried to fight," Tom Lyle said. "They wouldn't take me. They wouldn't take me because our entire family depends on *me*."

Preston's face fell. No one depended on *him*. As far as the United States government was concerned, he had been expendable.

As Tom Lyle saw the change come over his brother's expression, he softened. "Preston, I admire your sacrifice for this country. I do. And I promise, I will take care of you as long as you live."

They shook hands.

On November 11, 1918, the Germans signed the armistice ending World War I. Ten million soldiers were dead, but the greatest losses were still to come. As the surviving soldiers returned home, refugees relocated, and populations shifted as a result of modern transportation, a deadly flu strain spread throughout the world in a pandemic that would eventually kill an estimated twenty to one hundred million people.

In Chicago, both TJ and Susan Williams fell ill. Mabel and Eva managed to nurse TJ back from the brink of death, but there was nothing they could do for their mother. Susan died the following spring.

Their mother's death hit the family hard—especially Preston, who needed her nurturing now more than ever. He sank deeper and deeper into apathy, spending his nights boozing, gambling and womanizing, joining the ranks of what would come to be known as the Lost Generation.

As for Maybelline, the company seemed to run itself during that difficult winter and spring as women, seduced by beautiful ads in popular magazines, clamored to buy its products.

But with increased prosperity came increasing demands from the family. The neighborhood where they all lived was becoming a battleground as Italian and Irish gangs fought for turf and control of criminal enterprises. With Preston gone almost every night and Noel and Tom Lyle preoccupied with work, the remaining three members of the clan felt vulnerable. Soon Noel, now vice president of Maybelline, moved with Frances and their baby girl into a brownstone not far from work, and Tom Lyle transferred the rest of the family to much better quarters: the Edgewater Beach Apartments, a beautiful new building overlooking Sheridan Road and Lake Michigan. It rented for an astronomical one thousand dollars a month, the equivalent of fourteen thousand dollars today.

The Edgewater's high ceilings and French moldings did not blend well with the simple, homey furniture from the old apartment, so Tom Lyle began redecorating. With Emery's assistance he selected silk to hang on the walls, brocade drapes for the windows, and exquisite period furniture for each room. Framed art, chandeliers, and antiques added charm.

Tom Lyle had become quite a fashion plate himself, using his own image as a means of advertising his success. At the same time, he willingly traded in his beloved Paige for a larger automobile the whole family could use to drive along Lake Michigan.

Family was everything to Tom Lyle. He was "old reliable," keeping his immediate family together and regularly sending money to Bennie and Cecil in Kentucky.

Still, with the clan securely ensconced in its new home and the business humming along, my great-uncle for once turned his mind to his own happiness. He began socializing more with Emery and his theater friends, who introduced Tom Lyle to a liberal, chic counterculture of bohemians and intellectuals devoted to art, literature, and the esoteric theories of Sigmund Freud. Here was a world unlike any he had known or even imagined during his strict upbringing, and it intrigued and enriched him. He and Emery, with their matching pencil-line moustaches, became known as men about town.

Tom Lyle's refined-to-a-fault appearance annoyed Preston, who refused to be seen in public with "that mustache" even though he himself wore dark face makeup and even put a little Maybelline on his eyelashes, as many fashionable men did in the early 1920s. Our family photos of the time show him with his pomaded hair slicked back like silent film idol Rudolph Valentino's. To women, Preston played himself up as a war hero; they were moved equally by his tragic story and his freehanded spending. He liked to borrow Tom Lyle's car and disappear for days on end. Without a responsibility in the world, he sought to scrape up every small joy life offered him, roaming from bar to jazz club to back-alley gambling hall, the war still raging in his mind, every drink leaving a bitter taste in his mouth. Fetched frequently by Tom Lyle's driver from rooms in no-name hotels, Preston no longer talked of adventures out West.

Tom Lyle said nothing about Preston's antics, but TJ was a different matter. "Find a nice girl, Preston," the ex-sheriff said. "Settle down. Stop all this nonsense."

Tom Lyle tried to help in this direction by setting Preston up with a college friend of Emery's named Helen Clark, the first Maybelline model, her likeness appearing on the front of Maybelline's little red box. She was nineteen years old, tall and lithe, naive and demure, with doe eyes and brunette hair tucked neatly on top of her head: the girl next door. Rebellious bad boys like Preston appealed to her, but she was no fool: before she got too involved with him, she demanded he put a ring on her finger.

Ultimately, he did marry her—the price he paid to buy the family's acceptance. Tom Lyle's special fund paid for her diamond ring and the newlyweds' new apartment just a few blocks from Lake Michigan—close enough for the rest of the Williams clan to pitch in when Preston-sitting duties became necessary.

And they often did. Preston never went to work, but he continued to go other places, mostly at night, returning home only to sleep off his excesses.

Desperate, his young bride decided that getting her handsome husband a modeling job through her connections at Lord & Taylor might provide him with a schedule and the pride of earning his own money. Lord & Taylor executives were so impressed by the way he photographed in their tailored suits that they provided him with free clothes just to have him be seen around town wearing their label.

But Helen's efforts backfired; the additional money and attention only fueled Preston's cavorting lifestyle. The Jazz Age had begun, and he was ready for the good times. While Helen stayed home, her husband tramped through jazz joints—Louis Armstrong was playing his trumpet all over Chicago—and played cards for high stakes. Preston was known as a big spender, the Maybelline King, with a bourbon-filled flask in his hand and a showgirl on his arm, rubbing elbows with notorious mobsters like Al Capone—who was said to have copied Preston's flashy style of dressing in a dark suit and tie, llama-skin coat, and derby hat.

The fact that Preston was publicly associated with Maybelline mortified Tom Lyle, but even so, family loyalty prevailed. When Preston got in a bar fight or disappeared in an alcoholic binge and ended up in jail, it was Tom Lyle who bailed him out. When someone threatened to sue Preston over a pregnancy or act of mistreatment, it was Tom Lyle who settled matters behind the scenes.

Helen tried crying to her husband, reasoning with him—and finally screaming at him. She threatened divorce. But Preston didn't care. He had given up trying to please his disapproving father by staying with one woman, and despite her best efforts, Helen could not give him what he needed. For two years, he came and went at will, disappearing for weeks at a time, always searching but never finding what he was looking for. Probably never even knowing what he was looking for.

Until *she* found *him*.

Six

Triangle

For most Chicagoans, the Memorial Day parade of 1922 marked both the beginning of summer and an end to hard times. The grim chaos of war, the grip of the flu epidemic, and the ensuing suffering and loss were all in the past. The Twenties were beginning to roar.

For my family, that day would also mark another turning point: the moment when fate brought together the three titans who would dominate the family's destiny far into the future.

People of all social classes and income levels crowded the sidewalks to watch the parade that day. Flappers sashayed down the street with cloche hats over bobbed hair, summer dresses rose dangerously close to the knee, eyelashes fluttered, laden with Maybelline.

The younger generation was rebelling against the status quo: the system that had failed to prevent the horrors of the last five years. The so-called flaming youth—especially the young women who had won the right to vote in August 1920—were setting themselves free.

These new women were thought of as a little fast, a bit brazen. They went out together without a man to look after them; they sat in the backseats of motorcars, smoking cigarettes; they publicly held hands with men. During the war, the US and Great Britain had been the only combatant countries that didn't issue condoms to their soldiers. Returning soldiers must have learned about them, though, because condom sales doubled in 1920. A little freedom, it seemed, led to a whole lot more freedom.

Preston was there for the parade, of course. By that time, he had left his wife and moved back in with the family at the Edgewater. But Memorial Day held special significance for him, representing as it did that horrible day in the freezing Atlantic, the day that had changed his life. He had no idea that his life was about to take yet another drastic turn.

In my imagination, I see him out on the street that day—leaning against a lamppost, dressed in a white linen, single-breasted Gatsby suit with a pale pastel shirt and matching pocket square, topped off with an expensive tie. Who could resist a man in a suit like that? He smelled of Tom Lyle's French-milled sandalwood soap, shaving cream, and the pomade on his hair. When the military drill teams marched by, he wanted to shake hands with every one of them. He stood there as if waiting for his destiny, smoking a Camel.

Destiny arrived right on time, in the form of Evelyn Boecher and her sister, Bunny, a pair of beautiful young women sashaying down the sidewalk with the best of them.

Of his second daughter's five-minute birth in February 1901, John Boecher would say, "Evelyn entered the world in such a hurry because she never wanted to miss a thing"—a trait that would define her for the rest of her life.

Boecher, a first-generation German-American, had wanted a boy to whom he could pass his successful plumbing business; instead, he got three daughters. "All my boys are girls," he often joked.

With industrialization luring droves of people from farms to the city, housing shortages raised the demand for renovated older buildings. John Boecher had showed up first and worked hardest. Now he employed teams of stout lads all over the city, leaving him the leisure time and wherewithal to instill Old World graces and traditions within his young family.

Papa Boecher believed in the power of first impressions, and enlisted his daughters in reflecting his wealth and status, showering them with elegant clothing, jewelry, and French perfume. But of the three girls, it was the precocious Evelyn who stole his heart—turning him into the first of many men who would cater to her whims. She was soon known as "that spoiled-rotten Daddy's girl," a princess in a tiara, elbowing her way toward a crown of her own.

The Boechers wanted their daughters to be refined young ladies with charm, grace, and a musical education. At the Chicago Institute of Music, Bunny studied the trumpet, Verona the piano, and Evelyn the violin. Evelyn, however, really wanted to be a professional dancer. She enjoyed flouting her family's wishes, sneaking movie magazines into her schoolbooks and wearing theatrical makeup. She taught her sisters how to roll their hair in strips of torn rags to create long ringlets, and how to use beer to give their hair body and bounce. She even ran away briefly to join the circus, an experience that inspired her parents to allow her to join the ballet instead. Evelyn was always the first to try anything, from the newest fashion to catching a man's eye with her coquettish smile. It was easy for her to find admirers—but as she would learn, true love was much more difficult to come by.

Their first encounter was all in the eyes. Standing by his lamp post, Preston turned his head to see Evelyn's pale-blue gaze fixed on him from under a hat whose wide brim drooped flirtatiously to frame her gorgeous face. He noted her subtle eye makeup, her carefully applied rouge, the blood-red lipstick that defined a kissable pout, her curly bobbed hair, slinky dress, silk stockings, and her lean, muscular legs. She was stunning, petite . . . perfect.

She sized him up at the same time and nudged Bunny as they strolled past him. In a haughty yet flirtatious voice meant to be overheard, she said, "Look at that cad. He looks exactly like Valentino. Better, actually."

Preston liked her saucy attitude. "You!" he said, reaching out to tap her shoulder. "With the baby blues! Are you wearing Maybelline?"

She raised an eyebrow. "And if I am?"

"Allow me to introduce myself. I'm Preston Williams of the Maybelline Company. My brother founded the business."

Cocking her head, she said, "My name is Evelyn. And this is my sister Emma. Everyone calls her Bunny."

Preston pointed toward the balcony of his brother's penthouse apartment. "Would you ladies care to get a better view of the parade?" The two young women rode the elevator to the penthouse with him—a total stranger. Preston had that way about him.

As they entered the apartment, Evelyn and Bunny caught their breath. These girls had grown up in an extravagant brownstone with its own ballroom, but at parties they played their instruments to entertain guests in an atmosphere of old-world propriety and Teutonic pragmatism.

This apartment possessed an entirely different atmosphere. An enormous bouquet of white roses scented the entry hall. Sumptuous decorative touches graced the living and dining rooms. Contemporary art teamed with oriental rugs and tapestries depicting exotic settings. Sheer curtains over the tall open windows shifted like spirits in the breeze, while the late-afternoon sunlight glinting off Lake Michigan reflected golden light onto the chandelier crystals and the high walls.

Evelyn knew one thing instantly: this was the ultra-chic lifestyle she had always wanted.

She turned toward Preston and slowly took off her hat. She fluffed her hair, knowing that the sun's filtered rays would catch the honey highlights in the warm brown. The silk crepe of her dress became diaphanous, revealing the silhouette of her young body. She knew that, too.

Preston's gaze turned hungry.

As Evelyn let her own gaze wander over his wonderfully sculpted face, tan against his white linen jacket, the tension between them approached the snapping point. Less than a minute after the young man and woman set foot inside the apartment, the power of their mutual attraction set the ponderous wheels of fate in motion.

Cheers went up from outside on the balcony. Preston led Evelyn out there by the hand, Bunny following, to introduce the young ladies to his father and sisters, who were watching the parade. When TJ saw Evelyn, his eyebrows shot up—then he gave his son a nod of approval, suggesting that Preston had done something right for once. Although Preston was still married, even TJ had to admit that that was a doomed situation, while this one looked very much alive.

Preston left in search of champagne. TJ also excused himself, leaving the women alone.

Mabel explained that their father hadn't fully recovered his health since having the flu and watching his wife die.

"Oh, I'm so sorry to hear that," Bunny said. "The flu hit our family too. Evelyn had to leave the Ballet Russe to help nurse us all back to health—but then she came down with the flu herself and nearly died."

"Oh, you poor dear," Mabel said to Evelyn. Then, "You danced with the Ballet Russe?"

"For a time."

The four girls looked one another over for a moment. Mabel and Eva were painfully aware that at heart they were still country girls, while the Boechers were graceful, sophisticated young women who had been surrounded by wealth all their lives.

Then Preston returned, carrying two bottles of champagne in ice buckets. With skill born of long practice, he popped and poured, cupping Evelyn's hand in his as he passed her a crystal glass of cold bubbly. He and she could barely take their eyes off each other as they sipped, each moment a dalliance.

As Preston told his war stories with his usual flare, topping off Evelyn's glass from time to time, she found reasons to touch his hand or arm. She realized she never wanted to leave this magnificent world— or this handsome man who came with it. What more could a girl ask for?

"Will you stay for supper?" Preston asked, pleased to have stretched the afternoon into evening.

"Thank you," Evelyn said. "I would be delighted."

"I'm afraid I have to pass," Bunny said. "My boyfriend and I plan to see Valentino in *The Sheik* tonight; I need to get home and get ready."

"I'm sorry to hear that," Preston said, not sorry at all. "May I walk you to your car?"

As Bunny took the keys from Evelyn, she murmured in her sister's ear, "I'm not sure I should leave you alone with such a flashy character."

"Oh, I can deal with this jazzbo," Evelyn said, and walked with her sister and Preston toward the entrance that led to the elevator.

As they reached the outer hallway, a chime announced the arrival of the elevator. "Swell," Preston grumbled.

The front door opened and in walked a meticulously dressed man with a pencil-line mustache and a face that qualified him for the leading role in a movie. He raised his eyebrows. "Well, hello," he said.

Not since Bennie had Tom Lyle felt so overcome with attraction for a woman. He looked Evelyn up and down: her slender, almost athletic figure; her sense of style. The silk crepe dress skimmed her body perfectly. The scent of her perfume was mesmerizing. Like many of the actresses he so admired, she exuded a glamorous confidence that somehow reached out and included him. And above all, those eyes. With her perfect features and dewy complexion, Evelyn was the Maybelline ideal personified.

At that moment, a phrase leaped into his mind: *Eyes that charm*. He realized he had just found the tagline for his next ad.

Was the champagne making her giddy? Evelyn wondered. Two handsome princes in the same palace, and on the same day? First rugged Preston and now this elegant newcomer, even more striking in his own way. Years later, and many times over, Evelyn would say, "I don't believe I had ever seen a more distinguished-looking young gentleman in all my life."

Preston's voice held an edge. "Evelyn, meet my brother, Tom Lyle."

Suddenly, Evelyn was happy that she had parked the car more than two blocks away. It would take Preston a while to walk there and return.

Preston's gaze shifted between her and his brother. "I'll be right back," he said to her. Then, to Tom Lyle: "Fix her a drink or something, will you?"

And with one last glance, he closed the door behind him.

After a strained moment, Tom Lyle said, "Would you like a Manhattan?"

"Please," Evelyn said. She stood examining an Erté statuette as he walked to the liquor cabinet and began mixing two drinks. From the corner of her eye, she caught him looking at her from the corner of *his* eye.

He brought her drink, and as they talked about Erté and Art Nouveau, Tom Lyle lit a cigarette and kept stealing glances at her. Finally he said, "Forgive me for asking this, but have you ever been in the circus?"

She raised her eyebrows. "As a matter of fact, I performed ballet poses on horseback for a short while."

"I knew it! I believe I saw you in the ring once." He gestured for her to sit beside him on the sofa. "Just before Preston left for the war, the family went to the circus—and afterward, Preston and I both talked about the beautiful ballerina who rode bareback."

Evelyn laughed. "That could have been me, all right."

"How did you end up performing in the circus? Forgive me, but you don't really seem the type."

"Well . . . I ran away from home and joined up."

"Really?" He smiled. "I've heard of people doing that, but never met one before."

"It was because of my three old-maid aunts. My mom and dad are peaches, but Daddy's sisters . . . they drove me crazy. Three Miss Grundys, hovering over our every move—me and my sisters—always telling us we were going to hell. So of course driving *them* crazy became our favorite sport. They finally convinced our parents to send us all to music school. I didn't want to go, so I kissed my sisters goodbye and hit the road, as they say."

"But you came back after just weeks." He was facing her now, his elbow touching hers.

"Let's just say I found out it's not all candy apples and popcorn in the circus. Between the stench of manure, the hooting of crowds, the filthy roustabouts. . . ." She trailed off.

Tom Lyle touched her hand. "Someone tried to take advantage of a beautiful young woman."

"The ringleader's son-in-law. He pulled me inside his trailer, locked the door, and tried to assault me. But he was drunk, and I grabbed a board and slammed it over his head, then packed my things and caught the next train home."

"I'm very glad you escaped," Tom Lyle said. And then, changing the subject with a bright smile: "Your perfume is wonderful." He turned her hand palm up and drew her wrist to his nose. "A Houbigant?"

"Very good! *Quelque Fleurs.*"

"I've researched scents for—"

The door opened and Preston stepped into the room. He looked at them, and a look of surprise passed over his face.

Tom Lyle dropped Evelyn's hand. "Oh, good!" He rose to his feet. "Now that Preston is back, we can eat."

Preston said nothing.

"Car start okay?" Evelyn asked.

"Had to crank it," Preston said. Then to Tom Lyle, "Where's Emery?"

"I've no idea," Tom Lyle said. To Evelyn he said, "Emery is our friend and advertising director. I hope you'll meet him soon."

"Come and sit down!" Mabel sang from the dining room. "Time for dinner."

"No time!" Preston said, reaching for Evelyn's hand and hauling her to her feet. "We're going dancing."

Evelyn barely had time to grab her hat and call out the "nice-to-meet yous" before they were out the door. The moment they were alone in the hallway, Preston brought her wrist to his nose, as if curious about what Tom Lyle had found there. He breathed her in. "Nice."

Evelyn rewarded him first with her most alluring smile, and then with a long-anticipated embrace.

I never tired of hearing my grandmother, my "Nana," tell about meeting Preston and Tom Lyle Williams for the first time, any more than she tired of retelling the story. When I was a girl in my teens, moping over some unrequited crush, she would recount the tale, citing some particular part of it to illustrate a point. Whatever my crisis, Nana used the opportunity to relive that day. I have no doubt that, at the time, she believed she could have either of the Williams brothers—or both of them. She was definitely a have-it-all kind of gal.

She always said, "Time and place slipped away from me that night," but most likely she spent a little feverish time with Preston in the backseat of Tom Lyle's Packard. I suspect this because she never forgave my grandfather for revealing to both Eva and Mabel that he didn't bring her home until five-thirty the next morning—and the bars and dancehalls closed at three. As a result, Evelyn became the subject of family gossip that never quite ceased.

Yet whenever she fell into the memory of that holiday, the stars in her eyes turned into comets. "That was some day!" she would exclaim. "The day I fell in love *twice*."

Seven

Geometry of
the Heart

A daring spirit. Tom Lyle, Preston and Evelyn Boecher all shared this quality. All three had left home at some point in their young lives, determined to find a better future and satiate a hunger for something more. All three possessed a certain audaciousness, a willingness to pursue their dreams. Bold, beautiful, and brash, they became equals in a triangle that left the timid stay-at-homes gawking. Tom Lyle and Preston held an almost preternatural sense that Evelyn embodied their other halves, while Evelyn split herself in two to accommodate their love. It was a human geometry my grandmother thought she could sustain indefinitely.

With Preston, Evelyn entered the after-dark world of the city's glittering underbelly, a world wilder and more exciting than anything she had ever experienced. She plunged into it headlong, as if skinny-dipping in a moonlit pool.

To hold the interest of such a worldly man, she downplayed her proper upbringing and reinvented herself. She learned to drink like a man, shoot craps, and dangle a cigarette from her ruby-red lips. In smoky gambling dens, she perched at the edge of a table, shapely ballerina legs crossed, hem well above the knee, and rolled dice like a pro. Four-letter words salted her vocabulary, and she abandoned her proper grammar—which she would in later years insist was the mark of a lady—in favor of booze-hall slang. In this world, she didn't wince at being called a "doll," "tomato," "skirt," "sheba," or "bearcat," or object if a man admired her "chassis." With the looks of a femme fatale and an attitude to match, she convinced the denizens of the speakeasies that she was one of them.

Evelyn and Preston became a popular couple, and she basked in a sort of queen-of-the-hop limelight. Preston could always draw a crowd with his boisterous war stories, and Evelyn joined him at the center of the attention, prompting an adaptation of a popular joke: "Preston's a ham, but I hope his sugar cures him."

She discovered, to her delight, that Preston could dance well. Unfortunately, she had competition from the throngs of reckless young women eager to party all night. Despite—and, in truth, because of—the passage of Prohibition, drinking had become a sport, one that women played as well as men. As a precaution against the often toxic bootleg brews, the girls frequently brought their own "giggle water" in hidden hip flasks or unlikely containers that might be overlooked in a raid: coconut shells or hot-water bottles strung around their necks. Some of them knew the Maybelline King and tried to grab him away from Evelyn to dance. Preston charmingly declined, but my grandmother realized she had better stake her claim unequivocally.

There was a certain gangster, however, who was able to steal a dance from Preston's girl. He would grab Evelyn for a dance and jokingly say, "Cash or check, doll?"—meaning, "How do I pay you?" Coming from a man used to purchasing the affection of women, this wasn't even an insult.

"Sorry, Al," Preston would say, "the bank's closed," and he would waltz her away—smiling, of course; one stayed on good terms with Al Capone. It excited Preston that such a powerful and dangerous man wanted his girl; it made Preston want her even more.

Music filled those frenzied, wondrous nights. Songs such as "I'll Build a Stairway to Paradise," "Ain't We Got Fun?" and "Lonesome Mama Blues" were all the rage that summer, and Paul Whiteman caught on with "The Charleston," "Making Whoopee," and other hugely popular tunes that defined the era.

When Evelyn danced to such music, Preston watched her, hypnotized. Though my grandfather was a Casanova, my Great-Aunt Bunny said that in Evelyn's presence, he would nervously wring his fingers together. He bought her flowers and kissed her sweetly and gently, even if someone was watching. She was his queen, and their mutual passion became quite the bonfire.

Still, dates with Preston were only half the picture for Evelyn at that time. When she wasn't with Preston, she went out with Tom Lyle. With him she found respite from nights of debauchery, and could stop playing the role of the seductive girlfriend. She mingled easily and naturally with Tom Lyle's and Emery's friends, enjoying avant-garde theater and discussing her impassioned views about women's rights.

If Evelyn forgot which world she was in and told people in an exclusive club an off-color joke she had learned in a gin mill, Tom Lyle defended her in a way Preston never did: "She has moxie!"

Evelyn became Tom Lyle's regular date to the most fabulous upscale events in Chicago. She was always beautifully dressed and alluring in her Maybelline cosmetics. The two of them enjoyed dinner and movie dates and held long, animated conversations about ideas and events. They went to one of Harry Houdini's performances—not to see the magic but to discover the reality behind it. Houdini's knowledge of illusion fascinated Tom Lyle, a kind of illusionist in his own right.

Evelyn even offered some ideas about Maybelline. At midsummer, headlines proclaimed the winner of a beauty contest called the Miss America Pageant, now in its second year. Evelyn thought the new Miss Chicago could benefit from Maybelline products. "You should put her under contract, get some publicity."

"That's a good idea," Tom Lyle said. "But she's got nothing on you, Evelyn. I think of you when we're writing ad copy, you know."

It was not the first time he had said such a thing. An awkward moment passed between them.

As crazy as Evelyn was for Preston, she sensed that a future with Tom Lyle would prove more satisfying in many ways. He was attentive and seemed entranced with her. If only he wanted her in the overwhelming way that Preston did. But he didn't, and she thought she knew why. Tom Lyle already had an all-consuming mistress: Maybelline.

Then there was his past. He had told her about his son and his brief marriage to Bennie, and the dismay he felt at not being able to share their lives as husband and father. Evelyn suspected that loss made him keep his distance from other potential relationships. Or maybe he was simply holding back so as not to encroach on his brother's turf.

But who knew what the future held? More and more often now, Preston disappeared for a few days here, a few days there, without telling Evelyn where he was going or when he would return. Evelyn knew better than to reveal that she was upset by these absences; if she did, he might never return. But my Nana was an expert at playing the classic game, too; she simply acted as if she hadn't even noticed he was gone. That made him nervous enough to behave for a while.

An odd understanding developed between the two brothers and Evelyn— a sort of triple tie—no losers, no clear winners. Preston knew that Evelyn reserved her passion for him alone, and that in any case Tom Lyle would not make a play for her. Evelyn longed for Preston but believed that Tom Lyle was her soul mate.

For his part, Tom Lyle found inspiration in Evelyn; she generated a new spark of excitement in his advertising designs. Maybelline's continued prosperity was based on the premise that every woman desired to look her best, and Evelyn epitomized that philosophy.

But not everyone was so enamored of this newcomer. Although Mabel didn't mind having Evelyn replace her as the company muse, she did resent the way Evelyn monopolized her brothers. As an increasingly fervent Catholic, she also considered Evelyn to be a vamp.

Eva, on the other hand, admired Evelyn, and steered her toward Preston. Her own boyfriend, Chester "Chess" Haines, loved a good time, and the two couples often went out nightclubbing and dancing until dawn.

So, in the end, it was Preston whom Evelyn brought home to meet her family. The couple drove thirty-seven miles northwest from Chicago to the Boecher summer house at Lake Zurich, a resort area made newly accessible due to the paving of Rand Road. Evelyn's sisters Bunny and Verona visited as well, bringing along their more conservative boyfriends.

The young men listened attentively to Preston's war stories, but even on short acquaintance, the sisters warned Evelyn that she would get badly hurt by her new beau. Nor were John and Emma Boecher impressed. "Evelyn," her father said one morning at breakfast under the gazebo while Preston was off fishing with the boyfriends, "when you came back from that damn circus, we welcomed you with open arms. And we always supported your ballet career. But we can't understand why you would throw your talent away on this womanizer."

"I'm in love with him."

Her mother rolled her eyes. "You must stop fooling around with men who have bad reputations, Evelyn. Find someone substantial, from a respectable background."

"I'd be willing to send you to Germany to continue your career in music and dance," her father said.

"Thank you, Papa, but I'm not leaving Chicago. And I won't give Preston up."

Her parents exchanged looks. "Then I'm cutting off your allowance," her father said heavily. "You can still live at home, but don't count on us bailing you out when things get rough."

"And they will get rough," her mother added with a sigh.

Evelyn refused to believe it. Even without her own money, she kept partying with Preston and going out with Tom Lyle. Verona diverted the family's disapproval for a while by eloping with her boyfriend; but by the end of the year, Evelyn had to admit she was getting disheartened. She had still heard no talk of the future from either Williams brother.

Then she found out Preston would be the one leaving Chicago—and all thanks to Bunny's boyfriend, Harold. In early March 1923, the two men announced they were heading to Cleveland to work as hired scabs during the ongoing labor dispute between union workers and the railroads.

"But won't that be dangerous?" Evelyn cried. "Why would you do such a thing?"

"I'd rather make my own money than live on the family dole."

He said those words because they sounded both reasonable and responsible, but the truth was a bit more dramatic: he yearned for adventure. Here was a chance to get away from his family, go someplace he had had never been before, and fight for money—an activity worthy of a war vet.

When Evelyn kissed him goodbye at the station, she sensed that he was more distracted than passionate. His spirit was already poised for adventure hundreds of miles away.

Tears of frustration beaded her makeup-darkened lashes. "When will you be back?"

He shrugged. "Hard to say."

Although neither of them knew it yet, Evelyn was pregnant.

Eight

Leaving Chicago

The glamour of working as a scab in Cleveland quickly lost its luster. For one thing, Preston hated facing the furious shouts of picketers as he entered or left the rail yards. He hated being beaten by a group of them even less. Then there was the coal dust. It worked its way into his nose and ears, made his clothes filthy, caked under his nails, and sifted inside his boots. His muscles ached, and calluses soon replaced blisters.

But at least these were manly afflictions, and he bore them with secret pride. He had taken the job to prove he could stick to something and stand up to the call of duty—and he was succeeding. He might be sore, bloodied, and dirty, his nights might be lonely and his paycheck far smaller than he would have preferred, but at least he was an independent human being. He might never return to Chicago.

Eva wrote to warn him with that Al Capone had recently sent Evelyn a basket of South American long-stemmed roses. Preston tossed the letter away in disgust—surely not even Evelyn would go out with a gangster. Would she?

He couldn't get the thought out of his head. He wasn't under contract; he could pull up stakes at any time and head back to Evelyn, back to Tom Lyle's penthouse—back to his father's disapproving glare.

Forget it.

One evening after work, as he and Harold trudged through mounds of gray slush, a barrage of packed ice and garbage flew at them over the fence, along with the usual curses and slurs from union men.

"Scabs!"

"Lousy filthy rotten scabs!"

"You're taking food from my children!"

"Be a man! Fight the bosses!"

Some Pinkerton agents outside the fence rushed at the mob. Clubs rose and fell; warning shots cracked into the air. The picketers roared in protest and redoubled their bombardment of snow and ice. As Preston got closer to the fence, he realized that the picketers were also targeting a petite young woman standing there in a fur coat and hat, her gloved fingers clutching the fence wire. Dumb skirt. What kind of woman would be stupid enough to . . .

"Preston!" she called. "Preston!"

"My God! Harold, it's Evelyn!" Preston elbowed his way through his fellow strike-breakers. At the fence, he threw his arms around her and lifted her in the air. Amid taunts and lewd jeers from the strikers, he rushed her off into the darkness.

When they had gone what he considered a safe distance, he put her down. "What the hell are you doing here? Do you want to get killed?"

"I'm having your baby."

"You what?"

"I'm having your . . . *our* baby."

As my grandmother recalls that moment, the news took a few moments to sink in—then Preston pulled her to him and kissed her, deeply and passionately on the side of the road. Passing cars and trucks honked in ribald encouragement.

Finally they walked onward, hand in hand over the frozen slush. "But, Evelyn," Preston said, "I mean, how can we do this?"

"Do you love me, you fool?"

"I'm crazy about you." He hadn't realized how crazy until just now.

"That's how we're going to do it," she said.

Evelyn's fur coat hanging on a rack near the door of the Whistle Stop Diner was the most elegant garment the waitress had ever seen. Preston invested some of his hard-earned wages on pot roast, while Evelyn dipped a spoon into a small bowl of chicken soup.

"If you come back to Chicago," she said, "Tom Lyle will help get us on our feet, and you can work for Maybelline."

Preston's face darkened. "I'm already working here."

"The strike won't last forever, darling. I'm just suggesting you come home a little ahead of schedule."

"Evelyn, I have no intention of returning to Chicago at all. I want us to get married, but . . ."

"But what?" How could there possibly be a *but* to this?

"Legally, I'm still married to Helen. We didn't get a divorce yet."

Evelyn pushed her soup away and struggled not to show her desperation. Without a ring on her finger, her family would never accept her back, let alone help support an illegitimate child. Her old maid Catholic aunts would see to that. When she had confided her suspicion that she was pregnant to Verona, her sister had said, "You have to do whatever it takes to get Preston to marry you—the way I did with Charlie." Only then did Evelyn understand the reason for Verona's elopement: her son, who had been welcomed into the world as if he were a crown prince, hadn't been *born* out of wedlock—and that was all that mattered.

"Don't worry," Preston said. "I'll start divorce proceedings right away."

"But it will take at least a year to finish."

"Meanwhile, at least we'll be together." He kissed her hand. "Honey, we're going to be happy. You'll see."

In Evelyn's imagination, Preston whisked her back to Chicago and then went to work at Maybelline. Their home was a beautiful penthouse like Tom Lyle's.

In the real world, she moved into the cold, dingy flat Preston and Harold shared above a delicatessen in Cleveland. She had never had to cook for herself before, so the three roommates lived mostly on sandwiches from the deli below. There was little for Evelyn to do while Preston was at work, and no time or money for entertainment anyway. At least she got to sleep with Preston in the narrow bed with the yellowing sheets, while Harold slept on a cot. The height of luxury.

Still, in some ways things were good. When the weather got warmer, she sometimes met Preston after work and strolled home with him, arm in arm, stopping for kisses along the Cuyahoga River. Or they would have a picnic on the shores of Lake Erie.

Maybe Preston was right. Maybe they would be happy after all.

In early September the railroad strike came to an end, and Harold bought himself a ticket to Chicago. He asked Preston to have a drink with him while he waited for the train. In the bar, Harold turned his glass distractedly on the tabletop. "So, Preston, what do you plan to do now that the strike's over?"

"I'm not sure, except that I don't want to go back to Chicago."

"That's probably just as well."

Preston peered at him. "What does that mean?"

Harold cleared his throat. "Bunny wrote and told me Evelyn's been pretty much disowned by her parents, and doesn't plan to go back to Chicago until you marry her. Bunny asked me not to tell you."

"I'm glad you did," Preston said.

He stared at nothing as Harold hurried off to his train.

On November 26, 1923, William Preston Williams Jr. was born. My grandfather remained at the hospital for two days straight, not leaving even to shower, then sent Tom Lyle an ecstatic wire: "By God, I'm a father!"

Evelyn took heart in this. Perhaps her wild man would now grow up, move back to Chicago, and be a good father. Perhaps even a good husband.

Billy was the first boy born into the Williams family since Cecil eleven years earlier. Tom Lyle was so thrilled that he sent Evelyn not one but three baskets of red roses. At Thanksgiving time he ordered a cooked turkey with all the trimmings from the deli and had it sent upstairs to the apartment. He also shipped a package containing a silver teething ring with the baby's name engraved on it.

But apart from this, there was little communication between Cleveland and Chicago. Evelyn wrote often to Tom Lyle, but few letters came in return. The triangle seemed to have collapsed, although a new, more intimate one was growing to take its place. Preston adored his son and enjoyed watching little Billy suckling at his mother's breast.

But nothing is ever simple, and bit by bit, a teeter-totter motion began. Preston's love for his son propelled him to emotional heights matched only by the depths of his despair when Billy cried all night or Evelyn harped about getting married and going back to Chicago to work for Tom Lyle.

Instead, Preston leaped into a new career more suited to his temperament—boxing—only to discover that rather than bringing home a fifty dollar purse, he earned nothing but cut eyes and a broken nose.

In January, Evelyn received a letter from Tom Lyle describing Eva's plans for a romantic cathedral wedding with Chester Haines. Tom Lyle hadn't included a money order in the envelope or asked if Evelyn needed anything. But why should he? Tom Lyle didn't owe her anything. *She* was the one who had run away. Again.

But she had done it out of love. This mess she was in—that wasn't her fault. It had nothing to with her choosing the wrong man or ignoring the warnings of her family. Her parents were too old-fashioned, her miserable aunts too cruel.

Those were the problems. Those, and Preston himself. The man kept insisting on doing things *his* way when it was obvious he should do things *her* way.

If she ever hoped to have the life she deserved, she would have to get Preston to change. That was all there was to it.

In truth, even Preston knew change was necessary. Just looking at Evelyn, who on her deli diet of stale breads and hard sausages had lost her lovely curves, made him feel like a failure. He dealt with the sensation in his time-honored way: with booze and carousing.

One morning as he groaned in bed under the weight of a hangover, Evelyn asked him to take care of Billy while she went to the store. After she left, Preston tied one end of a string to the boy's cradle and the other end to his big toe so he could lie half-asleep on the floor and rock the child. The crying, crying, crying child.

He noticed that the faster he rocked the cradle, the quieter Billy became.

Faster. Faster.

Preston Williams, you're a genius.

The next thing he knew, Billy lay on the floor halfway across the room, purple-faced and screaming.

Of course Evelyn chose that precise moment to step in. She swept the baby up in her arms and whirled on Preston, tears flying from her eyes. "I'm through living like this! I won't do it anymore!"

Preston didn't ask what she intended to do instead. His head couldn't endure any more crying, shouting, or commotion of any kind.

In truth, Evelyn herself had no idea what she was going to do. She only knew that two things had become painfully apparent: she was going to have to leave this place . . . and she would never, ever be Mrs. Preston Williams.

Nine

A Ring and Roses

he only sign that the three-story building at 5900 North Ridge Avenue in the heart of Chicago contained something special was an elegant brass plaque attached to its glass door: Maybelline Co.

In 1924, twenty-eight-year-old Tom Lyle opened the door of his new headquarters, rode the elevator to the third floor, entered his newly paneled office, and sat down at his walnut desk.

He owned the entire building, which he had purchased with a check after both Noel and Emery began to insist that the company needed more space. That was how my great-uncle did things—he never bought anything he couldn't pay for on the spot. He was pleased with the building, although its purchase had severely depleted his cash reserves.

Fortunately, Emery had come up with a plan to restore them. Together, the two men hovered over photos of Mildred Davis, the first Hollywood silent film star they had contracted to appear in Maybelline ads. Emery had selected her because she had played the ingénue in most of her film roles, and he believed her wholesome image would appeal to the proper young ladies who still hesitated to wear Maybelline in public. Davis was thrilled to be chosen as a role model.

Mildred's photograph emphasized her wistful eyes, brought out even more by lashes heavily made up. The ad copy read:

**Girls and women everywhere, even the most
beautiful actresses of the stage and screen, now realize
that MAYBELLINE is the most important aid
to beauty and use it regularly.**

When Tom Lyle read the copy, he whistled. "*Girls?* You're suggesting we target an even younger market than we have been?"

"Absolutely," Emery said.

After Emery left, taking the Mildred Davis shots with him, Tom Lyle gazed at the one framed photo left on his desk. Not a movie star, but his son, Cecil.

He hadn't seen Cecil in months. The visits from Morganfield had become less and less frequent recently, a sign of Bennie's increasing surrender to her parents' grip. They still wanted her and her son to have as little as possible to do with the disgraced Tom Lyle—although he noticed they never sent back the support checks he sent as regularly as the phases of the moon.

He looked at his calendar, on which he had marked the days for Cecil's planned visit over the spring holidays—five glorious days—only to have to cross them off because of some problem or other with Bennie's parents.

Didn't these people understand the importance of family?

The phone on his desk rang. He picked up and the operator asked if he would accept reversed charges from a Miss Evelyn Boecher.

"Of course," he said. He hadn't spoken to Evelyn in ages; according to Preston, everything in Cleveland was going terrific, and Evelyn was delighted with her new station in life as a mother.

"Hello?" came a small, faded version of Evelyn's voice. In the background rose traffic noise and the wailing of a baby.

"Dear?" Tom Lyle said. "What's wrong?"

She told him, and he listened, increasingly annoyed at his brother and disappointed in himself. Had he known the truth of what was happening in Ohio, he would have wired Evelyn money long ago. How could Preston be such a colossal fool? The very things his brother refused to take care of were those that Tom Lyle longed for most in his own life.

Finally Evelyn ran out of steam.

"It's time for you to come home to Chicago, Evelyn," Tom Lyle told her. "With or without Preston. I'm going to make a few phone calls. I'll have a limo come for you and the baby and take you to the train station. Call me again in a half hour for the times. Be ready."

After hanging up, he decided to send Cecil a shiny new bike for Easter. With it he would include a note: *Hope to see you riding this soon, son. Love, Dad.*

Evelyn had barely managed to pack her meager belongings before a knock sounded on the apartment door. She knew it wasn't Preston. He wouldn't knock; besides, she had told him she didn't want to see him for a while. He had left meekly, perhaps even eagerly.

The driver carried her things downstairs to a shiny black limousine parked in front of the deli. People from the neighborhood stood and stared at it as if it had dropped down from outer space. Wrapped in the fur coat that had kept her and Billy warm throughout the bitter winter, Evelyn climbed in.

In Chicago, another limousine was waiting for them at the train station, and it whisked them directly to Tom Lyle's penthouse.

Tom Lyle greeted them with a warm embrace—and a beautiful new white wicker baby buggy, with a blue silk pillow and a blanket the color of Evelyn's eyes.

"I'll take care of everything you need," he said.

To fight back tears, Evelyn looked around and said, "Where is everybody?"

"Oh, Eva, Mabel, and TJ have moved into a place of their own close by. I'm sorry to say that Mabel's latest relationship didn't pan out, so until someone better comes along, she'll stay home and care for our father." He smiled into her eyes. "Evelyn, it's wonderful to have you back."

"It's wonderful to be back," she said, and this time could not restrain the tears.

Over the following weeks, Evelyn put back on the weight she had lost, and little Billy flourished. On sunny Sunday afternoons, Evelyn and Tom Lyle strolled down the avenue with the baby in the wicker buggy. They had picnics on an oversized gingham blanket in the park. They engaged in lively conversation over dinners in the penthouse or in the finest restaurants of Chicago. This was what they both had always wanted—a happy family, or at least the semblance of one.

But Preston called daily, begging Evelyn to return to Cleveland. She refused. She still loved him but knew he hadn't signed his divorce papers. She wasn't about to return to him and take away his motivation for finalizing the divorce. She was still a single woman. Looking at little Billy, happily gumming his silver teething ring, she knew she wanted more of a life for him than Preston could provide.

And not just for him. She also wanted—and deserved—more of a life for *herself*. And she knew just how to get it all.

Late one afternoon, she put on her nicest dress, ordered a sumptuous dinner for two to be delivered to the penthouse at the hour that Tom Lyle ordinarily got home, and made up her face with care. When the elevator bell rang an hour later, she expected the deliveryman—but it was Emery who emerged.

"Evelyn, dear, good to see you looking like your old self again." He strolled past her without waiting to be invited. Using the nickname he had bestowed on Tom Lyle, he asked, "No TL? I thought he'd be here by now."

"Me, too." My old self?

At the liquor cabinet, Emery made himself a drink. "You know, I've seen women wearing new spring frocks that would look great on you. They're right out of *Temporary Marriage*."

"So Mildred's look is the stuff right now?" Evelyn hadn't seen the latest Mildred Davis movie, but she didn't want to sound out of touch.

Emery sipped his drink. "Oh, yes. With her as a model, our sales volume has never been higher."

Outside, the elevator pinged again and Tom Lyle walked in. "Oh, good, Emery, you're here. I have a surprise for you downstairs."

"For me?"

"Just a little something. Want to see it? You can come too, Evelyn, if you'd like."

The elevator carried the three of them to the garage. When the doors opened, parked in front of the elevator was a new black Packard convertible. Tom Lyle drew a set of keys out of his pocket and handed them to Emery. "The whole Mildred Davis campaign was your idea. You're an absolute genius, my friend. Thank you."

"My Lord, TL, this is . . . this is just . . ."

"Best of all," Tom Lyle said, "I also bought one for"—he gestured toward the gate where an identical car was parked—"myself!"

Evelyn watched in shock. It wasn't like Tom Lyle to be so extravagant. Of course she knew Packards were his weakness, and he loved giving gifts, but still—why had Emery gotten a beautiful new convertible while she had no means of transportation at all?

"Let's take them for a spin," Tom Lyle said.

"I can't because of Billy," Evelyn said, and then realized they hadn't really meant to include her.

She watched as the men jumped into their separate cars and sped off, waving goodbye like a couple of schoolboys.

As they wound out of sight, Evelyn went back upstairs—just as the delivery man arrived with her splendid dinner. She put the food directly into the icebox and sat down to nurse Billy. *Temporary Marriage*, she thought. She didn't need to see the movie to know that such a thing was not what she had in mind for herself and her son. Not at all.

Over the next few weeks Emery visited the penthouse more and more, and his conversations with Tom Lyle included Evelyn less and less. She found herself retreating to the room she shared with Billy.

She was not familiar with a situation like this. She was used to being the focus of any man's attentions, not feeling like some kind of intruder. She wasn't even satisfied with being Tom Lyle's "beautiful muse," as he sometimes called her. She wanted a *husband*—a role Tom Lyle had seemed to have auditioned for more than once, only to decline the part when it was offered.

Somehow, she wasn't surprised when, a few nights later, he suggested it was time for her to contact her parents.

"This is no place for a young mother and her child to live," he said. "You should be around family. I promise, your parents miss you—and it must be killing them to not see their new grandson. I know it would kill *me*."

She sighed. "Maybe you're right. Maybe I can work up the nerve to ask them. But Tom Lyle, if they tell me to go away, I don't think I can stand it."

He rested his hand on hers. "And I don't see how they could resist you, Evelyn. The trick is to not call first; just go and knock on the door."

The next day, Evelyn put on an elegant and proper peach-colored dress Tom Lyle had bought her for the occasion, wrapped Billy in a new silk blanket, and stepped into Tom Lyle's Packard. The driver took her to her parents' home, twenty minutes away. She asked him to wait at the curb in case things went badly.

When she stepped into the house, little Billy in her arms, John and Emma rushed into the front hall and welcomed them both with open arms and teary eyes.

Three days later, another unexpected visitor arrived at the door of the Boechers' brownstone. He was handsome, dashing, and carried two dozen red roses.

"Preston," Evelyn said when she saw him, fighting back the tears.

She accepted the flowers and invited him inside, then was stunned when he thrust an envelope toward her. "The divorce came through, sweetheart."

As she unfolded the documents, to her amazement, my grandfather took off his hat, dropped to one knee, pulled an exquisite engagement ring out of his pocket, and asked her to be his bride.

She hesitated just long enough to quell her wary voice of reason with the thought that life would surely get better now. Then she leaped into the air. "Oh, Jesus! Yes, yes, for God's sake, yes!"

They were married in the Boecher ballroom, surrounded by both their families. Evelyn wore a short, white silk dress and her mother's wedding veil and carried a white Bible with red roses attached to it. Preston vowed to love her for the rest of his life. Even Tom Lyle and Emery had tears in their eyes when the handsome young couple kissed under an arch covered in red roses and baby's breath.

At that moment, Evelyn knew that a full and happy life was, at last, within her reach.

Ten

The Godfather

The Boechers owned several apartment buildings in the neighborhood, and John Boecher provided the newlyweds a place of their own just down the street from his and Emma's brownstone. Tom Lyle was so thankful that Preston had returned to his family that he put Evelyn on the Maybelline payroll, even though he expected her to report to work only on an as-needed basis to perform minor marketing duties.

As for Preston, he seemed determined to fulfill his role in just the way Evelyn had imagined. He went to work at Maybelline and happily minded the baby when Evelyn did odd jobs for Tom Lyle. He drank only at home, and in moderation. Still, when Evelyn was up alone with the baby at night, she would remember the drunken rages back in Cleveland. What if he reverted to his old habits and ruined everything?

At the next family gathering, Evelyn privately approached her new brother-in-law with a question. "Tom Lyle, will you be Billy's godfather?"

His grin belied the catch in his voice. "I would be honored."

In a ceremony far more elegant than Evelyn's wedding had been, ten-month-old William Preston Williams Jr., was baptized in the Catholic Church.

Although Evelyn's Lutheran parents were displeased with her decision to accept the Williams's religion for the boy, she didn't care. This way, no matter what happened, Billy would be taken care of as a member of the Williams clan.

In this instance, Tom Lyle's agenda didn't veer far from Evelyn's. Now, at last, he had a child to watch over from day to day. Little Billy would be like another son to him. And Evelyn—his feelings for her were complicated, but he wanted her in his life.

Loved ones were worth holding on to.

At Eva's wedding that October, everyone danced the Charleston. Maybelline was thriving as more and more women entered the workplace and exercised their purchasing power. The company's advertising budget had reached fifteen thousand dollars a month, while profits accumulated at ever-growing rates. The family was thriving, too. Evelyn gradually came to believe that Preston had gotten past the trauma of the war and his failures in Cleveland and was really ready to take on life's challenges. "He's not drinking as much," she told family members on both sides. Even they began to think she was right when Preston rented a cabin on Lake Zurich for the summer, near the one belonging to his in-laws. "It wasn't an act," my grandmother insisted later. "I know that man was happy then."

Prosperity and good times enveloped the entire family, and no one enjoyed it more than Tom Lyle. Cecil came to visit in 1926, and photos reveal a thirteen-year-old boy with an eager expression, neatly tucked shirt, carefully cut hair, and a strong young body. Bennie's parents were grooming him to become a minister, and he seemed keen on the idea.

Tom Lyle had nothing against the clergy or going to church—he remained a devout Catholic all his life—but he wasn't so sure about his son being pushed into a religious vocation; he suspected the Gibbs's were more concerned about shutting the still-yammering mouths of their Morganfield neighbors than they were about their grandson choosing his life's direction only after exploring the wider world and expanding his interests.

"Sure, we can go to the library, son," Tom Lyle said. "But first, how about if we go to the baseball game?"

"At Cubs Park?" asked Cecil. He had never seen a professional ball game before.

"Well, they just renamed it Wrigley Field, but yes."

"Wrigley—for the chewing gum?"

Tom Lyle smiled. Maybe his boy wasn't as cut off from life as he had feared. "Well, after the man who created the gum, yes."

Dressed in suits, Tom Lyle, Emery, and Cecil piled into Emery's new Packard and headed to the north side of Chicago. Soon Cecil forgot all about the library, studying the Bible, or getting to bed by sundown. He gaped at the fourteen thousand cheering Cubs fans, far more people than he had ever seen in one place before. The first few times bad calls from the ump brought a roar of obscenities from the crowd, Cecil shrank back in shock; but by the sixth inning, he was yelling along with everyone else. "Ya blind bastard! That was no strike!"

At the end of the day, Emery leaned close to Tom Lyle and said, "Cecil became a real boy today."

Tom Lyle beamed. "He's a bona fide Williams, that one."

On August 17, 1926, thirty-four-year-old Mabel Williams applied a bit of the eye makeup she had inspired, donned a lovely white dress, and married Chet Hewes at a High Mass. The ceremony was followed by a catered luncheon at Tom Lyle's penthouse, where the families and several Irish priests from the parish toasted the couple with shots of whiskey. A radiant Mabel waltzed with her new husband to the music of a three-piece string ensemble.

Evelyn had dressed three-year-old Billy to hold his own among his cousins. Unable to pronounce "Uncle Tom Lyle," he shortened it to "Unk Ile," which was soon what everyone at the wedding was calling Tom Lyle. The nickname would prove to be permanent.

One month after the wedding, Cecil returned to Chicago to celebrate his fourteenth birthday. Tom Lyle had a great surprise: tickets for Cecil, Emery, Preston, and himself to attend the biggest sports event in the world—the fight for the world heavyweight title between the champion, Jack Dempsey, and the challenger, Gene Tunney.

"I don't think Dempsey can be beat," said Preston, who had once been flattened by Dempsey back in Cleveland after his stint as a strikebreaker. "But I'm putting my money on Tunney anyway. The man was a marine in the Great War."

The Williams party took the train to Philadelphia, where one hundred and twenty thousand fans crowded around the outdoor ring to watch the Fight of the Century. The seats Tom Lyle had bought placed the group among governors, congressmen, and celebrities, including Hollywood cowboy star Tom Mix, who had rented a train to bring five hundred of his best pals to experience the thrill of this fight.

Preston bought the first round of beer, and Cecil pondered the sweating cup in his hand. "Dad," he yelled over the noise of the crowd. "I can't drink this!"

Preston grinned. "Then just hold onto it, kid."

The bell rang, and the crowd went wild as Tunney slipped and darted around the ring, dodging Dempsey's iron blows and responding with quick, stinging jabs. Round after round, Tunney wore Dempsey down. Tom Lyle, Emery, and Preston jumped up and screamed while Cecil, without realizing it, gulped down his beer.

Finally Tunney threw a massive left from which Dempsey couldn't recover, winning the heavyweight title and shocking the world. At the same time, Tom Lyle stopped worrying that his son might one day grow up to be a sissy. Despite the fact that Tom Lyle had never been an athlete like Preston and liked to wear Maybelline to fill in his brows and tint his eyelashes, mustache, and sideburns, he nevertheless considered himself to be manly and wanted to encourage manliness in his son.

For the next two years, Preston demonstrated his ability to be a good husband and father, and Tom Lyle rewarded him with an executive position at Maybelline Company: Head of Sales. Evelyn was delighted to see her husband get up each morning, put on a suit, and go off to work like a regular person.

"Oh," she told me wistfully, "he looked like a million bucks every day, and even had his own office right next to Tom Lyle's and Noel's. It had SALES DEPARTMENT printed on the door."

"IN GOLD," we would say in unison, and laugh.

My grandmother described these years as "heaven." Unfortunately the time was about to come when her husband, as she put it, "Led us out of the happily-ever-after and into the depths of hell."

Part 2

The Eyes Have It
The Start of Something Big
(1927–1936)

Eleven
Doctor's Orders, Darling

Late in the spring of 1927, Preston began complaining of general anxiety and severe stomach pains. By then he was drinking again; in fact, drinking more heavily than ever. Worse even than back in Cleveland. When his doctor suggested he visit the Mayo brothers' clinic in Rochester, Minnesota, for tests, my grandmother gladly packed his bags and waved goodbye to him as the train pulled out of the station.

She might have behaved differently if she had known what lay over the horizon.

As Preston sat in the waiting room at the Mayo Clinic, reading a *Photoplay* magazine, he heard a voice say, "So, who's the latest dish in Hollywood?"

He looked up at the dapper young man sitting across from him. "Viola Dana; she's what's happening right now."

The man grinned. "She's a real looker, and I should know; she's married to a good friend of mine." The man stretched out his hand. "I'm Charlie Chase."

Preston shook his hand. "Preston Williams. So you know the dame, too?" Preston spoke as if movie stars were common visitors in his life. "She works for my brother and me."

"You're in the movie business?"

"No, cosmetics. We own a little eye-makeup company called Maybelline. Viola's been doing our ads for several years now. Appeals to the flappers."

"Well, I'll be damned. Maybelline, eh?"

Preston was studying his new acquaintance. "I've seen you in a movie or two, right?"

"Very likely." Chase described his career as a silent film comedian and director. Preston was fascinated. Like Preston, Chase was at the Mayo Clinic to have tests for severe stomach pain. He suggested Preston come to warm, sunny Southern California later to regain his health.

Preston laughed. "I'd need orders in writing from the doc to get that one past my wife!"

"That shouldn't be a problem. Listen, I don't like eating alone. Are you staying at the Kahler Grand by any chance?"

"Absolutely."

"Want to meet up at six in the Lord Essex?"

"Assuming the doc doesn't recommend a diet of dry toast, sure."

Chase laughed. "I'm sure their toast is great, too."

At dinner, the two men ordered as if they could eat anything. "The doctor told me my nervous condition affects my gut," Preston said. "He said a change of scenery and some rest would do me good."

Chase laughed. "Did you get that in writing?"

Preston didn't laugh.

"What's a man like you have to be nervous about?"

"Well, for starters, I hate my job." Preston described the intolerable situation of dressing in a suit and dragging himself to an office each day—to sell women's cosmetics.

Chase gave him a long, searching look. "You ever done any acting?"

"Only when I want to get my wife to believe I'm sorry for drinking and staying out late." They both laughed. "Actually, I did model for Lord and Taylor for a while."

"What else can you do besides sell cosmetics?"

Preston focused on the things he loved most. "Hunt, fish, ride horses—and I used to box for prize money."

"Hell, you're a perfect fit for Hollywood! You're good-looking and have the kind of face that can pass for all-American or Latin with the right makeup. I've got lots of connections in the business; I could introduce you around. Since Valentino died, no one has stepped in to replace him, but you look a hell of a lot like him, you know. Might be an opening for another great lover in Hollywood."

Preston's gaze turned inward.

"But you'd really be perfect in action movies," Chase went on. "I just finished shooting a couple of two-reelers, *Crazy Like a Fox* and *Dog Shy,* and I have a pending project with Universal called *Movie Night.* I'm sure I could get you a bit part or some stunt work. Interested?"

This time, Preston didn't hesitate at all. "Hell, yeah."

Back in Chicago, he pitched a trip to California in terms of regaining his health.

Evelyn felt as if she had stepped off the edge of a cliff. "California? But what about Billy and me?"

Preston busied himself with his suitcase, putting in only the lightest-weight clothes he owned. "I should only be gone for a few weeks. No need to uproot you and Billy."

"How can you just take off and leave your family?"

He gave her a serious look. "Evelyn, I've got to do what the doctors advised."

Tears filled her eyes. "Please don't leave us, Preston. It's not safe for a woman alone in Chicago. Who will take care of Billy and me?"

The truth was, Preston hadn't really given that much thought, but now that he did, he still couldn't worry about it. The burden would simply fall on her parents or, of course, Billy's godfather, good old reliable Tom Lyle.

Still, he couldn't meet her gaze. "Look, once I'm settled, I'll send for you. How does that sound?"

Evelyn said nothing. Preston had gone to Cleveland without her, and he would do this, too, whether she liked it or not. The question was, how soon could she reverse it this time?

When Preston's train pulled into the station in downtown Los Angeles, the sun was shining in a clear blue June sky. Beautiful women strolled around in shorts and sundresses. Preston felt better already, excited in a way he hadn't been since going to war.

The next day, he rented a bungalow in Hollywood, and soon after that, Charlie Chase phoned him with an invitation. "Get ready to go to the Beverly Hills Hotel and meet none other than Viola Dana and 'Lefty' Flynn, one of Hollywood's golden couples."

Preston phoned Tom Lyle. "I'm going to need some money, TL. I have to buy a few things to wear. They dress differently out here."

Tom Lyle dutifully wired the money, and the next day, Chase sent his driver to take Preston shopping. He returned from his excursion with boxes of shirts, casual pants, and Italian shoes.

And a pair of riding boots.

A Hollywood director could not have ordered a more perfect setting to launch Preston's new life. The Beverly Hills Hotel was an oasis of palm-covered patios, bougainvillea-draped Spanish archways, architectural flourishes, and a well-lit pool. Outside, the air smelled of roses and orange trees; inside, of perfume, and the smoke of good cigars. Women wore pearls and satin dresses with slinky silk fringe. Fur stoles slipped down to reveal bare shoulders. The casual elegance stood in radical contrast to the humid Midwest with its stodgy architecture and grimy speakeasies—well, Preston would always love those; but still, this place felt right to him.

Chase saw him and approached, but Preston could look at only one person—the woman standing by a column, chatting and sipping something in a martini glass: Viola Dana. Though only four feet eleven, the woman looked even more beautiful in person than in her Maybelline shots.

Chase nodded toward the man in a suit who stood a foot taller than Viola. "That's my buddy Lefty Flynn, the stuntman and actor I mentioned. You'll like him. Never call him Maurice, even though it's his real name."

The way Nana described it, a mini Brat Pack of its time formed that night. "Lefty could have been Preston's twin," she sighed. "They were both heavy drinkers, womanizers, and athletes." In fact, Lefty had gotten his nickname for kicking the football with his left foot as a star football player at Yale—before being thrown out for running off and marrying a showgirl, only to divorce her eleven days later.

When Lefty heard that Preston loved horses, he asked a fateful question.

"Hey, how would you like to go riding with Tom Mix?"

Twelve

The Stetson

People everywhere loved Tom Mix and his portrayal of cowboys in the Wild West, but to Preston, Mix was a hero. Back in 1911, nickelodeon operator Tom Lyle used to bring home stories of Mix's films to his twelve-year-old brother—probably the only time Preston ever listened in utter fascination to what Tom Lyle had to say.

So Preston was more than ready when he, Lefty Flynn, and Charlie Chase pulled up to a Spanish-Moorish Mansion at 1010 Summit Drive in Beverly Hills. Preston's jaw dropped. He was used to the sumptuous beauty of Tom Lyle's penthouse on the lake in Chicago, but this place rocked him like one of Dempsey's haymakers. Tom Mix was just driving up in his white Rolls Royce with the famous Diamond TM Bar brand embossed in the tire treads. Nineteen years Preston's senior, but still a boy at heart, Mix wore a gigantic white cowboy hat. He honked and waved to his friends and then parked the car in the garage space between his Stutz Bearcat and his Duesenberg convertible coupe. Preston knew he was going to like this guy.

Mix got out of the car. He was decked from head to toe in cowboy gear. Chase offered his hand and said, "Always the Cadillac of Cowboys," a press nickname for Mix.

Mix shook Preston's hand. "So I hear you're the Maybelline King."

"Oh, no, not really. That's my brother, Tom Lyle. I'm just hired help."

Mix grinned. "Well, then, we'll call you Prince Preston."

At that time, Tom Mix was the highest-paid serial matinee cowboy star in the world, earning a minimum of seventeen thousand dollars a week—a jaw-dropping sum for the mid-1920s. And he wasn't shy about showing off his success. He ushered the group into a mountainous house that by modern standards might seem a bit schizophrenic. Spanish arches, white stucco walls, and a floor-to-ceiling rock fireplace defined Tom's space, while his fourth wife, actress Victoria Forde, had a separate living area featuring stained glass French cathedral windows.

It all looked terrific to Preston. He would later write to Tom Lyle, "Brother, you look like a poor paperboy next to the wealthy out here. I mean, you MUST get out here!"

If Preston was starstruck, Mix seemed to find something memorable in his new friend, too. Before Preston left that night, he was given the present of a big white Stetson hat.

One day, this hat would be passed on by Preston to his son, Bill, my father, who would keep it all his life. Dad seemed mesmerized by what it represented—a life that had so fascinated his father that he never came home for good again. Oddly, my own father idealized those times, while my grandmother cursed them.

Late in June, Mix invited Preston onto his sixty-nine-foot yacht, Miss Mixit, to go to Catalina Island with the boys to practice riding and roping. "I'll teach you some showmanship tricks, and if it works out, I might be able to use you in my next picture," he told Preston.

Preston's horsemanship must have impressed Mix, because shortly after the Catalina trip, he asked Preston if he had ever played polo.

"Always wanted to try it," Preston answered.

"Great. My friend Will Rogers is looking for another team member."

If Preston thought about his family during this time, he rarely let them know. Any phone call home meant having to listen to Evelyn's complaints, so he simply didn't call; instead, he settled for sending occasional letters, saying that the weather was making him feel better. In reality, my grandfather was roaming the hills on horseback by day and going to parties, trendy nightclubs, and the Santa Monica Beach Club at night, arm in arm with bathing beauties, starlets, and teenage girls. He worked on a few movie sets. His looks attracted paparazzi. He posed in publicity shots for movie magazines. In fact, it's possible he justified his partying and womanizing by telling himself he was seeking contacts for Maybelline—he was, after all, still on the payroll.

Although Preston didn't open his wallet very often, one day at the beach club, Lefty caught a glimpse inside it and said, "Who's the dame?"

Preston hesitated, then pulled out a small photo of Evelyn. "My wife. Think she could make it in pictures?"

"You ain't kiddin'! But why the hell are you here when you have a honey like that waiting for you at home?"

Preston looked out at the ocean and did not answer.

Thirteen

This, You Gotta See

In late August, after almost two months in California, Preston finally placed a call to Chicago. But not to his wife. Instead, he called Tom Lyle. "You've got to get out here and see this place, TL. It's the goddamn glamour capital of the world! Come out and stay at the Pink Palace, the Beverly Hills Hotel. Place is swanky. You see movie people right there in person."

"Maybe sometime," Tom Lyle said. "But Preston, you need to . . ."

"I went to a party the other night," Preston interrupted. "A Hollywood party. They had, uh, they had all types of people there. I saw two women kissing each other off in one corner and a guy dancing with another guy who was wearing lipstick and jewelry and a pink shirt. And nobody thought a thing about it."

In Chicago, Tom Lyle nearly dropped the phone. There was a time when he had feared that his younger brother wanted to beat him up for not being what he considered a "regular guy." For Preston to say something like this was a real paradigm shift. Could this really be the result of the lifestyle out there in Hollywood?

"I'll think about it," Tom Lyle finally said. "But Preston, you need to call Evelyn. It's not right that she's alone.

"I know, I know. But you just can't imagine what this pain in my gut is like. It's getting better out here, but not as fast as I'd like, and Evelyn is—well, the pain gets worse when I'm around her. I told her I'll send for her when I'm feeling up to it, and I will." Now it was Preston's turn to change the subject. "Hey, have you seen *It*?" He described meeting Clara Bow. "Her eyes are gorgeous. I think she could do as much for Maybelline as Mildred Davis and Viola Dana. Maybe even more."

"Yes," Tom Lyle said, "I did see the movie. Clara Bow. Hmm, you may be onto something, Preston."

"I told you this is the place to be. Emery isn't the only one who comes up with brilliant ideas."

Tom Lyle knew where this was going, but he was not about to reward his freeloading brother the way he did Emery. "When did you last speak with Billy?" he asked. "He really misses you."

"Yeah, I know, I know. I'll call. I will."

But he didn't.

Tom Lyle pondered his brother's invitation to come to California for a visit. This might be a good time to do it. On a professional level, everything was fine in Chicago. Even though the city sweltered in the August heat and humidity, several of the new air-conditioning machines kept the Maybelline building cool. They provided far more than just personal comfort, too. Recent improvements in what was called "man-made weather" had revolutionized the four-color printing process used in Maybelline ads, solving the problem of humidity variations that caused the inks to be absorbed differently and paper to shift, creating a fuzzy image. More importantly, the eye-makeup products themselves remained far more stable in a temperature-controlled environment, without the previous problem of oil separating from the dry ingredients and forming dewlike beads on the surface. Unfortunately, Tom Lyle's apartment building still lacked artificial weather, and he was beginning to feel a bit like a melting cake of makeup himself. Perhaps the cooling breezes of the Pacific Ocean were just the ticket.

As was his habit, he weighed the factors. The economy seemed vigorous, the market rising; more and more women could afford to spend seventy-five cents on a Maybelline product. In fact, millions of women were purchasing more than one product each year, choosing between the ever-popular solid and the newer liquid form in black or brown. Surely he could leave the business under Noel's capable direction for a while, especially with the excuse of going out West to meet with actresses who might be willing to pose for future ads.

But he had to admit, what intrigued him more than the weather or potential future business relationships was Preston's description of the Hollywood lifestyle. Could it be true that the people in that corner of the world were really so much more progressive in their thinking than what he was used to in Chicago?

Tom Lyle took Preston's advice and booked a bungalow for himself and Emery at the Beverly Hills Hotel, where he soon discovered that Preston had been right: there were no comments or raised eyebrows as he and Emery swam and sunbathed and dined together; they didn't even bother timing their comings and goings so that they were not seen at their shared lodging at the same time. No newspaper reporter snapped photos of unmarried Tom Lyle or pointed out that he appeared so often in the company of another man.

Also as predicted by Preston, at the Polo Lounge Tom Lyle and Emery did meet glamorous people, notably Gloria Swanson—one of the biggest stars in Hollywood—and over lunch discussed the possibility of her doing some print work for Maybelline. While they chatted, Charlie Chaplin sat down at the next table with a group that included Will Rogers and Viola Dana, Maybelline's very own top model. Neither Tom Lyle nor Emery had ever met her in person.

Tom Lyle took the opportunity to see what she looked like in real life. She was quite beautiful but nowhere near the knockout who appeared on the film screen or in Maybelline ads. Tom Lyle was not surprised. Over the years, as he studied the photos of actresses, he had discovered there was a special breed of photographer in Hollywood: artists who heightened the beauty of their subjects with dramatic lighting, evocative costuming, and cosmetics. One of the best such photographers at that moment was Walter F. Seely, whom Tom Lyle had hired to shoot all of Viola Dana's poses for Maybelline.

Now Tom Lyle asked a waiter to deliver his business card to Miss Dana. When she read it, her jaw dropped, and she scanned the room until her gaze fell on Tom Lyle. He waved, and she blew him a kiss. She was wearing a black silk sash around her head tied in a floppy bow over her right ear, flapper style—which held her wildly curly short hair away from her face and drew attention to her enormously expressive blue eyes. Tom Lyle and Emery approached her, and the three of them moved to the pool to talk. Tom Lyle told Viola he would like her to do another ad for him as soon as she was available.

"I'd love to," she said.

Emery grabbed a napkin and started scribbling. He said he could picture her at her vanity, holding a little red brush. The ad would say, *Miss Dana, world-famous for the beauty of her expressive eyes, has used Maybelline for years.*

Movie stars. Glamour. Gorgeous setting. Tom Lyle and Emery felt at home here in a way they never had in Chicago, even around Tom Lyle's family. Here they could be themselves.

The next day, they drove north up the Pacific Coast Highway. It was a mid-September afternoon, and the blue Pacific compelled them to stop the car and stroll in the sand.

"What do you think, Emery?" Tom Lyle finally said. "Think we could do our part of Maybelline's work from here in California?"

"The only problem I see is the autograph hunters. I can't believe so many people think we're movie stars."

"That's only because they see us chatting with movie stars. It wouldn't be like that if we lived outside Beverly Hills. We'd have weather like this, access to starlets when we need them, and the privacy to work all at the same time."

"And where exactly would this perfect spot be?"

"The Malibu Colony," Tom Lyle said promptly. "Clara Bow just built a house there, right on the beach. She'll lease it to us while we search for a place of our own."

Emery laughed and clapped Tom Lyle on the back. "As usual, you've thought of everything. Let's do it."

Although Preston lived only a few miles away, his circumstances were very different from his brother's. He wasn't driving anywhere in the decrepit old car he had bought; it was in the shop having a fender repaired—he had sideswiped a telephone pole while driving home drunk. Even before that, the vehicle had been in the shop so often that Preston sometimes had to ride the bus to movie sets. Not that he had worked much since late June. He had gone to the *Wings* set and done a little work; he had even met Clara Bow, whose strong Brooklyn accent had surprised him. But *Wings* itself had troubled him. It was a romantic drama set during World War I, in which two young men—one rich, one poor, both fighter pilots—fall in love with the same woman. The story was moving, but it brought Preston back to his own days of flying in the lead-filled skies over the Atlantic. And that made his stomach pains worsen again.

Still, pain or no pain, he had to find more work. The paychecks from the studios had been smaller than he had hoped, and he couldn't seem to hang on to the money Tom Lyle sent him.

He took the bus to the studios and checked for work, but had no luck. Will Rogers was filming in Europe, and the director of the latest Tom Mix movie was shooting scenes that didn't require extras. Dejected, heading back home empty-handed, Preston noticed a young lady and younger boy sitting across from him on the bus. The girl was pretty, and Preston struck up a conversation with her. It turned out that she spoke almost no English, yet she managed to convey that she and her brother had just arrived from Argentina. Her name was Virginia and she was sixteen years old; her brother was fifteen. They were desperate to find work—she hoped to become a live-in maid and cook, preferably in a place that could use her brother's help around the yard.

Preston considered this. After three months living as a bachelor, he had managed to turn his quarters into a pigsty, and he never cooked for himself. It would be nice not to eat at restaurants every night or get by on alcohol and pretzels.

"Would you like to come to my place?" he asked Virginia.

A few months later, on an evening in November, Tom Mix invited Preston, Lefty, and Charlie Chase to his house. Mix's wife was away, so it was just the cowboys. They played poker for a while, but Mix had something else on his mind, as did most of Hollywood. *The Jazz Singer* was showing in local theaters, and to see it, people were standing in lines that wrapped around entire city blocks. It was the first movie to include brief segments of sound and dialogue: "talkies" were on their way.

Mix was worried about that. Insiders were saying that silent films were dead, and the stars who didn't have the "right pipes" would see their careers end. "Hell," Mix said, "actors like Will and me, we ride and do rope tricks. I don't want to memorize any damn lines."

Preston shrugged. "Personally, I don't understand what all the fuss is about. I saw *The Jazz Singer,* and there's only a few minutes of anybody actually talking."

"No," Mix said, "things are changing, and I don't like it. You know, the Sells-Floto Circus keeps making me offers. A cowboy could live well doing those shows, traveling all over the country in a private railroad car, riding and roping."

As I imagine this encounter, I can picture the look of raw longing that must have passed over my grandfather's face. Traveling all over the country, riding and roping. And I can imagine something else, too. I can imagine that if Preston Williams had run off to join the circus with Tom Mix, he might have lived a much longer life.

After drinking all night at Mix's get-together, Preston couldn't eat or drink much of anything for several days; his stomach hurt too much. His young housekeeper, Virginia, tried to help him, but she wasn't feeling so well herself. She kept throwing up, especially in the mornings.

Fourteen

The Business of Family

By Christmas, Evelyn had moved with Billy into the home of her sister Verona and her husband, Charlie Stroh. Evelyn simply had to get herself and her son out of the neighborhood where she had been living. It had become too dangerous; the gang wars of Prohibition were in full swing, with killers firing Tommy guns at one another from passing cars.

Money was also a problem, one made far too vivid during the holidays. For Christmas, Verona bought her son, Will, a new bicycle and her daughter, Arvis, a tricycle. She had also asked Charlie's permission to purchase Billy a new bike, but Charlie said no. "Just to make Verona mad," according to Evelyn.

The best my grandmother could do was paint Billy's old kiddy-car red and put it under the tree. So when the kids came out to see what Santa Claus had brought them, Will and his sister sped outside on their new wheels, while Billy studied the little red toy that was just like the blue toy he already had. He turned to his mother with a plaintive stare. Why had Santa done this? Hadn't he been a good boy? Didn't Santa think he deserved a new bike or at least a new tricycle?

Evelyn tried not to cry as Billy solemnly examined his car, then pushed it outside, got in, and pedaled furiously to catch up with his cousins.

Tom Lyle and Emery returned to Chicago just in time for New Year's Eve.

When the workweek began, Evelyn called the Maybelline office and told Tom Lyle what was on her mind. "It's obvious Preston isn't coming back home and doesn't care to talk to me, so I need you to tell him something for me."

"I thought you did have a chat with Preston on the phone. He told me you did."

She laughed bitterly. "That was weeks ago, right after I saw a picture of him in *Photoplay* with some young tart on his arm and a grin on his face. I'll tell you, he didn't look sick to me. I called him and refused to hang up until he answered. When he did, he sounded like he'd been on a real toot the night before."

"What did he say?"

"Oh, he said it was just a publicity shot; it's his job to smile and look happy, but really he's in a lot of pain and needs more time to get better. The same things he says in his letters."

"I'm sorry, Evelyn, but it's true about the pain. He's got a real problem, and—"

Evelyn cut him off. "Tom Lyle, I've made up my mind to file for divorce. That's what I need you to tell him. I'm filing for divorce."

She heard Tom Lyle's breath catch. "Evelyn, darling, please. It's not right to leave him when he's so ill."

She wanted to dissolve into sobs; she wanted to ask him to comfort her. Instead, she cut him off again. "What's not right is that Billy and I have had to move in with Verona and Charlie because our old neighborhood is too danger- ous. What's not right is that I've had to start working for my father's plumbing business. What's not right is that—"

It was Tom Lyle's turn to cut in. "I know how hard it's been on you, dear, and I'm sorry I wasn't better about looking after my godson and you over the holidays, but I'll make it up to you. I'm sending you a check right now. Just say you'll reconsider, please."

"But why?" Although Evelyn was willing to accede to Tom Lyle's wishes with the words "sending you a check," she still wanted to go through the drama of being convinced.

There was a pause, then Tom Lyle said, "I was serious about Preston's health. He likes to think he's healing, but really, he's getting worse. But I'll talk to him. You're right; no matter what, he needs to come home and be with his family."

"That's all I've been saying."

"I'll make it worth your while on a continuing basis—just please, promise me you won't leave Preston."

A personal check arrived for her that afternoon. I never learned the amount, but it pretty much floored my grandmother. In addition, she was now certain that Preston would catch the next eastbound train; who could resist the maneuvers of Tom Lyle? That night she wrote Preston a letter saying how excited she was that he was coming home, signing it *Your loving wife, always.*

It took Tom Lyle considerable effort to reach Preston, and when he did, he told his brother about Evelyn's threat. "Preston, you've got to come back. Your office will be waiting, and I'll double the salary you were making when you left."

Silence.

"Preston?"

"I have some . . . uh . . . business to attend to here."

"Such as?"

Preston sighed. "Shit. I got a real problem." He explained about his new roommates, the live-in maid from Argentina and her brother. "She, um, really moved in."

Tom Lyle instantly made the connection. "My God, Preston, a sixteen-year-old girl? What the hell were you thinking? You need to get back here on the next train."

"I can't. She's pregnant."

For a moment Tom Lyle couldn't speak at all. Then he said, "Holy Mother of God. Evelyn will kill you."

But Tom Lyle, always the fix-it man, took charge once again. He and Emery rushed back to California, where Tom Lyle offered Virginia enough money to take care of herself until her baby was born. Meanwhile, Emery, who knew he would never have a child of his own, committed to financially supporting Virginia and the baby as if they were his own kin. Like Preston, Virginia would be put on the Maybelline payroll.

This solution seemed perfect in every way, except that Virginia begged Preston to stay with her until the baby was born, five months in the future.

"What will you tell Evelyn?" Tom Lyle asked his brother. "She's already about to blow."

"I'll think of something."

"She can never know about this arrangement, you know, or she'll kill me, too."

"I said I'll think of something."

That night my grandfather called Evelyn at the Stroh residence. "You see, honey, I'm in the middle of shooting a movie out here. I promise, as soon as it's done, I'm coming home."

To Evelyn, this meant no more than a few weeks—but the time stretched through the driest winter and early spring on record. Only the regular checks from Tom Lyle soothed her concern.

At the same time, living with the Strohs turned out to not be much safer than living downtown had been. Charlie owned a laundry, and gangsters harassed him constantly for insurance payments—meaning a portion of the laundry's profits. This did not go over well with Charlie, whom my grandmother called a "tough, hard drinking, womanizing bastard who carried a gun and wouldn't take shit from anyone." One evening, as he drove Evelyn and Billy home after picking them up at her parents' home, he shouted "Get down!" Evelyn glimpsed a sawed-off shotgun pointing at them through the window of a passing black sedan. She hurled Billy onto the floor and dove on top of him, screaming. But she wasn't screaming in terror or even cursing the gangsters. What came out of her mouth was: "God damn you, Preston! God damn you!"

The last straw came in May, when a couple of gangsters barged straight into the Stroh home, demanding that Charlie pay up. Little Billy was standing in the hallway, so terrified he wet his pants. Charlie whipped out his pistol and shot one of the men point blank. The other fled. When Evelyn came in and swooped her son into her arms, before her lay a man bleeding to death on the living room rug.

That did it. Without notifying anyone, Evelyn started divorce proceedings against Preston. As soon as the papers were ready, she and Bunny went to the courthouse, where she signed the papers, and had them sent to Preston. On the way home, my tough-as-nails grandmother finally fell apart and sobbed. "What am I going to do now? What am I going to do now?"

Bunny and her husband wanted to help. Unable to have children of their own and adoring "sweet Billy," as they called him, they offered to adopt Evelyn's son.

Although my grandmother's anguish and fear were real, her next move was entirely calculated. She phoned Tom Lyle once again, telling him about the shooting at the Stroh home and about the divorce papers on their way to Preston—adding that his godson, little William Preston Williams Jr., was about to become William Cotter.

Fifteen
The Deal

om Lyle was a worldly man, so he probably knew Evelyn was bluffing—but he was also compassionate and he understood her intolerable situation. This time, when he reached Preston by phone, he didn't bother with greetings. "Get home now, or you will not only lose your wife and child, I'll take you off Maybelline's payroll and give your entire salary to Evelyn."

With Preston, money talked when all else was mute. Knowing Tom Lyle would make sure his new family received at least the basic necessities of food and shelter, he promised to catch a train to Chicago within the week.

Only after Tom Lyle was sure Preston was on the train, did he call Evelyn. "Evelyn, I pledge that I will support you for the rest of your life if you stop the divorce proceedings, keep our little Billy at home with you, and help Preston as best you can."

Evelyn heard most clearly exactly six of those words: *for the rest of your life.*

I don't think there was ever any question that Evelyn would accept Tom Lyle's offer, but in her mind, she did it on her own terms. Being Mrs. Preston Williams was now strictly business. She didn't halt the divorce proceedings because she was a lovesick fool. No—she did it is as a mother sacrificing her own happiness for her son's welfare. She did it as a savvy businesswoman collecting a fat paycheck.

By the time Preston arrived in Chicago, he had been gone for more than a year. Tom Lyle and Emery were about to leave for their beach house in California for a couple of weeks, but first Tom Lyle wrote Preston a bonus check along with his regular pay, so he could rent an apartment that his family could all move into.

Preston found a nice little place on north Clark Street, just around a sharp corner from the Maybelline Building. He moved right in—but didn't call his wife to let her know he was there.

He had been forced to give up California, his teenage lover, and his new baby—who, of course, also needed him—to suit Evelyn. Fine. Let her make the next move.

Of course Evelyn was also stubborn. Although she had heard Preston was back in town, she continued to live with Verona and Charlie until a particularly loud fight in the next room woke her and Billy one night. Billy started to cry for his daddy, and Evelyn knew she had to make a move.

The next day, after finishing her work at Maybelline, looking professional yet flirtatious in a light summer dress, she walked around the corner and pushed the doorbell outside a two-bedroom apartment. Preston opened the door. He was dressed to go out, but when he saw Evelyn and the way she looked, he grinned and gestured for her to come inside. "Evelyn, honey."

She said nothing, just walked in and looked at the whiskey bottle on the table in the little dining area, with a flask and small funnel beside it.

He caught her cold stare. "Need a belt?" he asked, with another knowing grin.

"I do," she said, stone-faced.

He handed her a drink and poured another for himself. As Evelyn sipped, she walked from room to room, pointedly scrutinizing. The Kelvinator refrigerator hummed along in the kitchen. The stove was a white enamel gas-burner. Preston caught her looking at it.

"With a thermostat," he boasted. "Now you won't have any excuse for burning the chops."

Preston followed her into the larger of two bedrooms, where she inspected the closet and the white cast-iron bed.

"You look as gorgeous as ever," Preston murmured from close behind her.

She turned, ducking away from his grasp. How could he claim to have been sick? He looked tan and wonderful. Damn, it was good to see him, with his maddening little grin. She knew he was undressing her in his mind, imagining their bodies moving together. She felt the powerful pull between them but resisted it. She was doing her duty here, nothing more.

Tossing down the rest of her drink, she got ready to lay down the new terms and conditions of their lives. Preston would have to agree to stop running around at night, and . . .

In a swooping motion, he pulled her to him and pressed his lips to hers.

She lay down, all right, but not to dictate terms and conditions.

The next morning, she and Billy moved from the Strohs' brownstone to the north Clark Street apartment.

At first, Billy was shy around his father, but after Preston put on the Stetson and performed some bow-legged quick-draw cowboy silliness, his son began to laugh. Preston then put the huge hat on the boy, who clowned a bit and then grabbed hold of Preston's leg, clamping fiercely on to his daddy. Preston pried him off and carried him around, the family reestablished.

Or so it seemed. He was reporting for work at the Maybelline Building, but as the days went by, Preston couldn't get Hollywood out of his mind. Evelyn got sick of hearing him say things like, "Charlie Chase thinks that the talkies are . . ." or "Tom Mix once said to me . . ." or "Will Rogers said my riding ability is good enough to . . ."

Worse, Preston seemed to focus his frustrations on Billy. Every time the four-year-old cried, Preston grew increasingly upset.

"Somebody's got to toughen the kid up. He needs to learn to defend himself." Preston started staging fights in the empty lot next door with the other kids in the building. When Evelyn found out, she shooed the children back home and turned on her husband. "Are you crazy?"

She couldn't understand him. He had everything right here in his grasp, practically thrust upon him. Why couldn't he be more like Tom Lyle? Whenever she brought Billy with her to the Maybelline offices, Unk Ile would hold his arms out and cry, "Is that my little June bug? Junie, come in. I have something here for you." Then he would click his fingers and say, "You have a bug in your ear," and pull a shiny new quarter out of the air behind Billy's ear.

Tom Lyle made Billy feel important, but Preston always had to make himself the center of attention. He earned his way back into the family's good graces by charming the cousins with adventurous stories about the war, cowboys, gangsters, and movie stars. Cigarette dangling, hat tilting as he hammed his lines, he was a one-man show. He would chase the kids around and throw them into the air. According to my grandmother, Preston had to create as much drama in his life as possible to feel alive. Of course, in this instance, I believe Mrs. Kettle was insulting Mr. Pot over their shared MO.

Preston had his theatrical side, too. He liked to dress up in a black trench coat and put on dark makeup, so he looked as if he had just arrived from Hollywood with a great tan. He would accent his sideburns and eyebrows with Maybelline. Eva's husband, Chess, adopted the same look. Chess had a lovely singing voice, and, for a while, Preston presented himself as Chess's manager, getting him gigs at private clubs in return for a few bucks or some free drinks. At first Evelyn raised a stink about these shenanigans, but the truth was, as long as she and Eva were included in the charade, she secretly loved it.

There was a special, shadowy thrill to living in Chicago during that era. Evelyn and Eva took every opportunity to dress in fur coats with strings of pearls dripping down low-cut, black silk flapper dresses short enough to expose their legs. Although Evelyn loved Tom Lyle's lifestyle and sensibilities, it was the excitement of Preston that kept her addicted, a junkie in need of ever more thrilling fixes.

He always needed more, too, especially after the glamour and excitement of California. Every day, he found less and less to like about Chicago—the weather, the social life, the family, the job, or as he called it, "busy work." His main responsibility as sales manager was to visit drugstores with samples of Maybelline in a six-pack container and suggest that the vendor purchase two packs at a time and place them near the cash register or soda fountain. Not exactly riding horses in a Tom Mix film. Then, once the orders were in, he would send them to Uncle Chess in the shipping department so a Maybelline truck could drive all over the city and beyond to drop them off. He would have almost preferred to drive the truck himself.

On Valentine's Day in 1929, a news flash brought him some excitement, Chicago-style—the St. Valentine's Day massacre, an episode of gang violence in which seven men were shot to death execution style in a warehouse on north Clark Street.

When Evelyn heard how close by the murders had occurred, she immediately proposed a move to the suburbs. But Preston saw the killings differently—as an opportunity for adventure. He called Chess, who had also just heard the news, and said, "Meet me on the corner in fifteen minutes. We've got to get over there." He told Evelyn he was taking Billy out for a soda and would be back in an hour or so.

Clark Street was a mob scene, jammed with cars and spectators. It looked impossible to get through, but Chess had had the foresight to bring some fake press passes he had used before and gave one to Preston to put in the hatband of his derby.

"Good thinking, pal." Preston threw Billy up on his shoulders.

When they got to the police lines, Chess tipped his hat, showing the fake pass, and said, "Press." A young cop ushered him through. Then Chess came back and distracted the cop while Preston, carrying Billy, sneaked by. They managed to get close enough to see the blood splattered all over on the brick wall and concrete floor where the victims had been machine-gunned.

"This is brutal," Chess said. "Shouldn't we get Billy out of here?"

"In a minute." Preston patted Billy's leg. "You okay, son?"

When they returned home, Billy promptly told his mother about the policemen and the blood, and Evelyn exploded.

"You bastard! What are you trying to do? Scare him to death? What's next, a shot of bourbon?"

"Why not?" Preston said. "When I was five I snitched some of TJ's Old Granddad."

"Well, that explains it. No wonder your brains are burned out and your guts are on fire all the time."

To his son, Preston acted more like a rebellious older brother than a father. To his wife, he acted more like an itinerant lover. He gave her occasional moments of intimacy and delight, but in between those highs, Evelyn could never be sure what terrible thing he might do next.

Or already had done.

Sixteen

Who's Virginia?

*W*hen Herbert Hoover was inaugurated as president in March 1929, consumer spending on credit stood at an all-time high. More and more people spent money on entertainment, especially movies. Preston certainly did and also kept tabs on his buddies back in Hollywood. He found out that Tom Mix had opted for a contract with the Sells-Floto Circus. He found out that Lefty Flynn's mother had committed suicide. He found out that Flynn and Viola Dana had gotten a divorce. On the other hand, Charlie Chase's career was going gangbusters. He had completed one of his last silent films, *The Booster*, and was currently shooting *Modern Love*, a partial talkie. The directors liked his voice, so he even got to do some singing.

Hearing this news, Preston fantasized about coat-tailing his way into a film career in talkies—if only he could buy a one-person, one-way ticket back to his beloved California. And when he got there, he could reconnect with his new baby boy and the young, compliant, sweet-natured girl he had left there.

In April, he received an engraved invitation to an awards ceremony that a newly formed Hollywood group called the Academy of Motion Picture Arts and Sciences was holding to honor movies and the people who created them. Preston was invited because of his small part in the movie *Wings*, which had been nominated to receive an award. The shindig was black tie and would be hosted by Douglas Fairbanks and Cecil B. DeMille at the Hollywood Roosevelt Hotel.

Delirious with joy, Preston showed the invitation to Evelyn. "You'll love this, baby. You could get a swell new evening gown for it."

Evelyn didn't hesitate to buy a smashing outfit. She'd show those Hollywood honeys what they were up against! Train tickets were purchased. Everything was ready, but Evelyn was not as thrilled as she pretended to be. She had missed her last couple of periods and was beginning to throw up in the mornings. As the time for their departure to the coast approached, she told Preston she had the flu, then contacted a nurse she had visited more than once since Billy had been born. She simply refused to have another child with the undependable, unsteady Preston. The problem was that while abortions had been quite common and easy to get earlier in the 1920s, the authorities had recently begun a crackdown. Evelyn learned that her nurse had stopped performing abortions for fear of prosecution.

Desperate, Evelyn turned to her sister Verona, who had some familiarity with the same issues. The next day they drove to a ghetto area of the city and parked in front of a run-down tenement building. They climbed a dark stairway lit only by a naked light bulb, and Evelyn went alone into a dingy apartment. The abortionist used a coat hanger and alcohol, and when Evelyn cried out, the woman stuck rags in her mouth and told her to be quiet.

When Preston came home from work that evening, he found his wife lying in bed, pale, weak, and shaky.

"I'm calling Dr. Rogers," he said. "You can't travel like this."

"Already saw him," Evelyn lied in a faint voice. "Preston, I have to stay in bed for two weeks."

"Oh, no, babe. Maybe if you get a good night's sleep, you'll feel better."

But after two days, Preston saw no improvement at all. He paced, wringing his hands. "Can you get Bunny to come look after you for a few days? You know how much this trip means to me."

"Preston. Please don't leave me. Don't leave us again. I won't make it if you do."

And, amazingly, Prince Preston stayed. I suspect that my grandmother told her husband she had had a miscarriage. Certainly she didn't tell him the truth; that would only have given him good reason to rush off to California and never return.

Whatever she told him, it worked. Preston gave his invitation to the awards ceremony to Tom Lyle and stayed home to care for his wife and son.

To Evelyn, this was a sign that he truly did love her and Billy, and all would be well.

Thirty-three-year-old Tom Lyle happily accepted Preston's invitation to replace him at the Academy Awards. By that point, he was spending $200,000 a year on advertising, with Maybelline ads appearing in forty popular magazines, as well as Sunday newspaper supplements and specialized journals such as *Theatre.* Between 1915 and 1929, he had spent over a million dollars to advertise Maybelline. Everywhere, close-up photos of eyes darkened with Maybelline projected a provocative—but no longer perceived as sinful—eroticism.

In fact, Tom Lyle had just launched his 1929 *"Springtime is Maybelline Time!"* campaign, featuring an idealized lovely young miss looking up adoringly at her man with starry eyes. The offers to vendors pitched display cartons, each holding a half-dozen eye makeup containers, and urged druggists to try product placement by the soda fountain for "forcing extra sales." Tom Lyle felt that the ad would assure continued prosperity for the company, meaning he could afford to leave Maybelline in the hands of Noel while he and Emery headed out to California for a few days.

On the night of May 16, 1929, two hundred and fifty people—actors, producers, directors, professionals, and their guests—attended the first annual Academy Awards celebration. Tom Lyle and Emery wore black tuxedos with tails. Glamour ruled the night. Emery, always starstruck in the presence of his idols, nudged Tom Lyle constantly, pointing out Douglas Fairbanks Jr., Wallace Berry, John Barrymore, William Haines, Tom Mix, Will Rogers, and Ronald Colman.

Chaplin's film *The Circus* won special honors, as did Warner Brothers, the studio that had produced the first talking picture, *The Jazz Singer.* Then came the moment everyone had been waiting for. The emcee announced, "And the final Golden Statue of the Academy for 'Most Outstanding Production' goes to the epic silent film, *Wings.*"

Tom Lyle cheered and later phoned the news to Preston from the Roosevelt Hotel. He also asked how Evelyn was doing.

"She seems stronger," Preston replied.

That night, Tom Lyle couldn't get Evelyn off his mind. If she had been here with him, dressed to kill, she would have caused a sensation. He had studied the eyes of Clara Bow, Viola Dana, Marion Davies, Mildred Davis, Lillian Gish, Mary Pickford, and Gloria Swanson. They were the most beautiful women in the world—but not a one, he believed, was more stunning than Evelyn. How unfortunate that she wasn't a movie star; he couldn't risk basing an ad campaign on photos of her, however alluring she might be.

The lease was up at the beach house, so Tom Lyle and Emery spent the next few days looking for a home to purchase; a large place where they could have an office to work from. When Tom Lyle learned that Rudolph Valentino's

Mediterranean villa in the Hollywood Hills was available, he leased it for a couple of years, although he had no doubt that he would one day buy it. To him, the Villa Valentino represented the American Dream come true.

When Tom Lyle returned to Chicago, Cecil arrived for a visit shortly afterward, and Tom Lyle couldn't believe how tall he had grown and how handsome he was. It was the summer before Cecil's senior year of high school, and to my great-uncle's delight, he not only excelled in academics, he played football and was good-natured and popular. Tom Lyle made an appointment at the best photography studio in Chicago and ordered portraits in profile of himself and his son. He also painstakingly applied Maybelline to their eyes and sideburns. The picture came out as a masterpiece that would thereafter hang in any home where Tom Lyle lived.

Tom Lyle had never been happier. His son loved him. Profits were soaring. His accomplishments afforded the freedom he desired. Life was good.

Then, one day at work, he got a call from Evelyn.

"I hate to bother you, TL, but I just heard Noel's secretary saying something about sending a monthly check to a woman in California. I didn't know we had anyone on the payroll in California. So I was just wondering, who's Virginia?"

Seventeen

Miss Maybelline
and Mr. Hyde

"Virginia? Oh, she does some scheduling work for me when I'm in California."

"But you're not in California now," Evelyn said, "and Virginia is still receiving monthly checks."

She listened as Tom Lyle mumbled something about a bonus and said he would look into it.

Evelyn hung up and stared at the phone. Then she treated Mary—the secretary—to lunch. "She got grilled along with the cheese," was how Evelyn later put it.

During the meal, she learned that the mysterious Virginia had been receiving checks for about a year and was the only L.A. employee on the payroll. Evelyn consulted her mental calendar. That meant the mysterious Virginia had been receiving payments for much of the time Preston had been in Hollywood.

At home, Evelyn started checking Preston's pockets every night—and soon discovered a postcard addressed to the Maybelline office with a return address in Hollywood. On the back was a scrawl of crude printing.

Baby walking.
When you come see us?
Virginia

Evelyn's heart thundered and her cheeks burned. What kind of scheduling assistant could barely write?

The moment Preston walked in the door, she confronted him with the postcard. "I believe this is yours. Who is it from?"

"Toots, it's nothing." He scanned the front and back. "Virginia is just some girl I met on a bus out there one day. She and her brother needed a place to stay, so I hired her to cook and clean for me."

"She lived with you?"

"She and her brother. To cook and clean."

"How old is this Virginia?"

"Oh, eighteen or so."

"Eighteen. And her brother?"

"Fifteen."

"When did they move in?"

"I don't know. Not too long after I got out there, I guess."

"And her baby's just now walking."

"I guess so."

"What's his name?"

"Tony."

"Is he yours?"

"What?"

Evelyn stared into her husband's blinking eyes. "Is he your child?"

Preston drew himself up. "How can you ask me that?"

And he stormed out of the apartment.

Noel said, "I assure you, Evelyn, there is no child belonging to Preston in California."

Then he held his breath. When Evelyn had made an appointment to see him, he had assumed the subject would be something about Maybelline business, not this. To make matters worse, he knew why she had chosen him: because she trusted him. Good old scrupulous Noel, the faithful husband, the dependable father, the man who would never lie.

And he did hate to lie. But he had agreed to his brothers' deception and even understood its necessity. An honest reply to Evelyn's question would have terrible consequences for the family and also for Emery, who was supporting little Tony and Virginia. There were bigger matters at stake here than Evelyn's feelings.

But he wasn't a good liar, and Evelyn's expression told him she wasn't convinced—so he threw in a deflection that also had the advantage of being true: "By the way, Tom Lyle and I have been discussing something special for you in the company."

"For me?"

"How about we talk about it over lunch tomorrow in the tearoom at the Edgewater Hotel—you, me, Tom Lyle, and Preston?"

"I'd love that."

"I turned every head when I walked in," was the way the ever-modest Evelyn described her arrival at the Edgewater the next day.

All three brothers jumped up to pull out her chair. She loved the feeling that she not only had their attention but was somehow in control of the day's proceedings.

Noel started things off by talking to Preston, casually suggesting that his youngest brother hire an assistant to help in the sales department.

Preston played it cool. "I'm doing okay. I can handle it alone."

"I think you should have help, too," Evelyn chimed in. "The weight of it is taking a toll on you, Preston." She caught their expectancy and added, "Darling."

"Hmm. I don't know, baby."

"Just as long as your assistant's old and ugly," Evelyn joked.

"Or young and gorgeous," Tom Lyle said. "Someone with a great sense of style and flair; someone familiar who establishes long-term relationships with those druggists and keeps them positioning Maybelline in the best spots. Someone like you, Ev."

"Me? Are you kidding?"

They were all smiling at her.

"Sure, you." Preston grabbed her hand. "We'd be great together, a real team."

For my grandmother, these words provided the perfect antidote to the previous night's misery. They presented her with a clear choice: huff and demand the truth about Virginia and Tony—and perhaps end up living alone with Billy again—or shut up and enjoy a sweet deal.

She smiled. "Where do I sign?"

Evelyn soon found herself doing most of Preston's work. He often complained of stomach pains and couldn't travel, so she would hop in a company car and spend the day driving to stores all over the city by herself.

Her new career had another facet to it as well. She was expected to peruse the magazines that advertised Maybelline products, analyzing articles and other advertisements to discover the trends that appealed most to the new breed of women entering the workforce. She would write up a summary of her research for Tom Lyle, who would then make decisions for his next ad campaign.

It was a full day's work, and she came home tired, only to find a full-time job there, too. Both Preston and little Billy seemed to need constant emotional support. "I felt like I was holding up the whole world," my grandmother later described those times to me.

In November, she was also asked to make up flyers to be mailed to dime stores around the country. As soon as they were ready, she set out to walk the few blocks to the printer to pick them up. Being out on the downtown streets with its drive-by shootings and crude, loud-mouthed gangsters made her nervous, but it was broad daylight, and she was determined to do the job right.

The day had turned chilly and windy, and she wore her fur coat along with her high heels, giving her the appearance of an executive's wife more than of a marketing assistant. As cars passed, men whistled and horns honked, but that was okay, even a welcome ego boost. She picked up the flyers and headed back, this time into the famous Chicago wind. It ruffled the fur her coat and blew her hair into her eyes, but she teetered onward, clutching the armload of Maybelline flyers.

She was halfway back when a black sedan screeched around the corner. As it passed her, its engine backfired, the sound like a gunshot. Evelyn jumped as if electrocuted, throwing her arms reflexively into the air. Maybelline flyers exploded into the sky and flew everywhere, swarming like fallen leaves over drivers' windshields. Horns blared, tires squealed, cars thumped into one another in a drum crescendo.

A journalist happened to be nearby, snapping photos of a new building. At the sound of the backfire he turned, also crouching for self-protection, and happened to snap a shot of Evelyn staring in dismay at the swirl of papers.

Evelyn was close enough to the Maybelline Building that everyone came running out to see what was going on. Tom Lyle, Noel, Preston, Chess, and Chet all looked at each other as someone said the obvious: "Only Evelyn could cause such a commotion."

The next day, a newspaper headline read: *Miss Maybelline Stops Traffic* above a photo of Evelyn standing amidst a shower of flyers.

Tom Lyle laughed. "Evelyn, with that one photo you've accomplished more for marketing Maybelline than any flyer ever could."

After that, Evelyn would forever be known as "Miss Maybelline."

During the following week, orders poured in. Preston should have been enthusiastic about this, but he was too sick to notice. In fact, he fell into another of his depressions and quit going to work at all. Every day when Evelyn came home, he was drunk and melancholy, unshaved and unkempt. His hair hadn't been cut since the tearoom lunch at the Edgewater. He had lost all pride in his personal appearance. Seeing him looking like a bum horrified Evelyn.

One night, after putting Billy to bed, she made some soup for herself and tried to get Preston to eat a little. He ignored her until she sat down to relax a bit with her own meal; then he started groaning. Alcohol fumes wafted off him and he turned a red, bleary eye to her. "Why are you out so late every night?"

"I'm working, Preston. One of us has to."

"You're cheating on me, aren't you?"

"That's insane. The only man I'm spending time with is your own brother at work."

"You've always loved him more than me."

"That's in your own warped mind. If I loved him more than you, why would I be here at all?"

"I don't know. I've never known why you stay with me."

"At this point, I don't know either."

Setting her bowl aside, she went to bed.

At around one in the morning, Preston woke her. "Would you make me some soup, babe?"

Although she was exhausted, she figured she had better do it; this might be her only chance to get food down him.

Soon she set a plate of nicely scrambled eggs in front of him and watched in dismay as he drenched them in ketchup. "That doesn't seem like it could be good for you," she said.

"It's the only way I can eat them." He took one bite, then dropped his fork, bent forward, and clutched his stomach in his arms. "Oh, God!"

Evelyn reached for him. "What can I do?"

"Nothing!" He lunged to his feet, grabbed the tablecloth, and ripped it off the table, smashing dishes on the floor, spilling yellow eggs and red ketchup onto the linoleum. "God, I can't take this anymore! I'd rather die than stay here! I'm like a cripple! I can't live like this!" He grabbed a butcher knife and stalked out of the kitchen. "If I'm going to die, you're both going with me!"

He was heading toward Billy's bedroom. She threw herself in front of him and bared her teeth. "You'll have to kill me first!"

Perhaps her words reached him. Perhaps his pain was so debilitating he couldn't muster enough ferocity to do the deed. Or perhaps he recognized the insanity of what he had said. In any event, he dropped the knife and staggered to the couch, where he curled up and whimpered like a baby.

Evelyn poured him a little peppermint schnapps, brought him a hot water bottle, and eventually convinced him to go to bed.

She spent the rest of the night startling at every sound he made.

Eighteen
Crashes

Two days later, she called Tom Lyle. "I know we had a deal," she said, "but Preston is just . . . I can't tell you how awful things are. He's drinking and crazy with pain. I can't stand by him anymore."

"Don't say that, Evelyn. He'll snap out of it. I've seen it a million times; be patient with him."

Patient. The word made her want to scream. "It's too hard on me to raise a child, take care of a sick man, and work at the same time. I can't even walk the streets of this city alone. It's terrible out there, and Preston's no help. What would happen if I got shot? Who would take care of things?"

"You know I'll help, Evelyn," Tom Lyle said.

A few days later, when Evelyn showed up for work, she noticed a brand new sedan parked in front of the Maybelline building. Noel met her and handed her a set of keys. "It's yours." He grinned. "Feel like an executive now?"

Upstairs, he showed her Preston's office door. Except it wasn't Preston's anymore. His name had been removed. In its place, the sign read, in gold: *Miss Maybelline.*

Evelyn attacked her new job with her usual single-mindedness. Although she had many specific duties to perform—things to keep her busy, involved, happy—to Tom Lyle, her primary role was still to act as his eyes into a woman's world. After all, the company's most successful ads were the ones that Evelyn said would prompt her to buy the products. The faces that appeared in print might not be hers—they were either artists' idealized renderings or photographs of movie stars—but Evelyn remained the spirit and inspiration behind all of Tom Lyle's advertising campaigns.

And soon, he would need all the inspiration he could get.

On October 29, 1929, a news flash announced that the Dow industrial average had fallen almost 23 percent, and the stock market had lost a total of sixteen billion dollars in value in a month.

Sixteen billion dollars.

Tom Lyle knew the economic crash would be devastating for the country in general and would certainly ruin many companies. Although Maybelline, as a family-owned business, was not directly affected by the Wall Street disaster, there was no question that the aftermath would be devastating. Who would choose to buy cosmetics over food?

Despite his worries, in an act typical of my great-uncle's thoughtfulness and generosity, Tom Lyle asked Noel to double the amount of money Bennie and Cecil received each month. He wanted to make sure they were as insulated as possible from the hard times that had arrived.

The prosperity and opulence of the Roaring Twenties were gone, disappearing along with the vamps who had loaded up with Maybelline's seventy-five-cent product. Tom Lyle knew he would have to find ways to keep his product in the public eye, yet at a price women could afford, if he wanted to maintain his company in the years to come. The flashy flapper look was quickly devolving to a more demure look fit for austere times. Viola Dana remained a Maybelline favorite—but now, instead of representing the flapper, she portrayed the queenly matron revealing her beauty secrets to the world.

This ad pleased Tom Lyle, and despite the national situation, he felt good about the future. In fact, when Noel showed him a story in the *Wall Street Journal* about a brand-new skyscraper being constructed over the old Waldorf-Astoria Hotel in New York—the Empire State Building, the tallest structure in the world—Tom Lyle took it as a sign that the bad economy would be only a temporary dip in the road.

He was rarely so wrong. When Emery suggested an ad tie-in to the Empire State Building—*Things Are Looking Up,* featuring young women with gorgeous eyes gazing up at a new skyscraper—Tom Lyle backed it enthusiastically, until it became clear that for most of the country, things were looking very much down. They abandoned the new ad campaign as the market continued to decline, wages plummeted, and credit dried up. When industrial production collapsed as well, many businesses went with it.

But not Maybelline. While innovative and widespread advertising was responsible for a lot of the company's success over the years, that was not the whole story. Constant innovation in the lab also played a big part. That spring, thanks to the introduction of an improved waterproof eye makeup, total sales rose to $750,000—at a time when most businesses were struggling simply to stay afloat.

In fact, the Maybelline team even prepared to expand their product line. Evelyn had long admired makeup artist Max Factor's use of eye shadow on Hollywood actresses, so Tom Lyle hired chemists and sank a great chunk of capital into producing blue, black, brown, and green eyebrow pencils and eye shadows.

After launching the new products, Tom Lyle and Emery felt confident enough to take a trip out West to their new California home, the Villa Valentino. The Villa was also the perfect place for Tom Lyle and Emery to figure out what to do next.

What they did was develop a whole new look for upcoming Maybelline ad campaigns. Artists, designers, and architects—especially in the film industry—were at that time being powerfully influenced by a new decorative style that had grown out of Art Nouveau in France. Later, this style and others that shared similar aesthetics would be lumped under the label for "decorative arts"—art deco.

Tom Lyle and Emery loved the style, its opulence and complexity, and considered it the perfect vehicle with which to launch the company's new products. From California, Tom Lyle commissioned a gorgeous Maybelline ad that would come out in the October issue of *Photoplay* and other magazines. It featured an idealized woman in heavy eye shadow and deco spit curls. Draped in white fox, one shoulder bare, she would make women want to *"take these 3 easy steps to instant loveliness"*—Maybelline's eye shadow, lash darkener, and eyebrow pencil.

Despite the beautiful new ads, mail orders for the new Maybelline products didn't come in as expected; the economy was still in decline, a trend reflected in society at large. The movie stars and socialites who favored glamour over understatement were no longer viewed positively. Although four out of five women continued to use powders and skin creams, only one out of five used eye makeup.

So Tom Lyle and Emery adapted. Their next Maybelline ad campaign focused on a young woman, shoulder bare, with a neat coif and heavily made-up eyes—idealized and beautiful, but rather more demure than in previous ads.

**You can have eyes that are soulful pools of loveliness . . . eyes
that are bewitching and fascinating far beyond the power
of words to describe. And easily! And instantly . . . just as
though a magic wand had touched them.**

Though Emery may well have been inebriated when he wrote this preposterous ad, products flew off the shelves. The low price helped, too. Maybelline
still sold for only seventy-five cents, keeping it profitable while other cosmetic
companies that charged more fell by the wayside.

But the trouble was far from over. The holidays were bleak, with people
standing in lines to find work rather than the latest cosmetics. Religous zealots
lobbied "to put women back in their proper places." Who was responsible for
the sad state of affairs in America? Frivolous flappers, debauched film actresses,
women displaying themselves on the streets like harlots, that's who.

One morning at Maybelline Company headquarters, Evelyn walked into
Tom Lyle's office and slapped a magazine down on his desk. She opened to an
editorial. "Look at this!" Her eyes had a way of flashing fire when she got angry.
"This calls makeup—especially eye makeup—'fit only for tarts from the wrong
side of the tracks.' Who do these high hats think they are? And look at the drab
broads in these pictures! What a bunch of goody-goodies."

Tom Lyle folded his hands on top of the magazine. "It's even worse than
that. Now Hollywood is jumping on the bandwagon. Do you know Norma
Shearer? She called eye makeup 'the province of whores.'"

"Norma Shearer? She even *plays* goody-goodies. What, she's pretending she
doesn't wear makeup?"

"Not exactly. Right now, Ponds Cold Cream and Helena Rubenstein
makeup are considered high class, but dark lashes and eyelids are low class. And
that's the look associated with Maybelline."

"Hypocrites. That's all I can say. They're just a bunch of hypocrites."

In a way, the world had reversed itself. For most of Tom Lyle's life, ordinary
people had looked to the larger-than-life faces on the silver screen for guidance
on matters of appearance, dress, and deportment. Now it worked the other
way around. Now the film industry modeled its output increasingly on the
concerns and needs of the everyday citizen. The realities of financial depression,
job loss, and hopelessness were reflected in the symbolic language of film and
what would become iconic images of out-of-control monsters: *Dr. Jekyll and
Mr. Hyde, Dracula,* and *Frankenstein* all came out that year.

As the economy continued to slump, even Maybelline began to feel its
effects on the bottom line.

For Tom Lyle, "pick me up" came when Cecil made an early summer visit
to Chicago. The tall, dark, handsome young man who stepped off the train

was scarcely recognizable as the adolescent Tom Lyle remembered, and he had come on a man's errand. After graduating with honors from Morganfield High, he had been offered football scholarships by a number of universities, and he wanted Tom Lyle's help in selecting the best one.

"Mom wants me to go to Duke University because it was founded by Methodists and Quakers," he said. "And it offers a highly respected degree in divinity."

"That's still the direction you want to go?" Tom Lyle asked. "To become a pastor?"

"Yes, sir."

"Then Duke's a wonderful choice." He didn't add that the university also boasted one of the best athletic programs in the nation and a large and diverse enough student population to expose his son to a range of influences far removed from those of northwestern Kentucky. Tom Lyle enrolled Cecil at Duke for the fall of that year, paying extra so his son could have a private dorm room.

On the day Cecil left, Tom Lyle stepped forward to hug his son as he had always done—but Cecil was quick to offer a handshake instead. Tom Lyle hesitated, then smiled and took his son's hand in a warm clasp. Although issues of sexual orientation were never discussed between father and son, Cecil had obviously gained a greater understanding of his father's relationship with Emery, the man he called Uncle Dutch (after the then-popular term "Dutch uncle," meaning a stern mentor). Cecil loved and admired them both, but was clearly redefining how comfortable he felt with physical contact.

In September, Tom Lyle called Cecil from the Durham train station to announce that he and Emery were in town and would like to drop by with a few things. Cecil was pleased—then dismayed as his father and Uncle Dutch showed up with a wardrobe of top-quality clothing and all manner of athletic equipment. "Where am I going to put it all?" he asked, gesturing at his small dorm room closets.

Tom Lyle smiled. "I'm sure you'll figure it out, son."

A few weeks later, Tom Lyle and Emery surprised Cecil once again, this time by traveling to Durham to watch Cecil play in a football game. But instead of taking the train, they drove east from Chicago in Emery's classic 1924 Packard roadster, still showroom perfect. Tom Lyle called his son down from his dorm room, and Emery handed the boy the keys to the car.

Cecil's jaw dropped as his gaze shifted from one man to the other. "Uncle Dutch, you can't . . ."

"Oh, but I can," Emery said, grinning.

Tom Lyle said, "There's a woman's college and a nursing college on this campus now. Don't you want all those coeds to see you driving around in a classy car like this?"

Cecil forgot all about keeping a physical distance, and hugged both men as hard as he could.

Back in Chicago, Tom Lyle and Emery renewed their marketing efforts. Despite Hollywood's current preoccupation with bland, virtuous women being saved from evil by equally bland, virtuous men, the partners knew there was still a niche for glamour and beauty. There always would be. Even people with severely restricted incomes wanted to emulate their favorite stars, so offering advertising contracts to the most beautiful Hollywood actresses still made sense. No matter how bleak the economic outlook, Tom Lyle believed, women would never lose their desire for beauty and sex appeal and would always pay for an affordable cosmetic product of good quality. He and his staff saw themselves as keeping the spark of glamour burning in those dark, drab times, so Maybelline continued an aggressive advertising campaign with full-page magazine ads in color.

The most recent ads featured Natalie Moorhead, a Hollywood newcomer whom Tom Lyle and Emery had met over the summer; her slim figure was made for the semi-sheer, slinky gowns created by the Russian/Parisian designer Erté, whose work exemplified the art deco trend that Tom Lyle and Emery loved so much. Erté's exquisite, flowing creations melted along her curves and pooled at her feet. Platinum-blonde, vampish Moorhead did not possess the demure prettiness of the virgin, yet neither could anyone accuse her of being a flapper tart from the wrong side of the tracks. She was a statuesque, sophisticated comedian, who wasn't afraid to be her own woman. I can just hear my grandmother chortling, "Norma Shearer, eat your heart out."

If this campaign couldn't turn things around, nothing could. Moorhead introduced Tom Lyle's new Non-Smarting, Tear-Proof Maybelline, with a copy that read:

> BEAUTIFY YOUR EYES, THIS MARVELOUS, NEW,
> EASY WAY. Give them a dense, rich fringe of dark, long-
> appearing lashes instantly with the new MAYBELLINE.

The ad showed Moorhead with heavily laden dark lashes against white alabaster skin. This appealed to the more mature woman who still preferred a touch of glamour to the plain depression worn look now being seen everywhere.

Cecil was needing a makeover as well.

During Cecil's first term at Duke, Tom Lyle received a letter from his son with an unusual request.

Dear Dad and Uncle Dutch,

I'm working hard here at the university in my studies and for the football team. I think I'm "giving them what their looking for," as you say, Uncle Dutch. We won our last two games. I'm meeting all kinds of folks.

They sure do talk about people's "bloodlines" here. This guy from my dorm says his family is related to Robert E. Lee. One fellow in my history class is getting straight As, and I think it's partly because his great-grandfather was related to John Wesley somehow. His paper didn't seem much better than mine, and I only got a C+. The professor knows I'm from a tiny town in Kentucky, yet I drive a better car than he does! (Thanks to you two.) I truly admire his faith and his high standards, though, and the way the deans talk about training their graduates in fields that will "uplift mankind." But I was wondering what kind of "bloodlines" we have. Are there any distinguished ministers in my family? That would be grand.

Love, Cecil

Tom Lyle undoubtedly read the message between the lines: the aristocracy at Duke favored old, established wealth, and Cecil was seen by some as a hick with a *nouveau riche* daddy. But the letter reminded Tom Lyle of TJ's endless sermons about his ancestors coming over on the Mayflower. He wrote Cecil that Emery was going to start immediate research into the Williams family genealogy, and Cecil could expect the results to be rewarding.

At about that same time, back in Chicago, mobster Al Capone was convicted of income tax evasion and sentenced to eleven years in prison. Everyone—especially Evelyn—hoped that now gang crime in the city would finally die down, and things would improve.

But not even removing Capone from the streets could salvage the economy. By Christmas 1931, two years after Black Tuesday, the economy plunged to such depths that the city government of Chicago couldn't meet its payroll and issued IOUs to municipal employees.

Soon after that, Tom Lyle received the worst possible financial news. The president of Chicago Guaranty Trust called to tell him that his personal financial ship had sunk. The banks closed, taking his fortune with them. On paper, at least, Tom Lyle was no better off than the guys selling apples on the street corner.

Once again, he was broke.

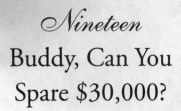

Nineteen

Buddy, Can You Spare $30,000?

om Lyle saw his company going up in smoke as product sales continued to drop off. Nor could he use his personal fortune to buttress his crumbling empire, since that $2.5 million had evaporated overnight. How could he continue to keep up with his overhead and support his family?

As he sat at his polished walnut desk, he heard the click of high heels in the hall. He raised his head. "Is that you, Evelyn?"

She stepped into his office. "Sorry, I had to come back for my purse."

"How much have you got in there? I might be asking you for a loan," he half joked. Normally Tom Lyle never burdened the family with his problems, but that night, according to my grandmother, he needed to talk.

She took off her coat and sat down as he poured them each a drink. "I'm going to have to lay off the extra employees for sure," he said, his mellow voice wavering with emotion. "I might even have to close the doors if the economy doesn't pick up."

Evelyn looked into his eyes and then leaned forward. "Tom Lyle, if I have to sell everything I own and scrub floors at night, I will never let you close the doors of this company. I will work for nothing and sell my wedding ring, the car, and all my beautiful clothes if it will help."

Nana did love theatrics, but her heart was in her words. My grandmother was a survivor with claws, and she inspired Tom Lyle with her gumption.

The next day, they strategized with Emery and Noel.

Noel quoted dismal sales figures and passed around a typed paper. "TL, mail orders have always served as our mainstay, but you can see that those sales have dropped to a trickle. Our drugstore and dime-store customers are buying at a higher rate, but not quite enough to make up the difference."

"So even if we can cut the mail-order department down to bare bones," Tom Lyle said, "there's no guarantee we'll get enough customers in stores to replace our mail-order volume."

Evelyn leaned forward. "I think we can. I've made calls on drugstores where I had to ask if they sold any Maybelline products. Getting some of those stodgy old men to stock eye makeup is tough. They think it's just something silly and stick it in a back room. But the buyers in stores that use our display cartons are always glad to see me."

"That's it, then," Emery said. "I could design a more eye-catching display carton. Use brighter colors."

Tom Lyle raised his hands, palms up. "That sounds great, except that we have thousands of the old display cases on hand. We'd have to invest in new ones, print, ship, deliver, and repack. Then there's distribution. Switching from mail to direct sales requires a vast distribution system and lots of local sales people. We're talking about a huge capital outlay, and I don't even have enough to pay the people I already have."

"Could you get a loan?" Evelyn asked.

Everyone stared at her. Tom Lyle rubbed his forehead and sighed. "I pay cash. I've never asked anyone for anything."

Noel had to smile. "What about those five hundred dollars you borrowed from me sixteen years ago? That did you some good, didn't it?"

They all got a much-needed chuckle out of this.

"Problem is," Emery said, "who has money to loan? The banks sure as hell don't."

"Ask Rory Kirkland," Noel said. "He knows we can turn things around."

"Rory engineered the Post Keys Gardner stipend for us."

"And we made good on it."

"What does it hurt to ask?"

"I'll do it," Tom Lyle said.

For the Williams family, Kirkland's loan of thirty thousand dollars was like Tom Mix leading a posse to the rescue. The funds kept Maybelline afloat while the company launched a fledgling distribution network under the management of Eva's husband, Chess. Meanwhile, Mabel's husband, Chet, continued to supervise production.

At the same time, Tom Lyle and Emery came up with a brilliant idea to keep the mail-order business alive: to their ads they added coupons reading: *Send ten cents and coupon for a trial size.* These proved enormously popular; in fact, Tom Lyle came to realize that a significant market sector seemed to prefer the little ten-cent size.

Evelyn's involvement ranged from helping make executive decisions to being a general gofer. In her role as a representative for the Maybelline Company, she softened her makeup a bit and took on a more modest appearance as she went out every day to talk with people in department stores and drugstores and keep Tom Lyle current with the word on the street.

She also worked to get Preston back on the team: sober, dressed in a suit and tie, and out on the streets using his famous charm to sell, sell, sell. Like everyone else, she took less pay and worked longer hours.

Evelyn often made sandwiches and brought them to work for everyone, and she became famous for her "almost meatless meatloaf." Her optimism, ready laugh, and quick sense of humor infected everyone; for many years, family members would tell tales of these special times.

Frugality continued at home. Evelyn stopped buying fancy outfits and instead mended her existing clothes. When she had to purchase items for Billy, she bought them a size too big, put them on him, and made him stand still for what seemed like hours as she took in cuffs and waistbands, only to let them out again as he grew. To Evelyn, Billy's appearance reflected on her parenting, just as her father had lavished beautiful clothing on her as a statement of his family's station in life. He had also conveyed the notion that he had thereby made Evelyn admirable and lovable, so Evelyn could do no less for Billy, who never looked less than perfect when he was out with his mother.

Even as Evelyn, Tom Lyle, Emery, and the rest of the team worked round the clock, Emery somehow found time to complete his work on the genealogy report for Cecil. He sent the boy a tome of twelve handwritten pages that established a definite blood link to Benjamin Franklin and a probable link all the way back to Roger Williams, the co-founder of the state of Rhode Island. On Tom Lyle's mother's side, a common ancestor proved to be a grandfather of George Washington. The end of Emery's letter read:

> This is one of the letters that should be read on the installment plan, but hope you will be able to make something of it. I think you are doing splendidly in school. Don't feel discouraged if you don't get A's right off, for you tackled a pretty stiff proposition when you jumped from Morganfield High to Duke, and

we are all aware of it, so don't feel that everyone is expecting you to head your
classes on your first year.
  Lots of love from your Uncle Dutch

Cecil would treasure the letter always, and, as predicted by Emery, he went
on to do well in his classes.

It helped, no doubt, that he was unhampered by the poverty gripping the
rest of the country. By May 1932, most people were doing whatever they could
just to survive. A killing drought had begun in the Great Plains states. Hobos
rode the rails, looking for seasonal jobs. Regular folks stood in long soup lines
and begged for work. The crime rate soared.

And 1932 was a particularly sad year for Kodak, the company that put
affordable cameras in the hands of the average citizen and whose invention of
roll film provided the basis of the entire film industry. After two years of intense
spinal pain, George Eastman, the company's founder, committed suicide. His
note said, *My work is done. Why wait?* During his life, he had donated over
a hundred million dollars to charity—the equivalent of a 1.5 billion dollars
today—a fact that impressed Tom Lyle, who would himself prove to be extraor-
dinarily generous to the less fortunate. Tom Lyle also felt he owed a personal
debt of gratitude to Eastman by putting a camera in the hand of practically
every American. Women especially wanted their faces to look nice in photos to
be preserved for posterity, and turned to eye cosmetics to help create their best
image.

As always in times of trouble, the human spirit asserted itself in many ways.
Little Shirley Temple, at age three, appeared in her first movie role. Bing Crosby
began to croon. A strong man living only by his own resources made people
feel empowered when *Tarzan of the Apes*—an enduring favorite hero of Billy's—
played in movie houses. Groucho Marx made folks laugh. After starting out as
a ditzy dog, Betty Boop became a completely human female cartoon character.
People tuned in to *Amos and Andy,* a nightly radio show broadcast out of Chicago. They identified with Little Orphan Annie in the funnies. A children's
book published in 1930 was gaining popularity: *The Little Engine That Could.*

After just four months, Maybelline—the Little Company That Could—was
back in the black. New sales strategies and wider distribution for point-of-sale pur-
chases turned the Erté/deco glamour ads into profit, and Tom Lyle made contact
with several department-store chains in hopes of further expanding the market.

He soon paid back Rory Kirkland, with interest, and would match Kirkland's loyalty thereafter by maintaining their professional relationship for the
next thirty years.

Although the name Miss Maybelline remained on the door of the office in the Maybelline building, Evelyn and Preston worked from there together—when Preston was feeling well enough to work at all. At first, the enforced intimacy brought the couple together; despite all the long hours and hard work, Evelyn would remember these times as good ones.

On the down side, Billy had become a latchkey kid, having to return to the apartment after school and then stay there alone until Evelyn returned. Either that or he would walk around the corner to the Maybelline offices, where Tom Lyle encouraged him to think up ideas that could make money.

My grandmother told me that in those days, my father loved to polish the chrome on Unk Ile's car. In return, "Tom Lyle always gave him a quarter. Billy thought he'd figured out a way to get even more quarters, so he started polishing all the cars on the street! He was so proud of himself, only to learn it had all been for nothing."

Later, Billy sold magazine subscriptions to win a new two-wheel bike. He was having trouble competing with the other boys until he made the rounds at Maybelline, where he sold half his orders in one day. He saved Unk Ile's office for last, and was overwhelmed with joy when Unk Ile wrote him a check for the entire amount.

It was about this time that both Tom Lyle and Evelyn noticed Billy's remarkable talent for drawing. He often had to sit waiting for his mother after school, so Uncle Noel gave him a pad of paper and pencil to keep him busy. He began to draw pictures of the objects around him—a chair, a desk—then went to look out the window and capture images of trees and the people walking by.

When the family discovered this natural talent, they encouraged Billy to be an artist. He never quite did that, but in time my father would use his artistic skills to design and build beautiful homes. Even as a boy, he wanted a big house so badly that if he couldn't have it in real life, he at least imagined it and drew it room by room.

Evelyn was not unhappy as a working mother, but she hoped and believed that Preston would soon start to work reliably, which would allow her to slow down and spend more time with their son. But Preston's stomach continued to give him problems, and he occasionally lapsed into a drinking binge, which only compounded the workload for Evelyn.

And then Evelyn, now thirty-one, discovered she was pregnant again.

Maybe this time she would keep the baby. After all, her dear sister-in-law Mabel had just given birth to her third child, Thomas Randolph—Tommy for short—and Eva was also expecting a third child. Evelyn thought that if she had a second son, she would name him after Tom Lyle rather than Preston.

She began unpacking some of Billy's baby things that she had saved. The soft infant smell lingered in the blue silk blanket Tom Lyle had given her. There were the booties and caps Bunny had knit. Yes, another baby, perhaps a second son, a second chance. . .

One evening she came home from work and discovered that Preston was gone. So were his clothes.

Twenty

After the Roar

When Evelyn walked into his office a few days later, Tom Lyle was shocked at how worn she looked. For the first time, she seemed to have lost her lovely youth, or at least the flirtatiousness, the mischievous twinkle, the spunk, the color—everything that made her Miss Maybelline.

He was almost as surprised when all she asked was if she could move into one of the two apartments in the basement of the Maybelline building. He suspected that another divorce attempt was in the making. Not that he could blame her. Tom Lyle knew exactly where Preston was, and why. Before departing, his brother had said he wanted to be with Virginia and Tony. Seeing that there was no point in trying to stop him, Tom Lyle had simply written him a check.

Still, he felt terrible about not being honest with Evelyn. "Of course we'll set you up downstairs," he said gently. "That way I'll know you and Billy are safe while I'm gone, and you'll be near Noel if you need anything."

Evelyn fought back tears and nodded her gratitude.

The next day, Tom Lyle and Emery departed for California, and Evelyn and Billy moved into an apartment in the Maybelline building. Movers carted in some of Tom Lyle's own furniture, oriental rugs, and artwork, and Evelyn gloried in the luxury.

Noel, Frances, and their three children came to welcome Evelyn and Billy into their new home. Evelyn took one look at Frances's swelling belly and thought of the baby she had intended to have until she saw Preston's empty closet. She broke down in tears.

"What's wrong, honey?" Frances was sympathetic.

"I'm just so happy for you," Evelyn managed to say.

Frances chuckled. "I'm a bit mortified at what people must think about a forty-two-year-old woman having another child."

"Well, people do talk," Evelyn said. But not as much as they would have talked about what she had done only a few days before. At least the practitioner had been a real doctor this time. Although abortions remained illegal, in these hard times, the procedure had once again become common, if still stigmatized.

After Noel and his family left, Billy asked the question he would from then on ask daily—maddeningly, repetitively, a question that was unanswerable: "When is Daddy coming home?"

"I don't know, honey," Evelyn would say. And it was true. This time she refused to even ponder on the answer, because such speculations led inevitably to thoughts of Virginia and Tony—people whose existence in Preston's life would mean too many things she didn't want to face.

When Tom Lyle called Noel from the Villa Valentino for a progress report, he received gratifying news: "Our sales levels are solid, TL, with cash reserves accumulating in the low six figures after expenses." At last, Tom Lyle felt like he could relax and spend a little money. He not only purchased the Villa Valentino, he decided to fully remodel and refurnish it.

One day, while browsing through an antique store, Tom Lyle and Emery met the shop owner, a one-time actor named William "Bill" Haines, and his lover, Jimmy Shields. Haines let it be known that he had designed Joan Crawford's mansion in Beverly Hills. It happened that Tom Lyle was at the time courting Crawford for a Maybelline shoot, so at their next meeting, he asked the actress about the flamboyant Haines.

She lit a cigarette and raised one of her famous eyebrows. "Men like Bill are a real problem for the studios; they want everything to look hunky-dory and on the up-and-up. Back in 1926, the usual solution was to force an actor with Bill's preferences into a sham marriage. Well, Bill wouldn't cooperate. He was a big name at MGM at the time, but he refused to play by Louie Meyer's rules and give up Jimmy Shields. So, of course, the acting roles stopped coming. That's when I asked him to design my mansion, and he did such a beautiful job everybody's using him: Claudette Colbert, Carole Lombard, William Powell, George Cukor, even Jack Warner."

Tom Lyle promptly hired Haines to decorate the Villa, and the two couples became friends.

Still, Tom Lyle felt compelled to live a lifestyle almost as two-sided as that propounded by Louis B. Meyer, and for similar reasons. It was all about public perception. The difference was that unlike movie stars, Tom Lyle did not court the limelight for himself—but for his line of eye cosmetics.

It was a dangerous line to walk, even in Hollywood, where a large gay culture thrived just offstage. If a homosexual lifestyle had been tolerated as part of the overwhelming roar of the previous decade, the Great Depression brought about an entirely different mindset. People turned to God for help in ever-greater numbers, and this religious renewal included the persecution of homosexuals. The word "fag" stopped being slang for "cigarette" and came to be a pejorative term for homosexual men. "Pansy Club" referred to the gay lifestyle. Antigay legislation proliferated nationwide.

Although Tom Lyle had always preferred to keep his secret life exactly that, a secret, he and Emery lived in an even more covert manner during those years. They provided no interviews at all; few people even knew who owned Maybelline. In public, Tom Lyle preferred to be associated with the female stars he signed for magazine ads and was actually offended by overt displays of homosexual behavior. This was one difference between him and Emery, who was more flamboyant. Emery had, in fact, developed a separate circle of friends who were more like him, although he still took care not to attract the wrong kind of attention.

My grandmother, as she would for the rest of her life, refused to acknowledge that Tom Lyle and Emery were a "true couple"; she continued to believe that Tom Lyle's commitment to her was almost as strong as that of a husband to a wife. She made sure Billy spent as much time as possible with his uncle when Tom Lyle was in Chicago, and when he wasn't, she had her son send him little notes signed with Xs and Os.

Tom Lyle had another reason to keep his head low: his son. Cecil was uniquely vulnerable, having already established a high profile at Duke. He was now meeting nice young girls from conservative religious families, and he would be mortified if his father's lifestyle ever became common knowledge. This was something Tom Lyle could never allow to happen. Hadn't his son already suffered enough ostracism thanks to Tom Lyle?

That didn't stop him from seeing Cecil whenever possible, though. In early September 1932, Tom Lyle and Emery went to Duke for a short visit. Cecil's sophomore year was just beginning, and he was everything Tom Lyle could have wanted in a son: tall, strong, intelligent, an offensive end on the Blue Devils football team. Tom Lyle could not have been prouder, but he could tell something was on Cecil's mind.

He didn't push it, and sure enough the truth came out at dinner. "Dad,"

Cecil said, "I was just wondering. Would it be a huge hassle for me to change my name?"

Tom Lyle didn't know what he had expected, but it wasn't that. "Change it to what?"

Cecil looked his father in the eye. "To Tom Lyle Williams Jr. Because that's who I am."

Tom Lyle blinked for a few moments. Then, "Dear boy! Dear boy! Oh, my dear son." His voice choked and broke. Heads turned in the restaurant and then looked away in embarrassment.

For once, Tom Lyle didn't care about being a public spectacle. He threw his arms around his son and laughed with sheer joy. "Emery, I've got a junior!"

"A sophomore junior," said the new Tom Jr.

Tom Lyle's happiness utterly unhinged him. He felt that his sheer lightness of spirit had to be expressed in some material way—but what on earth could possibly equal the delight that Tom Jr. had created in his heart?

Well, his son's dorm room was a mess, with far too little space for all his things. And all that dingy old furniture and dreary plaid—it just wouldn't do.

Tom Lyle called his Hollywood decorators, Bill Haines and Jimmy Shields.

Then came endowments to the college—tax-deductible contributions that would ensure his son a certain deference, an attitude the opposite to what Tom Lyle had experienced when he was in school. The famous Duke Chapel was still under construction, a soaring cathedral, really, that would seat sixteen hundred people. When completed, this structure would become the main image associated with the university.

Tom Lyle hastened that day by twenty-five thousand dollars before he left for Chicago, and made sure to donate the money in honor of his son.

Three weeks later, the director of administration called Cecil, informing him that a team of designers was waiting in the dorm lobby along with a truck full of furniture. Dozens of students gathered around the truck as three men unloaded bookshelves, a hand-carved desk with an executive chair, and a massive headboard with Tom Jr.'s new initials carved in it. So many students followed the furniture up the stairs that the campus police had to be called to clear the hallways and restore order.

"Who is this guy?" Tom Jr.'s fellow students asked.

"Beats me," one said, "but I think I'll get to know him."

Word eventually spread that Tom Jr., the modest divinity major, was the son of Tom Lyle Williams of the Maybelline Company, and he became a bit of a campus celebrity. He wrote his father that he had been chosen as captain of the football team, although only a sophomore.

To see his son so well liked, happy, and admired made Tom Lyle feel that he might float up to the moon.

As the weather turned bitter, Tom Lyle and Emery decided to winter in California, away from the cold and the misery of the rest of the country. By this time, people were struggling to save a dollar to buy a new pair of shoes from the *Sears, Roebuck* catalogue. Cars sat up on brick blocks, unused, because their owners couldn't afford to pay the license fees. People walked hundreds of miles for jobs, and no one knew that the worst suffering still lay ahead.

To most of the population, the only people who seemed to be flourishing were criminals, starting with the gangs who made, smuggled, and sold liquor. A vast majority of the population was already sick of Prohibition and all that came with it: the gang wars and the battles with police officers who had to enforce laws a majority of the people didn't want or obey.

This was also the era of celebrity bank robbers, such as Lester M. Gillis, aka "Baby Face" Nelson; John Dillinger, with his Robin Hood cachet; and "Pretty Boy" Floyd, whose robberies were so successful that bank insurance rates in Oklahoma doubled. Even a psychopath like Clyde Barrow took on glamour as he and his girlfriend, Bonnie Parker, rode around the Midwest, robbing and killing. Whole families, such as "Ma" Barker and her boys, turned to crime. Even Al Capone remained powerful, even though he now ran his operation from prison.

In the November presidential election, Franklin Delano Roosevelt's promise of a New Deal brought him 57 percent of the popular vote, and he carried forty-two of the forty-eight states. The mood of the country grew more hopeful, even though the realities were still grim, and poverty was actually spreading. Depression had fallen over the whole world.

By now, Evelyn had learned to always make the best of things. Still, between Preston having abandoned her yet again, Tom Lyle focusing more and more on his own son, and Noel and Frances being so busy with their four children, Evelyn felt increasingly sidelined.

Just before Billy's ninth birthday, the bicycle he had earned by selling magazine subscriptions was finally delivered. Evelyn fixed her hair and makeup, put on her best frilly dress, told Billy to don his dress-up outfit, and took a picture of the two of them posed with the bike. She sent a print to Tom Lyle, along with Billy's usual Xs and Os, hoping to hold onto their places in his heart. A short note came in reply, but Evelyn realized she and her son would be spending the approaching holidays entirely with her relatives and not with any of the Williams clan.

On the first working day of the New Year in 1933, construction began on San Francisco's Golden Gate Bridge, a signal that the country was feeling a resurgence of confidence in anticipation of its new president. History would show the optimism to be premature. At the end of the month, a man named Adolf Hitler became chancellor of Germany, while in Chicago, machine politics were getting underway. Voters had elected Democrat "Pushcart" Tony Cermak as mayor, and he had quickly fired three thousand city workers and replaced them with his own people. He then brought in a burly Irishman, Pat Nash, who was chairman of the Democratic Party. Later, when the new mayor was visiting President-elect Roosevelt in Florida, an assassin took aim at Roosevelt and instead hit and killed Cermak. His job as mayor of Chicago was filled by a man named Ed Kelly—and the infamous Kelly-Nash machine was born.

After Roosevelt was safely inaugurated in March 1933, Evelyn heard one of Preston's old Hollywood acquaintances, Will Rogers, on the radio, commenting on the new president: "America hasn't been this happy in three years as they are today. No money, no banks, no work, no nothing, but they know they got a man in there who is wise to Congress, wise to our so-called big men. . . . If he burned down the Capitol, we would cheer and say, 'well, we at least got a fire started anyhow.'"

Twenty-One
Brave Fronts

*E*velyn was raising Bill alone again and she didn't like it. She felt guilty about leaving him unsupervised every afternoon after school. Also, he needed a room of his own; a one-bedroom apartment was no place for a boy his age.

Worse, he was handling his feelings of isolation and anger about his father's absence by getting into all sorts of mischief, wandering around looking for adventure in a city where the crime rate continued to rise. Evelyn knew he needed supervision and structure, and sooner rather than later.

Finally, she called Tom Lyle in California and asked his opinion on the matter. Bill was, after all, his godson.

For once, Tom Lyle provided pop psychology instead of a practical solution: "Our Billy should have a strong male role model and activities that expand his talents."

What did that mean? Knowing my grandmother, I suspect she was hoping Tom Lyle would say he would be on the next train to Chicago to help with Bill or that Preston would be coming home forthwith. When neither of these things happened, she looked elsewhere for a source of structure and discipline for her son. She found it in the Tower Hill Military School in Dundee, Illinois.

She registered Bill there for the fall term.

On the last Sunday of August, Evelyn drove Bill forty miles east of Chicago to the school. Tom Lyle had returned from California and came along for the ride. At the academy, the trio toured the flat, tree-lined grounds, which included a dormitory building, stables, a swimming pool, and tennis courts. Tom Lyle and Evelyn encouraged Bill to take advantage of the facilities and opportunities. His mother gushed, "You're going to have the time of your life with other boys your own age."

"You'll be safe here," Tom Lyle said. "And it will help you develop into a fine young man."

All Bill knew was that first his father had abandoned him, then his mother, and now even Unk Ile was prepared to dump him out here in the middle of nowhere with a bunch of strangers in uniforms.

Evelyn would always remember the sadness in the eyes of her only child as he watched her drive away. She waved and smiled, acting brave for both of them, all the while masking her rage at Preston, whose continued absence had, she felt, forced her to do this thing.

Tom Lyle was hiding something as well. While in California over the summer, he had visited Preston, Virginia, and Tony more than once. Although Evelyn probably suspected as much, she hadn't dared bring the subject up. She didn't want to know about her husband's other life two thousand miles away, just as she didn't really want to know about Tom Lyle and Emery's other life.

She still wanted to believe she was the Queen of Hearts to the both the men she loved—even if they couldn't, for different reasons, love her in return.

On the last Monday in August 1933, Tom Lyle and Noel sat in the Maybelline building discussing the company's prospects. As the economy had continued its downward spiral, so had Maybelline's fortunes. The air conditioning had been turned off to keep costs down, and Tom Lyle worried that the cakes of lash darkener stored in the warehouse were "sweating" and changing consistency. The more complex the industry became, the more headaches Tom Lyle faced. What with changing chemistry, harassment from religious zealots, and the still-bleak economy, he wasn't sure how long he could keep going.

To make matters worse, the combination of people needing fast money and Maybelline's widespread use made the company susceptible to lawsuits involving such things as eye infections, stabs in the eye with mascara brushes, and various other ailments caused by alleged defects in the product. That year a fifty-two year old woman was fatally poisoned by one of Maybelline's competitors, Lash-Lure, a mascara substitute, which only encouraged more lawsuits.

This produced an onslaught of bad press that frightened the public and urged women to boycott cosmetics. Tom Lyle was seriously thinking about selling the company and retiring to California when fate took a hand.

While in L.A., he had met with representatives of a pharmaceutical company that had expressed interest in buying Maybelline. But now they seemed to be in no hurry to complete the deal.

"I think all the Lash-Lure litigation has scared them," he told Noel wearily.

"But that doesn't make any sense. Every complaint against Maybelline has been resolved in our favor."

"So far. But trust me, these people aren't done. What kind of sales figures are we getting for August?"

Noel passed him the report. "Slow. We can cover expenses and payroll, but there isn't much left for advertising."

Tom Lyle shook his head. "With numbers like these we'll lose our buyer for sure." He slumped in his chair. "Did you know Emery and I met Jean Harlow this summer? She has an image that I'm sure would drive more women back to glamour, and I was aching to offer her a contract, but I didn't know what we were going to do. And now we don't have the money to make the offer."

With a knock at the door, Mary entered. She handed Tom Lyle a typed paper. "There's a young man here looking for a job."

"We've got nothing to offer," Tom Lyle sighed but glanced at the résumé anyway.

Harold W. Ragland. "I know this man," Tom Lyle said. "He's sales manager for a women's magazine we've placed ads with before. Hmm. Says here he's got a degree in business. I had no idea. Maybe he's after your job, Noel."

"Very funny." But in fact, both brothers were impressed. No one in their family had extended their education beyond high school; Tom Jr. would presumably be the first. "And look here," Tom Lyle added. "He worked his way through school playing saxophone and clarinet in a jazz combo. That takes energy and imagination. What do you think?"

Noel took the résumé and glanced at it. "It can't hurt to talk to him." With that, Harold "Rags" Ragland walked into their lives—his pockets empty, his new baby waiting at home, his mind teeming with ideas. The men shook hands all around and sat at the table. "Gentlemen," Rags said, "I know you're busy, so I'll get right to the point. I've been watching the Maybelline Company for over two years now. I've checked stores where Maybelline is sold, talked to managers and sales people, and been amazed. Here's the biggest name in the eye cosmetics field, the best product at the lowest price—and it seems to always be stocked in a limited fashion or displayed to disadvantage compared to its competition.

I thought, 'These people are missing buyers because of the way the displays are set up.' And I wondered why that was."

Tom Lyle glanced at Noel again. "Well, to be honest, Mr. Ragland—"

"Call me Rags, please."

"To be honest, we're a family-run business. Always have been. I handle the advertising along with one other man, and my brother here manages the business on a day-to-day basis. My other brother and his wife take care of sales, including the store trade you're talking about, and that's all we have at the executive level. That's how we like it."

"What if I told you that you could double your sales in six months? Well, you couldn't, but I could."

Tom Lyle blinked. "Double?"

"In six months?" Noel said.

Rags spread his hands. "Right now, except for mail order, Maybelline is only available in the Chicago area. That's old thinking, gentlemen. You need a sales and marketing strategist, someone to market Maybelline regionally, nationally, even internationally. I'm telling you, the opportunity is there. You have no real competition if you make your move now, and make it strong."

Tom Lyle sighed and thought about the fact that he was secretly thinking of selling his company. "That sounds wonderful, Mr. Ragland, but I'm sorry; we simply have no position for you at this time."

"Six months," Rags said. "Hire me for six months, and if I don't double your business in that time, fire me. That's all I'm asking."

Tom Lyle opened his mouth, closed it again. Although he couldn't be more than six or seven years older than Rags, he felt as if he were looking back at himself the day he arrived in Chicago, full of determination and energy. "Would you mind waiting outside while I speak with my brother?" he asked.

"Certainly." Rags snatched up his hat and marched out.

After the door closed, Tom Lyle sighed. "He's right, you know. Evelyn's doing her best, but it's difficult for her, with Bill and all. I guess I keep hoping Preston will come back and help us out."

"Me too," Noel said. "But it doesn't look likely. And sales are down to $359,000. If we're going to have a prayer of hanging on to the company or getting it in shape for a buyer, we've got to have a solid marketing department."

"I just hate to bring in an outsider."

"I understand, but Kirkland wasn't family, either, and he saved our behinds. Look, TL, you're an A-number-one self-made man, and we all think you're a genius, but . . ."

"I know. The company can't continue on its own momentum. We need real direction and expertise."

"And this Rags fellow certainly seems to have ideas."

"Yes, he does. So—six months?"

Noel pulled over a pad of paper and did some hasty math. "At seventy-five a week, we can afford him."

"And if things haven't changed by March first, he's gone."

"Right."

"Then let's tell him the good news."

Rags Ragland started work that very day. His first act was to suggest the company do away with mail order altogether. "Focus on displaying your products in stores in a more dazzling way. Catch a woman's eye, and she'll buy on impulse."

He also took one of Evelyn's duties—paying personal visits to stores that stocked Maybelline—to extremes never dreamt of before. Rather than visiting stores and chatting with their managers, he traveled to the headquarters of retail chains. And there, rather than speaking with head buyers, he would meet with the owners themselves. Nobody had done something so audacious before.

Well before the six months were even over, Maybelline sales doubled. And they kept climbing.

As a reward, Tom Lyle gave Rags a permanent position at a hundred dollars a week. A few months after that, as sales continued to rise, Rags was placed on commission at one-half percent of total gross sales. Not net, gross—a terrific number.

The next step was for Rags to replace the Preston-and-Evelyn sales team entirely, taking full charge of sales and sales promotion. He was the first and last person to hold this position for the company.

Feeling optimistic with Rags at the helm of a more-official marketing department, Tom Lyle and Emery flew back to Hollywood to work with Jean Harlow, who had just finished shooting her latest film, *Bombshell*. Emery, ever the celebrity watcher, was especially enthusiastic. "Do you realize her fans are a ready-made market for Maybelline? She's the reason you see so many platinum blondes around these days."

"I know," Tom Lyle said, "and this ad will be special. I met an art director from MGM studios named Buzz Ellsworth. He has men who are geniuses at retouching photos to make everything look especially sharp and perfect."

"That's outstanding," Emery said. "But we have to make as many November and December magazines as possible. Our gals see the movie. Then they see the ad in their favorite magazine, and then they head directly to Woolworths—and see Rags's new displays. How can it fail?"

Tom Lyle was less sanguine. Ever the perfectionist, he was disappointed with the first Harlow shoot. Fortunately, the actress was between roles and available to squeeze in a second session the next day. Even after that, Ellsworth's artists redrew the chosen shots several times before they met Tom Lyle's standards; he simply wouldn't send out anything containing even the slightest flaw.

He had scraped together every liquid asset he had left to finance this ad campaign. The future of the company depended on its success.

Twenty-Two

Rags and Riches

*J*ean Harlow was the "Blonde Bombshell," the latest in a parade led by Natalie Moorhead. Unfortunately, Harlow had also earned an image as a floozy among the critics, so the new Maybelline ad's success or failure would depend on whether they kept up their snooty reviews of her.

As it happened, she had developed a gift for comedy that charmed reviewers. That, combined with her independent spirit and reckless elegance, entranced the public. She was not ashamed to flaunt her body under lustrous bias-cut silk. Her worldly air and exotic sex appeal was exactly what Tom Lyle was looking for to attract women who had the guts to use their own style and beauty—enhanced with Maybelline, of course—to stand out. He believed that a woman's greatest asset was her ability to capture a man's imagination with mystery and keep him fascinated with her. Harlow represented that vision. Once again, Tom Lyle's finely tuned instincts paid off.

Magazines across the country carried the full-page, glossy color illustration of Harlow, artfully made up with Maybelline. Women rushed to copy her shaved, pencil-line arched eyebrows, platinum blonde hair, and smoky eye shadow above thick dark lashes. Maybelline flew off the shelves. At a time when most cosmetics companies were collapsing under the weight of the Depression or lawsuits, Maybelline roared back to life, led by its new triumvirate of Tom Lyle, Noel, and Rags Ragland.

As for Evelyn, she continued to check stock levels in local stores and remained Tom Lyle's connection to women's trends, but if she had considered herself a career executive before Rags was hired, she certainly felt displaced now.

That wasn't all bad, though. With her salary uninterrupted and more free time on her hands, she was able to go shopping, dress beautifully, and enjoy her family—except for Bill. Although she brought her lonely son home from the military school for his tenth birthday and for holidays, she didn't see him nearly as much as she wanted to. While his Aunt Bunny and Uncle Harold drove up to the academy every other Saturday, Evelyn thought it best for Bill not to depend on her visiting every weekend. She wanted him to adjust to living away. This hurt Bill because he was often left alone on the weekends while the other kids were home with their families. Bunny always brought back reports about how well Bill looked and how strong he had grown playing sports. Bill had made friends with the daughter of the man who owned Tower Hill. She taught him how to be an aggressive tennis player and take out his frustrations on the court. Almost despite himself, he was learning discipline, good manners, and how to take care of himself. Although Evelyn was happy at Bill's success, the news did not cheer her. She missed raising her son and watching him mature. She missed her boy.

FDR's famous alphabet soup of programs under the National Recovery Act had finally halted the downward freefall of the economy, and the ratification of the Twenty-first Amendment had repealed the Eighteenth Amendment, ending Prohibition. The combined legislation nudged the country away from the brink of collapse.

In 1934, taking advantage of Maybelline's singular position of strength, Tom Lyle scooped up any little eye cosmetic company that came on the market, until "Maybelline" became synonymous with "glamorous eyes" all over the world. Soon Tom Lyle's "Wonder Company," as it became known in the trade, had no competition at all, and its annual sales rose to $510,000.

But Tom Lyle was just getting started. His next move: radio. The company sponsored a radio show, The Maybelline Hour, on WFNT out of Chicago, hosting the "Penthouse Serenade," which featured Freddy Martin and his orchestra. Each show began with a supposed elevator attendant saying, "First floor, going up." A member of the Williams family would step into the imaginary elevator and have a conversation with the operator while riding to the penthouse at the Edgewater Hotel. The elevator door would then open, and the band played "Penthouse Serenade." Evelyn, in her role as Miss Maybelline, was a regular on the show, while other members of the family appeared on occasion. The public got to know Tom Lyle; Mabel, who had just had her third child; Eva and her baby boy, Bobby; Noel and his family—and, according to my father, eventually even Preston.

Out at Tower Hill, Bill and his friends sat around the radio every afternoon, waiting for the elevator door to open to a band playing the latest popular music. Bill loved listening to Unk Ile talking about home and his cousins. On the nights Evelyn was on, she always said something that was secret code to Bill for *I love you, darling.* The other boys didn't know this voice on the radio was Bill's mother. Bill didn't tell them because the family told him not to tell people who he was for fear of his being treated unfairly by some jealous teacher, administrator, or fellow student, or worse, being kidnapped.

To cover for Preston's absence, the elevator man established that Preston was ill. When he asked Evelyn how her husband was doing, she would reply, "Oh, he's better," or "He's having more tests at the Mayo Clinic"—or, if she was in an ornery mood, honestly: "Your guess is as good as mine."

It was during this time that the word "mascara" first came into use. Until then, most women called any eyelash-darkening product "Maybelline," as in, "I put on my Maybelline and my lipstick." But now, with increasing product differentiation, a new word was needed. It's believed that Tom Lyle, who still remembered the old hair dye product for men's facial hair, Mascaro, simply adapted the name for feminine usage. In any event, the industry snapped up the new term.

By whatever name the product was called, Maybelline continued to capture the lion's share of the market. Again, Rags Ragland led the way. He was the first to think of selling mascara in grocery stores; he was the first to think of selling it in chain drugstores. He chose to eliminate department stores, which took bigger commissions. Instead, he concentrated on high turnover by ensuring product visibility and affordability; in fact, he was the one to coin the phrase "sensibly priced," which would grace Maybelline displays and packaging for many years to come, along with the famous cameo portrait of the Maybelline girl. He also suggested that the larger box of seventy-five-cent Maybelline should be stocked in a smaller quantity, in favor of racks displaying more of the ten-cent trial size of mascara, eye shadow, or eyebrow pencil.

At this productive time, Tom Lyle also came out with Maybelline "Eyelash Grower"—working the description carefully to comply with consumer guidelines; there would be no more Lash-Brow-Ine debacles. In fact, this new product received the highest honor in the cosmetic field, the Good Housekeeping Seal of Approval, for purity and quality. Mothers trusted it not only for themselves but also for their teenage daughters—who could afford to spend ten cents for a small container. Maybelline Eyelash Grower thrived, creating future buyers for Maybelline products yet to come.

With this success in place, Tom Lyle and Emery headed for Hollywood in the early spring of 1934, leaving a noticeable gap in his penthouse visits on *The Maybelline Hour.* Because Evelyn's charisma came through even on radio, she represented Tom Lyle in his absence. If talk shows had existed in those days, she would have been a standout.

Still, there was one bit of family news—contained in a letter from Tom Jr. to his father—that wouldn't make it on the air for a while yet:

> Dear Dad and Uncle Dutch,
>
> I've met a beautiful 17-year-old brunette with piercing blue eyes, a real Southern Belle from Georgia in her freshman year.
>
> She doesn't seem to be impressed with the fact that my father is a cosmetics magnate and certainly isn't impressed with money. She doesn't give a hoot about glamour, fashion, or flashy movie stars; and can you believe she's more impressed with my bloodlines and the long line of American patriots, pioneers, and noted statesmen in our family tree? She's a real humanitarian and very involved in civic activities and organizations. Unfortunately, she isn't a Methodist, but being an Episcopalian is OK with me.
>
> I'm proud to say that her roots go back to the American Revolution, the Civil War, and WWI, and she appreciates history, religion, and education just like me, more than image. I have been invited to meet her family who live in Thomasville, one of the most beautiful resort towns on the Georgia-Florida border. I think I'm in love with her. And if all things work out, we will marry in April of 1936.

Life was good for the Williams family, but elsewhere, tough times continued. Hot, dry winds swept through the drought-ravaged Midwest, lifting an estimated 350 million tons of topsoil skyward. Easterly it blew, until by evening, Chicago was choked by a dark blizzard. Two days later, when the winds died and the airborne dust finally settled, twelve million pounds—four pounds for each resident—covered Chicago. In the farmlands to the west, matters were far worse; hundreds of thousands of families became refugees of what came to be known as the Dust Bowl.

Everywhere the land sweltered. In Chicago, the summer of 1934 stands as the hottest on record, with temperatures reaching a hundred degrees for many days and over ninety degrees for a solid thirty-four days.

On one such day, a certain man decided he wanted to get out of the heat and watch a double feature in the air-conditioned Biograph Theater. As he stepped back outside, John Dillinger encountered an FBI ambush and was shot to death. His location had been betrayed to the police by a female companion who wore an agreed-upon orange dress, although the press preferred to call her the splashier "Lady in Red."

Two months earlier, police had also killed bank robbers Bonnie Parker and Clyde Barrow. It seemed that the crime wave was finally about to end as the chaotic economy continued its slow grind into stability.

At the same time, a different headline upset the Boecher family, which still maintained and celebrated its deep German roots. German president von Hindenburg had died, leaving no one to stop Adolf Hitler from taking over their beloved Deutchland.

Distress, and change, were in the air.

Being in Hollywood was rarely a true vacation for Tom Lyle and Emery; they were too busy looking for new actresses to model for Maybelline. Finally, they decided to seek some cooler weather and genuine relaxation and rented a mountain cabin in Big Bear.

When they arrived, however, they discovered that so had the film crew and stars of *Forsaking All Others,* a romantic comedy starring Joan Crawford and Clark Gable. Tom Lyle saw an opportunity he could not pass up. Crawford's screen characters often represented hard-working girls just trying to get by—and her particular mystique, unlike Harlow's slinky sex appeal, had created a cult of young women who identified with her rags-to-riches story lines. When Tom Lyle found Crawford, she was approving some publicity stills and asked his opinion.

"I'd like to make your lashes look a little heavier," he said. With his practiced eye, he could tell Maybelline would give Crawford's sexuality a wide-eyed quality that would appeal to even the most discerning of women.

"They'll have to touch up the shots later," she sighed. "I can't use Maybelline; my contract won't allow it. I'm under an exclusive contract with Max Factor, so I can't represent another cosmetic company."

"I look forward to the day your contract with them runs out," he said. "Meanwhile, would you mind if I made up your lashes and took a few pictures for my own use?"

"Of course."

As Tom Lyle slowly put on coat after coat of Maybelline mascara, his vision of Joan Crawford became reality—her eyes sparkled with an intensity regular stage mascara never produced.

Emery photographed her with his Kodak, and after the film was processed, compared it to the shots taken at the studio on Technicolor film.

He shook his head. "This still isn't the look we want."

"It's the film," Tom Lyle said. "It's perfectly fine for home photography, but it can't capture the look we're going after. I want something that's never been seen in advertising before—half photo, half illustration: the perfect version of whoever's wearing our products."

"The only way we're going to get that is to somehow use Technicolor on our ads," Emery said.

"Then that's what we'll do," Tom Lyle said. And he meant it. He was spending more money on advertising than any other company, regardless of industry, and expected the highest quality for his money.

Although Tom Lyle was extravagant with his promotional budget, he remained conservative when it came to spending money on himself—except for his one indulgence: convertible Packards. While in Hollywood, he purchased a custom-designed new convertible with gold chrome—an unheard-of idea—and oversized white-wall tires. That fall, he and Emery drove this vehicle from California all the way back to Chicago, where along the way it was undoubtedly the most ostentatious car ever seen driving through small towns and past poor farms. Tom Lyle did not do this out of self-aggrandizement; in fact, he believed that showing off the vehicle would signal economic growth. "All people need hope," he said, "and this car gives hope that things are getting better, and we'll all be prosperous again soon."

In Chicago, he parked the Packard in front of the Maybelline building for passersby to admire. Today, the car would probably be stolen or vandalized in short order, but at the time, the display was received in the intended spirit.

When Bill saw the car, he hovered around in a continual state of gee-whiz awe, polishing and repolishing its amazing golden trim. At the same time, he had to fight back tears at the thought of returning to military school in a few days.

Inside Tom Lyle's office, he accepted his usual quarter for polishing the Packard, then worked up his courage to ask the question that had been preying on his mind since Unk Ile's return in that magical car.

"On *The Maybelline Hour*," Bill said, "Aunt Eva said my dad was working out West. Did you see him when you were in California, Unk Ile?"

"No, Bug, I didn't." Tom Lyle managed to speak the lie sincerely, although it broke his heart to do so. Then he had an inspiration that he hoped would silence all further questions. "Say! How about if I play hooky from work tomorrow and drive us in the new Packard over to see the World's Fair?"

"Keen!" Bill said. "That'd be aces!"

The next day, Tom Lyle, Emery, Grandpa TJ, and Bill toured the Chicago World's Fair with its rainbow buildings and art deco style. Most attractions featured technology, but there were also clever tableaus depicting scenes from

Chicago's history and exhibits that would shock people today: a "Midget City" of "Lilliputians"—costumed dwarves and midgets—and live babies in incubators. But mainly, it was the new technology that dazzled visitors: model homes with the latest appliances, dream cars, and streamlined trains.

The displays weren't the only things attracting attention. TJ noticed more than a few people giving long looks at his son and Emery as they strolled down the Midway. Of course, Tom Lyle and Emery had, as usual, penciled in their sideburns, mustaches, and eyebrows to look perfectly manicured. TJ's sheriff instincts kicked in, and he countered any hint of aggression with direct eye contact, at the same time shielding Bill and shepherding him away from the gawkers and one drunken fellow who openly leered at Emery.

Later, as Tom Lyle dropped off his father at Mabel and Chet's, TJ asked for a private word with his son.

They went alone to the porch. After a moment's hesitation, TJ cleared his throat. "I think Bill's reached an age where he's going to start asking some questions about you and Emery."

Tom Lyle felt as if he had been skewered on a stick. He had no idea what to say.

"I know you heard the ugly talk today," TJ went on. "So did Bill." He looked Tom Lyle straight in the eye. "The boy's got enough on his plate already; he shouldn't have to fight certain battles. You and Emery are walking targets. You stick out and attract people who figure you're fair game."

"I would never do anything to hurt my godson."

"Of course not. Not on purpose—but remember what happened to Max Factor's half-brother, Jake the Barber. He was kidnapped."

Tom Lyle stared out at the street. "Dad, with all due respect, that whole deal was a hoax. You know that."

After a moment, TJ rested a hand on Tom Lyle's shoulder. "Son, I think it's time you and Emery considered living permanently out there in California."

"What?"

"It's not like you have to be here in Chicago. Noel and Rags can handle their part of the business without your help."

"But one of the reasons I haven't already moved out there is so I can stay close to my family—including Bill."

"Then there's one more thing you ought to consider."

"What's that?"

"You're getting well known around here. What if some smart guy decides to make a quick buck off you? He sees you with Bill. He waits, then grabs Bill off the street and holds him for ransom."

Tom Lyle felt the breath leave his body.

His father squeezed his shoulder. "Some people might not even care, son. Some people might say you brought it on yourself."

"Oh, that can't be right."

"Maybe you haven't noticed, but what with first the Depression, then the Dust Bowl, and now more trouble brewing in Europe. People are worried. They wonder what causes bad times. They want to know who's to blame. And you know how that goes: once people start looking for a scapegoat, they generally find one."

Tom Lyle was silent.

His father was right.

More right than he even knew. But Tom Lyle knew. In a way, Maybelline had become a victim of its own success. The press wanted to know how one little makeup company had not only survived but thrived during the bleak years of the Great Depression. Well, how else but by pandering to vanity and pride, the worst qualities of a suffering population? The tabloids of William Randolph Hearst's newspaper empire were particularly eager to report on every lawsuit against the cosmetics industry, the implication being that companies like Maybelline were responsible for what the papers called "America's moral decline." Never mind that Hearst himself kept a mistress, Marion Davies, who wore as much rouge, lipstick, and eye makeup as the flashiest of her fellow Hollywood actresses.

Even respectable magazines such as *Vogue* and *Ladies Home Journal* began to glorify grooming approaches acceptable in the Victorian age and refused to run cosmetics ads, no matter how much cash the moguls of makeup offered them.

The assault extended beyond periodicals. A former newspaper reporter named Malcolm L. White published a book based on what he claimed was a three-year study of the cosmetics business. His conclusion: homosexual executives in the beauty industry were bent on corrupting American womanhood. This, he warned readers, was precisely how ancient Rome had been brought to its knees.

Influenced by such editorials, irate husbands and clubwomen lobbied the US Congress en masse. They believed that men like Tom Lyle Williams were debasing respectable women and girls with the paints of ancient Rome and Babylon. As a result, Congress drafted two bills, which would have empowered a special commission to censor makeup and take a long, hard look at homosexual influences in the industry, with the aim of purging them wherever possible.

Once people start looking for a scapegoat, they generally find one.

Sure enough, things had quickly gotten personal. Both Max Factor and Charles Revlon had hired public relations firms that used photos and serious newspaper articles to awaken readers to the fact that their clients were real men who were being pilloried because they had strayed into a woman-dominated industry. After all, nobody complained about Helena Rubenstein, Merle Norman, or Lydia Pinkham, all of whom hawked similar products.

Max Factor had himself photographed as a white-coated scientist, tinkering in his laboratory, inventing serious products to, as he put it, "cover flaws which nature inflicted on millions of women." His publicist distributed photo layouts of Factor with his family gathered before the hearth, playing board games and working on jigsaw puzzles. Revlon, the matinee idol of the business, was shown playing polo or tennis, sporting a deep tan and tight clothing that accentuated his manly, muscular body.

Acting as his own publicist, Tom Lyle also chose to play up his image of respectability. As often as possible, on *The Maybelline Hour* and elsewhere, he took pains to mention being Catholic and previously married—the proud father of a son.

Unfortunately, there was another angle from which he was vulnerable: his well-known affiliation with the film industry. That same year, a man named Joseph I. Breen had been appointed to head the new Production Code Administration (PCA), which would become more popularly known as the Hays Code, an attempt at self-regulation in the movie industry. Through Breen's notorious censorship, reference could not be made in movies to alleged sexual perversion—such as homosexuality, which was listed right alongside pedophilia. Among the literally hundreds of forbidden subjects were childbirth, miscegenation, nudity, and erotic dances. Even the popular cartoon character Betty Boop had to lose her sexy flapper look and wear an old-fashioned housewife skirt. The Hays Code made it impossible to be openly gay, even in Hollywood, and many stars such as Cary Grant and Randolph Scott had to endure well-publicized married lives no matter how miserable they were.

Scapegoats . . .

Tom Lyle looked at his father. "Remember when you forced me to leave Morganfield?"

TJ hung his head. "I never have forgiven myself for that."

"No. It was probably the best thing that ever happened to me. And now I'm going to do it again—for all of us."

Twenty-Three
The Prodigal

On the evening of November 12, the phone rang at the Villa Vallentino. When Tom Lyle answered, he heard a hoarse, desperate whisper rise on the other end of the line. "Help me, brother."

"Preston?"

Tom Lyle and Emery leaped into the Packard and raced to Virginia's bungalow. Once inside, Tom Lyle was shocked to see Preston's thin arms flailing in nervous agitation as he sat rocking himself on a leather sofa. Virginia, now a lovely young woman of twenty-two, stood wide-eyed in the hallway with a terrified-looking little boy peeking out from behind her—Tony, of course.

Virginia pointed at Preston. "'E ees seek! No sleep. No eat. *Trés días.*" She held up three fingers.

After finishing her workday and shopping for Bill's birthday present, Evelyn returned to her apartment in the Maybelline building. She slumped down on a chair. What a week. Three days earlier, Tom Lyle had phoned her from Los Angeles to let her know Preston had once again been sent off to the Mayo Clinic for stomach tests. Well, she had thought, isn't that a terrible shame? The poor, poor, suffering man . . . and by the way, care to tell me where my so-called husband has been for the last two years? But she hadn't said it. Why bother? Preston could die for all she cared.

She put him out of her mind—something she had had plenty of practice doing, after all—and tried to think good thoughts about the immediate future. That wasn't as easy. Bill's birthday would fall on Monday, November 26, and Evelyn dreaded the long, solitary drive out to Dundee. Neither did she look forward to a birthday celebration without Tom Lyle.

When the phone rang, she started to reach for it, then halted and stared at it for a couple of rings. She felt a strange sense of destiny about picking up the receiver. As if just thinking about Tom Lyle had conjured him up on the other end of the line.

Finally, she grabbed the receiver. "Hello?"

"I've missed you, baby," rasped a voice, slightly hoarse yet still unmistakable. And not Tom Lyle's. "Missed you so bad."

A great wad of anger stuck in Evelyn's throat. If not for the utter desperation in Preston's voice, she would have hung up on him immediately. "If I could just see you again, that beautiful mug of yours." No apologies. No explanations. No testing the waters. Not even a "hello."

Yet Evelyn felt tears welling up. She swallowed hard and made sure her voice came out even harder. "I'm sorry to hear about your illness, Preston. But if you want to see someone, it should be your son. I had to send him to Tower Hill."

"Military school. I know. Mabel told me."

"Mabel?"

"That's where I am now. I'm back. I'm staying with them."

Evelyn felt her chest tighten. *I'm back.* But then she blurted the question she had been grappling with for two years. "How could you abandon Bill for so long? How *could* you?"

Hearing the pain and fury in her voice, Preston couldn't answer. Perhaps he didn't know the answer. More likely, he knew it and couldn't face it: he was ordinary. He had tried to be a hero, and failed; he had tried to be a movie star, and failed; he had tried to be a business executive, and failed. He had no clue how to be anything other than ordinary and had substituted alcohol for accomplishment. Why had he fled to California? So he could be with a woman who didn't expect more of him, a woman who saw him as important and special just as he was. And he wanted to be a father to little Tony.

He could say none of these things to Evelyn, of course.

So he came up with a simpler version of the truth: "I've been an idiot in a lot of ways, Evelyn."

"No argument there."

She hadn't hung up, though. She was still on the line. "I was hoping we could drive out to Dundee together," he said. "Pick Bill up and whoop it up a little for his birthday, maybe have a nice Thanksgiving dinner somewhere."

She still didn't hang up. But she did call Tom Lyle, who was also in town, and asked if he and Emery would go with them to visit Bill. Tom Lyle agreed, pleased at the prospect of seeing his godson, and offered to drive them up himself.

Preston and Evelyn got through the ride to Dundee without my grandmother screaming at my grandfather every inch of the way, mainly because Emery carried most of the conversation talking about California and all the movie stars. Preston normally would have been upset hearing about the good life in the sun, but he was on powerful pain medication and half-asleep most of the way. When Emery finally wound down, Tom Lyle asked Preston what the doctor's report was, and he told them the latest diagnosis from the Mayo Clinic: the only way they could extend his life was to remove some or all of his colon. He didn't know what to do. He was terrified. Evelyn had no comment, but Tom Lyle knew he had to do something to bring Bill home so he could be with his father.

In Dundee, Evelyn soon discovered that Bill, in the misdirected logic of children, resented her for sending him to military school far more than he resented Preston for abandoning him. The second he saw his father, he ran at him with shouts of joy. A photo from this time shows a thin but smiling Preston with a cigarette in his hand, a beaming Bill in the driver's seat of TL's Packard, and Evelyn with her foot on the running board, as if trying to get closer to her son and farther away from her husband.

Back in Chicago, Preston stayed with Evelyn and Bill in the Maybelline apartment, although Preston slept on the sofa. On Sunday, the two males roughhoused until Evelyn chased them outside to the nearest park. Preston said he didn't feel up to a grand family gathering, which was probably true—but even more, he didn't want to face Evelyn's family or his own father.

So on Monday, Evelyn baked Bill's birthday cake, topped it with eleven candles, and they shared it, just the three of them. Bill pronounced everything aces, keen, and swell.

For Thanksgiving, the trio ate a low-key dinner in a local restaurant, nothing but soup for Preston. Outside, the weather had turned miserably cold and windy.

Bill begged to not go back to Tower Hill.

Evelyn said, "You'll understand this better someday, Billy."

"Bill! I'm not a baby. I just want to live at home."

Preston said, "It won't be for long, son. Your mother and I have a few things to work out, but I promise you, things will get better soon."

Evelyn spent the rest of the afternoon in a frosty silence, furious at Preston for making promises she knew he would never keep. Bill sulked. After he finally fell asleep, Preston stood at the door to Evelyn's bedroom, watching her pack clothes into Bill's suitcase.

"I was happy with us all together again," he said.

Evelyn didn't look at him. "Good."

"I quit drinking, you know."

"For now."

"This time I mean it."

"It's been a long day." She moved toward the door and gripped the knob. "Good night, Preston."

She waited until he backed away, then closed the door.

The next morning, Preston felt well enough to drive Bill back to Tower Hill alone. Evelyn let some time pass, then called Tom Lyle.

If he was hoping to hear a heartwarming story of family reconciliation, he was disappointed. "I was shopping a couple of weeks ago," Evelyn said, "and I noticed all the mannequins wearing little veiled hats. Very smart-looking. I went in and tried several on, and the saleslady said how much they called attention to my eyes. I started thinking, why don't we show some models wearing these hats? I mean, why wear something that draws attention to eyes that don't stand out?"

"Excellent suggestion," he said. "We could get Emery to write something that says, more or less, 'Don't bother wearing a stylish hat without Maybelline to enhance your eyes.'"

They chatted along these lines a bit more, then Tom Lyle cleared his throat. "Preston called me yesterday. I understand you and Bill and he had a nice Thanksgiving."

Evelyn had already carefully chosen her next words. "Bill loved the ten-dollar bill you sent him for his birthday. He'll write you soon."

"The boy needs to be with his dad, Evelyn," Tom Lyle said gently. "And Preston is so bad off . . . he needs you both. If you reconcile one more time, I'll bring you all out to California as soon as possible for a fresh start. How would that be?"

Twenty-Four
Oh, Preston . . .

Bill had become quite an equestrian at Tower Hill Military School, transforming himself into a competent and self-confident boy. He couldn't wait to show his father how well he could handle a horse.

Most of the other boys hadn't yet returned from their Thanksgiving holiday, so the stable master agreed it would be okay for Preston to go riding with his son. The man didn't know Preston was on heavy pain medication that dulled his reflexes. Bill, excited to show off, took off at a gallop through the snow and called back to his dad, "Hurry up!"

The great Tom Mix had admired Preston's riding skills, and Preston had played polo against Will Rogers and held his own, despite never having even seen the sport before. Laughing, he charged off down a slope after his son.

All went well at first. Clouds hung in a low blanket, and air in the twenties nipped the nose, ears, and cheeks. Snowdrifts slowed the horses, but the wide-open countryside worked its magic, and Preston felt like a young man again.

The dizziness came out of nowhere. One moment he was riding high in the saddle; the next, he was being dragged through crusty snow and over frozen earth, his foot caught in the stirrup. The torture seemed to go on forever before the horse slowed to a stop and Preston was able to work his mangled foot free. He collapsed on the frigid ground and passed out.

He awakened to find his son standing over him, face pale, eyes wide. "Broke my foot," Preston moaned. "Can't walk. Can't ride. Go get help, son."

After Bill galloped off, Preston lay back and stared at the gray sky. Half-frozen, every inch of his body throbbing in agony, he found himself thinking back to his grim hours in the frigid Atlantic, clinging to pieces of wreckage while he waited for help. Wondering if it would arrive in time.

A couple of days later, Evelyn arrived to bring Preston back to Chicago. She helped him inch into the passenger seat, his face bruised, his movements stiff, his fractured ankle in a heavy cast. As she took her place behind the wheel, it occurred to her that she was the only person who could possibly take care of this poor excuse for a man.

"I want you to move back in with me, Preston," she said.

Her businesslike tone didn't invite an emotional reply, and Preston was in no shape to make one, anyway. He responded with a nod.

"When your foot heals," Evelyn went on, "Tom Lyle said we should all come out to California and be near him. All three of us. He'll help us get a fresh start out there."

Back at Tower Hill, Bill simply didn't understand why he couldn't be with his parents now. He wrote his Unk Ile, begging to leave school. Tom Lyle wrote back, asking his godson to try to understand how sick his father was and how his mother couldn't work and take care of Bill and Preston too, and the crime rate was still high in downtown Chicago; it was too dangerous for a boy to be living there.

Be a soldier for me, Bug, Tom Lyle wrote. *Someday things will be different, just wait and see.*

But Preston was already back at the Mayo Clinic, forced to return by ongoing weight loss, agonizing stomach pains, and frequent panic attacks. At first he refused to have the radical gastric surgery recommended by the doctors, but when an X-ray of his foot showed that it was finally mending, Preston cheered up a little. If he could survive being dragged halfway across Illinois by a horse, surely he was strong enough to endure a little surgery. Anything to end the unremitting pain.

That same month, February 1935, TJ Williams died in his sleep at age seventy-seven. With the exception of Preston, the entire family gathered for a beautiful funeral paid for by Tom Lyle. Nearly a hundred people paid their respects on that frigid day.

Preston used his upcoming surgery as an excuse, even in his own mind, not to attend the funeral. In truth, he was simply too distraught about the fact that he and his dad had never resolved their differences. Thanks to the success of Tom Lyle and Noel, Preston had lost his father's respect. TJ had gone to his grave thinking of his youngest son as a failure; Preston was sure of it. And now he would never be able to change that. Overwhelmed by loss and emptiness, he slipped into emotional blackness. His nausea and pain intensified, and his surgery was postponed. The doctor said his colon was covered with pre-cancerous polyps and wanted to remove the whole thing—a last resort even for doctors on the leading edge of surgery. Preston didn't want to be a guinea pig. Even if the surgery was successful, did he want to live as an invalid under Evelyn's care for the rest of his life?

On April 2, 1935, Preston's doctor wrote Tom Lyle a letter advising sanitarium care for Preston. After all, he wrote, there was nothing the clinic could do if their patient wouldn't undergo the operation.

Preston immediately checked out of the clinic and went back to Chicago. He had no intention of spending his last days in a sanitarium. He wanted to spend them with Bill, trying to make up for his two-year absence, for the boy being sent to military school, for all of it.

When he explained this to Evelyn, she blinked back tears. "Oh, Preston." But she chose not to ask him why he hadn't reached this decision while they still had time to build a life together. Instead, she said, "I guess it's time to take Tom Lyle up on his offer."

She reached Tom Lyle by phone and filled him in on all that had happened.

He was distraught by the news about his brother but pleased that they would be moving to California as soon as arrangements could be made and Preston felt strong enough for the long cross-country drive. "And the timing couldn't be better," Tom Lyle added.

"What do you mean?" Evelyn asked.

"Oh, Evelyn, I'm walking on air. Tom Jr. is considering coming to work for me instead of becoming a minister down in Thomasville! Since you'll be moving out West, I'll offer him the apartment you're in now. It's like it's meant to be, isn't it?"

"Oh, yes. Yes, it is," she said. *No, no, it isn't,* she thought. "I guess this means I'll be resigning from Maybelline."

"Not at all, darling. You'll stay on the payroll, and, after you move out here, I can consult with you anytime. Your advice about the hats was spot-on, by the way. Women are wearing hats everywhere now. Joan Crawford said the best hat designer is Lilly Daché. We're going to get her involved."

"Terrific." Evelyn ached to be a part of this campaign but knew she had to let it go. She was a consultant, nothing more. An opinion expresser, not a decision maker.

As for Tom Jr.—well, his father might be dancing on air, but Evelyn Boecher Williams's feet were planted firmly on the ground, and she knew exactly why the prodigal son had decided to switch careers in midstream. Not because he had discovered that he loved business more than God, but because he had realized that on the wages of a minister he could never provide his fiancée with the comfortable lifestyle to which she was accustomed.

The sort of lifestyle Evelyn herself wanted and deserved.

She said none of this, of course. She and Tom Jr. had always had a cordial relationship, if not a warm or close one, and so it would remain. At least she wouldn't have to live and work in Chicago, forced every day to acknowledge the boy's new position alongside his Uncle Noel at the helm of Maybelline. Instead, she would have to adjust to the fact that once again, her life was about to change.

In Hollywood, Tom Lyle and Emery kept their heads down, avoiding publicity even as they pushed Maybelline to ever-greater heights of visibility. Despite the best efforts of yellow journalists and reproachful preachers, women both young and not-so-young streamed into the dime stores across America in search of Maybelline. In the mid-1930s, fashion began to pull away from early Depression frumpiness, offering a fresh appeal to the younger generation, who gravitated toward a style of their own. Victorian plainness had grown tiresome, despite the heavy influence of class-conscious women's magazines, and young women eagerly thrust themselves into the full flow of twentieth-century style. The sophistication of femme fatale movie stars such as Jean Harlow, Joan Crawford, and Marlene Dietrich was changing fashion, and Maybelline offered an important key to the look.

Tom Lyle had not merely been flattering Evelyn when he pointed out she was right about hats highlighting a real change in trends. There was nothing sexier than flirty eyes slightly hidden behind the veil of a chic little hat worn to lunch with friends or at a cocktail party in some penthouse. Through Rory Kirkland's agency, Post Keys Gardner, Tom Lyle had contracted a photo shoot with the rags-to-riches fashion icon Lilly Daché, who had first made a splash in the 1920s by taking style beyond chic into flamboyant absurdity. In the '40s, she would become notorious for designing Carmen Miranda's towering turbans covered with flowers, birds, and the contents of entire fruit bowls. But even in the mid-thirties, Daché's hats were among the most outrageous of all—and women loved them.

Daché herself appeared in a Maybelline ad—tasteful yet glamorous, showcasing her combination of celebrity and fashion with a new line of Maybelline products, including Cream Form Mascara. To capitalize on impulse buying,

Rags Ragland created new cards to hang on special displays right at the front doors of dime stores. Magazines across the country carried a full-page ad of a younger woman in a fashionable Lilly Daché hat, eyes made up with Maybel-line, along with an autographed photo picture of the famous milliner and copy designed to capitalize on the word *chic*.

> **The shallow sailor crown lifts the hat off the eyes, and to achieve real chic, it is important, of course, to reveal the eyes at their best—in eye makeup, as well as through hat design. Modern eye makeup is as necessary to chic as the smartest hat.**

Targeting the fashion-conscious young woman brought in a whole new breed of buyer—in droves.

Twenty-Five

Paradise West

"How's the remodeling coming?" Evelyn asked, pitching her voice above the rumble of the surf. Tom Lyle and Emery had invited her, Preston, and Bill's new friend, Jimmy Langhorn, to a rented house in the Malibu Colony. They were staying there while the Villa Valentino was undergoing refurbishment. "The remodel is going fine," Tom Lyle said. "But I'm afraid to go over there very often."

"Why's that?"

"Women!" Tom Lyle laughed. "With everything torn up, scavengers are sneaking in and hunting for souvenirs that might have belonged to Rudolph Valentino. They're after a piece of his history, if not the man himself, and they'll take anything they can get their hands on, including the toilets!"

This time they all laughed. Evelyn couldn't remember the last time she had felt so relaxed. She could even understand why Preston had fallen so in love with California, although she often missed the noise and frenzied activity of Chicago. She also missed her apartment in the Maybelline building; it might have been too small for her and Bill, let alone the three of them, but at least it had been elegant and stylish. Now they lived in a small apartment in Hollywood, which was not exactly the glamour spot she had expected it to be.

But Bill was happy; that was the main thing. He had met Jimmy Langhorn at the Gardner Street Elementary School, where he was enrolled for the last couple of weeks of the term before summer. The two boys had become fast friends. They were out in the blue water, getting tan and blond.

Preston looked better, too. He was still too thin, but at least the sun had given him a kiss of color.

She sipped her cocktail. Preston had a beer by his side—apparently drinking beer was not the same as "drinking." More likely, his stomach couldn't handle the hard stuff. But never mind. It was all right. He didn't get drunk anymore, and Evelyn would take whatever she could get.

Even the drive out from Chicago had been good—a slow trip in her over-loaded car. First, she and Preston had headed up to Cheyenne, Wyoming, where they had collected Bill from the train he had been put on by his Aunt Bunny and Uncle Harold after school. The three of them had then turned south, cruising through chilly mountains on roads paved and unpaved. At night, Evelyn and Bill slept in a pup tent, Preston in the car. In New Mexico, they had stopped at Indian reservations, where Evelyn had purchased turquoise jewelry, hand-woven blankets, and handmade pottery. In Arizona, they had marveled at the red rocks and desert vistas. When the car broke down, they had stayed at a cheap motel until Tom Lyle could wire them money.

Mile by mile, the landscape had changed. Everything had changed. They seemed to have left the bad times behind them at last.

She became aware of Tom Lyle talking about the one hundred palm trees he was having his gardener plant around the Villa during the remodel. The trees would be beautiful and elegant there, he said, and of course that was true, but Evelyn suspected he had another motive for the landscaping: the foliage would help screen the estate from the view of neighboring hillsides and homes.

Evelyn shifted her gaze back to the ocean, where Bill and Jimmy chased one another through the shallows. It was one thing for a grown man like Tom Lyle to decide to . . . well, to live that way, but it was something else entirely to expose a young boy to it. Tom Lyle never would; he was a most circumspect and private man. But by coincidence, Jimmy Langhorn was the nephew of Bill Haines, the flamboyant antiques dealer Tom Lyle had engaged to redecorate the Villa. Haines supported his father, sister—Jimmy's mom—and Jimmy, while living only a couple of blocks away from them in a big colonial house with white pillars and a huge front porch. Bill and Jimmy were over there all the time, and Evelyn was not comfortable with that. Haines and Shields had a reputation for the most blatant type of behavior, something she did not want her son exposed to. He might start asking difficult questions. He might even ask about Unk Ile. So far, he still thought of his uncle and Emery as just close friends who lived together, and Evelyn would like to keep it that way for everyone's sake.

Bill had reported that Jimmy's mother dated lots of handsome men who drove big flashy cars. Evelyn closed her eyes and imagined it: a handsome, sharply dressed man pulling up to her house—not her apartment, her house—in a Cadillac or maybe a convertible Packard like Tom Lyle's. "Evelyn!" he would call, waving a huge bouquet of flowers. "Come on, let's go!" And she would come dancing down the front steps in a sharp dress and sexy veiled hat.

"Sweetheart?" Preston said. "How about grabbing me another beer?"

Preston wanted to live in a house, too. Things had changed since he was here the other two times. Now he had his wife and son with him, of course. Now his health was in the dumps. Besides, even if he wanted to, he could no longer seem to connect with his old Hollywood friends, the few who were still around. Hell, he couldn't even visit Virginia and Tony. Virginia had married someone else and even had another child; why would she want to see the withered ghost of her first lover? Besides, if Preston started going over there, how long would it take Evelyn to find out? Two seconds? And then what would happen? Forget needing surgery; Evelyn would rip out his intestines on the spot.

He wanted a house, but not just any house. This might be his last summer as a fully intact man; he would love to spend it living in a place on the beach. But the prices were too high in Malibu, so they decided to look farther south. In the end, they found a beach cottage in San Clemente. Father and son bodysurfed together while Evelyn sat under an umbrella, careful not to let the sun touch her face. Several weeks of relaxation brought the family together in a summer paradise, including almost a second honeymoon at night after Bill fell asleep. But those days were bittersweet; Preston could hardly eat a thing without complaining that his guts felt like they were on fire, and his health continued to decline, along with his weight.

Tom Lyle and Emery drove down several times, even though the trip took half a day of wending their way along the coast highway. They loved to lower the car's top and wear sunglasses and hats, which made them stand out in the small village on the water, where very few people from Hollywood ever visited. They didn't care. In fact, they let their hair down and relaxed in a way they never did in Los Angeles. I'm even told that Tom Lyle and Emery slept on the couch or the floor—an image I find almost impossible to picture.

In late July, Preston and Bill took the train to Los Angeles, where Tom Lyle picked them up. At the Villa, Preston asked his brother for a favor. "Could I take your car out one more time, like old times, and show my kid a few sights?"

As always, Tom Lyle couldn't refuse Preston a thing. As he handed over the keys to the Packard, a look passed between the brothers that Tom Lyle would remember for the rest of his life. In that moment, it was as if all the pain and insanity between them fell away, and they stood there as two souls who were precious to one another, grateful for their time on earth, and fearful that each moment might be the last.

Then Preston and Bill climbed into the car and cruised down the winding hill onto Hollywood Boulevard. From there they drove to Wilshire and Fairfax, stopping at Gilmore Stadium to see Preston's old friend Will Rogers, who was serving as grand marshal at a rodeo.

But Rogers didn't recognize Preston, a ghost of the man he had known six years earlier.

Preston grinned. "We played polo together once. Our pal Tom Mix used to call me Prince Preston."

With a whoop, Rogers extended a hand across the grandstand, and the two men started chatting. Bill kept tugging on his dad's elbow, waiting to be introduced.

With his characteristic humble style and dry humor, Rogers parodied himself when he said to Bill, "I never met a kid I didn't like."

Bill asked for his autograph, and Rogers not only signed the program for him but invited father and son to sit in his private seats closest to the stage.

"You can tell your grandchildren about this," Preston said to Bill. "You just met one of the great ones."

On the way back to the Villa, Preston told Bill—apparently without irony—how much he admired the way Rogers put his family first and never got caught up in the glamour of the bright lights, even though he was a box-office draw second only to Shirley Temple. Preston described how, at Bill's age, he had dreamed of going out West to ride horses and rope steers. Bill loved horses as well, and learning that his dad was a wannabe cowboy created an indelible bond between them.

On August 16, Will Rogers and his pilot, Wiley Post, were killed in a plane crash while attempting to take off from the mud flats outside Point Barrow, Alaska. Preston was devastated. He had taken Bill to say goodbye to Rogers when Rogers was leaving California, but they hadn't been able to get through the crowd at the airport.

Bill's reaction was even stronger; he cried for days, as if he had lost his dearest friend. The real cause ran even deeper than that, though. He had never before realized that a person could die before his time—vibrant and alive one day and gone the next. If it could happen to a famous, successful man like Will Rogers, it could happen to anyone.

Twenty-Six

The Man in the
Llama Coat

By Christmas 1935, Preston was injecting several hypodermics of morphine just to get through each day, and needle marks left tracks like highway maps on his arms and legs. Still, he could not keep food down, and suffered three to four bouts of diarrhea a day.

In early January, the pain became so severe that the doctor ordered him to the Mayo Clinic for the surgery he so feared.

The medical reports of January 15 described Preston as "very nervous and irritable," with a diagnosis of "anxiety neurosis and possible addiction to narcotics." Special nurses were hired to watch him twenty-four hours a day. On January 17, he turned thirty-seven years old. Four days later, he went in for a preparatory surgery.

Meanwhile, Evelyn and Bill took a train to Chicago so that Bill could stay with his Uncle Noel, Aunt Frances, and favorite cousin, Allen, while his father was in the hospital. As soon as Bill was settled, Evelyn headed straight back to Rochester. The temperature was below zero as she stepped off the train and saw the strangest thing: a man in a llama coat just like one Preston had, leaning against a lamppost in the snow, smoking a cigarette and looking at her as if he had been waiting there for her. She was reminded of the first time she ever saw Preston, at the Memorial Day parade in Chicago almost fourteen years earlier.

The man lifted his head and grinned. She gaped. "Preston? My God, Preston! What are you doing out here?"

"I snuck out of the hospital."

"But—"

His kiss silenced her. He led her across the street, out of the frigid air, and into a steamy pub where he ordered drinks. "I want to talk to you, Evelyn, and I don't care what the doctors say." He paused. "When I come out of this operation, I won't be a whole man."

She knew what he was referring to. Having a colostomy meant he would spend the rest of his life wearing a bag outside his body to contain his wastes. "Preston, that's ridiculous. Of course you'll be—"

"Evelyn, I need you to listen. This is important to me. I want to still be whole when I tell you this." He took her hand, removed her glove, and kissed her knuckles. "I still love you, baby. And I'm sorry for all the pain and trouble I've caused."

She was shaken to her soul. Preston almost never apologized for anything; this was a terrible sign. Still, she refused to respond emotionally, because if she did, she would start sobbing with no possibility of restraint. "I love you too, Preston," she said—but even then she couldn't go so far as to say that given the chance, she would make the same choices again. "I do love you."

When they returned to the hospital, the doctors told Evelyn that Preston's condition was so critical he would need a blood donor before they could perform the surgery. Noel had the same blood type as Preston, so Evelyn called and asked him to come to Rochester as quickly as possible.

"You'd better bring Bill with you," she added, her voice catching.

Two days later, when Bill saw his dad lying in bed, skeletal under the sheets, he began to cry.

"You've got to be brave, son," Preston said. "The surgery will be a success. I know it. When I get well, we'll all return to California and be happy again."

Bill wiped his tears on his cuff. "You mean it, Dad?"

"What do you mean, do I mean it? Why, I already have a dog picked out for you as soon as we all get home."

"Mom, did you hear that? My own puppy! That's swell, Dad. I love you!"

Preston's colostomy, one of the first ever performed at the Mayo Clinic, was a success. Evelyn phoned Noel and Tom Lyle with the good news.

But after a week, complications set in. Preston couldn't fight off pneumonia, and he slipped into a coma. On February 15, 1936, after Evelyn had sat with him all day, the nurse told her to go to her motel and get some rest. She struggled through the snow to her room, undressed, and plunged into a restless sleep.

The phone rang in the middle of the night. It was the nurse. "Come quickly, Mrs. Williams. Your husband probably won't make it through the morning."

Evelyn threw on her clothing, called Noel at his hotel, and fought her way back across the snow. The wind nearly blew her off her feet. In Preston's room, she was appalled at what she found. The around-the-clock nurse was dozing in her chair while Preston struggled to breathe.

Evelyn kicked the nurse out of the room and screamed for the doctor. "Can't you see he's dying? Please, please, please do something!"

The doctor looked at her sadly. "I'm sorry, Mrs. Williams. There's nothing more we can do. He's in God's hands now."

After the staff left, Evelyn threw herself across Preston's chest. "Don't leave me! Preston! Don't leave me!" She was hysterical. She loved him. She hated him. Most of all, she wasn't prepared to lose him.

With her ear on his chest, she clearly heard the castanet rattle of his fluid-filled lungs. She thought about how he had clung to life during the war and how powerless he had felt not being able to save his pilot from drowning. Now he was the one drowning, and she was just as powerless. It wasn't right. It wasn't fair. Thirty-seven was too young to die.

His breathing stopped. His chest sank, sank, and became still. Evelyn stared hard at what she thought she saw next: a thin vapor leaving his body. It floated to the ceiling and disappeared, and that was when she knew Preston was gone.

Years later, she still swore this was true.

Preston Williams was buried in the Mount of Olives Cemetery in Chicago, on a hill overlooking Lake Michigan. An American flag covered the coffin as the fallen hero was honored for his service to his nation. A sailor played "Taps" on a bugle while others fired off a twenty-one-gun salute.

Bill Williams did not attend the funeral. In his loss and pain, he blamed Evelyn for his father's death. "You made him have that stupid operation. He never even wanted it."

After the service, Evelyn sat in the limo beside Tom Lyle, thinking about her return to California and hoping Bill's sullen attitude would fade along with his grief.

Tom Lyle squeezed her hand and offered her a small black box. She opened it and stared, stunned, at a boulder of a diamond ring.

"Two karats," Tom Lyle said.

"But—what does this mean?"

"My darling Evelyn, this is a token of my devotion and appreciation for your staying with Preston all these years and trying so hard to make the marriage work. Let's vow to each other that we'll be a family, together, for Bill and for each other."

"Oh, yes." For a moment she thought Tom Lyle might actually embrace her. Or perhaps she should make the first move . . .

He raised her hand and placed the diamond on the ring finger of her right hand. On her left hand, she still wore Preston's smaller diamond, which she had always suspected had also been paid for by Tom Lyle.

Tom Lyle looked into her eyes. "I vow to love and care for you and Bill, and I'll never turn down any request."

"And I vow I will always stand by your side, Tom Lyle. Apart from Bill, you are my whole life."

As strange as all this was, it didn't feel to her like a betrayal of Preston. It felt right.

Still, vow or no vow, there was one thing Evelyn couldn't tell Tom Lyle: she was pregnant.

Part 3

The Third Front
(1937–1949)

Twenty-Seven
Miss Mom

*I*n March 1936, my grandmother rented another bungalow on the coast, this one in Laguna Beach, already a tourist town because of the well-known artists it had attracted. Evelyn and Bill didn't care about the art. They moved there to heal. Evelyn didn't particularly care for the isolation of Laguna Beach, but being near the ocean seemed to be the one source of comfort for her son.

As Bill slept in his own room, Evelyn stood in her underwear before an oval mirror. I imagine her angling left, then right, and then in full profile, appraising her reflection. This would probably be her last chance at motherhood and certainly her last chance to produce a Maybelline heir. What would a baby brother mean to Bill? He had barely spoken to her that evening or, for that matter, at any other time since Preston's funeral. He hadn't forgiven her for sending him to military school, and he still accused her of killing his father. Evelyn felt hurt, ashamed, and, above all, fearful. Would Bill consider a sibling yet another betrayal or, like her, a sign of hope?

Pop! . . . Pop! . . . Pop-Ping!

The noise was loud and seemed to be coming from awfully close by. Someone outside playing with firecrackers? A car backfiring? But it hadn't sounded like it came from outside.

She threw on a robe and hurried down the short hall, feet thudding on the bare wooden floor, and stopped at Bill's door. Better not just barge in; he'd pitch a fit if she woke him up. She tapped on his door and then entered slowly. A scuffling sound came through the darkness.

"Honey? What's going on?"

"Nothing. You woke me up."

She shuffled toward him, hands waving in front of her. "My gosh, Bill, your window's open. It's too chilly."

"I like it open. Can't I even have my own window open if I want?"

"All right." She groped for his covers and started to pull them up.

"No!"

"Okay! Okay!" Evelyn peered out his window and smelled something like smoke, but she couldn't see anything out there. The nearest streetlight seemed to be out. "Unk Ile and Emery are coming down next weekend; I'm making them Gramma Boecher's Sunday dinner. Won't that be nice?"

"Sure." He turned his back on her.

The next night, Evelyn woke from her sleep with a jolt, clutching her belly. She began cramping, then hemorrhaging. Utterly alone in her misery, she lost the baby. She would mourn this secret for years to come.

Pop!

Evelyn woke from a deep sleep.

Pop! . . . Pop! . . . Pop-Ping!

There it was again. She'd heard the sound more than once in the last couple of weeks, and had figured out what it was. Now she was feeling well enough to do something about it.

She tore into Bill's bedroom without knocking, to find him aiming his BB gun out the window. She even knew what he was shooting at: the streetlights. She had noticed broken glass in the street.

Still, it was terrible to see the truth with her own eyes. "Bill! What do you think you're doing? This is crazy! Unk Ile will be so disappointed in you. This is just terrible!"

Bill glared at her. "I don't like lights in my face; I can't sleep." He dropped the gun and sobbed in a way Evelyn hadn't heard since Preston died.

Although she knew she would never be the world's greatest mother, she realized that her son was grieving. She walked over and rubbed his shoulder. He shrugged her off. She sighed. She didn't dare take away the gun; it had been a present from Preston.

"Okay, honey," she said. "I'll get darker curtains for the window."

Bit by bit, Bill's attitude improved. Tom Lyle and Emery visited as often as they could. The three males swam in the ocean and lay on towels in the sun, chatting while Evelyn chimed in from the shade of an umbrella.

As always, Emery was full of the latest Hollywood gossip. "Did you hear Clark Gable was just voted King of Hollywood?"

"I heard that," Bill said.

"Well, guess who was voted Queen?"

"Myrna Loy," said Evelyn and Tom Lyle simultaneously.

"That's right. She's just the hottest thing right now. Evelyn, did you and Bill catch her in *The Great Ziegfeld*?"

Bill huffed. "They show the same two movies for six weeks straight here in Laguna."

Emery laughed. "Well, there's a new *Thin Man* movie in the works; we'll have to all go see it up in L.A. She's terrific in those."

"Look at her eyes," Tom Lyle said, holding open a movie magazine to a photo of Myrna Loy. "Now look at this." He showed them a groundbreaking Maybelline ad built around before-and-after photography. The "touch of Maybelline" transformed ordinary young women into beauties right there on the page. "Rags is building a whole marketing campaign around this idea," Tom Lyle said.

From her position in the shade, Evelyn carefully hid her expression. All this talk of marketing and ads and movie stars made her long to be back where the action was. Once upon a time, she had worn nice clothes to work, met interesting people, and helped run a multimillion-dollar company. Now, as Bill healed and needed her less and less, she found her sense of isolation growing. Not that she wanted to move back to cold, grimy Chicago, not anymore, but still.

Near the lifeguard tower, a group of teenage girls in bathing suits giggled as they rubbed cream on their skin. Bill was staring at them, Evelyn noticed. Tom Lyle obviously noticed, too. He winked at Evelyn and turned to his godson. "Bill, I'm going to see if I can work out a deal with the studios to promote up-and-coming teenage starlets in Maybelline ads; we figure it will attract more teenagers. What do you think of Deanna Durbin and MGM's new girl next door, Judy Garland?"

Bill's summer tan pinked up a bit around the cheeks. "Cute girls."

When school resumed in the fall, so did Bill's behavior problems. He was late to class every day, and at night, he once again took aim at the streetlights outside his window. When Evelyn tried to reason with him, he would either simply walk away or slam the door in her face and then cry in private.

One evening, desperate, she spoke through his closed bedroom door. "Your birthday is coming up. Would you like me to call Jimmy Langhorn's mother and see if Jimmy can come down for the weekend?"

After a pause, the door opened. Bill peered out, his eyes sparkling instead of brooding and introspective. "You mean it?"

"Sure; we'll show him the sights. Come on, let's go for a walk and talk about it."

But that wasn't what Evelyn really wanted to talk about. As she strolled side by side with her son on the cool sand, she tried to think of a way to broach the subject. Finally she decided to leave it up to him. "What's going on, Bill?" she asked.

"Nothing."

From his tone, she knew "nothing" meant "I miss my father." But he almost never brought the subject up, and she knew that was her fault. She hated to talk or even think about Preston and avoided doing so whenever possible. She felt too many conflicting emotions about him and the way he had treated her—and Bill.

For a while, the silence was broken only by the crashing waves. Then Evelyn reached out and clutched Bill's hand. "I miss him, too," she said. It was the plain truth.

That was all he needed to feel connected once again to his mother. They both had a good cry there in the thundering dark and walked home with their arms around each other. At last, a truce had been struck.

At least temporarily.

The next weekend, Jimmy Langhorn rode the Greyhound bus down to Laguna Beach from Hollywood, arriving with one change of clothes—and his BB gun.

Evelyn took the boys to Balboa Island, where they rode the ferry to the Fun Zone. She let them eat hot dogs on a stick and the frozen ice cream on a stick called Balboa Bars. That night, both boys got ill, and she made them take turns holding a hot water bottle on their aching stomachs and an ice pack on their heads.

But it was worth it. By the time Jimmy went home Sunday afternoon, Evelyn believed Bill had worked through all his problems. From now on, her son would be communicative, happy, and well behaved.

A few days later, the Laguna Beach municipal maintenance department sent her a bill for eight broken street light bulbs. Bulbs that had been shot out over the last two nights.

Evelyn was livid. She had tried being patient, she had tried being understanding, she had tried being nice—and look how her son had repaid her.

Her parenting instincts swerved, as usual, from warm and fuzzy directly to cold and angry, without pausing in any kind of middle ground. Storming into Bill's room, she snatched up his BB gun and cried, "That's it! No more BB gun! No more being late to school! I mean business!"

And she did. The next day she packed up the car, shoved Bill inside, and drove a half hour north on the Coast Highway to the Balboa Peninsula, where she found another beach house. This one had one compelling attribute that the Laguna house had lacked: it sat directly across the street from a Catholic School. Our Lady of Mount Carmel wasn't quite the Tower Hill Military School, but it was close enough. If a bunch of nuns couldn't discipline her son, no one could.

Now that Bill was in the hands of God, Evelyn decided she was free to live a bit more as she wanted to. For starters, she began sleeping late in the mornings. With no one to wake him and help him get ready for school, Bill rarely showed up for class on time. And whenever he was at home, he complained. He hated the new house. The Linoleum floors got so cold and wet he didn't like to step on them. The place was too small. "I want to live in a big house like Jimmy does," he said.

Evelyn shook her fist at him. "You'll wind up living in the Big House if you keep this up."

The line would one day become a standard joke between them.

But not then.

Somehow, she and Bill muddled through the holidays and all of the following summer before Evelyn made her next move.

In the fall of 1937, she called Tom Lyle and asked if he would help her and Bill move to a home nearer Villa Valentino.

"Of course, Ev," he said.

She smiled. It was time for a change.

Twenty-Eight
Miss Maybelline Is
Back . . . Sort Of

The ivy-covered bungalow Tom Lyle bought them on Kelton Avenue in West Los Angeles wasn't exactly the big house Bill had wanted or the snazzy mansion Evelyn would have preferred, but the old, established neighborhood did offer Bill something he had never experienced before: access to people his own age outside a school environment. This was Tom Lyle's idea; he wanted his godson to grow up like a regular kid and make lasting friends, but still live close enough so Unk Ile could regularly keep an eye on him—attention that would prove to be increasingly necessary.

Tom Lyle furnished the little place with comfy overstuffed furniture, a modern radio, and all the newest kitchen appliances advertised in popular magazines. He believed that both Bill and Evelyn would benefit from living in a nice, cozy home.

But my grandmother itched with the feeling that life had more to offer. Much more. She discovered that she had nothing in common with the stay-at-home wives in the neighborhood, so most days while Bill was in school, she drove to Hollywood and watched movie matinees. In them, young, beautiful women were adored by handsome men willing to fight for them and shower them with love and attention.

She looked at the huge diamond on her finger with longing and regret. The next man in her life wouldn't be Tom Lyle, no matter how much she might wish otherwise. So she had to move on. And she had to start now.

It didn't really cross her mind that the new shape of her future didn't leave a lot of room for her son. After the last two years with Preston, followed by two years of living in isolated beach cottages for the sake of Bill, she had had all the responsibility she could handle.

It was her turn to live.

For Christmas that year, Tom Lyle had the Villa decorated to surpass the splendor of Macy's department store. Inside, lights covered a fifteen-foot fir tree; outside, they twinkled from the trees surrounding the estate.

On Christmas Day, he brought out a little basket and presented it to Bill. Out squirmed a beautiful golden cocker spaniel puppy, which Bill clutched in delight. He had begged his mother for a puppy since he was a little boy in Chicago, but she had always made excuses why it wasn't the right time. His father had promised him one but died before he could fulfill the promise.

Now Bill looked at Evelyn. "You mean it, Mom?"

Tom Lyle and Evelyn answered with one voice: "It's time."

They named her Lady.

They ate Christmas dinner together, then Tom Lyle played his wonderful piano rendition of "Turkey in the Straw."

Bill would remember that Christmas as the holiday highlight of his youth.

Day by day, a previously hidden side of Evelyn began to emerge—the side that wanted to experience the same careless freedom that had once so infuriated her in Preston.

First, it manifested itself in a compulsion to change her look to coordinate with the stunning but secondhand clothes her sister Verona was sending her and with the Lilly Daché cocktail hats she found in stores and boutiques throughout Beverly Hills and Hollywood. To maximize the effect of the hats, she even cut her hair.

She admired herself in the mirror. "Welcome back, Miss Maybelline!"

But where should she strut her new stuff? She called Tom Lyle and asked if he would mind her visiting stores in the area and talking to the salesgirls on behalf of Maybelline, the way she had in Chicago.

"Why not?" Tom Lyle said jovially. "You're still on the payroll, and I've always appreciated your insight."

"I'll start tomorrow," she said.

Evelyn slid smoothly into her Miss Maybelline persona, even though she was at best a lame-duck employee. The company marketing department was now run completely by Rags Ragland in Chicago, and she had no direct communication with him. It was frustrating.

Still, she looked terrific as she left the neighborhood on her self-appointed rounds. She looked like an actress or a woman of means—and if she drew too much attention from married men in her neighborhood, and too much gossip from their wives, what of that? She preferred the company of the salesladies in Westwood Village.

One of them told her about the tea dances at the Biltmore Hotel. "A live orchestra plays, and people have tea and crumpets and dance. It's all very elegant. Anybody who's anybody in Hollywood shows up for publicity shots and that sort of thing."

But Evelyn couldn't imagine going to the Biltmore Hotel alone, not as a single woman of thirty-seven. She thought of Jimmy Langhorn's mother, Beverly, who was always dating wealthy men.

The next day, the two ladies showed up at the Biltmore dressed to knock 'em dead. The experience was everything the salesclerk had promised it would be. Evelyn was asked to dance again and again. Many of her partners bought her cocktails and asked her where she had been all their lives.

When she came home that night—late that night—her self-confidence had skyrocketed. It took her almost an hour to remember to check on Bill. He was in his room, asleep. Well, of course he was. He was a big boy. He didn't need his mother hovering over him every moment of the day and night.

As my grandmother blended into the Biltmore crowd, she quickly tired of her made-over outfits. Unfortunately, she didn't have money for new clothes because although Tom Lyle kept her on the Maybelline payroll, her salary wasn't enough to pay for the kind of clothes she wanted for frivolous adventures. So she settled for dying her hair red and wearing dark red lipstick, rouge, blue eye shadow, and heavy black mascara, even in the daytime.

One afternoon, she spun before Bill, her face painted for the night, and said, "Darling, what do you think?"

He dared not answer honestly—that he was shocked and embarrassed by her. He remembered about how his buddy Joe Montel had reacted when he saw Evelyn for the first time. "Oh my God! Is that your mother or your sister? She's goooorgeous!"

"You look okay," he finally said.

Twenty-Nine
True Confessions

*M*ovies had affected the entire family. They had provided Tom Lyle with his first understanding of glamour. They had tantalized Preston into thinking he might replace Rudolph Valentino—a dream so powerful that he abandoned his family on and off for years. Now they inspired Evelyn to create a more exciting persona for herself, one that would attract men willing to shower her with admiration. And movies offered Bill a way to escape his loneliness and find a haven in adventure and exotic passion. He especially loved the block-buster *The Hurricane,* starring Dorothy Lamour, who was twenty-three going on thirty-five. What her body looked like in a sarong made Bill tack up a few pictures of her in his room.

"Glamour," Lamour was quoted as saying, "is just sex that got civilized."

Tom Lyle would have agreed. His dream was that all women, maiden or matron, would discover glamour through Maybelline. Sarongs aside, he saw what the movies did for Dorothy Lamour's exotic eyes and still wished there were some way to capture the same magic in his ads.

It was all about the Technicolor.

Technicolor was a sophisticated film process based on a double-negative lamination system in which colors on the red-orange-yellow end of the spectrum were photographed on one negative and blue-green-purple hues on the other. A full-color range was filmed by employing a three-strip camera.

Surely, Tom Lyle thought, there was a way to get individual shots using the same process—but no one he spoke with had any idea how to do such a thing. Kodak had just introduced Kodachrome, the first color still film, but a single roll cost five dollars—the equivalent of three hundred dollars today. Even at that price, while Kodachrome worked wonderfully for scenery, it showed flaws and tended to exaggerate uneven skin tones in close-ups of human faces.

So, for the time being, Maybelline continued to use black-and-white photos for its actresses and color only in ads featuring illustrations of idealized women. But the Technicolor vision remained a powerful dream for Tom Lyle.

On the marketing and production front, the company's graphics designers came out with a modern metal Maybelline box in red and gold, as well as a leather pouch holding a tube of cream mascara and a tiny red brush. To support this new look, Tom Lyle planned Maybelline's most ambitious advertising campaign yet, one that would blanket the newspaper and radio markets in addition to the usual glamour and movie magazines. But before he launched this audacious new campaign, he needed one more thing: the right face, the right image, the right cachet.

One morning, he called Bill. "There's someone I want you to meet, Bug. Pick you up in a half hour."

Soon Tom Lyle and Emery pulled up in a black convertible Packard with red leather upholstery and gold chrome—the Maybelline colors. Bill hopped in, and they cruised to Beverly Hills, where they stopped in front of an elegant estate. A butler ushered them into an oversized entry, where a few minutes later, a woman wearing white gardenias in her long dark-brown hair descended the winding stairway. Bill stood gawking at Dorothy Lamour.

Emery closed Bill's mouth with his palm while Tom Lyle introduced Bill as his nephew. Dorothy put out her manicured hand and commented on what a handsome young man he was. He blushed.

During the short, no-nonsense meeting that followed, no drinks were offered, and the guests didn't linger. Lamour signed a contract for a full-page color photo of herself to be used with ad copy proclaiming Maybelline as her eye makeup of choice, then bid her visitors a cordial farewell.

In the Packard, Emery said, "Well, Bug, a penny for your thoughts."

"She's the girl of my dreams." He let out a long sigh. Then, "Can we go to Musso and Frank's?"—one of the oldest and most popular restaurants in Hollywood.

Although Bill could not stop talking about meeting Dorothy Lamour, to

Tom Lyle and Emery, the outing was just another day in Paradise. Celebrities needed Maybelline exposure as much as Maybelline needed them; it was a win-win relationship. They accepted one another, regardless of foibles, oddities, or bizarre lifestyles—all was tolerated, even admired.

Bill would also get to meet Hedy Lamarr, Joan Crawford, and Carole Lombard—but no one excited him more than a young woman whose name never did reach iconic status: Eleanor Fisher.

At that time, *True Confessions* magazine topped the sales charts among teenage girls, and it struck a deal with Paramount and Maybelline to do a sweeping marketing campaign to attract an even larger youth market. In a brilliant move, the magazine held a "Miss Typical America" contest, the winner of which would win five hundred dollars and a trip to Hollywood.

The sponsors crowned young Eleanor Fisher as Miss Typical America, and Paramount gave her a small part in Carole Lombard's last film at the studio, *True Confession,* inspired by stories from the magazine. Again, Bill went along to the contract signing with Tom Lyle and Emery—and again, he was dazzled. At age fourteen, Bill was now officially girl crazy.

Maybelline splashed full-page color photos of Eleanor in magazines all across the country, congratulating her for being chosen from thousands of "America's most dazzling beauties." The ad stressed the role that her beautiful eyes, fringed in romantic lashes, played in her win. The same charm, the ad went on, "can be yours too, instantly, with but a few simple brush strokes of Maybelline Mascara."

The ad, together with the film and *True Confessions* magazine, expanded Maybelline's scope still further. Although prudes, yellow journalists, and religious fundamentalists still spouted their antiglamour rhetoric, no one was listening. Profits soared.

Evelyn's life would certainly have titillated the *True Confessions* readership.

One evening, Bill answered the doorbell to find a tall, handsome man standing on the porch. He was dressed in a sports jacket and white pants, holding a bouquet of flowers and a box of candy. "Hi, young man," he said. "I'm Charlie Lewis, here to pick up Evelyn for dinner."

Bill let him in and took the candy. "Thanks. You can give the flowers to my mother."

"Mother?" Charlie asked. "Evelyn? I thought she was your sister."

"Tell that to her. I'm sure she'd love to hear it—again."

While Charlie Lewis gaped at him, Bill opened the candy and stuffed a couple of pieces in his mouth.

Charlie Lewis billed himself as a freelance casting agent, a man with the connections to get aspiring starlets into the movies—in other words, he was a cliché Hollywood wolf. A regular on the tea dancing circuit, he swept naive young women off their feet and into his bed. He had good taste in clothes, cars, and women, and though he was typically most interested in young girls, he seemed to be impressed with Evelyn—he had watched her transform from a transplanted Easterner into a "California hot tamale."

Evelyn had noticed him, too, but written him off as a showoff until she finally stepped out onto the floor with him. By the end of a fast mambo, she was smitten with his wit as well as his moves, and by evening, she knew she was in love. Not a crush, not just one of those crazy things. The big L.

In her new fantasy, Charlie was a real catch. They became an item. He introduced her to his fun-loving drinking buddies—guys Preston would have loved. Charlie thought nothing of dropping by the bungalow unannounced with a few such friends, until Evelyn's little home turned into the Biltmore West, with loud music and Evelyn's shrill laugh ringing through the open windows while working neighbors were pulling into their driveways after a long day. Word got around that Evelyn didn't have a job and that a lot of men with party girls on their arms and flasks of booze in their pockets came and went from her home all day and half the night.

By this time, Evelyn had developed what became her signature look: flowing Harlow pants and kimonos, along with her own special touch—a low-cut corset draped over with scarves to create a daring bustier. She accented this costume with a cigarette holder and high heels. It was a good look for a high-class call girl in a movie, but for a single mother, it mostly provided fare for choice gossip.

Charlie began showing up at the house every day in his two-seater roadster. Sometimes he didn't come to the door at all. He would honk the horn and yell, "Hey girl, let's get going here! Time's a wasting—you're not getting any younger!"

"Oh, Charlie," Evelyn would cry, skipping out the front door. "You're so bad!"

The roadster would tear away down the street as housewives gawped out their windows—exactly as Evelyn wanted them to.

One evening, when Charlie and his friends came by, talk turned to playing the horses at Santa Anita, Del Mar, and the new Hollywood Park. An upcoming race was going to feature the famous thoroughbred Seabiscuit. "Only a fool would bet against that boy," Charlie said.

"But he isn't being ridden by his usual jockey," one of Charlie's friends said. "Red Pollard got smashed up in a big pileup a few races back."

"Doesn't matter. Nobody's beating Seabiscuit. What do you say, babe? Want to go to Santa Anita? All the movie stars have their own private boxes there. If

Arnold Anderson, Debbie Reynolds,
and Tom Lyle, 1950

Tom Lyle, Thomas Jefferson and Mabel in his first car,
a custom designed "Paige," Chicago, 1917 (cost: $1,800)

Mabel Williams—for whom Maybelline cosmetics was named. This
photo was taken at her wedding to Chet Hewes: April 17, 1926.

My make-up would not
be complete without
Maybelline Mascara,
Eyebrow Pencil and
Eye Shadow.
Merle Oberon

Merle Oberon, 1938

To Maybelline —
The eye make-up I find
so truly flattering →
Always
Hedy Lamarr

Heddy Lamarr, 1944

World War II ad

To Maybelline —
The eye make-up
I would never be
without —
Sincerely
Joan Crawford

Natural color photograph
by PAUL HESSE-Hollywood

Joan Crawford, 1946

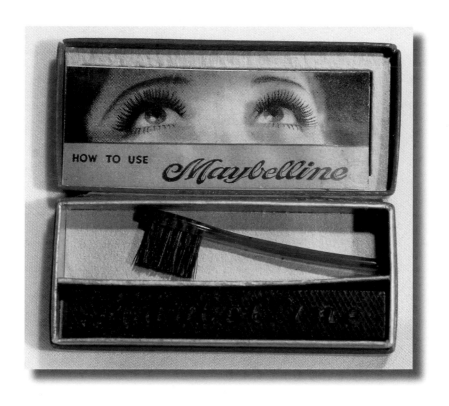

Original Maybelline packaging, 1917

To the girl with a soldier overseas...
How much do you really want him back?

Just how much do you miss your soldier—far across the ocean?

Do you miss him so much that you'll pass up that jeweled bracelet you've set your heart on?

Do you love him so much that you'll make your old suit last another spring?

Do you want him back so badly that you'll walk to the office and to the stores when you could take the bus—and sit home in the evenings when you might go to the movies?

You do? Of course you do!

So start saving, start denying yourself little "extras" and luxuries right now. And buy United States War Bonds with every single cent that you save!

War Bonds will help bring your soldier back!

War Bonds mean reinforcements for him right now—a reserve for you both in years to come.

War Bonds mean American bombers over Germany and submarines under the China Sea—they really mean a shorter war!

War Bonds are your ballot against inflation—your insurance policy for freedom—your savings bank book after the Armistice is signed.

And over and above all that, they're the most careful and cautious, the safest and most productive investment into which you—or anybody else—could possibly put your money. Start buying War Bonds for your soldier. And start buying them today!

SAVE YOUR MONEY THE SAFEST WAY—BUY U.S. WAR BONDS REGULARLY

Published in cooperation with the Drug, Cosmetic and Allied Industries by:

Maybelline
WORLD'S LARGEST-SELLING EYE BEAUTY AIDS

World War II War Bonds ad, 1943

Betty Grable in a cross promotion for the
20th Century Fox picture *Down Argentine Way,* 1940

Tom Lyle—with Salle Allen, Emery Shaver, Annette Williams, and Arnold Anderson—at his Villa Valentino home in 1945

Billy, Evelyn, Tom Lyle, and Emery Shaver, 1934

Tom Lyle in his custom designed Packard, Los Angeles, 1938

Evelyn and Preston, 1935

Tom Lyle, Bill and Evelyn, 1938

Tom Lyle and Evelyn, 1966

you play your cards right, I might arrange for you to sit next to Clark Gable or Spencer Tracy."

She threw her arms around him. "I'd love to." She didn't mention that while she had never been to a live horse race before, she knew plenty about betting—back in Chicago she had her own bookie. This should be exciting.

Seventy thousand fans crammed the stands at Santa Anita. Scanning the crowd with her binoculars, Evelyn saw Bing Crosby standing with his racing form, talking to a beautiful woman. "That was as close as I ever came to rubbing elbows with a celebrity at the races," she said in later years.

Like Charlie, most of the fans were there to see and bet on Seabiscuit. Evelyn, on the other hand, put twenty on a horse named Stagehand because she liked the name. Charlie got a good laugh out of that.

When the horses broke from the gate, Seabiscuit languished in twelfth place, forced to the outside by another horse. Charlie screamed until the veins stood out in his neck: "Move it! Move it!"

Finally, Seabiscuit broke loose, leaving the competition behind as he dashed ahead at record speed. Charlie bellowed, "I'm rich!"

"No, *I'm* rich!" Evelyn screamed as another horse pulled away from the pack and began to gain on the leader. "That's Stagehand!"

Stagehand finished first, and Evelyn spent her winnings on a new spring wardrobe.

Tom Lyle came to visit not long after that, bearing a bouquet of gardenias. As Evelyn greeted him, he shook his head and remarked on how impressed he was that Evelyn could manage her money and still look like a million bucks. Smiling, Evelyn bustled off to the kitchen to check the pot roast. Bill frowned but made no comment on the happy homemaker routine. His mother had told him to keep his mouth shut about certain things, and she could be pretty frightening when she felt threatened.

Evelyn lit candles, while in the background a Benny Goodman record played "Begin the Beguine." Over dinner, she and Tom Lyle discussed how terrible it was that *Time* magazine had named Adolf Hitler their Man of the Year.

She served Tom Lyle his favorite dessert, pineapple upside-down cake, and he asked her about fashion trends and what she felt would be the next big fad.

This was the cue she had been waiting for. Like Scheherazade, she related stories and observations she had gleaned from gossip at the Biltmore, the racetracks, the tennis club—all the while implying that the information came from her hard work interviewing salesclerks and reading movie and fashion magazines.

"Speaking of movie magazines," Tom Lyle said, "I recently had the pleasure

of meeting Alice Faye while she was making *Alexander's Ragtime Band* at Fox."
He spoke casually, but he was doing a little storytelling of his own. In reality, his
relationship with Alice Faye had begun more than four years earlier, when the
young singer first came to Hollywood to film a song for *George White's Scandals*.
Tom Lyle, who remembered hearing Alice's soulful voice on the radio show
known in Chicago as *The Fleishmann Hour,* had contacted her about doing a
possible Maybelline ad. Although she was relatively unknown at the time, he
recognized the star quality in her voice and her classic blonde beauty, and he
asked her to have dinner with him.

Thus began a strange and long-lasting relationship.

Tom Lyle signed Faye to a modeling contract with Maybelline, with the associated advertising campaign timed to the release of *Alexander's Ragtime Band*.
But the relationship didn't end there. Tom Lyle and the beautiful actress—nineteen years his junior—were seen together quite a bit in Chicago and New York
while Alice Faye's gigantic eyes looked down from the neon Maybelline sign
in the middle of Times Square—a sign that not only winked, but appeared in
the movie itself. Together, the glamorous pair helped each other market their
separate products. For Tom Lyle, the appearance of an intimate relationship also
helped him maintain his public façade.

"I love her new, softer look," Evelyn remarked, and they discussed Faye's
evolution from a singing version of Jean Harlow—the wisecracking showgirl
type—to a more mature and elegant woman.

Bill had an opinion, too. "I liked the baton twirler in *Alexander's Ragtime Band*. Unk, if you sign a contract with *her,* promise I get to go with you.
Wouldn't the guys go nuts, Mom?"

It was all so civilized, so 180 degrees opposite Evelyn's daily activities with
Charlie Lewis. My grandmother was a real dame, and I must make my own true
confession: I loved her for it!

Thirty
Technicolor

On September 13, 1938, British and French prime ministers Neville Chamberlain and Édouard Daladier met with Adolf Hitler and Benito Mussolini to sign the notorious Munich Pact. Less than two months later, Hitler ordered an official pogrom against Jewish citizens in Germany. SS men wearing civilian clothing and paramilitary groups such as the Brownshirts murdered ninety-one people, arrested and deported twenty-five to thirty thousand people to concentration camps, destroyed more than two hundred synagogues, and ransacked seventy-five hundred businesses and homes. All the shattered glass earned the ominous incident the name Kristallnacht—Crystal Night.

Tom Lyle was deeply concerned about the atrocities and anonymously sent money to several charities around the world, but Maybelline's success continued to be his primary objective. He was, after all, the one his family depended on.

One day, he rushed up to Emery, displaying a pair of photos. "Emery, look at this. Before-and-after shots of Merle Oberon. Tell me what you see."

Emery looked over the photos. He knew about Merle Oberon, of course—a beautiful actress of mixed Indian-English heritage who had been badly scarred in a terrible accident the year before. One picture showed her without makeup, every pit and indentation clearly visible. In the other, her skin looked flawless—and not just because of artful makeup and lighting. Something else was going on here.

He looked up at Tom Lyle. "How did they do this?"

"Technicolor," Tom Lyle said. "It has to be. Someone's figured out how to take still shots in Technicolor—just what we've been looking for."

He made an appointment with Oberon, who had just finished filming *The Divorce of Lady X,* and they met to discuss contracting her for a new ad campaign. It would be timed to begin in March 1939, just before the release of *Wuthering Heights,* in which Oberon costarred with Laurence Olivier and David Niven. Tom Lyle wanted to place a portrait of Oberon on the back of movie magazines—but not an ordinary photo. No, this would be a Technicolor masterpiece suitable for framing, with Oberon's signature and a personal message praising Maybelline.

This appointment proved to be even more monumental than Tom Lyle had expected. It led not only to a contract with the actress, but to a meeting with a man who would come to play a major role in the company and in Tom Lyle's personal life: Arnold Anderson, the talented young artist who had produced the photo that so captivated Tom Lyle.

Arnold explained that he had taken Technicolor footage of Oberon from its color negative, carefully developed it, and then, using a sophisticated airbrush technique, erased Oberon's scars and other imperfections through touchups with a unique paint, creating a lifelike painting. Although the technique would eventually become commonplace, at the time, it was absolutely groundbreaking.

In his typical understated manner, Tom Lyle looked Arnold in the eye and said, "You're a genius!"

For the Maybelline ad, Arnold had a Technicolor image of Oberon shot with ideal lighting, then personally walked the film through the lab in Hollywood and used the process he had developed to create a flawless still picture in brilliant color.

Tom Lyle was thrilled. He worshipped perfection. In Maybelline ads, he insisted that a star's facial contours remain unlined—even if she was smiling or raising her eyebrows—to allow her eyes to sparkle, virtually popping off the page. With his new technique, Arnold could disguise any wrinkle, any flaw. Tom Lyle simply had to have the skills of this young man, and asked Anderson not only to work for Maybelline, but to move into the Villa Valentino as well. Having a photography studio right there on the premises would, after all, be a highly productive arrangement.

Arnold agreed, and Tom Lyle immediately set up the new studio, containing equipment as elaborate as that found in any movie company. From then on, the three-man team ran what would become an advertising empire from the Villa.

But the change from a duo to a trio had other ramifications. Tom Lyle was infatuated with Arnold for more than his artistic skills. The truth was, Tom Lyle sometimes grew weary of Emery's incessant chatter and often-flamboyant behavior. Arnold was different. Although he shared Emery's quick wit and easy laugh, he didn't require as much attention and was therefore less of an emotional drain. Also, despite his boyish good looks, Arnold projected a more masculine façade than Emery did. For the same reasons Tom Lyle liked to be seen in public with Alice Faye and other actresses, he felt more comfortable going out in society with a man who appeared to be nothing more than a business associate.

Gradually, Tom Lyle came to spend more and more time with Arnold. A new balance became established as Emery kept busy with his theatrical friends, his hobbies, and the small antique shop in Beverly Hills Tom Lyle had opened for him. But one thing didn't change—all three were devoted servants of the one true queen: Maybelline.

Meanwhile, Bill required attention of his own. Not long before his fifteenth birthday, he called Tom Lyle and begged for a car so that he could be popular at school. Tom Lyle reminded him that he was still a year from having a driver's license but said he would think about it.

Bill knew what that meant: he had won.

Sure enough, on Christmas morning, when he took Lady out for her morning walk, he found himself staring at a black 1935 Ford convertible with a rumble seat in the back and a big red bow on the hood.

The car needed some work, and Tom Lyle insisted that Bill earn money for parts and learn to do the work himself. Bill went further, not only getting the car running but customizing it with the help of his friends. When he asked if he could take it for a spin, his mother shook her head. "Only after Unk Ile gives you some lessons."

The next time Bill came to the Villa, Tom Lyle drove him down Wedgwood Place in the Packard. He turned onto Hollywood Boulevard, demonstrating the proper hand signals, carefully changing lanes, explaining the rules of the road. Only when he saw the flashing lights of a police car behind him did he realize he had been gaining speed the entire time.

Back home, Evelyn asked how the driving lesson went.

Tom Lyle showed her his traffic ticket. "Bill should do very well, if he doesn't follow my example."

Bill was also growing up in other ways. One day, he noticed a pretty girl in the hallway of University High School, talking to the girl his friend Gene Benz was dating. He nudged Gene. "Who's that?"

"Oh, that's Pauline MacDonald, but you can't get near her."

"Why not?"

"She doesn't date—too busy dancing. Her father's some kind of big shot at MGM. She wants to break into the movies, so she's there all the time."

"A dancer, huh? No wonder she has such a great ass."

"Well, forget it, you'll never get near it. You won't even get past the three girls she hangs out with."

"We'll see about that," Bill said.

Watching her from afar, he realized that Gene was right. Nobody could seem to penetrate the gaggle of girls who surrounded her. Still, Bill began following her to class—at a distance—and waiting for her to show up for lunch in the cafeteria or stroll to the lawn where the girls sat with their friends.

Pauline MacDonald had captivated him. Unlike his mother, Pauline dressed in simple clothes and wore no makeup at all. Pretty square, but oh, those legs, and that beautiful smile, and something about her clear, sparkling eyes, even without any makeup.

Evelyn noticed Bill moping around and guessed the general reason, even if she didn't know the particulars. She decided to sign him up for cotillion.

"Cotillion . . . Mom, are you nuts?"

"You want to meet girls, don't you?" She pulled his sports jacket and dress shirt out of the closet.

"Girls, as in chicks! Skirts! Not squares."

"Nevertheless, cotillion is a good place to start, and you'll learn how to dance as well."

"I don't give a rat's ass about social dancing." Bill was beginning to feel desperate. "And I hate dressing up. That's for mama's boys!"

That gave Evelyn pause. She remembered Preston accusing her of turning Bill into a mama's boy and how he had gone to extremes to toughen his son up, as if he had known Bill would have to fight the world without a dad. She pushed the thought out of her mind and thought how proud Preston would be of their son now. "You're no mama's boy," she said.

On the night of the first cotillion dance, Bill walked into the ballroom and received a nametag. Uncomfortable in his cream-colored sports jacket, tan slacks, dress shirt, and tie, he kept his eye open for any attractive girls who might be dumb enough to be there by mistake. He didn't see many; most of the young ladies were just too plain for the guy Dorothy Lamour herself had called handsome.

A middle-aged matron took the microphone and announced that it was time for the first dance of the evening and would the boys and girls please pair up for the circle dance.

As Bill shuffled into position, he judged the distance to the door for a fast escape if things got too weird. Then he looked up—straight into the eyes he had spent so much time thinking about. Pauline MacDonald stood so close he could smell her freshly washed dark-brown hair, see the scrubbed shine on her cheeks and the beautiful golden flecks in her hazel eyes.

"Don't worry, I don't bite," she said, as she put her hand on Bill's shoulder.

Thirty-One
The Girl Who Was Not a Dame

*M*usic played as Bill awkwardly placed his right hand on Pauline's waist. He could not have named the tune. How tiny Pauline's waist is, he thought (it was all of nineteen inches). He could feel her dancer's poise, as if her weight didn't quite settle on the floor the way his did. His heavy wingtips seemed to grow larger as they slid around Pauline's dainty steps.

They didn't talk much, but there was something about Pauline that was naturally sweet, likeable, even wholesome. This was no future dame in the making.

When the dance ended—at 9:00 p.m. sharp—he walked her outside and asked where she lived.

The next day, Sunday, he pulled up in front of her parents' bungalow in Santa Monica. Pauline stood in the front yard watering the lawn, her skirtlike jumper shorts revealing her shapely dancer's legs.

Arm casually resting on the passenger seat, Bill called, "Want to go for a ride?"

She turned off the hose. "Nice car. I'll go ask Mom."

She hurried upstairs and after a few nerve-wracking minutes, returned with her mother, who hadn't bothered to remove her apron.

Bill leaped out of the car and ran over with his hand out. "My name is Bill Williams. It's very nice to meet you."

"Where did you get such nice manners?" Elna asked.

"From my mother, ma'am."

"She must be a very nice lady to have raised such a young gentleman."

"Um, yes, ma'am." He was pleasantly shocked at how unlike his mother Elna MacDonald was. Her graying hair lay neatly around a kind face without a lick of makeup on it. Still, her baby-blue eyes twinkled the way Unk Ile was always trying to get the eyes in his ads to do.

"Young man," she said, "you have my permission to take Pauline for a drive. But only if you stay for Sunday dinner with us when you come back."

"You bet! It would be my pleasure."

It was a gorgeous spring day in 1939, and the young couple cruised by Pacific Ocean Park in Santa Monica and then headed up the coast, listening to Glenn Miller playing "Tuxedo Junction," "I Got Rhythm" by the Five Spirits, and "I Hear the Angels Sing," by Benny Goodman and Martha Tipton.

In Malibu, Bill pulled into the parking lot of the Cliff House restaurant, and he and Pauline climbed out to watch the seals at play. As they walked down the shoreline in the bright sunshine, Pauline talked about her mother and father—the "big shot at MGM," as Gene Benz had called him. It turned out that Andy MacDonald was indeed a big shot at the studio, supervising set construction and designing special effects for all kind of movies, including *The Wizard of Oz* and *Gone with the Wind.*

Pauline told Bill that her father had been called in to create a controlled fire for the burning of Atlanta scene in *Gone with the Wind,* which had to be shot in one take and employed virtually every Technicolor camera in town. Pauline laughed. "My dad says that when the movie comes out, if you know what to look for, you'll probably see the gates of Skull Island from *King Kong* burning up in the background."

Bill laughed, too, then surprised himself—and her—by blurting, "You're lucky your dad is still around."

She looked at him.

"What I mean is, you're lucky to have a dad working in the movie business."

"What does your father do?"

Bill looked away. "He's dead."

Pauline listened silently, the wind lifting flyaway wisps of her hair—as it always did—while Bill unburdened himself about his father's life and early death. At some point, she realized she was holding his hand and couldn't remember who had initiated the contact. She didn't much care. This young man wasn't like most of the boys she knew. He was more polished and worldly, had better manners and great looks—yet there was this soft, vulnerable side to him, too.

After a few minutes, Bill brightened. "I might not have my dad, but I do have a wonderful uncle. Maybe I can take you to meet him sometime." He described Villa Valentino, which to Pauline sounded like something her father might have built for a movie extravaganza.

He asked about her dancing. She said that when she was small, her mother had signed her up for dancing lessons at Grace's Dance Studio in Culver City, where talent scouts watched for young girls they could audition for musicals at MGM. Pauline had grown up at the studio and become friends with all the studio kids who made movies at MGM—including Judy Garland and Mickey Rooney. By age thirteen, she had begun her dance studies with Bill "Bojangles" Robinson and Eleanor Powell. Soon, she hoped to audition for a movie role.

"That's my dream," she said. "What's yours?"

Nobody had ever asked him that before, not even Unk Ile. He had to stop and think about it for a second. Then the words popped out of him: "I'd like to design and build beautiful homes."

She squeezed his hand. "Maybe I could help you someday."

Back at the MacDonalds', the smell of roast beef, mashed potatoes, and a homemade apple pie reminded Bill of Gramma Boecher's in Chicago. A vase of fresh flowers sat on a white tablecloth amid platters of food and a pitcher of milk. Here was a family that valued simplicity, order, and structure, with a father who worked full-time and had brought home a regular paycheck in an era when many people were still broke and out of work.

Andy MacDonald, paunchy and balding, sat at the head of the table and said grace. As Bill joined in, he felt a sense of security he had rarely known in his own family life.

He marveled over the fact that Mr. MacDonald worked in the movie business yet had a wife who seemed unaffected by the glamour of it. Plain and pleasant, Elna reminded him of his Auntie Mabel, who no longer bothered with the makeup she had inspired.

Bill dug into his meal. It was delicious. He hadn't realized how tired he was of living on canned food and peanut butter sandwiches while his mother ran around with Charlie Lewis.

He had discovered the place he wanted to be every Sunday.

Bill and Pauline began double-dating with his buddy Gene Benz and Pauline's girlfriend Mary Eldridge. Along with hundreds of other young people, they drove downtown to the Palladium, where they learned the jitterbug and danced to the swing of Tommy Dorsey and Benny Goodman. This was their music. Jazzed and happy, young people were ready to party again.

The possibility of war in Europe seemed so distant. In June 1939, FDR refused to allow the cruise ship *St. Louis*—carrying 907 Jewish refugees who had already been turned away from Havana—to dock in New Orleans; most Americans paid little attention. The same was true in Canada, where the ship was also refused. Finally, it had to return to Europe, a situation Germany used as proof that no one in the world wanted the Jews.

Americans turned their heads. They had just regained a toehold on normalcy. No one wanted to deal with Adolf Hitler.

"Well, Bug." Unk Ile turned his head away from the phone to yawn. It was just after two in the afternoon, the hour Tom Lyle was usually just getting out of bed. He preferred to work into the early morning hours to be sure of uninterrupted quiet. "Of course I'm eager to meet your young lady. Bring her by at, say, three thirty?"

"Sure thing."

Tom Lyle hung up and looked across the patio to the swimming pool, where Arnold Anderson had just executed a perfect dive into the cool blue water to the applause of Emery and several younger men scattered around in the sun.

Tom Lyle smiled. Few people knew about the pool parties and barbecues that went on behind the locked doors and closed gates of the Villa. Through Anderson and Billy Haines, Tom Lyle had gained connections with many actors in Hollywood who looked and acted straight on screen, but in private were gay or bisexual. In fact, a secret demimonde known as "The Club" had grown out of the wild parties throughout this hidden community in Hollywood. At these soirees, pre-rolled marijuana and Benzedrine were served in candy dishes on silver trays. This, along with the cross dressing, drunkenness, and other wild behavior characteristic of such parties did not appeal to Tom Lyle. He preferred his own private club here at the Villa, where only the most discreet were invited, and even they tended to be mostly Emery's friends, like the group around the pool.

All handsome men—but to Tom Lyle, Arnold stood out among them like an Adonis. Sometimes, he thought Arnold might be the love of his life—except that Arnold showed disappointing signs of having a drinking problem. He was so different from Emery. But so was Tom Lyle. In fact, they were all different from one another, yet wedded by their shared love of work and creativity. If that made life complicated, well, what of it? Was anything worth having ever truly simple?

"Emery?" he called across the pool. "Sorry, but you're going to have to ask your friends to leave. Bill's coming over this afternoon with his first girlfriend."

"He's really something," Pauline whispered to Bill the moment Tom Lyle left them to get a couple of Cokes. She found him as impressive as any of the stars at MGM.

Bill grinned. "Told you so."

Tom Lyle returned with the bottles, straws sticking straight up from the necks. Lighting a French cigarette, he sat down and asked Pauline about her father's work. "I've been associated with the film world myself since 1911," he said.

"Really?"

"Oh, yes. That's when I ran the nickelodeon in Morganfield, Kentucky."

They all laughed.

On the way home, Pauline said, "That was wonderful. But when do I get to meet your mom?"

For a moment Bill didn't answer. Of course he had known this question was coming. He had become almost a tenant at Pauline's house, but she had yet to visit his. "Well," he said, "Mom's pretty busy these days. I'll ask her."

Someday.

Thirty-Two
Plaid Skirt Meets Silk Kimono

*I*s that music coming from your house?"

Bill and Pauline had just pulled into the driveway of Evelyn's bungalow and parked among a clutch of stylish cars. The moment Bill killed the engine, the wailing of saxophones and clarinets filled the air.

Bill swallowed. "Yeah. Mother likes to play it loud."

He knew this was a bad idea, but he hadn't been able to put it off any longer. Not only Pauline, but Evelyn as well, had been asking when the two of them could get together. His mother had been the one to suggest he bring his girlfriend to one of her Saturday parties. He had tried to think of a reason to get out of it—again. Evelyn and Charlie's Saturday soirées had become a ritual among the Biltmore Hollywood fringe hopefuls. The bar was always stocked with liquor, the record player with jazz, and the dice were ready for throwing across the hardwood floors. Fancy cars came and went late into the night.

Bill always tried to not be around as his kimono-clad mother entertained at these events, belting out oldies or kicking up her heels to Johnny Mercer singing "Too Marvelous for Words." He certainly didn't want to expose Pauline to them. But he knew he couldn't avoid having Pauline meet Evelyn forever, so he mentioned his mother's invitation to Pauline—and unfortunately, she accepted with joy.

So here they were. Bill got out of the car and went around to open Pauline's door for her. She stepped out in her Scotch plaid skirt, white blouse, and black patent leather pumps.

"This way," Bill said, and led her around to the back of the house, where they went inside through the French doors. Inside, twenty or so people danced, drank, and yelled "snake eyes!" or "Give it to me, Lady Luck!" From the midst of the chatter rose Evelyn's laughter, louder than the barking of the cocker spaniel.

That was when Pauline finally got her first view of Evelyn Williams: a beautiful woman setting her Manhattan down so that she could throw dice with one hand while balancing a cigarette holder in the other. She wore a black silk kimono, red silk pants, spike heels, and her signature bustier scarf creation.

Evelyn saw Pauline, too. "Darlings! Everyone, look! Bill is here with his little girlfriend!" She rushed over, arms in the air, trailing kimono sleeves like wings.

Pauline gaped. Evelyn touched her chin. "Close your mouth, dear, you're catching flies."

Bill scrutinized the floor.

After the introductions, Evelyn looked Pauline up and down and from side to side. "Darling, let me give you a little makeover, a little before-and-after. You'll love it."

Bill stiffened. "Mother! Pauline looks great."

"Oh, no, Mrs. Williams," Pauline said. "Thank you, but no."

"I will not take no for an answer." Evelyn took Pauline's arm and led her into her bathroom.

Charlie handed Bill a Coke. "Would you like a shot of bourbon in it?" he asked, and then added, not unkindly, "Look, let her be—you know your mother."

"Yeah," Bill said. "And I'm not happy about it."

"I don't mean to be disrespectful, Mrs. Williams—"

"Call me Evelyn, darling. Mrs. Williams was my mother-in-law."

"Of course, Evelyn, but—"

"Have a seat." Evelyn turned on the lights around her enormous oval mirror and handed Pauline a glass of Scotch. "Just relax."

"Oh, no, thank you. My mother would never let me drink liquor."

Evelyn chuckled and got out her kit of Maybelline. "Hold still, dear, and don't blink." She applied mascara to the girl's lashes, added blue eye shadow, penciled her eyebrows, powdered her face, rouged her cheeks, and applied lipstick to her already perfectly shaped lips.

Overwhelmed, Pauline submitted until Evelyn parted her hair down the middle and pulled the sides up with combs. "Ouch!"

Evelyn caught her gaze in the mirror. Evelyn was not smiling now. "Dear, remember this: it hurts to be beautiful."

Jimmy Dorsey's saxophone was playing in the background when Evelyn opened the bathroom door and out stepped a fifteen-year-old goddess in a long black gown, her face glowing with artfully applied color, a white gardenia behind her ear.

"Holy crow," Bill whispered.

The roomful of beautiful people erupted into claps and whistles. "You did it again, Ev!" someone said. "You've got the golden touch."

Pauline's face reddened so much that the rouge disappeared, but her smile lit up the house. Bill took her hand and whispered in her ear, "Sorry about my mom. But I gotta admit, you could be a pinup girl."

Before she could reply, Charlie Lewis snatched her from Bill's grip and took her for a spin across the hardwood floor, the crowd clapping in time to the music.

When Pauline walked into her own house, her mother's eyes widened, but not with joy or amazement. "Wash that greasepaint off your face immediately! You're only fifteen years old, for God's sake!"

"It's okay, mom," Pauline said. "Bill's mother did it. It was all in fun, and I think I look beautiful."

"You don't need makeup to be beautiful. You are beautiful. Being young is beautiful." Elna marched toward the bathroom to search for cold cream. "What was that woman thinking?"

Pauline followed her. "She was just having fun. It was all in fun."

"Fun." Her mother found the jar and handed it to Pauline. "I don't appreciate Bill's mother taking it upon herself to make my daughter look like a tart. She better never do it again."

When Bill heard about Elna's reaction, he made his mother promise she wouldn't do any more makeovers on his girlfriend.

Evelyn gave her hand an airy wave. "So, when do I get to meet her parents, anyway?"

"I'll mention it to Pauline," Bill said.

Someday.

Thirty-Three
Black Velvet
Meets Apron

Something was wrong in the MacDonald household. Bill could feel it at Sunday dinner. Everyone was quieter than usual, and Andy had not given Bill his usual hearty handshake and shoulder chuck. At the table, he didn't look up from his pot roast and rolls. Elna was pleasant enough, as usual, although Bill noticed she didn't speak to her husband at all.

Perhaps they were upset by the news from Europe; Bill's mother certainly was. Germany had invaded Poland, and Great Britain and other Commonwealth nations had declared war on the Boechers's beloved Hinterland. Who knew what would happen next? Would America once again be drawn into a terrible conflict on foreign shores?

But that wasn't the problem at all. While Bill and Pauline did the dishes after dinner, Pauline explained that her mother was upset because she wanted to move into a bigger house like the one they used to own, but her father didn't think now was a good time.

"Where did you live before?" Bill asked.

"We had a beautiful Spanish-style place in Cheviot Hills. Mom and Dad used to throw some really fancy parties there."

"Why did you move?"

"Dad fell on a nail at the studio and got such a bad infection, the doctor wanted to cut his leg off."

"No!"

"Well, Dad knew that would mean the end of his career, so he begged the doctor to try something else, anything else. For nine months he lay in bed, and nurses removed a cup of pus a day. He got to keep his leg, but right then the stock market crashed, and we had no way to pay for our house, and nobody would buy it, so the bank foreclosed. On top of that, Dad was also supporting his sisters' families and several of the men at MGM who couldn't work."

Bill nodded. "Unk Ile took care of my family during the Depression."

"It actually worked out okay," Pauline said in her optimistic way. "Mom seems to get more enjoyment out of helping others like she does now than she ever got from putting on parties. But I guess now that Dad's sisters' families aren't dependent on him anymore, she wants to have a nicer house again."

"But not too far away, I hope," Bill said.

On Thanksgiving Day that year, Evelyn got her chance to meet the entire MacDonald family—in their new home, which was actually much closer to Bill's place than the old MacDonald house had been.

When Evelyn stepped inside, she looked around with considerable interest. She had often admired this gracious home from the street and, in fact, had dreamed of one day owning and decorating it herself. And she would certainly have done a better job than this. Where were the lavish furnishings, the rich rugs, the beautiful details like silver candlesticks and crystal vases?

She classed the joint up just by being in it. She had dressed in a black velvet dress that showed a fashionable bit of skin, and had bracelets jangling on both wrists. In one hand, she carried a bouquet of roses; in the other, a nice bottle of wine.

She glanced at the woman—apparently Pauline's mother, Elna—who had let them in. The woman had greeted them at the door wearing an apron, for God's sake, and carrying a damp dishtowel. One would expect the wife of a big shot at MGM to at least have a dash of lipstick on, if not some mascara.

"You'll have to excuse me," Elna said. "I'm just taking the turkey out of the oven."

"Why, of course, Mrs. MacDonald," Evelyn said, handing Elna the wine and roses. "No need for excuses. I'm so very pleased to meet you."

In the living room, Andy MacDonald sat in a big brown leather easy chair, reading the paper. He heaved himself up to meet the much-talked-about Mrs. Williams, winking as he offered her a glass of punch with a splash of rum in it "for holiday spirit."

Hmmm. Was that wink a conspiratorial acknowledgment of the rum or something flirtatious? Oh, well. Lots of men winked at her.

Although impressed by Andy's position at MGM, Evelyn was less taken with how such a short, fat, bald man could be unaffected by showbiz glamour. She thought about the letter she would write to Verona describing this house of drab people and drab furnishings, and took a drink of her rum punch. This was going to be a long night.

Evelyn was not the only one who felt underwhelmed. Her theatrical mannerisms failed to impress the MacDonalds, including Pauline's brothers, Fred and Bob. Fred, who was only ten years younger than Evelyn, arrived dressed conservatively in a suit with argyle socks and wing-tip shoes. Evelyn zeroed in on him instantly, told a few off-color jokes, punched his arm, and laughed too loudly.

Out of earshot, Fred nudged his sister and said, "Pauline, these people have no class. You can do better. That woman was making passes at me!"

Pauline glared at him. "At least she doesn't cry all the time like Mom does."

After that he stayed silent, scowling.

The evening was long, long. Evelyn had been right about that. She didn't get it. She had arrived armed with fashion, flashy jewelry, insider gossip, a quick wit, and a ready laugh. None of that seemed to impress these people; in fact, the more she turned up her charisma, the more the conversation dimmed, while people focused puzzled attention on her, then resumed chatting as if she hadn't spoken. How could they be bored with her?

Evelyn watched Bill and Pauline as they gazed into one another's eyes, smiling secret smiles and pressing their shoulders together as they leaned in to catch a comment or pass something at the table. What the heck did her son see in this girl, anyway? What was it about this plain little mouse and her mousy little family that had him so mesmerized?

Thirty-Four
"I'll Never
Smile Again"

Three days after Christmas 1939, *Gone with the Wind* premiered in Los Angeles. Bill and Pauline sat spellbound in seats that were a little too close to the screen, and, at the end, they stood up and applauded along with the rest of the audience. In their excitement, they, like most Americans, didn't realize that in the real world, they were themselves at the early Scarlett O'Hara stage: "Fiddle-dee-dee. War, war, war. This war talk's spoiling all the fun at every party this spring."

When the film was released in London in April, the British packed theaters to see it. In that city, the movie would run continuously for the next four years, through blitzkrieg, blackout, and missile strike.

Another inadvertent American contribution to the war effort appeared in 1940, with the release of Tommy Dorsey's song "I'll Never Smile Again." For the first half of the song, the vocals were handled, as usual, by the Pied Pipers, but then a new solo voice rose up, crooning, "I'll never love again, I'm so in love with you, I'll never thrill again, to somebody new . . ."

Like a soft blue flame, that voice settled directly into the listener's heart and melted it. A young Frank Sinatra rocketed the song to the top—his first hit—and throughout the war years, "I'll Never Smile Again" would connect lovers separated by oceans and conflict. Winston Churchill would one day say to Frank Sinatra, "Young man, you belong to my people as well as your own. Yours was the voice that sang us to sleep in that infamous summer of 1940, when people were trying to get comfortable sleeping in the underground."

Bill and Pauline chose "I'll Never Smile Again" as their song.

That year, Bill got an after-school job at Ocip's Drugstore on Pico Boulevard, delivering prescriptions and making malts. Unfortunately, the pay wasn't high enough to finance the good times he wanted with Pauline, so he started dipping into the cash he collected delivering prescriptions. Just a few cents at first, then as much as a dollar at a time. Ocip's fired him, and Evelyn gave him another lecture about the Big House. But Elna and Andy's reaction was far worse: they refused to let him see Pauline anymore.

Pauline fought back. "He didn't steal that much, and he only did it because his mother spends all their money on clothes and doesn't give him any allowance."

The MacDonalds realized there wasn't much they could do to stop the romance. Besides, life was about to hand Bill a second chance. With the military hurrying to prepare in case the United States was drawn into the war, Douglas Aircraft Company began hiring that summer. Bill got a job working the swing shift.

Meanwhile, Pauline continued to work toward her future in the movies. One day, when Bill picked her up after work, he could see that she was about to burst with excitement. "Grace told me that she and Eleanor Powell think I should audition for Busby Berkeley!"

"Great!" Bill said. "That's wonderful. Aces!" He was thrilled that his girlfriend might become a star. Of course he was, but he had to wonder—would she still have time for him then? Would she even want him?

Already there was a problem. Bill had gotten into the habit of picking her up after his shift, then taking her out dancing at the all-night clubs. That was now out of the question; she had to get up extra early in the mornings to rehearse. So one night he called his old buddy Gene Benz instead, and they headed downtown, driving faster and faster as the radio blasted. A cop clocked them going seventy-five miles an hour in a forty-mile-an-hour zone. When he pulled them over, he found beer in the back seat.

Bill spent six days in jail. At his hearing, Evelyn pleaded that he was the sole support of his family, so the judge allowed him to keep his job—provided he return to jail each day between seven in the morning and three in the afternoon.

"So," Evelyn said, as she picked him up from jail to drive him to work, "you're finally living in the Big House. How's the chow?"

"A little better than at home," he said.

Evelyn was in no mood for any sarcasm but her own: "Listen, buddy. You shape up, or I'll lock this car away in Unk Ile's garage."

Bill took a deep breath. "Mom, I am. I will. I made a mistake, okay?"

"You're darn right you did. And you owe me. From now on, your paychecks go straight to me, and I'll give you an allowance."

"Fine."

"The worst thing is the beer they found. Beer? In your car? Don't you dare turn into an alcoholic like—"

"I won't." *Maybe I'd be different if you hadn't pawned me off on everyone else and spent time with me instead.* He didn't say those words, although they formed the unspoken subtext of most of his arguments with his mother, then and well into the future.

He and Evelyn established a pattern. After work, Bill would sleep for a few hours in his bed at home. Evelyn would wake him at 6:00 a.m.: "Darling, it's time to get up and go to jail!"

Bill paid off his fine in a month, but Evelyn insisted he continue to turn his paychecks over to her. "I'll put everything except your allowance into a savings account for you."

Bill had a bad feeling about that offer, and rightfully so. As it turned out, if his mother felt she needed to make a trip to the department store, she would dip into Bill's savings to, as she put it, "keep the house running." Although Tom Lyle continued to cover her living expenses, he provided nothing for extras.

She thought about getting a job like Pauline's mother had decided to do, even though money was never an issue because of Andy's job. Elna was bored sitting home with nothing to do while Pauline was occupied with school, dancing, and Bill. Andy worked day and night at the studio and Elna wanted to be more productive as well. She got a job in the nursery at Culver City Hospital, spending three days a week tending to new babies and their mothers.

As Evelyn thought about it, she decided a job wouldn't be a good idea, not yet when she was still so busy having fun.

One evening, when Bill had a night off, he took Pauline to Villa Valentino. Tom Lyle encouraged his nephew to visit the Villa with his friends, preferring to have them close at hand rather than running wild in the city. Like Evelyn, Tom Lyle worried that his nephew might follow in Preston's footsteps, which would be unbearable.

That evening, Pauline and Bill danced to their song on the jukebox, while Tom Lyle, Emery, and Arnold worked their usual evening schedule. Bill clutched his girl extra close, grateful for her loyalty and devotion and relishing the chance to hold her instead of being locked in a cell with drunks, derelicts, thieves, and other unsavory fellows. He could smell the gardenias in her hair.

As they danced past the big window into the living room, Pauline looked up and saw Tom Lyle standing by the grand piano, holding a framed portrait. There was something wistful about his expression, even his posture. With the last line of the song, he set the picture down beside a bouquet of red roses, turned and went about his business.

Later, Pauline checked to see whose face had so captivated Tom Lyle—and was surprised to see it was the actress Alice Faye. Although she knew that Alice and Tom Lyle had gone out publicly many times during the filming and promotion of *Alexander's Ragtime Band,* she had never thought there was more than a business relationship between them. Now she wondered.

She wouldn't learn the truth for many years. No one in the family would, because Tom Lyle kept it a secret from everyone, especially Evelyn, with whom he wanted to maintain the fiction that he would have married her if it weren't for his devotion to Maybelline.

The truth was that over the years since *Alexander's Ragtime Band,* Tom Lyle's relationship with Alice Faye had developed into more than just a façade to throw off the suspicious. In addition to attending galas together, they shared intimate dinners, confidences, and dreams. He recognized her vulnerability and wanted to protect her from the harsh realities of the film industry; she sensed his passion and warmth and wanted to be enfolded in them.

Still, they were more often apart than together, and things change. Tom Lyle had been disappointed when Alice married the singer and actor Tony Martin in 1937, then saddened—but not surprised—when they divorced three years later. The parting was rough on Alice, and, to make things worse, she felt that Daryl Zanuck expected her to perform like a wind-up doll. Prone to pneumonia in the days before penicillin, exhausted, fighting depression, and suffering from an abdominal pain that her doctor recommended she deal with surgically, she felt that she couldn't go on. Yet she had already signed a contract and begun preliminary work shooting a script that she found delightful: *Down Argentine Way,* featuring a new costar, Carmen Miranda, whom Alice had admired on Broadway.

Alice wanted to do the film but broke the contract to take care of her health. Zanuck claimed her surgery was elective and threatened to sue. Two weeks later, Alice was replaced by another pretty, talented, blonde young woman who was relatively unknown: Betty Grable.

Later, with her health and spirits on the rebound, Alice turned to her good friend Tom Lyle, and they picked up where they had left off. After only a few months, the delicate equilibrium of this relationship was disrupted; Alice told Tom Lyle that she was falling in love with him. To his shock, he felt something very powerful for her as well. Love? Why yes, he decided, yes, I do love her, too. She's wonderful, adorable, divine. But . . .

Not since the day Evelyn had breezed into his life had he longed for a deeper connection with a woman than what he had working with the actresses who posed for Maybelline ads. But Alice Faye seemed to trigger something in him that made him think that perhaps, through her, he could join the world of society-approved relationships. Imagine—no more need to hide behind shuttered windows and one hundred palm trees. No more need to pretend to family members that Emery and Arnold were just business associates and nothing more. Being married to a wonderful woman like Alice would make life easier in so many ways.

He agonized over what direction to take. Could he stand to give up what he had with Arnold? Could he risk pushing Emery away after twenty years?

As usual, there was no simple answer. Arnold himself dated women, did he not? And his drinking was getting worse, not better. In fact, it was almost as if Arnold had stepped in to continue the emotional chaos created by Preston. At one point, Tom Lyle had asked him, "Why is everyone I love an alcoholic?"

That wasn't quite true, of course. Emery was no alcoholic—but he did love to party far more than Tom Lyle did. Yet he was still a wonderful man, a beloved friend.

How confusing everything had become.

Emery noticed him moping around and said, "Come to Palm Springs with me this weekend, TL. One of my stage plays is being produced at the Palm Springs Theatre."

Tom Lyle agreed that a getaway weekend sounded perfect.

While driving through the desert, the two men discussed things they hadn't had time for recently: the worsening situation in Europe and Japan, fashion, advertising, literature, psychology. Emery was an avid reader, an intellectual, and worldlier than Tom Lyle, who cloistered himself within his research and evaluations of American trends. The more they chatted, the more Tom Lyle realized that he needed Emery, depended on him, and, ultimately, Tom Lyle remained devoted to him. He couldn't just walk away from their relationship.

But that meant he would have to end things with his delightful Alice—and probably Arnold Anderson as well.

Another complicated situation, and a delicate one. Alice deserved to know the truth, not some concocted story. But if knowledge of his true nature were to fall into the wrong hands, the scandal could ruin Maybelline.

In the end, Tom Lyle risked trusting Alice—and she never betrayed his confidence. She later married bandleader Phil Harris and went on to have a long and happy life.

Eventually, Tom Lyle took her picture off his piano.

In parting, Alice did Tom Lyle one more favor: she suggested he contact Betty Grable, her replacement in *Down Argentine Way*, to be a Maybelline model.

Tom Lyle put Evelyn on the trail. Asking around at the Biltmore, she learned that although Grable had the right looks, many of her previous movies hadn't done well at the box office. Nor had many people in Hollywood heard of Carmen Miranda, the wild woman with the fruit on her head. How would *Down Argentine Way* sit with Americans? Without Alice Faye's star power, it could easily bomb—and take Maybelline with it.

Tom Lyle had to give this issue some thought. An ad campaign was the single greatest expense of staying in business. Even a month of reduced sales volume would hamper launching subsequent campaigns, thereby initiating a downward spiral.

There were many reasons this might not be the best time to take a risk on a relatively unknown starlet. France had fallen recently to the Nazis, who had signed a pact with Italy and Japan. President Roosevelt was about to mandate a peacetime military draft, while Europeans suffered in misery. Cosmetics were all but irrelevant in the lives of most of the inhabitants of the world, so Maybelline's overseas sales had plummeted.

Tom Lyle weighed all this in his usual, careful way and made his decision.

Thirty-Five
Chica Chica
Boom Chic

Learn Betty's Secret for Beautiful Eyes, the ad read. Arnold had carefully retouched the before-and-after photos, producing illustrations that were more than photography to convey a smooth and beautiful complexion. The tiny "before" shot revealed a pretty girl with pale brows and lashes, while the "after" showed a lushly made-up young beauty. Tiny print mentioned that Betty Grable was featured in the film *Down Argentine Way.* This way, Tom Lyle reasoned, even if the movie tanked, the ad would still work since it didn't emphasize the film.

In the ad, Betty was quoted as saying, "It's easy to have lovely alluring eyes . . . The magic secret is Maybelline eye makeup." Emery's copy gave step-by-step application instructions, ending with: "Then, the joyful climax . . . when you form your brows in graceful, classic lines with Maybelline smooth-marking Eyebrow Pencil."

Tom Lyle wasn't the only one taking a risk on the film; so was Daryl Zanuck. Would a goofy, lighthearted romp set in Argentina appeal to Americans in a year when dramatic films like *The Philadelphia Story* and *The Grapes of Wrath* were taking most of the credits? The answer was hard to predict. A few westerns had done well, and Ginger and Fred were still dancing. Bing

Crosby, Bob Hope, and Dorothy Lamour had starred in the popular *Road to Singapore*—which had nothing to do with Singapore and was oblivious to Japanese imperialism in the Pacific. Fox Studios wanted something fresh, and if their stars couldn't cavort in Europe or the Pacific, they would have to take their fun and games elsewhere. South America seemed like a pretty safe bet. With that lively Brazilian music, moviegoers could transport themselves to a place where war didn't exist.

The gamble paid off. When the film opened in October, the public adored Betty Grable and newcomer Carmen Miranda in her outrageous costumes. Revelers everywhere, including Evelyn's crowd at the Biltmore, learned to samba to tunes like "Bambu Bambu." The age of Carmen Miranda movies and music had begun. *Chica Chica Boom Chic!*

At the same time, teens and young women in their twenties identified with Grable's saucy blonde beauty and lively spirit. In droves, they crowded into dime stores to buy Maybelline. Tom Lyle immediately featured his new bombshell in another full-page color ad. Although few people realized it at the time, the era of the pinup had begun. Soon women's faces and bodies were helping to sell everything from Dow chemicals to Lucky Strike cigarettes. Another change was that the promotion departments of movie studios began working out deals with companies to help coordinate the release of ads with relevant films. Filmmakers now came to Tom Lyle instead of him going to them.

Still, Tom Lyle took nothing for granted. He knew from his market research that if Maybelline didn't bombard women with new ideas, faces, and looks, buyers would quickly get bored and move on to a more interesting product or company. So he never let up in seeking ways to appeal to every sector of the women's market. Keeping Maybelline well ahead of the competition demanded more ads every day.

The teen market represented an ideal target: sales in the present and easier sales in the future as current customers continued to buy Maybelline. Fortunately, teen actresses were debuting in films at every major studio: Lana Turner, Deanna Durbin, Judy Garland, Shirley Temple, and Jane Withers all released films that year. Still, Tom Lyle continued to use the photo of Marjorie Woodworth, the young majorette from *Alexander's Ragtime Band,* which Arnold had airbrushed, achieving a look that captured the glamorous yet wholesome impression of the all-American coed. This long-running ad proved to be quite a moneymaker. The teenage girl of 1940 filled her cosmetics bag for under a dollar. She identified with her favorite stars, wanted to stand out in a crowd, and wanted to either attract a boyfriend or keep her current boyfriend interested. Maybelline promised to help with all these things.

One Saturday night in September, Bill drove home and was surprised to see his mother's car in the driveway. She usually stayed out late—sometimes all night long—on Saturday nights.

When he walked in, he found her standing in the living room as if waiting for him, a drink in her hand. He squinted at her. "You colored your hair."

"I got tired of the red and decided to try brown." She sipped the drink. "Do you like it?"

"I guess."

Another sip. "Did you and Pauline go to Tom Lyle's tonight?"

"Yes." Bill walked into the kitchen and poured himself a glass of milk.

Evelyn was right behind him. "What did you talk about?"

"Well, Pauline auditioned for Busby Berkeley today. He liked her routine and wants to set up a screen test for a new musical he's working on."

"And you went to tell Tom Lyle before me?"

Bill drank his milk. "I figured he'd be home."

"Was he impressed with Pauline's big news?"

"More than you seem to be."

"Well, I understand what it takes to make it as a dancer, that's all. I used to be with the Russian ballet, remember?"

"Well, Unk Ile was happy for her. He thinks she's great. He even gave her some Maybelline samples to use and pass out to her friends. Then he wants her to tell him what they think about the stuff."

Evelyn lowered her glass as if it were growing heavier. She forced one corner of her mouth up. "So, Pauline's wearing makeup now, no matter what her dowdy mother says? Good for her. Bet she's happy I showed her how to put it on, isn't she?"

"'Night, Mom." Bill picked up Lady, carried her into his room, and shut the door.

A moment later he heard a drinking glass shatter on the kitchen floor.

Evelyn swept the shards into a corner and left them there. She hadn't thrown the glass; she had had a few too many drinks and lost her grip on it.

She got a fresh glass from the cupboard and poured herself another drink. In its swirling depths, she viewed her life. She would turn forty in four months, and she was not living the life she had planned to have by this age. She had thrown away most of her youth on Preston and wasted the last few years flirting around town with pretty boys who were, let's face it, going nowhere. Like Charlie Lewis. She knew it now: the man was all show with no money to back him up, just a loser looking for a wealthy sugar mama to take care of him. That's why Evelyn had ended their relationship a few weeks ago.

Now the only men she had in her life were Bill and Tom Lyle. She couldn't lose either of them or, for that matter, Tom Lyle's financial support. That meant she couldn't let anyone—anyone at all—come between her and Tom Lyle.

Yet here was this mousy little Pauline creature, first stealing her son's heart and now reeling in Tom Lyle! Imagine a savvy businessman like him turning to a bland high-school girl for market research!

She went into her bedroom and stared at herself in the full-length mirror. She still looked great—as good as Joan Crawford or that new girl, Carmen Miranda. She wasn't out of the race of life yet, not by a long way. If Little Miss MacDonald was Seabiscuit, Evelyn Boecher Williams was Stagehand.

Thirty-Six
Shattered

After that, Evelyn insisted on going along every time Bill and Pauline visited Unk Ile. While at the Villa, she suggested that he design ads featuring mature women—women who were still attractive and glamorous as they aged. Although he continued to hit the youth market hard, he did follow her advice. When Evelyn saw her touch in print, she became a bit less fearful that a young girl would take her place in the affections of Tom Lyle; still, she knew her time was limited, especially as Pauline's big audition approached and all attention centered on the girl.

Dance instructor Eleanor Powell gave Pauline tips for her upcoming screen test. Eleanor was already working on a film that Pauline might get to dance in, a Hollywood version of George Gershwin's stage hit, *Lady Be Good*. Just the tagline for this movie—"The tap-happiest, swing-singiest, melodic miracle since *Ziegfeld Girl*"—made Pauline want to get to work filming.

Supercharged with excitement, she practiced her routine constantly, perfecting a jazz interpretation of "Trees," in which her supple body moved like leafy branches swaying in the wind to the beat of Gene Krupa's drums.

Her father, Andy, ever the pragmatist, asked around MGM to see what others thought about his daughter's chances. Both Cedric Gibbons and Busby

Berkeley told Andy they thought his daughter had an excellent chance of making it. She was talented and easy to work with, and everyone liked her.

Pauline MacDonald was going places.

A delay in production pushed Pauline's audition back until December 28, 1940—an eternity of waiting for a sixteen-year-old girl—but finally the calendar reached the day before the big event.

Hardly able to contain herself, Pauline drove Bill to work at Douglas Aircraft, dropped him off, and then drove his car to a movie theater on Imperial Boulevard. She sat through the show, although not a bit of the plot stuck with her, then climbed back into the car, checked for traffic, and pulled out onto the street—just as a car driven by a drunken soldier and two girlfriends careened around the corner, striking the Ford head-on.

Seatbelts wouldn't be widely available until the 1950s. Pauline wasn't wearing one. The impact halted the Ford, but not her. She hurtled forward and up, smashing through the windshield and flying through the air as both cars folded up below her like accordions. A moment later, Pauline plunked onto the pavement, rolled a few times, and lay still.

The police arrived within minutes, along with two ambulances. A paramedic knelt over Pauline's motionless form and noticed a sad irony: a blood-spattered white gardenia still clung to her hair. Her face was a red mask, glittering with shards of broken glass, but he could appreciate what she must have looked like only minutes earlier. "What a shame for such a beautiful girl to have died so young," he said to his colleagues, and they pulled a sheet over her.

But as they raised her into the ambulance, spitting sounds came from under the sheet. They yanked it back and saw Pauline trying to spit out her shattered teeth.

By chance, Pauline was rushed to the same Culver City hospital where her mother happened to be working that night. When Elna ran into the emergency room and saw the white gardenia in Pauline's hair, she almost fainted. Her daughter was alive, thank God, but the doctors didn't know if she would make it. Pauline had suffered internal injuries and had glass embedded in her face. And even if the girl lived, her upper thigh had been shattered by the steering wheel. Pauline would certainly never dance again. She might not even walk.

At Douglas Aircraft, Bill waited outside for Pauline to pick him up. When she didn't show up, he finally went back inside—just in time to hear an announcement asking Bill Williams to come to the office at once.

Andy MacDonald picked up Bill at the factory and drove him to the hospital. There, they were told that although Pauline was alive, the doctors wouldn't know how bad her internal injuries were until morning.

When Bill was finally allowed to see his girlfriend, he sank into a state of shock.

After several days in a light coma, Pauline woke in terrible pain but with no memory of what had happened. She learned that her father had invented and built a traction apparatus that pulled her thighbone out of her hip, where it had been wedged tight. A stainless-steel plate and sixteen screws held her leg together.

When she was allowed to have visitors, Bill came to see her every day and kept her current on all the activities at school. Andy also visited regularly, trying to hide his heartbreak at seeing his little girl crushed, not only physically but also emotionally. Although she said nothing—for a while she could barely speak at all—they both knew her dream of dancing was over. He worried about how it would affect her in the long run.

He had other concerns, too. He had no health insurance, and the hospital bills soon piled up. Tom Lyle offered to help the MacDonalds pay the bills, but Andy was too proud to accept. He began working overtime, sometimes falling asleep on his feet at 3:00 a.m. in the studio that never slept. Elna, too, started working more shifts at the hospital, where she dropped by Pauline's room several times each day to do whatever she could.

Tom Lyle's floral bills mounted impressively. As soon as Pauline woke up, he sent three dozen red roses, followed by a dozen every week that she was in the hospital.

Evelyn visited as well. It took her a while, but she finally knocked at Pauline's door and asked to come in. Pauline's first reaction was shame and horror: how must she look to this flashy, beautiful woman? Pauline's repeatedly shaved scalp had grown an inch of hair by then, but tiny glass particles still pushed through her skin from time to time, her broken nose would have a permanent bump on the bridge, and she had lost several of her front teeth.

But Evelyn only smiled and looked around the room, which was loaded with get-well gifts and cards from school friends, fellow students from Grace's dance studio, Job's Daughters (a Masonic organization), people from church. There was even a giant get-well card that Pauline's father had had made in the art department at MGM and signed by over a hundred people, including Louis B. Mayer, Cedric Gibbons, Busby Berkeley, Judy Garland, Mickey Rooney, Shirley Temple, Eleanor Powell, Jeanette MacDonald, and Bill Robinson. Pauline saw Evelyn's gaze linger on the card for a moment, then slide over to Tom Lyle's latest bouquet, as if somehow recognizing its source.

Then Evelyn smiled and approached the bed. She didn't seem to notice Pauline's full-body cast as she raised a past issue of *Glamour* magazine and turned it over to display the full-page Maybelline ad on the back, featuring the beautiful face of Merle Oberon. Pauline looked at it, crestfallen and hurt, even a little sickened—had Bill's mother finally visited her only to remind her that she was no longer perfect?

Evelyn sat in the chair beside the bed and read some of the ad copy out loud: "Maybelline gives your eyes beauty you never even suspected. It gives your face a new personality, vivid and vibrant—inviting the man in your life . . ." Evelyn winked, "to discover a new, young, irresistible you!"

Evelyn set the magazine aside and pulled a cosmetic bag out of her purse. "Let's give you a look," she said.

A little later, Pauline's mother walked into the room and halted at the sight of Evelyn sitting beside her daughter's bed. Then she saw Pauline examining her face in a hand mirror.

Elna looked closer at her daughter's face. Looked at an open bag of cosmetics on the bed. Looked back at her daughter—and bit her tongue. Pauline was smiling.

Evelyn glanced at Elna, then turned back to Pauline. "Don't you worry one minute, dear; you'll come out of this just like Merle Oberon did. In time, your skin will expel the glass." She pulled a jar of Mud-Pack Masque out of the cosmetic bag. "Meanwhile, use hot compresses followed by mudpacks twice a day; that will help your skin to heal."

Elna stepped forward. "You do what she says," she told her daughter. She hesitated, then reached down and poked around in the bag. "And then maybe you can teach me how to use a little dab of eyebrow pencil."

They laughed. All three of them.

That fall, after a full year in the hospital, Pauline came home determined to walk again, although she was still wearing a cast up to her waist. One night, she even felt strong enough to escort Bill to the front door—but when he bent over to kiss her goodnight, she lost her balance, and in trying to catch her, Bill ended up falling on top of her on the hardwood floor.

She was rushed back to the hospital. An unhealed bone had become dislocated, and the doctors wanted to reset it in another surgery. Pauline refused, knowing that it might mean she would walk with a limp for the rest of her life. Elna and Andy were heartbroken, even more financially devastated than before—and furious at Bill for being so negligent.

Later, when Pauline was walking with the aid of crutches, Evelyn drove her and Bill out to Tom Lyle's for a special event. For $395—the equivalent of about $4,500 today—Tom Lyle had purchased something called an RCA TRK-12 television set, the name indicating its twelve-inch screen size. One of only forty TVs in Los Angeles at the time, this early device nested eye-up in a standing console. To view it, you lifted the lid to a favorable angle and watched a mirror image of the television screen.

Across the nation, only ten TV stations existed. Two of them, the early versions of CBS and NBC, were in Los Angeles. The day Evelyn brought Bill and Pauline over to see the television, Lowell Thomas broadcast the news, sponsored by Sunoco Oil. Ivory Soap sponsored a quiz show. A few blurry cartoons—*Felix the Cat* and *Popeye*—completed the programming that evening. Tom Lyle predicted great things for this new invention—and, of course, its likely impact on Maybelline sales.

Everything seemed to have an impact on Maybelline sales, and from their bunker in the Villa Valentino, Tom Lyle and Emery tried to monitor every change in the pulse of the world. Roosevelt had just announced an "unlimited national emergency" and ordered the seizure of all Japanese assets in the United States. Though still proclaiming neutrality, he also ordered the navy to shoot on sight any convoy threat in the North Atlantic. Skirmishes with the German U-boat fleet were already taking place; it was only a matter of time before the young men in America would be called up for the military draft.

This made Tom Lyle worry about Bill. The boy had graduated from University High, and although he still worked at Douglas, he was of prime draft age. Tom Lyle would find it unbearable if Preston's son had to suffer from the trauma of war as his father had—or worse, if he were to be killed.

Bill had a different perspective. His life was just getting started. He didn't want to go to war because he didn't want to leave Pauline, his friends and family, and his comfortable life in California to go shoot at Germans in Europe or "Japs" in the Pacific. That stuff was so far away; it just wasn't his problem.

But then, on December 7, 1941, a nationally broadcast hockey game was interrupted with the first televised instant news report. Japanese bombers had flown to the United States naval port in Pearl Harbor, Hawaii, and unleashed bombs and torpedoes on the American warships there. A large portion of the Pacific Fleet had been destroyed, and thousands of soldiers had been killed.

American complacency was shattered as well. Once again, the country was at war.

Thirty-Seven

"We Interrupt This Program . . ."

*J*ust over a month after the Pearl Harbor attack, popular actress Carole Lombard flew to her home state of Indiana for a war-bond rally. As she was leaving, she called out to her fans, "Before I say goodbye to you all, come on and join me in a big cheer! V for Victory!"

Her TWA DC-3 flew not to blacked-out Boulder City, Nevada, its usual stop on the way to Los Angeles, but to a well-lit Las Vegas-area airport that would later become Nellis Air Force Base. After a brief layover, at four on the morning of Friday, January 16, 1942, the plane lifted off for the final leg to California. The night was clear, but the plane was 6.7 miles off its usual course, and apparently no one thought to consider the height of the mountain range that lay just southwest of Las Vegas. Twenty-three minutes after takeoff, the plane crashed into 8,300-foot Mount Potosi. All twenty-two people aboard were killed.

When Evelyn heard this news, she immediately picked up the phone and called Tom Lyle.

His voice broke with emotion. "I just talked to her a few days ago. We were so excited about her next photo shoot."

"All I can tell you is, she inspired me," Evelyn said, "and I'm going to do what

I can to continue her work. It's Pauline's birthday today. Maybe she'll join me selling war bonds. I think it would do her some good to get out more anyway."

Tom Lyle gave the response Evelyn wanted to hear. "That would be wonderful, Ev. You always were a champ in a crisis."

And she was—but that didn't mean she didn't have an ulterior motive.

Evelyn called Pauline and wished her a happy birthday, then added, "I think you should get back into the swing of things, dear. No good staying home, feeling sorry for yourself. How about volunteering time with me in selling war bonds?"

Selling war bonds had become a popular way to support the war effort from home—so popular that an ad from the era dramatized the plight of a housewife who feared her husband's wrath because she had been so busy selling war bonds that she hadn't had time to fix dinner. No problem, the ad assured, just open a can of Chef Boyardee pasta and earn raves from hubby. Thus, eating canned spaghetti became an act of patriotism.

Pauline was reluctant to agree to Evelyn's request. She was getting better, although she still needed crutches to walk and had required the help of a tutor to earn her high-school diploma. But it took all her gumption to maintain anything resembling a positive attitude toward life. She was in constant pain, the scars on her face and nose were still livid, and she wore a dental bridge to replace the front teeth that had been smashed out.

Still, she wanted to prove to Evelyn that she had won the battle over self-pity. And there were bigger problems in the world than her appearance or even the end of her dancing career, weren't there?

"Of course I'll help," she said.

For a few hours, they stood in front of a department store selling bonds. Pauline felt pretty good about it, but on the way home, Evelyn had some advice. "Put a little more makeup on next time, dear. You'd look much prettier. That handsome young man would have paid more attention to you."

Pauline frowned. "I don't want to flirt."

"Oh, but you should flirt, darling. You should keep your options open." Evelyn eyed Pauline's crutches. "You just never know how things will turn out when you have a handicap."

Pauline felt the heat rush into her face. "I don't need to keep my options open. I don't want to be with anyone but Bill. He loves me, and I love him. And I'm not always going to need crutches."

"I'm glad to hear that," Evelyn said crisply. "That way you can get a job and pay Bill back for the car you wrecked."

Pauline felt as if Evelyn had just kicked her crutches out from under her, but she refused to let the pain show.

"You bet," she said.

The next time Evelyn next saw Bill at home, he faced her with a thunderous expression that reminded her—too much—of his father's. "You stay away from Pauline!"

"Sweetheart, she needs to—"

"She needs to be with me. Stop trying to split us up."

Evelyn softened her voice. Apparently Pauline hadn't mentioned the bit about paying for the car. "This is for your own good, darling."

"Mom, Pauline stood by me when I was in jail and her parents wanted to break us up. And if she hadn't been coming to pick me up from work that night, she'd be dancing in the movies right now. I'm sticking by her."

"Please, darling, listen to your mother. You're too young to settle for one girl without playing the field. And you can do better than Pauline anyway. A girl like her is fine for a high-school romance, but you're getting older now, and you're a Williams. For a serious relationship, you need to look for someone . . . Please, don't sign your life away to a cripple just because you feel guilty that . . ."

She fell silent, baffled by the expression that clouded her son's face. Was he upset with her for being honest? For having his best interests at heart? The nephew and godson of Tom Lyle Williams deserved a special girl, a girl who fit the Maybelline legacy of beauty, beauty, and more beauty.

Somehow, she would have to make him see that.

She was a persuasive woman. As the weeks went by, she kept dropping hints to her son that he could do better than Pauline—and bit by bit, he seemed to get the point. She could tell. Although he continued to claim loyalty to his sweetheart, his eye was beginning to wander, to scan around just in case something better than Pauline did come along.

World War II was going full force when the news came that rationing was about to begin.

"Three gallons of gas a week!" Evelyn moaned when she heard about the coupons for fuel. "I'll be stuck at home!"

Even Tom Lyle, a man not given to panic, was disturbed by the ever-expanding list of items to be rationed: gasoline, metal, rubber, and seemingly everything people relished in their diets—coffee, meat, cheese, butter, and sugar. In this atmosphere, people were already staying away from movies and restaurants and hunkering down at home, where few women bothered to wear makeup. Families were buying and hoarding necessities—which did not include mascara.

Then came a shocking phone call from Noel in Chicago: "We've got a production problem, TL. The president issued a warning to the beauty industry that they're going to start rationing certain raw products soon— including petroleum."

Tom Lyle groaned. Petroleum was still Maybelline's key ingredient. "That's all we need. We've got to do something fast or we'll sink along with the enemy battleships."

He, Emery, and Arnold put their heads together, and Emery mentioned a trucking ad he had seen: *They'll Never Bomb Us Out! . . . Trucks will always get through!*

"We need to get that kind of spirit into our ads," Emery said. "If we create enough demand for our products, we can get a message through to Washington. Remember how well 'Patriotism through Beauty' worked in 1917?"

"He's right," Arnold said. "The boys have got the insides of their Quonset huts covered with pinups—including most of our girls. They may say they're fighting for the flag, mom, and apple pie, but their wallpaper tells the truth."

Tom Lyle nodded. "If we could get the military brass to consider how many of those pinup girls are wearing makeup and how much the makeup affects their appeal. . ."

"That should get some attention in DC," Emery agreed.

Still, the next day, Tom Lyle called Noel and told him to buy as much petroleum jelly as he could before the rationing went into effect.

The first wartime Maybelline ad showed a housewife—her eyes perfectly Maybellined, of course—writing a letter to her husband at the front. The slogan read: *They're doing their bit by keeping their femininity. That's one of the reasons we are fighting.* Another ad showed an elegant young woman being admired by a military officer as he helped her on with her white stole. The caption read: *Just as he dreamed her eyes would be.* Another ad simply said: *War, Women, and Maybelline.*

In the spring of 1942, the Pentagon warned the White House that the war should not create a glamour shortage. A memo to Roosevelt advised that such a loss of beauty "might lower national morale."

Suddenly, petroleum flowed like water into Maybelline's vats. Tom Lyle's campaign had virtually saved the entire cosmetics industry for the duration.

On the home front, Evelyn's efforts to separate Bill and Pauline, which had once looked so promising, were beginning to backfire. At first she didn't see it. What she saw, instead, were the imperfections she was sure her son must also be focusing on. Although Pauline now used Maybelline and other makeup diligently to conceal the still-red scars on her face and minimize the visible damage to her nose, tiny glass fragments continued to erupt from the surface of her skin. Shock had caused her once-thick hair to grow back slowly and with less vigor. But worst of all—in Evelyn's eyes—the girl walked with a limp and always would.

Yet somehow, all of this worked against Evelyn's plan instead of aiding it. Pauline had signed up for business school and took the bus to Santa Monica every day to earn credits toward a business credential. She had, in fact, exceeded Evelyn's expectations for what should be the girl's best effort and refused to live the life of a cripple. Apparently, Bill found this determined attitude far more attractive than physical perfection.

When Pauline graduated from business school, Andy took her and Bill out for Italian food to celebrate.

"Do you remember Ronald Reagan?" Andy asked Pauline.

"Sure," Pauline said. She had met him several times at MGM, where Andy had built sets for *Knute Rockne, All American*—the last movie Bill and Pauline had seen together before her accident.

"Mr. Reagan has been called to active duty," Andy said, "and he's making training films for the military right there in Culver City. He remembered your accident and asked how you're doing."

"That's very sweet of him."

"There's more." Andy grinned. "I asked him if he had any job openings for stenographers, and he said he did—and would be glad to hire you." As Andy explained it, the Army Air Corps wanted Reagan to not only make training films, but also coordinate the training of camera crews who would actually go out on planes during combat missions. The production company was called "Combat Camera," and Pauline's job would be to view raw footage and type reports on each film's subject matter—all the while earning good pay.

Pauline pushed up out of her chair and hugged her father hard.

Bill beamed. "I can't believe my girlfriend is going to work for Ronald Reagan!"

In fact, women everywhere were earning the best paychecks they had ever received as they filled in for men now serving overseas. One hundred and fifty thousand women went further, rushing to enlist in the newly established Women's Auxiliary Army Corps (WAAC), where they took over military desk jobs and thereby made more men available for combat.

Because of this, Tom Lyle's early apprehensions about Maybelline's prospects during the war were unwarranted. All the new earning power and independence actually created more cosmetics customers, and Maybelline continued to target its ads to this market. Evelyn herself had become such a woman—active, supportive, and fiercely patriotic. But this new life came with a price. During the day, she was usually out selling war bonds, but at night—with Charlie Lewis ejected and Bill either working or off on a date with Pauline—Evelyn often found herself home alone. That was unpleasant enough, but the night the Japanese conducted a raid on the coastline of California in retaliation for Jimmy Doolittle's recent thirty-second bombing run over Tokyo, she truly realized how alone she was—no one to offer comfort in the blacked-out house, no one even to talk to. Even Tom Lyle was gone, visiting Chicago where his first grandchild, Diane, had just been born.

By the time that nerve-wracking evening ended, Evelyn knew one thing for sure: she wanted and needed a man in her life.

In October, Bette Davis and other Hollywood celebrities transformed an old livery stable-turned-nightclub at 1451 Cahuenga Boulevard into what would become one of the most famous wartime canteens and homes-away-from-home of the era: the Hollywood USO. There, stars and studio people volunteered their time alongside ordinary people like Evelyn, who had been screened and issued a volunteer ID card.

Evelyn talked to volunteers, young hostesses, and soldiers, and the experience sparked an idea that she pitched to Tom Lyle for a Maybelline wartime promotion. The resulting ad showed a pilot preparing to board a plane.

The headline cried,

> **To the girl with a soldier overseas . . . ,**
> **How much do you really want him back?**

The copy read:

> **"Help bring your Soldier Back!**
> **Start buying War Bonds right away."**

The only reference to Maybelline lay across the bottom of the page:

> **Published in cooperation with the Drug, Cosmetic, and**
> **Allied Industries by MAYBELLINE, THE WORLD'S**
> **LARGEST-SELLING EYE BEAUTY AIDS.**

By emphasizing patriotic themes like this, Maybelline not only stayed profitable throughout the war, but also found its respectability greatly enhanced.

At the Hollywood USO, Maybelline pinup girls including Betty Grable, Rita Hayworth, and Dorothy Lamour appeared often enough that the line of soldiers waiting to get in frequently wrapped around the block. Evelyn was especially eager to sign up for volunteer service on these occasions, although she never did anything to steal the stars' time or attention away from the servicemen. For Evelyn, it was enough to be asked to dance, to feel young again, to whoop it up for a good cause.

One early fall evening, Evelyn arrived for a stint at the USO and adjusted her double-breasted coat, which she had tailored short and tight to save on carefully rationed fabric. In the process, she dropped her handbag, spilling the contents across the paved area in front of the canteen. As she bent to pick everything up, she sensed someone watching her and looked up to find herself under the scrutiny of a distinguished-looking, silver-haired gentleman in his late forties. He smiled and bent to help her collect her belongings.

"Thank you," Evelyn said. "Were you going inside? You don't look like a military man."

He pointed to an office building next to the canteen. "Actually, I was just at a meeting with my lawyers, and I was curious to see if any movie stars were here tonight." He paused. "At first I thought you were Joan Crawford."

Evelyn smiled. She wasn't about to fall for a line like that. "'Lawyers, plural?'" she said. "Are you in that much trouble?"

He laughed. "No, they handle my company's litigation. My name's Warren Deuel. May I buy you a drink?"

Thirty-Eight
Miss Gold Digger
Meets Mr. Gold

*H*e had said the magic words: my company.

Now he said some more. "There's a new place down the street called the Mocambo. Have you tried it yet?"

Evelyn had been dying to go to the Mocambo. All the stars went there. Tom Lyle's decorator friend Billy Haines had designed the interior, which cost $100,000. A reviewer had described the nightclub as a "cross between a somewhat decadent Imperial Rome, Salvador Dali, and a birdcage."

"I haven't been there yet, no," she admitted. "But I'd love to go."

Perhaps Xavier Cugat or Desi Arnaz would lead the band in conga rhythms that night. Glass panels fronted aviaries where cockatoos and macaws cavorted. The celebrity columnists had gossiped about the lavish divorce party Myrna Loy had held there that year. Within the walls of the Mocambo, no wartime fear or sadness was allowed.

Warren Deuel mesmerized Evelyn with his refined appearance, impeccable manners, and good taste. Sipping a rum drink at the bar, Evelyn told him about herself—emphasizing her connection with and contributions to Maybelline. Warren invited her to continue their conversation over dinner: chateaubriand for two. This was extravagance on a breathtaking scale. Everyone complained about the complicated rationing system the Office of Price Administration had devised, based on an elaborate point system accompanied by an array of coupons and tokens. Although restaurants were partially exempt, Warren no doubt paid a stiff price for his steaks, and, ideally, both Warren and Evelyn would have turned in red ration coupons for a choice cut of beef—almost double the points for hamburger. But people everywhere rationalized that they could cheat for a special occasion, and, for Evelyn, this night certainly counted.

"Tell me about your company," Evelyn said.

Warren explained that he was a geologist who knew where and how to peer, blast, and probe for earth's treasures, primarily oil and gold.

Magic words.

Oh, the glory of first impressions, the heady novelty that commands the mind to take in only that which the heart and soul crave and blink away the clues that might recommend caution. Warren and Evelyn danced as if on their own private carousel. Danced, drank, laughed until their blood sang; they closed down the bar. Warren walked her to her car—and didn't ask for a kiss before they both drove off in their own vehicles, each far too drunk to be behind the wheel.

On their next date, Warren took her to another nice restaurant. After three or four drinks, Warren revealed that his wells and mines were not yet producing oil and ore at the highly profitable levels he anticipated. Oh, he added, "I'm married, Evelyn, but in name only."

Although Evelyn had also had several drinks by then, her lighthearted façade wavered. Then she made an admission of her own: "Well, I'm single, but on the financial side, I'm not exactly in the chips myself since I stopped working directly for Maybelline."

This didn't seem to matter to him, so why should his marriage to a distant, uncaring woman matter to her? By the next day, she had decided that her attraction to Warren was real, no matter what his situation.

By December, they were an item.

As the holidays approached, American morale rose a notch. After a horrendously long and bloody fight on the Pacific island of Guadalcanal, the Americans had finally turned the tide. For the moment, at least, the Japanese were in retreat.

Back home, most Americans strove to maintain an existence as normal as possible for the holidays. Movies like *Mrs. Miniver*, starring Greer Garson, showcased beautiful and patriotic women. Sure enough, Tom Lyle signed a contract with the actress, and soon her face lit up displays in dime stores around the country, inspiring housewives to remain beautiful while they waited for their men to return from the war. Maybelline also came out with an ad featuring a lonely wife sitting by her Christmas tree—but she wasn't shedding a tear; she appeared defiant. The copy read: *Maybelline helps women put on a brave face to conceal heartbreak. It gives them self-confidence when it is badly needed.*

Pleased with the success of the ads, Tom Lyle invited Bill, Pauline, Evelyn, and Warren to spend time with him at the Villa. He showed them photos of his granddaughter, Diane, and asked Pauline and Bill what movies they and their friends liked. Evelyn didn't care for the way this took Tom Lyle's attention away from her, but on the other hand, she had Warren to fuss over her.

The foursome spent Christmas Day itself at the MacDonalds', where Evelyn tried again to charm the family. Elna smiled and nodded and wished Evelyn well with her new man, although she noticed that Warren's glass was never empty for long.

Warren was not only a miner, he was a metaphysician. He believed that a single lifetime wasn't enough to finish one's work on earth, and often spoke to Evelyn about reincarnation and destiny. She found his arguments compelling and began to study metaphysics and read the books of Edgar Cayce, a psychic whose work would later heavily influence the New Age movement. Based on her research, Evelyn decided she and Warren had shared other lives together.

On New Year's Eve, Warren's resolution was to divorce his wife. At midnight, Evelyn kissed him, her mind swimming with dreams of the fun they would have in 1943—going to wonderful restaurants, classy charity events, and parties where she could dress up and feel young again. My grandmother was a wonderful person when she was happy, and at that moment she was happier than she had been in many years. She didn't even care about Tom Lyle being crazy over baby Diane or that Pauline seemed to now represent the target market for Maybelline as she herself had done twenty years ago.

She even tried to be more accepting of Pauline and her family. During a family picnic on a mild January day at the beach, Evelyn suggested she and Elna go for a walk. As they strolled along the shore, Evelyn opened up about her relationship with Preston and how hard life had been with him. She hoped that Elna would return this heart-to-heart talk, but Elna did not. Could not. She couldn't open up to glamorous Evelyn about why she cried all the time and why so many meals at the MacDonald table were now silent and grim. She hadn't even told anyone in her own family.

The truth was that after giving birth to three children, Elna had felt unattractive compared to the ageless beauties within her husband's glittering MGM social sphere. Although Andy tried to convince her that she looked fine, she chose to withdraw from the parties and premiers to become a homebody.

Meanwhile, Andy continued socializing and eventually met a woman named Mary Washburn. Mary wasn't beautiful, but she was smart, witty, and independent; she wore expensive jewelry; and she owned her own car and an exclusive boutique in downtown Los Angeles. Mary was hot pepper to Elna's salt of the earth.

Elna insisted Andy stop seeing Mary. Instead, he asked for a divorce. Elna begged him not to go through with it, after which his mistress called and said that she and Elna would just have to share Andy.

Elna had grieved ever since.

Now she listened to Evelyn jabbering on and on about her relationship with Warren Deuel. It made her sad for herself, but she felt happy for Evelyn until Evelyn said exactly the wrong thing: "Have you heard about reincarnation, Elna? Very interesting stuff. I believe that Warren and I were married in a former life, that's how strong our connection is."

"Really," Elna said in a voice colder than the January ocean. Andy had told her exactly the same thing about Mary and him. Apparently, Mary had even convinced him that Pauline had been his daughter with her in a past life! Reincarnation was proving to be quite a handy little philosophy for conducting extramarital affairs.

But Evelyn missed the sudden cooling in Elna's voice. "Unfortunately, he's still married, but that woman is just not right for him. He wants a divorce, and I hope he and I can get married soon."

Of this, all Elna heard was *he's still married*. She grew livid. She couldn't believe she had been walking along the beach for a half hour, listening like a sister to this . . . this whore, this home wrecker, this reminder of the witch who had destroyed her own marriage.

Evelyn finally realized that her efforts to woo Elna had failed—again. Well, then, she was done trying. Although the two mothers remained civil face to face, behind their opposing backs, conflict raged like a firestorm from then on.

And it exploded when the issue of Pauline's paying for Bill's car finally came to the surface.

Thirty-Nine
Private Feud
and World War

*B*y Evelyn's reckoning, because cars were so difficult to obtain and so expensive during wartime, Pauline should pay for the cost of replacing Bill's car now, not just what the old Ford was worth at the time it was wrecked. Pauline resented this money-grubbing attitude, but she also knew that Bill was heartsick at the loss of his car. So when she finally scraped together the four hundred dollars Evelyn demanded, she surprised Bill with the cash one afternoon before he went to work.

"What's this for?" he asked.

"A new car to replace the one I wrecked."

"What? Oh, sweetheart, you don't have to pay for that! Are you kidding?"

"No. Your mother told me I had to do it. So I did."

"My mother . . . *what?*"

When Bill got home, Evelyn was sitting alone in the living room, reading about Edgar Cayce.

"How could you make Pauline pay for the car?" Bill demanded without preamble. "How could you do that to her? She almost died. She could barely walk when she—"

Evelyn calmly laid her book aside. "I know it might look mean, honey, but it pulled her out of her misery and back into life, didn't it? I gave her a goal, and now she's fighting to complete it. Look how much better she's doing!"

"That's not because of that blood money! All I cared about was that she was alive; I couldn't care less about the car, and she knows it. And you didn't make her pay just to give her a goal."

"Well, of course I did, honey. Why else would I have done it?"

He stared at her, unable to find the words. Finally he blurted, "It's not even necessary. Unk would help me get another car if I asked him."

Evelyn stood. "Bill, you can't always go to your uncle with your hand out. He was never that kind of man. He pays all his own debts and expects others to do the same."

"This is different."

"Is it? Look at you: you're the man of this house, yet you live here rent-free and feel like you can preach at me. Well, that stops right now, mister."

Bill had pushed things too far. Now his mother not only insisted he accept Pauline's hard-earned money, but that he turn it over to her as a rent payment rather than put it toward a new car. Somehow, Evelyn had converted his righteous fury into defeat for him and profit for herself.

Things would only get worse if he resisted. Ashamed, he accepted the money from Pauline—and handed it to Evelyn without comment.

But inside, he smoldered.

Pauline's money probably found its way directly to Evelyn's dentist, along with whatever cash Evelyn got from hocking the ring TL had given her. She was in desperate need. Believing her teeth were too small, she had decided to do what Joan Crawford had done to ensure that she had a dazzling smile: she had all her natural teeth extracted and replaced with dentures.

When the procedure was over, Evelyn felt more beautiful than ever before— and judged Pauline's appearance with corresponding harshness. After all, being pretty wasn't good enough for a possible Maybelline family member—and Pauline was merely pretty. Evelyn still insisted that Bill could do better. Must do better. Somehow he had to learn that.

But Bill ignored her. He loved Pauline; hadn't he remained loyal to her the entire time she was recuperating? In fact, the only real problem they had was that he found Pauline too attractive—and she wouldn't "put out."

One evening, they double-dated with a buddy of Bill's whose girl specialized in putting out. Parked at Silver Lake, the other couple rocked the car with their night moves. In the back seat, Bill tried to get some of the same action going with Pauline. This time, when she tried to stop him, he ignored her. Somehow she managed to slip out of the car.

"Take me home," she said, her voice as cold as the moonlight.

Nobody argued with her, not even Bill. They drove back to Pauline's place in silence, and Pauline got out of the car and marched inside the house.

Bill hesitated, then followed her uncertainly as far as the front porch, where he stood wondering what to do. He felt terribly conflicted. He would have asked Pauline to marry him long ago if Evelyn would have allowed it or even if he had had enough money to support a wife. Meanwhile, he was a man, with a man's needs. Surely Pauline understood that. Surely—

The door burst open and Elna hurtled out with a frying pan cocked over her shoulder. Bill backed away fast, almost falling down the porch steps. Elna chased him, yelling, "Don't you ever to try to take advantage of my daughter again!"

Bill managed to escape with his skull intact, and later apologized to Pauline. She accepted his apology, and no more frying pans greeted him on the front porch. Still, he was angry, too. He loved Pauline, but how long did she expect him to go on like this?

Forever, apparently. "You've been running around on me!" she shouted one evening when he came over. "Everybody's talking about it."

"Pauline, you—"

She held up the cable-stitch sweater she had been knitting him and ripped it back to the yarn it was made of. "Get out of here! Get out of here!"

"Pauline, I—"

Andy MacDonald appeared in the doorway. Instead of a frying pan, he raised his fists and chased Bill down the street, bellowing, "Never bother my daughter again!" with the righteous indignation only the guilty can muster.

With Bill out of the picture, Elna encouraged Pauline to date a particular boy from church. He was going to become a minister, and he was very nice—but compared to the exciting ones with Bill, their dates fell flat. Still, Pauline refused to so much as speak to Bill.

On Bill's end, the separation was so painful he couldn't eat, sleep, or work. His buddies fixed him up with a few young women, but he tired of them quickly. They were just girls. Something to enjoy for a few minutes in a dark place. Pauline was different. She and her family had offered him a safe place to be real, to be himself—and except when it came to sex, Pauline always put his feelings before her own. She wasn't pretentious she never bragged about the big home she had grown up in or her wonderful life at MGM before the car crash. She never moaned about her lost career. In fact, she always tried to build up his spirits, to make him feel worthy and loved.

Without Pauline, life just wasn't enjoyable anymore.

Tired of seeing her son moping around the house, Evelyn finally called Tom

Lyle and asked him for enough money to buy Bill another car. A few days later, Evelyn drove Bill to the Villa and parked in the driveway next to a gray '36 Ford.

Tom Lyle handed Bill a set of keys. "She's all yours, my boy."

"Thanks, Unk Ile. That's keen."

He seemed grateful, but where was the joy? Where was the vast gratitude he must surely feel toward his mother? Nowhere. She couldn't believe it.

Even less could she believe what she did next: telephone the MacDonalds' house and ask for Pauline.

"Yes?" came Pauline's voice, utterly flat.

"Pauline, darling, I just called to say that I forgive you for ruining Bill's car."

"I see. Thank you."

Evelyn waited, but that was all. She sighed. "Pauline, Bill misses you."

"Oh?"

"He'd be very happy if you stopped by."

"Well, I don't think I—"

"Pauline, the truth is, he's been miserable. Nothing cheers him, not even getting another car."

"Another car?"

"From his Uncle Tom Lyle. Dear, that's not the point. Bill realizes he needs to be more of a gentleman; truly he does." Evelyn steeled herself. "Won't you please forgive him, and take him back?"

"I'll think about it," Pauline said and hung up.

And she did think about it. She even discussed the situation with her mother, but at first all Elna could think about was the nerve of some people. How could Evelyn force a young girl to make payments on the car that had almost taken her life, in an accident that hadn't even been her fault—and then forgive her for wrecking it? On the other hand, at least the wretched woman had been forced to come crawling to Pauline, asking for forgiveness for her son. That was something. Especially since Pauline really had been miserable without Bill in her life.

"Call him," she said.

For Evelyn, "crawling to Pauline" had been nothing more than a calculated risk. She wanted her son happy but was still convinced that he would eventually come to his senses and look for a more appropriate girlfriend. It was only a matter of time.

As for her opinion of Pauline, that had not changed at all: here was a nice, ordinary girl made for a nice, ordinary boy—but not her boy. Not William Preston Williams.

But the wait for Bill to come to his senses turned out to be much longer than she had anticipated. Pauline's limp steadily improved, until she and Bill could dance together again. She even resumed some favorite pastimes, including roller skating and ice skating. The night Bill saw her lace up her skates, he knew that the old Pauline was back. When the music played and she spun out on the ice, nobody would have guessed that one of her legs was shorter than the other, far less that she had almost died in a terrible accident.

Soon Bill and Pauline were back jitterbugging at the Palladium, and although Pauline still privately mourned the loss of her dancing career, she vowed to stand behind her boyfriend and help him make his dreams come true. She had seen the shape of them: Bill had shown her his little drawings of the kind of dream house he hoped to build for them someday.

Tom Lyle had his own doubts about Bill's recent choices, not those concerning Pauline, but those concerning bigger things, matters of life and death. He feared that his nephew was so focused on Pauline that Bill might end up working for the rest of his life at Douglas Aircraft, or, worse, be drafted and lose his life in the war.

One night, Tom Lyle took his nephew to dinner at Romanoff's on Rodeo Drive in Beverly Hills. No burger or chili and malt here—Bill knew Unk Ile had something on his mind. They were seated at Tom Lyle's favorite booth, right next to Humphrey Bogart's. Bill saw Louis B. Mayer having dinner with Frank Sinatra and Lana Turner. He sure wished Pauline could be there.

"Bill," Tom Lyle said, "there's something I want to say to you: It's time you went to college."

"College? But I hate school. And Unk, look at you—you didn't go to college."

"And that's something I've always regretted. I'm lucky to have two college boys working with me—Emery and Arnold. I'm telling you, Bug, if you graduate from college, I'll be able to open doors for you in advertising. And believe me, advertising is the future; it's the American dream come true."

Bill folded his arms. "I want to make money now, not waste my time in a classroom."

"Make money doing what?"

"Maybe working at MGM in the art department, painting backgrounds for movies. Maybe working my way up to art director."

"You're thinking Andy MacDonald has the connections to get you hired on."

"Well, yeah."

"Connections are good, Bug, but I know Andy would prefer you get a degree in art first."

"But why? I can draw and paint right now."

"Getting a degree proves you can stick to a difficult task for four years; it shows you've got guts and determination. Look at Tom Jr. He graduated from Duke, and now he works at the Maybelline Company—not only because he's my son, but because I know he's got what it takes."

"But I just don't see myself as a college boy, Unk Ile."

Tom Lyle sighed. "In that case, Bug, I suggest you join the Coast Guard right away. I've asked around, and all you'd have to do is show up for guard duty in San Pedro on the weekends. And being in the Coast Guard would keep you out of overseas combat duty."

Bill's eyes widened. "I hadn't thought of that."

Tom Lyle might have wanted to protect his nephew from the bloody reality of combat, but he didn't hesitate to capitalize on the romantic aspect of young men and women separated by war. Over the next two years, he generated a parade of ads featuring dreamy models of all types, with eyes of blue, brown, green, or hazel staring into the eyes of the beholder in lifelike portraits to be carried even into battle—representations of the girl to come home to. Movie-star pinups remained popular, of course, selling Maybelline to the girls stateside who sought to emulate the stars in their favorite magazines.

Betty Grable, Rita Hayworth, Hedy Lamarr, Elyse Knox, Jane Russell, Lana Turner, Linda Darnell, Maria Montez, Susan Hayward, Virginia Mayo, and Barbara Stanwyck—Tom Lyle contracted all these beauties to appear in full-color Maybelline magazine advertisements. Grable, said to hold a million-dollar insurance policy on her legs, was particularly desirable, the embodiment of the girl next door with moxie. Her accessible beauty inspired young ladies every-where to save their grocery money to buy a little sex appeal.

Toward the end of 1943, Tom Lyle came out with a series of ads featuring officers from all branches of the service, wearing their dress uniforms, smiling at beautiful, elegant women in formal attire with faces made up to look like movie stars. The copy read:

> In moments like this, lovely eyes
> can say more than any spoken words.
>
> Perhaps today, your hero is far from the things he
> loves most—you, home, and the country he is
> fighting so bravely to protect. Yet you are always
> near him in his thoughts and in his dreams.
>
> While he's away, he wants those eyes he adores to be
> bright and smiling. When he comes back to you, your eyes
> can be just as he pictured them in his fondest dreams.

These days more than ever, millions of women are grateful for
the soft, glorifying effect of Maybelline eye makeup. You will
be grateful, too, once you see what a difference it makes!

Bill joined the Coast Guard in August 1944, shortly after the D-Day offensive pushed the Nazis back from the shores of the English Channel. He could have posed for one of his uncle's ads in his dress uniform: black with gold trim and gold buttons and a white hat with gold trim.

As proud of the uniform as he was, he lost it when he failed to report for duty one Saturday morning after a night of partying.

He was immediately drafted into the US army.

In Europe, the Battle of the Bulge had just begun, and would prove to be the single bloodiest engagement of the war, with more than nineteen thousand American deaths out of eighty thousand casualties. Things were little better in the Pacific Theater, where the Japanese continued to fight to the death for every square inch of land, and kamikaze pilots rained down. A young, freshly trained soldier en route to either locale did not face optimistic prospects.

Evelyn was terrified for her son and hadn't seen him so downhearted since his father's death nine years earlier. Still, he packed his duffle bag like a good soldier, kissed his mother and his girl goodbye, and caught a train to Fort Riley, Kansas. Tom Lyle wrote him there, using the salutation, "Dear Bug."

> . . . even though I know it is very strenuous . . . I feel sure that the training will be good for you. . . . Bug, I hope that you won't become discouraged and listen to the gripes of the goldbricks—you'll always find that type in every walk of life, and particularly in the Army—those who are so dumb that they think it is smart to try and get away with breaking all the rules. I know you well enough, Billy, to be sure that, no matter how tough the breaks seem, you've got what it takes to see it through and be a really good soldier. It will mean a great deal to you and all of us for you to come out of the Service with a fine record that you can always be proud of.
>
> Remember that anyone can be a good scout when everything is easy sailing, but it takes the real stuff to make the best of rugged going. I know that you are going to miss being at home at Christmas, and we are certainly going to miss you, too, Bug, but . . . remember those thousands of poor guys who are spending their THIRD Christmas away from home, and overseas, at that. . . .

In early January 1945, the rigors of boot camp began in earnest. Bill wrote Pauline almost every day. She wrote him twice a day, every day. He carried her picture in his wallet and was so homesick he wanted to die.

In February, Elna wrote Bill a fateful letter:

> With you gone and without her dance career to look forward to, Pauline needs a stronger connection to see her through, and you do, too. You've been together seven years now, and if you want to make sure she's here for you when you come back, you need to do the right thing and get married. If she remains single and available while you're gone, she may lose trust in your loyalty, and she just might meet someone else.

Bill mulled these words over for a week, then wrote to Pauline, proposing marriage. She accepted eagerly.

Evelyn was not pleased. She tried to convince Bill to wait until he got back from the war before committing to marriage. She even went to Tom Lyle and begged him to take her side. He tried his best, because he honestly still felt the boy should go to college before taking on the responsibilities of marriage and children.

But in the end, none of it mattered. Every time Bill imagined Pauline meeting some other guy while he was gone, a green streak of jealous rage ignited in his heart.

The wedding took place on March 16 at the Westwood Congregational Church in Los Angeles, where the MacDonalds had been members for years. Since there had been no time to send invitations, Reverend Hoag presided over a very small service. The MacDonald family was there, of course, but not Tom Lyle, and not Evelyn. Although Tom Lyle loved Pauline and respected Andy MacDonald, he had begun to shy away from any non-Williams gathering that did not take place at the Villa Valentino or one of the places he knew would respect his privacy.

Evelyn was a different matter. She told the MacDonalds that she couldn't attend because she had dropped a bowling ball on her foot.

The young couple had time for only a one-night honeymoon in Lake Arrowhead. Bill had to get right back to Fort Riley to join his unit, which would be shipping out to the Pacific in a few days.

This caused a problem of its own. Pauline wanted to drive to Kansas with her new husband, but that didn't seem possible. For one thing, she was afraid of having to drive back again by herself. But more importantly, even if they combined their gas ration stamps, they didn't have enough for her to make the round trip anyway.

That just didn't seem right, so Bill called his old buddy Gene Benz and asked for help. Their brilliant plan: break into fancy parked cars in Beverly Hills in search of gas stamps.

When the cops spotted them, Gene escaped but Bill did not. At the station, he couldn't decide on whom he would feel the least humiliated to use his one phone call. His wife? She'd think she had married a loser. His mother, with all her jokes about the Big House? No. Tom Lyle? Even if Unk Ile were available, could Bill stand telling the great man what his godson had done?

"You gonna call or not?" the sergeant demanded.

Bill called Pauline.

It turned out to be her father who, through his connections at MGM, came to the rescue. One of the studio lawyers, whose job was to keep stars who got in trouble out of the papers, agreed to help—although much to Bill's annoyance he insisted on Evelyn's presence at the police station.

When she walked in, everyone turned to look at her, as usual. Bill noticed that by some miracle, her bowling injury appeared to have healed.

The lawyer managed to get the night sergeant to reconsider Bill's case. He asked Evelyn, "Will you sign a statement ensuring that your son will report for duty at Fort Riley on Wednesday morning?"

"Yes."

It was three in the morning by the time they headed home. Bill thanked his mother and said he would write her when he got to Kansas.

"Oh, I'm coming with you," she said. "How else are you going to have the gas rations to get the car back?"

Nothing would change her mind. No doubt she was pleased at this excuse to come along on the ragged remnant of her son's honeymoon. This could be the last time she saw her son, after all. Apart from the very real possibility of his dying in combat, there was the likelihood that if he returned, he would remember Evelyn's shabby treatment of his new bride and choose to start his married life somewhere far from his mother.

With the three of them crunched miserably together in the front seat of Bill's little '36 Ford, they set out eastward on Route 66. The car had no heater, and the back window was broken, letting in most of the mid-March cold from the high deserts and the western plains. At night, the trio shared a motel room—not exactly the ideal honeymoon for Bill and Pauline.

The moment they arrived at Fort Riley, Bill had to check in and see the lieutenant about a possible court-martial because of his recent arrest. When Pauline and Evelyn kissed him good-bye, they had no idea if they would ever see him again.

Evelyn expressed her grief and fear as anger at Pauline. All the way back to California, Pauline's new mother-in-law harangued her about forcing Bill into marriage. Evelyn showed no kindness, compassion, or affection for her new relative. "You'd better not be pregnant," she said—again and again, mile after mile, as if Pauline having her son's child would somehow be shameful.

Pauline didn't understand. She thought if Bill were killed, the birth of his baby would be a blessing for her and Evelyn alike.

By the end of that long, long drive, the enmity between Evelyn and Pauline had been irreversibly set.

With Bill's court-martial still pending, he pulled out of Fort Riley with the rest of his troop, heading for Fort Ord in Oakland, California, just outside San Francisco. Once there, he was called into the lieutenant's office, where he was told his jail experience had to be reviewed before he could be assigned orders to go overseas.

To Bill's shock, the review resulted in a court-martial.

Once again, he had to call his wife and mother to deliver bad news. Evelyn said she would come up to Fort Ord immediately, but Pauline refused to accompany her. Not understanding the circumstances, Bill cried, "But you're my wife! I want you to come!"

"I didn't say I wouldn't come. Don't worry, I'll be there."

Pauline traveled north, alone, on a Greyhound bus and arrived at Ford Ord exhausted and looking much the worse for wear in her plain plaid skirt, oxfords, and bulky hand-knit sweater. Her hair was unwashed, and she didn't have on a speck of makeup.

To her disgust, Evelyn was already there, perfect as a fresh rose and looking appalled at Pauline's appearance. Bill didn't care about that. He was just thankful that Pauline had arrived.

The morning Bill shipped out, his wife and mother stood shivering in the late March fog, wiping their tears and waving as Bill shuffled up the gangplank in his military prison uniform and handcuffs. At his official court-martial proceeding, the judge had not been sympathetic to his excuse that he had broken into parked cars for gas stamps so his new wife could drive to camp with him. He was on his way to war, but departing in disgrace rather than honor. Thankfully, it was a summary court-martial, which would result in a thirty-day imprisonment and wouldn't leave a permanent blot on his record.

Evelyn was horrified to see her son treated like a criminal even as he set off to help defend his country. As for Pauline, she simply prayed that her husband would come home safely.

Bill was heading for the Philippines.

Forty

"Most of You Will Be Killed"

By the time Bill's troop arrived in the Philippines, they believed their duties would basically be a mop-up. General Douglas MacArthur had just led American forces and Filipino guerillas in the Battle for Leyte, where Allied forces suffered relatively low casualties for once, compared to some fifty thousand Japanese Imperial forces left dead. The rumor was that a handful of Japanese soldiers were still hiding up in the hills and would need to be cleared out. That didn't sound terribly threatening to Bill, and his first few letters home casually mentioned a special mission he would be going on.

The mission was based on a technique the army had developed to locate hidden Japanese bunkers, most of them loaded with explosives. Commanders would send a reconnaissance plane over the rolling tropical hills outside Manila to identify active areas, after which army sorties would move in, sweep the forest, and capture any enemy soldiers. To facilitate this mission, the army had converted part of an old plantation into a small landing field. They needed someone there who had experience working on planes. The limited knowledge Bill had gained at Douglas—all in riveting—proved to be his ticket to the plantation. It was a lucky break for him; nobody else in his squad had any knowledge of planes whatsoever.

Every day the plane went out to scout. When it came back, Bill would run out on the field, anchor the aircraft, refuel it, check it for bullet holes, and help the mechanic work on it, if necessary. The lieutenant who flew the reconnaissance plane in return took Bill to the PX for supplies that were unheard of for most GIs: sheets, blankets, pillows, and—the greatest prize—a real toilet seat for the outhouse. One of Bill's duties was to clean the outhouse by pouring gasoline down the hole and lighting the waste on fire. Not exactly the stuff of heroics, but Bill didn't complain.

Two months later, the recon missions ended, and Bill was sent to join the other end of the job—making sorties into the jungle to capture Japanese soldiers. His pup tent joined the long lines of others sagging under the pounding rain of tropical downpours. Mosquito nets were required at night to avoid malaria.

Pauline wrote to Bill every day, and he also got occasional letters from her parents, his mother, Tom Lyle, other relatives, and whatever friends were still home or who had already returned from the war. He also got a steady supply of goodies. The MGM Studio Club sent packages filled with chewing gum, candy, cigarettes, socks, stationery, shaving cream, combs, chocolate, and newsletters with photos and messages from MGM actresses—some of which Bill shared with friends. He wrote to Pauline that the guys kept their morale high by covering any surface they could protect from the rain—like the insides of their lockers and their helmet liners—with their girls' pictures or with pinups. Pauline started sending him glamour shots of herself. Bill wrote back that she was the "prettiest of them all."

Finally, Bill was sent out into the jungle for the first time. At first, he was excited to see some action, although he had heard that Japanese snipers were adept at hiding and planting mines along lines of approach. They could sneak up on a soldier from behind and kill him without being detected. Bill knew guys who had gotten killed while standing right next to a buddy.

As Bill's squad reached the map coordinates reported to be a Japanese hiding spot, he thought he saw something dash across the path up ahead.

"Halt!" he shouted. "Who goes there?"

The only answer was the echo of running footfalls.

"Halt!"

More footfalls. Bill raised his rifle, pointed it at a quivering bush, and pulled the trigger. A figure collapsed onto the trail.

Bill and the other men approached the fallen enemy slowly. There had been many stories of a Japanese soldier faking death, only to lie in wait for his enemy's approach and shoot him pointblank.

But this one was dead. Bill saw the face of a boy, no more than a teenager. But still an enemy, and for a soldier, the first kill is a rite of passage. Bill grabbed souvenirs from a corpse that would never be buried: Japanese money, pictures, cards, letters. He grabbed an aluminum canteen etched with the image of a peaceful Japanese garden—something he would think about often in later years.

The soldier also possessed a Japanese flag, binoculars, watch, compass, bayonet, and knife. Finally, Bill reached for the belt, only to stick his hands into a spot full of warm guts. But he was not repulsed. Pumped with adrenaline and relieved he wasn't the one who had been killed, he simply got up and headed down the hill with his fellow soldiers.

When Bill told his commanding officer about the enemy soldier he had killed, the captain said, "You did the right thing. That slant was probably getting ready to ambush all of you."

Back home, Pauline had her own horrors to struggle with. In her job with the Combat Camera production company, she began to review footage from the liberation of German concentration camps: human bodies stacked in piles of two and three hundred, starved, beaten, or gassed to death. She wrote up summaries concerning places called Dachau and Auschwitz. The images were indelibly etched in her mind.

They also made her focus on the cheer to be found in life. Bill's cousins from Chicago, Will Stroh and Noel Allen Williams—whom everyone called Allen—happened to be stationed in California and spent much of their free time at Pauline's parents' house. Pauline had wonderful parties for them almost every weekend, serving homemade dishes built around the allotted two-pound weekly meat ration and some vegetables from her mother's victory garden. Andy served the boys drinks from a special bottle of bourbon he kept under lock and key, doling out a toast and a joke with every swallow.

When Evelyn got wind of these gatherings, she felt unfairly excluded; was Will Stroh not her nephew? Unfortunately for her, while in San Francisco, she had badmouthed Pauline to one of Pauline's uncles in an attempt to enlist his help in splitting up the marriage—a strategy that backfired decidedly, prompting Andy MacDonald to refer to Evelyn as "that highfalutin' dame." Now the MacDonalds looked magnanimous and had a great time with her relatives, while she was left in the cold.

Rescue came in the form of her boyfriend, Warren Deuel. After many attempts, he finally persuaded her to get out of her usual social circuit, put on a pair of pants, and go with him to see what he did for a living—travel around the West doing geological research for big companies looking for oil or mineral deposits. On one trip to Bakersfield, he taught her about dolomite, the evolution of crystal from the cooling of the earth, and how fossils developed over time.

And Evelyn listened. Warren's quiet wisdom convinced her more than ever that they had known each other in a different time and place, perhaps Atlantis.

Their love seemed ancient; it transcended physical limitations. They were soul mates—even though he, despite his New Year's resolution, was still married to someone else.

So she listened when he said, "Darling, Pauline and Bill have their own destiny, and it is not for you to interfere. Simply accept it."

Whether on the road or back in Los Angeles, Warren and Evelyn talked and drank and drank and talked, until they couldn't turn their minds off without consuming enough alcohol to put them to sleep. In fact, Warren's habit grew to the point where he drank in the morning so that he wouldn't have to face a hangover and be unable to work. Then it reached the point at which he complained that bugs were crawling all over him. Warren, like Preston, was an alcoholic. On the other hand, unlike Preston, he had no rage in him. Evelyn decided she could help the dear man.

And he helped her in return. With his guidance and encouragement, she managed to say enough of the right things to the MacDonalds that they finally invited her to their Saturday night dinner parties. Either that, or the MacDonalds, despite the resentment they felt over Evelyn's treatment of their daughter, were simply gracious to their cores.

In any event, Evelyn showed up wearing sweetheart necklines with chokers or clingy dresses with flirty gathers at the bust or hip, reprising her Miss Maybelline persona. She staged this little show in front of Bill's cousins in hopes that when they went back to Chicago they might tell Verona and Noel how great she looked and that she had a successful boyfriend in the oil business.

Even as her son slogged through the jungles in the Philippines, image remained everything to Evelyn. No matter how much Warren or Edgar Cayce urged her to rise above her ego, she still loved to strut her stuff.

Bill read about all the activity back home in Pauline's treasured letters and, like all GIs, prayed the war would end before he got killed. He knew that in Europe, Hitler had committed suicide and VE day had been declared. But here in the Pacific Theater, everyone feared that the worst was yet to come: the invasion of Japan.

Bill's company commander told his men: "Most of you will probably be killed."

On August 6, 1945, President Harry S Truman ordered an atomic bomb, equaling twenty thousand tons of TNT, to be dropped on the Japanese city of Hiroshima. Three days later, another exploded over Nagasaki, for a combined death toll of more than two hundred thousand people. The Japanese surrendered unconditionally.

Bill and his outfit were loaded onto a ship and sent to Tokyo Bay for the signing of the Armistice. As the vessel entered the bay, Bill looked around and saw hundreds of enclaves with heavy artillery flanking their entrances—the Americans would have been annihilated if they had attacked this place. As the ship pulled up alongside General MacArthur's, a surge of excitement rolled like armored tanks through thousands of cheering men. Bill could feel the vibration through his feet.

He watched Japanese emperor Hirohito sign the Armistice. Witnessing the end of the cataclysm that Japan had unleashed on the world was something he would talk about for the rest of his life.

That autumn, a man who came to be known to the family as Milford was discharged from military service. Shell-shocked and looking for menial work, he knocked on Unk Ile's door. Tom Lyle was a sucker for a sob story. Although he couldn't turn down anyone who asked a favor, he had a unique policy about lending money: he wouldn't do it. If he decided to grant a financial request, the money never had to be paid back. Unk Ile believed in the power of giving, and the return he got from his generosity often prompted him to say that the more he gave away, the more it came back tenfold.

In this case, he used a different approach: he hired Milford to be his doorman. Milford eventually became the main houseman, running the entire Villa with the help of Oma, the housekeeper and cook for the rest of Tom Lyle's life.

Forty-One
A Queen
and a Princess

Far too many young Americans did not return from the war, while too many reports of unimaginable atrocities did. Perhaps this explains why, following the end of hostilities, many young Americans developed a craze for a more manageable form of terror: horror movies.

The portrayal of girls in these films took a certain drift. Rosie the Riveter's muscles had been acceptable during the war, but now she must not get too big for her bandana. In the new horror movies, powerful women became the villains, while nice docile girls needed male protection to avoid becoming the Evil Woman's victims or, worse, become like her.

Lois Collier, who starred in low-budget thrillers including *Weird Woman*, *Cobra Woman*, and *Jungle Woman*, was suddenly quite the rage, particularly among college girls. Tom Lyle featured her in a full-page 1945 Maybelline color ad, showing Collier in two contrastingly lit pictures to illustrate different makeup tricks for day and evening.

By daylight or candlelight, keep your eyes aglow with
Maybelline. Lovely Lois Collier, Universal star, shows how
important it is to use flattering Maybelline eye makeup in

**bright daylight, as well as in the softer lights of evening. . . .
For the finest in eye makeup—insist on Maybelline!**

Maybelline still sold the ten-cent sample sizes that appealed to this age bracket, while more mature women preferred the seventy-five-cent size. Profits continued to pour in, but nobody in Chicago or Los Angeles was taking the future for granted. In fact, to use Rags Ragland's words, "Patriotism and pinups won't bring in buyers anymore."

"We need a different approach," Tom Lyle agreed. "A new look that elevates women above the pinup."

"What about Ava Gardner?" Emery asked.

Tom Lyle considered. He had kept track of young Ava Gardner for years as she was being groomed for stardom and going in and out of tumultuous marriages. "She's not quite there yet," he said.

But on January 19, 1946—Tom Lyle's fiftieth birthday—he got a phone call that gave him a present he had been waiting ten years for.

"Hallelujah!" he said to Emery after hanging up the phone. "Joan Crawford has completed all her print ad obligations to Max Factor and is ready to sign an exclusive contract with us!"

"That's beautiful," Emery said.

"I think we should return the courtesy," Tom Lyle said.

"You mean—but what about all our other stars? Do you really think we should hitch our wagon to only one?"

"Yes, since she happens to be the biggest star in Hollywood!"

Tom Lyle, Emery, and Arnold met with Crawford for photo shoots several times at the Hesse Studio. Tom Lyle had chosen Hesse to photograph Crawford because he knew Hesse, who had made glamour his trademark, could capture the smiling eyes for which Maybelline was famous, eyes being the key word. In almost none of Tom Lyle's ads did the models show their teeth. He didn't want anything to draw attention away from the eyes.

After reviewing hundreds of pictures of Crawford in different hairstyles, makeup, and clothes, Tom Lyle selected a sophisticated shot that he felt would appeal to both the young and more mature markets. The photo featured Crawford wearing a breathtaking shoulder-padded V-necked dress, thick with white sequins; a black choker at her neck anchored a dazzling diamond and ruby pin. The background of blurred iridescent sequins created a twinkling effect that called attention to the arresting beauty of her eyes. She autographed the finished product: *To Maybelline—the eye makeup I would never be without — Sincerely, Joan Crawford.*

Tom Lyle timed the release of the ad to coincide with Crawford's Academy

Award for Best Actress—her virtual coronation as Queen of Hollywood. Crawford became the face of Maybelline around the world. She would be Tom Lyle's exclusive Hollywood representative through the rest of the decade, carrying the company to a level untouched by any competitor.

Of course, he also continued to use anonymous models and painted illustrations to reach out not only to the ever-increasing numbers of college girls, but also to all the young women who were welcoming their men home from war, getting married, and having babies. Such lifestyles required a more natural, clean, and wholesome look—that of the all-American girl.

To target this emerging market, Maybelline tried a new advertising approach featuring subtle natural lighting, soft pastel shades, and understated makeup. No more Technicolor for dramatic hues, no strong lighting with heavy makeup, no more Paul Hesse glamour shots for Arnold to enhance.

One before-and-after ad used this copy:

> **Mary had a little inferiority complex. It followed her
> everywhere she went. Boys looked past her—not at her.
> Girls liked her—because she was no competition!
> She was dainty and sweet. Her nose was always carefully
> powdered, and she used the right shade of lipstick,
> but the kindest thing you could say about her eyes
> was that they were—well, just a washout! One day,
> Mary read a Maybelline advertisement, just as you
> are doing, and look at Mary now! Moral: many
> a girl has beaten her rival by an eyelash!**

Although Evelyn identified more with the glamorous Joan Crawford than with the all-American girl, she too began to rethink her image. Since Bill and Pauline were living in Tacoma, Washington, while her son finished up his military service, Evelyn continued to join Warren on visits to his work sites. She often showed up at the mines dressed in a fringed leather jacket worn over pants and hiking boots, with a cowboy hat shifting on her hair as she stumbled over chunks of granite. She spent most of her time on these trips at Harrah's Casino in Reno, gambling. Warren joined in as often as possible, watching Evelyn and suggesting moves on the tables while chain-drinking straight Scotch.

Later, Evelyn and Warren would sit together among the Granite Mountains of the Sierras, enjoying the magnificent air and long panoramic views of the Nevada basin.

"Honey, look at this," Warren would say, showing her an ordinary-looking rock. "Can you imagine how this was made?"

"No darling, tell me."

"Nevada landforms date back about twelve thousand years to the glacial period. These mountains were covered with ice, and when it melted, the valleys became lakes, which then dried up, leaving this beautiful desert filled with minerals."

"Like gold," Evelyn said. That was the part she understood best.

In November 1946, Evelyn called Bill from Reno to wish him a happy birthday—but he was the one to announce a major surprise.

"I've got some big news, Muddy"—at some point he had dropped "Mom" and started calling Evelyn "Mud" and "Muddy." "Next June, you're going to be a grandmother!"

Silence stretched between them for almost two seconds before Evelyn started harping about the huge responsibility they were taking on, where would they live, and how did Bill intend to support a baby?

He sighed. "Aw, Mud, I'd thought you'd be happy. We're happy as hell. See you for Christmas."

Evelyn hung up and told Warren. "Guess we'll have to forget about going to Las Vegas for the opening of the Flamingo for New Year's. The kids are coming home. And Pauline's pregnant."

Warren hugged her. "I never thought I'd be sleeping with a grandma."

"I'm only forty-five!"

"Forty-six in February, dear."

The moment Bill received his honorable discharge from the army, he and Pauline headed back to Los Angeles. Despite Evelyn's exaggerated protests, the young couple moved in with the MacDonalds. Bill hoped to get work at MGM, constructing sets or painting backgrounds, but the studios were in the midst of a labor dispute over wages, hours, and working conditions. Andy couldn't allow his son-in-law to cross the picket lines without putting his own job in jeopardy.

Not being able to work at MGM depressed Bill, but he had another option. Pauline's brother Fred, a construction contractor, was swamped with work slapping together postwar bungalows. He invited Bill to join him as his painting foreman. Bill gave it a try, but lacked the discipline for the job. Or, to put it his way, he resented his brother-in-law's "big shot attitude."

Unemployed and frustrated, Bill began to drink. On June 10, 1947, Pauline Williams gave birth to Sharrie Lynn Williams: me. My name came from my father's misunderstanding of the French word *chérie*, which appeared in the last line of one of Frankie Laine's signature songs, "That's My Desire." When my father heard the song, he leaned over to my mother and said, "If we have a little girl, I want to name her Sharrie."

At birth, I weighed a mere six pounds, six ounces, and what little hair I had was strawberry-blonde; eyes, blue. Pauline noticed my right foot, which turned in slightly due to a minor deformation. In other words, an imperfection. My mother was heartbroken. She had hoped her daughter would one day be a dancer—but according to the doctor, there was a chance I might not even be able to walk.

Evelyn fretted about this physical defect for a different reason: it might reflect negatively on the family. "We're ruined," she said.

My mother, the twenty-three-year-old ex-dancer thought differently. She started me on an exercise routine, massaging my legs and forcing me to do little push-ups with my feet. Soon I was able to pull my whole body up, and at nine months, I ran across the room for the first time.

Unk Ile invited us up to the Villa so he could witness my great talent. After we arrived and walked past "Aspiration," the outdoor statue that looked up at the sky, Milford the butler led us into the living room. There at the windows stood Unk Ile, cigarette in hand, admiring the lights of Hollywood spread out below him. The glow from recessed lighting fixtures cast a romantic ambiance throughout the room.

Unk Ile turned and smiled. "Have any of you ever noticed how low lighting makes everyone look more beautiful?"

This was the world into which I was born.

After the hugs and kisses, Tom Lyle asked Milford to serve cocktails and then brought out a little box, which he handed to my mother. Inside was a perfect Tiffany baby's ring, with a diamond in a gold art deco setting. She placed it on my finger.

"Only one other princess has a ring like that," Unk Ile said. "My granddaughter, Diane."

"Now there are two little princesses," Pauline said proudly.

We couldn't afford a house of our own, but I now wore a diamond ring I would outgrow in a few months. To the Williams clan, this made perfect sense.

At least I—the slightly deformed little princess-in-training—didn't swallow the ring.

Forty-Two

Tony

$\mathcal{B}$y 1947, commercial television offered thirteen stations nation-wide. New York and Washington, DC, were connected by coaxial cables, and new microwave technology transmitted TV signals via "repeater" stations situated every twenty-five miles in populated areas. Tom Lyle eagerly considered using this new medium for advertising but chose to hold off until more Americans actually owned a TV set. He knew that time would come soon; commercials insistently asserted that to truly partake of the American Dream, every family needed a television in its home.

Although Joan Crawford was still Maybelline's Hollywood representative, she appealed to a relatively small demographic, that of the sophisticate. Tom Lyle was still aggressively pursuing the all-American girl image, so when fresh-faced Norma Christopher was crowned queen of the 1947 Tournament of Roses, he set out to contract her for a before-and-after Maybelline ad. They met at the Carlyle Blackwell, Jr. Photography Studio in Hollywood to do a series of shots with natural lighting to capture the demure, uncomplicated, understated look desired by brides-to-be.

The final ad portrayed Norma before—looking okay—and after—looking like a princess bride.

The copy read:

The top of your face is important, too! Look what happens
when you stop halfway through. In contrast to those
red lips, the eyes seem a bit dull and blank, don't they?

Now see what a few soft touches of Maybelline mascara,
eyebrow pencil, and eye shadow can do. . . .

The cultural changes in America following the end of the war were nothing compared to the personal changes Tom Lyle was about to experience. Gardenias were still in bloom on the autumn day when he opened his mail to read that his beloved Villa Valentino lay directly in the path of the new Hollywood freeway that was being constructed to link downtown Los Angeles with Hollywood.

Tom Lyle stared at the notice, trying to find words in it that meant some other nearby home was in jeopardy and not his Villa. Here was where he had expected to spend the rest of his life.

There were no such words. He finally sank onto a chair, stared out at his magnificent view, and wept.

The war had halted construction of the Hollywood freeway—part of California's State Highway 101—but now eminent domain carved its swath through many of Hollywood's loveliest neighborhoods. The former home of Rudolph Valentino would not be spared even as a historical site; no amount of money could change that. Tom Lyle had one year to relocate.

Although still barely recovered from the shock, he and Emery began looking for property in Beverly Hills, Bel Air, Brentwood, and Pacific Palisades—the finest real estate in the area. Tom Lyle preferred the hills and the sweeping vistas they offered. The sparkle of city lights inspired him more powerfully than the ocean's blackness at night, partly because he still slept most of the day and worked throughout the hours of darkness, and partly because lights meant people, and people meant activity, art, music, money, glamour.

In Bel Air, he found the perfect piece of property on Airole Way. He decided not to try to replicate the old Hollywood charm of Villa Valentino; instead, he hired Arnold's brother, an architect, to design an ultramodern home for him.

That last summer at the Villa, Tom Lyle called Bill and Pauline and asked them to come up for lunch, saying, "I have someone I want you to meet."

When they got to the Villa, Milford let them in and they found Tom Lyle out by the pool. As they walked past "Aspiration" and down the winding brick steps, Pauline asked Bill, "Who is that boy in the pool?" Bill looked over and saw a muscular young man with thick auburn hair and naturally dark skin lying on a float in the water while Tom Lyle sat on a chair nearby, legs crossed. No one else was around.

"I have no idea," Bill said.

As Unk Ile saw them approaching, he stood, smiled, and swung a hand toward the young man. "Bug," he said, "this is Tony, your half-brother."

Bill didn't know what to say or do. He had never known Tom Lyle to play a practical joke before.

Then he saw his uncle's eyes. They were warm but direct. Serious eyes.

The young man rolled off the float, swam smoothly to the edge of the pool, got out, and flashed a big toothy smile their way. Bill could see his father in this kid, just as he could see him in his own reflection—and for a second Bill didn't know whether to hit Tony or hug him. He couldn't believe his mother had kept this a secret from him. On the other hand, at least he now understood why she was always so merciless about his father and why she often said she hoped he was turning over in his grave as he watched her recapture her lost youth.

Tom Lyle launched into the story: Preston coming to California for his health, getting into the movies, meeting Virginia. One thing leading to another. Tony being born, being supported by Emery, then sent off to Chicago at the age of ten to be raised by Tom Lyle's sister Eva and her husband, Chess.

"I've decided it's time to tell you the truth," Tom Lyle went on, "because Tony just graduated from high school. He's almost a man, and he wanted meet the half-brother Eva told him he had out here in California. Since your mother is out of town with Warren right now, it seemed the perfect time to introduce you boys to each other."

At least now Bill understood how his mother had kept this a secret from him: it was still a secret to her.

He looked at the young man dripping by the side of the pool. *Your half-brother.* He grinned and held out a hand. "Pleased to meet you, Tony."

Despite his shock, Bill instantly bonded with Tony; brotherly love at first sight. Pauline's family told Tony he was welcome at their home any time.

The moment Evelyn returned, Bill asked her how it was possible she couldn't know he had a half-brother. Despite Warren's calming presence, Evelyn shrieked out her feelings of betrayal—not at her first husband, about whom she had had plenty of suspicions, but at Tom Lyle and his entire extended family.

"How could they? How could the entire Williams family hide this bastard child and not tell me?"

White-faced and clutching her chest, she insisted Bill tell her the whole story. Then, "Tom Lyle actually introduced him to you? As your half-brother?"

"That's right. Because he is. Mom, calm down."

"No, I will not calm down!" Hands shaking, clutching her hair, pacing, she seemed to be in six places at once. "Promise me you will never, ever allow that bastard in this house, or stay in his presence at Tom Lyle's. Promise me!"

"Okay, okay!" Bill was ready to say anything to stop her hysterics.

But he broke this promise repeatedly over the summer. Tony would often drop by the MacDonalds' on the new motorcycle Emery had bought him and stay for dinner with the family. I was eighteen months old at the time, and Tony loved playing horsy with me, bouncing me on his knee and singing me songs. When he came by, he always had a little gift for me—a gold bracelet with my name on it or a stuffed animal—and chocolate kisses for my mother. He was kind, loving, and affectionate, and he had the Williams sense of humor. Bill was overjoyed to have a brother; he didn't care what his mother thought. One day, Bill and Tony were helping Unk put some belongings into boxes for storage. Pauline was there as well, and had brought me along. Tony kept hiding among the boxes and jumping out to make his little niece laugh.

Just then, Evelyn's car swung into the driveway.

"I thought she was in Bakersfield!" Pauline cried.

"So did I," Bill said.

"Quick, Tony," Pauline said, "hide in the coat closet."

Sheepishly, Tony obeyed. But the moment Evelyn came in, she knew something was up. She was savvy that way. "Who's here?" she demanded.

Bill shrugged. "Nobody."

Evelyn knew he was lying. She started snooping and soon enough went to the coat closet and opened the door. Abashed, Tony smiled at her, and she instantly knew exactly who it was. She could see Preston in his face.

"Get that bastard out of here!" she shrieked.

Bill stood his ground. "No, Mother. You get out."

This was the first time that Bill had ever openly defied her. She was shocked silent. At that moment, Tom Lyle walked in. Evelyn glared at him, her face unrecognizable in its rage and anguish; then she snarled, "I will deal with this later," and stormed out.

Tom Lyle sighed, apologized to Tony, and told him it would be best for him to go visit his mother in Las Vegas until things calmed down. Tom Lyle needed to talk to Evelyn and let her know that this didn't change a thing between them or with Bill.

Emery gave Tony some cash, and he set out for the desert on his motorcycle. Although he could not have felt happy at his treatment by Evelyn, or about being paid off to hit the road—even temporarily—he did not argue.

It was dark by the time Tony left L.A. He made it most of the way to Vegas but apparently started nodding off a few miles outside town. The police said he ran head-on into a truck and was killed instantly.

With the exception of Evelyn, the family was devastated. Tom Lyle and Emery blamed themselves for what had happened, and Bill blamed his mother.

As for Evelyn, in the darkest part of her soul, she felt justified in feeling relief that the son that should never have been born was gone and that her own son would now be the sole heir to Preston's legacy.

There was a small funeral, at which Bill and Pauline met Tony's mother—a sweet, quiet, humble woman, the complete opposite of Bill's flamboyant, outspoken, drama-queen parent.

Tony's coffin, covered with gardenias, was quietly placed in an unmarked grave in Santa Monica.

Pauline, who had herself come so close to being killed in a head-on accident, took Tony's death the hardest. She felt eerily connected to his spirit and felt his presence when she smelled the white gardenias covering his coffin, flowers just like the white gardenias she had worn in her hair the day she herself almost died.

For weeks after the funeral, she awakened in the night, convinced that she smelled gardenias. Tony's death made her wonder why she had lived and he had not. Haunted by her own memories, she told Bill that Tony's spirit was trying to tell her something. Bill told her she was crazy, and she started getting up at night to take a shot of bourbon so she could sleep—which probably wasn't the best thing for the baby growing in her womb.

When news about the imminent appearance of another Williams child made the family rounds, Elna was delighted, but Evelyn let it be known that she thought Pauline should have an abortion. Evelyn insisted this new child was coming along too soon after Sharrie and that having two children would be too much responsibility for Bill, who didn't yet have a job or own a home.

She was ignored. Bitter about how the whole family conspired against her, she huffed off to join Warren at his mines.

Reenergized by the new life inside her, Pauline suggested to Bill that they get a GI loan and buy a home of their own. On October 10, 1948, they purchased a prefabricated bungalow in the suburbs of Culver City, a few blocks from the MGM studios. Tom Lyle gave them the money for the down payment, and Bill promised to pay the fifty-dollars-a-month mortgage.

Andy brought French molding and leftover tropical wallpaper from the studio and helped Bill customize the house with Bill's original architectural designs. Bill and a buddy hung the wallpaper, and Elna made beautiful drapes from a matching tropical fabric. Tom Lyle gave them the bamboo sofa and chair that had been in his sunroom, and Andy re-covered the furniture with the same tropical fabric, creating a darling little nest that welcomed the young family to their home—just as Tom Lyle was losing his.

Tom Lyle and Emery spent an afternoon taking a last walk around the Villa's empty rooms, listening to the comforting creaks of the beautiful oak floors that would have easily lasted for years alongside the elegant tiles. Sunlight filtered through the bougainvilleas at the windows. The studio where the advertising magic happened—would Tom Lyle's muse know how to find them if they were no longer here? They strolled the grounds they had stopped tending, paused at the brown gardenias that still gave off a faint scent. The saddest sight was the semi-drained pool that had seen so many exclusive parties.

Tears slipped down his cheeks as Tom Lyle watched the last sunset from the verandah where he had enjoyed intimate dinners with Alice Faye. The loss of Villa Valentino tore at his heart as powerfully as if a loved one had died. And one had, of course; Tony, that sweet young man.

All his money could never heal the grief of that moment. It seemed that his life was disappearing as the new generation set up camp.

In January 1949, shortly before Bill's new baby was due, engraved wedding invitations arrived for the extended Williams clan. Noel and Frances's son, Noel Allen, was getting married the following month, in a full mass in one of Chicago's oldest cathedrals. Bill's favorite cousin was marrying Jean Kilroy, the daughter of a tavern owner from the wrong side of the tracks. Auntie Frances was not happy about it, not at all. She told the family they needn't bother to make an appearance.

Pregnant Pauline couldn't have gone to Chicago even if they had had the money, and Tom Lyle avoided huge, semi-public gatherings whenever possible, so he would not attend. Still, Pauline felt sorry for the bride; she knew exactly how it felt to be boycotted by a mother-in-law who would never consider any girl good enough for her golden boy.

Still, family was family. The California branch of the Williams family would respect Frances's feelings and stay away.

The wedding of Noel's boy and the Kilroys' only daughter was a grand affair that cost a fortune, but the absence of the Williams clan hurt the bride and groom deeply. When the young couple headed to Florida for a honeymoon, Allen promised to shield his wife from his mother's snobbery, even if it meant leaving Chicago.

But a few days later, Frances called him, hysterical, insisting that he and Jean return home immediately. Noel was in intensive care, fighting for his life after suffering a serious heart attack.

The newlyweds rushed back to Chicago. Tom Lyle caught a plane as well and waited, with Mabel, Eva, Tom Jr., and the rest of the family, praying.

What would Tom Lyle do if his brother didn't make it? Noel had been with him from the beginning. In fact, there would have been no Maybelline without

Noel's steady guidance, confidence, competence, and unfailing good cheer—not to mention his original five-hundred-dollar investment.

Tom Lyle felt he could not face a future without Noel in it.

Part 4

Fantasy vs. Reality
(1950–1969)

Forty-Three
Rio and Reds

Fortunately, the time had not yet come for Tom Lyle to face that future; Noel woke from his coma and began a slow recovery. He wouldn't be able to return to work for several months, however, so Tom Lyle invited him and Frances to Los Angeles.

"Yes, yes," Noel said, "as soon as we tie up this deal with Brazil, I promise we'll catch a plane and get out there."

The deal with Brazil was the result of Tom Lyle's first trip outside the United States. The previous spring, he and Emery had traveled to Rio de Janeiro to investigate exporting Maybelline cosmetics to South America. Maybelline had been in Canada and Europe since the 1930s, but the demand for affordable eye makeup had been expanding at an incredible rate in Brazil, where during the war the United States had established military bases to support Allied actions against forces in North Africa. Once the war ended, the demand for Maybelline continued, and Tom Lyle wanted to take advantage of that.

Still, family was a priority. "Noel, let Tom Jr. take over that project from here—the negotiations are over; all that has to be done is the paperwork."

That was no comfort to his brother, who knew that even as he grew weaker, Tom Jr. was turning into a young lion. The boy—well, he was now thirty-six—not only had a business degree from Duke, he had already put in thirteen years at the company.

Noel insisted on seeing the deal through to its conclusion before taking a vacation, and Tom Lyle reluctantly agreed.

While Tom Lyle was enthusiastic about the Brazil arrangements, he was a bit less sanguine about his son's more ambitious dream of opening Maybelline offices all around the world. Tom Lyle had turned fifty-three and wanted to relax a bit and enjoy the fruits of his thirty-five-year career, rather than deal with foreign countries and their business politics.

But Rags Ragland sided with Tom Jr. He pointed out that he, Rags Ragland—not Noel or even Tom Lyle—would be the one dealing with the international trade. He was already well connected with the decision makers in cosmetics markets around the world, so why not take the next step? It would expand Maybelline's business, as well as prepare the company for the big launch of television advertising that was about to begin.

But Tom Lyle held his ground. "I realize Brazil has become the United States' most important trading partner and foreign investor, but to go as far as opening international offices is out of the question. We can ship from here."

"TL," Rags said, "you know I always defer to you with the utmost respect— but Tom Jr. is right: distribution will eat us out of house and home if we have to ship all over the world from Chicago."

That must have resonated a bit; after all, Tom Lyle's first independent business venture had failed down in Florida thanks to shipping costs.

Evelyn also put in her two cents' worth. Although there had been some distance between her and Tom Lyle since the incident with Tony, the bond between them remained strong. They sometimes spent a pleasant evening together, discussing their children and anything else on their minds. Tom Lyle mentioned his doubts about his son's desire to establish international offices. Evelyn talked about how Bill had decided to give up the college courses he had been taking in architecture and interior design and instead find a way to support his family following the birth of his second daughter, Donna. "He and Pauline are going to start their own dry cleaning business," Evelyn said.

"That's terrific!" said Tom Lyle. "But Bill's only twenty-five. Can he and Pauline juggle two babies, a new business, and their first home all at the same time?"

Evelyn smiled. She had her own doubts, but she had to give him a sly little nudge. "Why, TL, what are you saying? Think what you were doing at age twenty-five."

He chuckled. "True. I must be getting old. Or tired."

"Nonsense. Fifty-three is the prime of life."

"Almost fifty-four."

"That's nothing." She looked Tom Lyle straight in the eye. "TL, you're at the top of the heap. Thanks to your ads, there's a worldwide market for women who want to beautify themselves according to the American ideal. The Maybelline ideal. But it's only just starting. You have to move quickly to capitalize on America's new clout as a world economic power."

He simultaneously smiled and shook his head. "Why is it you're always able to convince me of anything?"

"Because I'm always right."

They clinked glasses in a toast, but then a shadow passed over his face. "There is one problem with all this."

"What's that?"

"Maybelline is already the major producer of women's eye cosmetics in the world. Everyone is watching us, and everyone wants a piece of us—including our own government. They're rumbling about breaking up monopolies."

To this Evelyn had no quick response. No wonder Tom Lyle was so reluctant to launch into international expansion and make Maybelline all the more dominant in the marketplace. The company was a family-owned business. If the government decided it was also a monopoly, they could break it into pieces.

And that would be the end of everything Tom Lyle had worked for.

The year 1950 marked a sharp rise in the American economy. As GIs returned from the war, went to college, and began settling into prefab homes in the suburbs, the nation returned to being a consumer society built on credit and boom times. The public was bombarded with advertisements, not only on billboards and in magazines but now on television as well. The mass production of black-and-white TV sets had brought commerce directly into the privacy of the living room, creating the perceived need for families to acquire everything possible to participate in the American Dream.

But under the surface of this materialistic utopia lurked a growing fear of anything that might threaten it—particularly an enemy called communism. In the year 1950, McCarthyism took hold of society, and the communist witch hunts began. In fact, anything deemed anti-American was suspect. Homosexuality fell into this blurry category, particularly if the gay person was in a position of influence.

Tom Lyle dealt with the stress the way he always did: by continuing to make Maybelline grow.

That year, the company turned its biggest profit ever—almost two million dollars. That summer, Noel kept his promise, flying with Frances to California to have a look at Tom Lyle's new estate. When he saw it, he was stunned. The over-all design ethic was Chinese Modern, the opposite of Villa Valentino's romantic Mediterranean flavor. Tom Lyle looked like a wizard on vacation as he stood at the double doors of his glass-and-metal home in his elegant yet casual California attire, his brown eyes twinkling.

Inside, slate floors covered the entryway and extended down a long hallway flanked by bedrooms filled with multicultural art and beautiful modern furniture. At the end of the hall was the studio where Tom Lyle, Emery, and Arnold still produced the magazine ads that reached all around the world.

Out back, the entire city of Los Angeles, from downtown to the Pacific Ocean, spread out for the onlooker's enjoyment.

Noel smiled, took off his suit and tie, and donned a short-sleeved shirt.

After two weeks of visiting the sights from Santa Barbara to San Juan Capistrano, Noel understood why his son Allen—who had been stationed in San Diego during the war—wanted to move back to this area. Still, he and Frances didn't want him to leave Chicago, so they asked Tom Lyle what he thought about having Allen join the company. They pointed out that Allen had a business degree from Loyola and already lived in one of apartments in the Maybelline building's basement. On top of that, he was a born salesman, dripping with charisma—he would be perfect company representative to send overseas as Maybelline expanded.

Tom Lyle thought this was a great idea, although he suggested that before hiring Allen into the company, they first let Tom Jr. and Rags create an official position for him.

Like Tom Lyle's house, the next Maybelline ad campaign had an Asian feel to it. The new face for the 1950s was not that of the movie star, pinup girl, or idealized girl next door, but a woman with vaguely Asian features, an expression of worldly confidence, and icy-cold beauty. This was the image that Maybelline would broadcast around the world through television commercials. The ad was even shot in black and white rather than the glossy color Maybelline had become famous for; in its dramatic austerity, it seemed to say, "I have it all. I don't need anything else. I am Beauty."

Emery also created a slogan that replaced Rags Ragland's long-running "Sensibly Priced" (which Emery had already edited to "Quality, yet Sensibly Priced" some years before). The new catchphrase was "Maybelline, Preferred by Really Smart Women the World Over." The rest of the ad stated: *Achieve the New EXOTIC Eye Makeup with MAYBELLINE*—"exotic" being the key word, appearing in a typeface meant to evoke what was known in those days as the Orient.

As usual, Maybelline was ahead of the cultural curve, if not helping to define it. It was the first cosmetics company to advertise via the new medium of television, and sales immediately broke every record in the industry. At age fifty-four, Tom Lyle had altered everything about his life: letting go of the Villa and the past it represented, striking out into international expansion, and embracing a future where the sky was the limit.

Then he received a phone call from Chicago; it was five o'clock in the morning and he had been about to turn in for the day. The moment he heard Noel's voice, he knew the news was bad.

"We've been contacted by the government. They plan to investigate the Maybelline Company as a monopoly."

Forty-Four

Cover-Up

A new anti-monopoly law had gone into effect that year, and privately owned companies were at particular risk of being investigated. Because Maybelline controlled the lion's share of the eye cosmetics business both nationally and internationally, it was an obvious target for such an inquiry. Tom Lyle also had personal reasons to fear attracting the government's spotlight: The House Commission on Un-American Activities was taking full advantage of its power to make and break lives, and Tom Lyle's personal lifestyle, not to mention his list of acquaintances, would give "Tail-Gunner Joe" McCarthy plenty to aim at.

Noel's policy had been to keep most of his dealings with the government secret from Tom Lyle, for fear his brother would become so unsettled that he would sell the company. In fact, Rags and Tom Lyle had already taken several trips to New York City to talk to potential buyers, but when offers were made, Rags always nipped them in the bud: "TL, the sky's the limit here." Not that Rags had to worry about finding a job if Maybelline were sold; he was still being courted by every other cosmetics company out there.

So it was Noel who took the brunt of the stress every day. He began staying all night at the other company apartment so that he could work around the clock composing letters, gathering records, and putting together a case to prove that Maybelline was engaged in no unfair business practices. One route of attack he had to defend against was the claim that Maybelline produced inferior products at such low prices that emerging eye cosmetics firms had no chance to get off the ground. Noel was able to show that Maybelline's success was based not only on the reasonable price of its products but also their quality—and the company had the Good Housekeeping Seal of Approval to prove it. And yes, Maybelline products were sometimes used as loss leaders by dime stores to bring in customers who wound up spending much more on other products—but Maybelline stood on its own quality, never paying commissions for salesgirls to promote its products, thanks to Rags Ragland's insightful relationships with the ever-expanding drugstore companies.

Another complaint was that Maybelline might become a complacent giant or simply buy up any little company that tried to step on its toes. Together, Noel and Rags were able to prove this allegation false as well. In fact, they shot down every allegation except one: the fact that a single family owned and controlled almost all of the eye-beautifier market.

Finally, after months of sleepless nights, stressful days, and constant begging from his wife to "let go and retire before you have another heart attack," Noel called Tom Lyle and said, "You've got to step in and do something about this immediately."

Tom Lyle considered his options. It was true that Maybelline was the largest privately owned cosmetics company in the world. The only non-family member in an executive position was Rags Ragland, who comprised the marketing department.

So Tom Lyle's response to the governmental threat was to restructure the business. He drew up papers naming Mabel's husband, Chet Hewes, sole owner of a new and separate company, Deluxe Mascara, which would be responsible for the production and distribution of that single, crucial product. Although Maybelline would purchase all its mascara from Deluxe, that was beside the point from a legal point of view. Since Chet was a member of the family, this simple move prevented the Maybelline Company from being dismantled without weakening it.

From that point on, Chet ran mascara production as a separate business, although under the table, all profits were combined in the family pot.

With the monopoly nightmare behind him, Tom Lyle bought his first thirty-second TV time slot on CBS, to be aired during a new show called *I Love Lucy*. Even he was amazed at how popular the program would become. He reinvested the resulting profits in advertising time on CBS and NBC, focusing on prime-time shows, such as *Texaco Star Theater, The Philco Television Playhouse, Arthur Godfrey's Talent Scouts,* and Ed Sullivan's *Toast of the Town*.

But none topped the success of *I Love Lucy*. Its star, Lucille Ball, became the image of the American housewife who wanted more glamour and excitement in her life. With her long false eyelashes and heavy eye shadow, Lucy sold more Maybelline than any film actress ever had. Television was the greatest advertising tool ever invented, and, thanks to it, in the 1950s Maybelline's popularity continued to soar.

Tom Lyle was eyeing the new but still-expensive color television as a future advertising tool when, on November 1, 1951, he received another unexpected phone call from Chicago.

"Dad, it's Tom. Noel had a massive heart attack. He didn't survive. He's gone."

Tom Lyle fell into a deep depression. Noel was dead, whisked away from his adoring wife, children, and grandchildren. And why? Tom Lyle saw only one answer: because he, the younger brother, had bowed to demands that he expand the company internationally. It had been too much. He shouldn't have done it. He had known Noel would never stay away from his desk despite the risk to his heart. And he had been right.

Tom Lyle had now lost three brothers: Pearl at age eighteen, Preston at thirty-seven, and now Noel, the cornerstone of the family, the rock, the pillar of strength, at only sixty.

Sixty. Not so many years older than Tom Lyle himself.

Sitting there in his Bel Air estate, Tom Lyle gazed out over his adopted city, and for the first time did not see a future among the glittering lights.

Once again, it was Evelyn who stepped in. As soon as she heard the news about Noel, she drove to Tom Lyle's house, bearing his favorite foods: home-made German pepper steak, sweet and sour cabbage, and pineapple upside-down cake. Although Tom Lyle didn't eat much of the meal, he appreciated her thoughtfulness and her mere presence. They reminisced about Noel.

"I'll never get over it," Tom Lyle said. "And how am I going to face Frances? She begged me for two years to do something about his workload."

"What could you do? Noel's life was the company. You know that."

Tom Lyle nodded. "There would be no Maybelline without him. He was Maybelline."

"No, TL. You're Maybelline, and you have to keep the company going, if only for Noel's memory. That's how he'd want it."

Tom Lyle looked at her. "This whole family would perish without Maybelline, wouldn't it?"

She had never thought about it that way—and she didn't want to think about it now. "That's not what I meant. Don't say that."

"No, you don't understand. You're right—Maybelline has to go on. So I'm going to make a change. I'm going to incorporate the company and seal the family in as stockholders in honor of my brother and everything we've built together. No more covering things up; it's all about blood now."

Evelyn squeezed his hands. "It always was, darling; it always was."

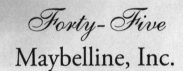

Forty-Five
Maybelline, Inc.

As Tom Lyle had feared, Frances was bitter at the prospect of facing the future without her husband of thirty-five years, but rather than focusing her grief and anger on Tom Lyle or even Maybelline, she chose a different target. "Allen, sweetheart," she said to her son, "you know Jean only married you for your money. Look at her family. Her parents are tavern owners, for God's sake, and old man Kilroy is a bookie. Evelyn used to book with him twenty years ago."

"Mother, I don't want to hear this anymore," Allen snapped. "If you don't stop this, you'll have no son at all, because I'll pack up my family and move to California."

"You can't do that. Tom Lyle wants you to work for the company here, in Chicago."

Allen hesitated. "I'm considering turning him down."

"What?"

"Nobody else in the family has been invited to join the executive ranks. Not even Bill. I don't want to cause jealousy. Plus if I accept the job, I'll be stuck here in Chicago for the rest of my career. I'm not sure I want that."

Frances moved straight from anger to tears. "But you have to take the job, sweetheart. Blood is everything. Your father believed that with all his heart."

"Yes, Mother," Allen said, "and it killed him."

That summer, Allen visited Tom Lyle in Los Angeles and enjoyed tanning a golden brown while he lay by the pool, contemplating the city skyline and once again considering the generous offer his uncle had made him. Caught between his love for California's laidback lifestyle and his mother's despair, he didn't know what to do. Even convincing Jean to leave Chicago would be difficult—she had no friends or family in California. There were no real prospects for work here, apart from being a salesman. On the other hand, a career with Maybelline guaranteed wealth, success, and a solid future.

Aware of his nephew's dilemma, Tom Lyle left him alone to work things out.

Allen drove to Culver City to visit Bill and Pauline at their home and, after one look at the place, decided that dry cleaning must be the business to be in. Then he found out that Bill spent all this spare time working on his little home, applying Uncle Noel's credo that "It's one thing to have a nice house, but it's the landscaping that makes all the difference." For the front and back, he had designed old brick planters, strategically filled with beautiful tropical foliage and palms, to create an effect reminiscent of Villa Valentino. Together, he and Pauline had planted and maintained a lawn of *Home and Garden* perfection.

Not that the inside had been neglected. To Allen, it resembled a movie set, with its art deco furniture, red rugs, and sterling silver lamps that Tom Lyle had given them from the Villa. Bill pointed out the decorative moldings on the ceiling and walls, the exotic tropical-print drapes hanging across the walls and the windows, and Bill's most prized possession, a cherry-wood cabinet from MGM's prop department, modernized with a built-in radio and record player.

Allen had grown up surrounded by beauty and wealth, Chicago style—but this was life lived on a scale he had never imagined possible, one based on only a little money and a lot of good ideas. Even more impressive was the fact that Bill was thriving on a personal level. He loved running Hill Top Cleaners. He loved being his own man.

Back in Bel Air, Allen told Tom Lyle that he had made up his mind: with thanks and regrets, he was turning down the offer to become part of Maybelline. Instead, he intended to work for Standard Oil in Chicago for a couple of years, then transfer to California with his family. He told Tom Lyle that he didn't believe it would be fair for him to take a position with Maybelline when Bill had never had the same opportunity.

Tom Lyle looked at him through the smoke of a cigarette. "Bill didn't go to college or show any interest in the business—but I understand."

Allen didn't know if Tom Lyle really understood or not.

He also didn't know how deeply his decision would affect any family members who, in the future, might want to join the Maybelline Company.

Other futures were also changing. That same year, my grandmother taught me to fall in love with my own reflection.

I was five, and our family had gathered at Unk Ile's new home in Bel Air for what was meant to be an ordinary get-together. The living room was spacious, with a high ceiling and recessed lighting. The wall-to-wall carpeting and walls themselves were cream-colored. The fireplace was set between two rooms, and when it was lit, its glow extended into both the dining room and the living room, which was graced by a grand piano and adorned with a dozen roses in a cut crystal vase and pictures of beautiful movie stars.

Everyone sat in the living room while Tom Lyle talked about makeup. He told us that Maybelline was going to do a before-and-after demonstration live on TV—another industry first.

I didn't know or care what that meant; for me it was enough to be sitting there drinking a Coke and feeling like part of the adult conversation. Then I saw my grandmother looking at me. She gave an eyebrow a mischievous lift. "You, dear, come with me. Your Nana has an idea."

My baby sister, Donna, followed us as Nana took me by the arm and led me into the master bathroom, where she flicked a switch with her exotic red nails. A long row of Hollywood bulbs lit up, illuminating the wall-to-wall mirrors in a space the size of our living room at home. Unk Ile's bathroom was the most lavish thing I had ever seen. Ivory and beige marble tiled the floors and several walls. My eyes popped at the life-sized alabaster statue of a nude man standing in the center of a step-down spa.

"Now then, darling," my grandmother said, perching me atop the marble vanity and shaking a bejeweled finger at me, "you be good for your Nana so we can show Unk Ile just how pretty you are."

I nodded. My grandmother intimidated and bewildered me. Even at age fifty-one, she was what my uncle called a bombshell. She pranced around in her strawberry blonde hair and turquoise eye shadow. She never wore her signature kimonos at Tom Lyle's and had opted instead for a stylish silk blouse, linen skirt, and high heels—still demanding to be the center of attention and still succeeding.

In awe, I waited while she carefully arranged bottles and tubes around the sink, as if preparing her palette. My sister kept trying to lick the lipsticks.

Nana shooed her away. "Donna, darling, no. These are not candy." She turned to me. "Now, look at what Nana has to show you."

She reached into her pocketbook and removed a small red box with long cursive letters scrawled across the top. I couldn't read cursive, of course, but I did recognize the first letter from one I had seen on my daddy's papers at home. It was an M. Nana held the box before me as if bestowing a gift. "This little box, Sharrie, is your future."

When she opened the box, I wondered what all the fuss was about. My future, as far as I could tell, was a tiny brush and a smudge of black goop.

She must have seen the disappointment on my face. She cocked an eyebrow. "Just wait and see."

She called the black goop *Maybelline mascara* and told me it was my uncle's creation, "Named after your Auntie Mabel"—she peered intently into my eyes—"and me." With the little brush, she stroked a thick coating of black onto the top lashes of my left eyelid—and then onto the tiny lower lashes.

That, I couldn't stand. I squinted and pulled away, causing her to smear mascara across my cheek. "Ouch, it hurts!"

She jerked me back into place by the ruffles of my bathing suit skirt. "Sit still, darling, don't blink." She looked me straight in the eye. "If you remember anything, Sharrie, remember this: It hurts to be beautiful. But it's worth it."

She sounded so serious, even Donna paid attention.

For what seemed to me like an eternity, Nana painstakingly painted every lash on my eyes. Then she rubbed blue eye shadow—a shade matching her own—across my upper eyelids. She dipped a cotton ball into a powder of creamy white and dusted it lightly across my face, tickling my nose. A little color on the cheeks, a dab of orange on the lips, and she stood back to examine her work.

"Now blot," she told me, rubbing her own lips together to show me how. "Yes. Well, go ahead, Missy. Look."

When I turned to the mirror, I gasped. There I glimpsed my future, a version of who I might become.

"Nanaaa!" Donna tugged at my grandmother's silk sleeve. "Make me pretty, tooooo!"

I kept staring at my reflection, gazing from different angles. The outer transformation was amazing, but I felt different inside, too—so grown up, like one of the movie stars in the photos I had seen in Unk Ile's office.

We made our way back into the living room, Nana beaming behind me, letting me walk in first—the only time I can remember her letting anyone walk ahead of her. My parents and Unk Ile waited, unaware, clinking the ice in their Manhattans, talking and laughing, playing the piano. But as I made my entrance across the ornate Oriental rug, they looked up one by one; my parents, Emery, Unk Ile—and for once, they were all staring at me. For the first time in my life, I felt important.

"Well, well, what's this?" My father feigned bemusement.

My mother rolled her eyes. "Here we go again."

Unk Ile rose from his position at the piano and walked over to me. A giant to me, standing so straight and tall, with his perfectly tailored gray slacks and short-sleeved gray-and-white-striped shirt, his Italian loafers, his pencil mustache. "My, my," he murmured in his gentle, resonant voice, kneeling in front of me and peering from behind his specs. "There's nothing more beautiful than Maybelline on virgin eyelashes, is there?" He took hold of both my arms and leaned in to whisper in my ear. "When you grow up, Sharrie, you are going to be a beautiful woman. I can tell."

This was the most profound moment in my short life. From then on, I lived to get that same recognition, approval, and overwhelming attention from him again. If being beautiful was the most important thing in the world to people as magical as Unk Ile and Nana, well, being beautiful was what I wanted more than anything else in the world.

After years of waiting, Warren finally divorced his wife and was free to marry Evelyn.

It was a very simple ceremony. Following "I do," the next words Evelyn spoke as Mrs. Warren Deuel were, "I have to call Tom Lyle."

As she left the chambers of the Reno justice of the peace, she finally felt complete satisfaction. What she did not feel was guilt for stealing her husband from another woman. Warren's "in name only" first wife hadn't been the one to nurse him through his alcoholic binges and DTs, had she? No, Evelyn had. A lesser woman would have given up the job years ago, but Evelyn had seen his potential. And she had been right. Warren had finally raised enough money with his partners to own their own oil wells at Edison Field, which in 1951 produced 1,400,000 barrels of oil. Evelyn knew she and her new husband would be rich beyond their dreams, if she could just keep him sober.

The honeymooners rented a cottage in Kern County, where Evelyn was happier than she had ever been before—no longer concerned about the past or with her son's middle-class little life in Culver City. Every day, she woke singing with the sunrise and was dressed, made up, and serving Warren his coffee by six. By seven they were on the road, checking their wells in Bakersfield or driving out to mineral excavations in Nevada.

The 1950s were sure to bring Evelyn the prosperity and success she had dreamed of all her life. Best of all, she finally had a man she loved securely by her side.

In early 1952, Evelyn and Warren pulled into Bill and Pauline's driveway, honking the horn of their new black Cadillac convertible. They bore armfuls of gifts for the girls: dolls that could walk, cowgirl outfits with holsters and guns, bags of hard candy, and a box of oddly shaped rocks collected from all over Nevada.

"Tungsten, darling, it's called tungsten," Evelyn said, spreading the rocks across Pauline's dinner table.

"What's it used for, Mud?" Bill asked. To him the rocks didn't look like much.

"Everything, darling. Light bulb filaments, x-ray tubes, rocket engine nozzles—anything that has to withstand high temperatures."

"Which is why Adlai Stephenson had better win the upcoming election," Warren said from the kitchen, amid the sounds of glasses clinking. "Speaking of which, aren't the debates on TV?"

"Pointless to watch them," Evelyn said. "Eisenhower is just going to bluster about how if he's elected, he'll turn the war over to the South Koreans."

Bill raised his eyebrows. "What does any of this have to do with tungsten?"

"Everything." Warren returned to the living room with a tray of drinks and ice. "If Eisenhower wins, he'll end the Korean War—and that would be a disaster."

"A disaster?" Pauline said.

"For us, yes," said Evelyn. She added plenty of water and ice to Warren's drink.

"But, Mother, the country's tired of war," Bill said. "To me, General Eisenhower is a hero."

Warren tipped back his glass. "If the war ends, so will America's prosperity."

"Are you kidding?" Bill said. "The Democrats have been in office for twenty years, and look what they gave us: depression, war, and shortages. It's time to give the Republicans a chance."

"Honey," Evelyn said, "if Stephenson is elected, we'll be so rich you won't ever have to worry about money again. Why, we'll buy Donna a horse and Sharrie a big house with a swimming pool in the backyard. Would you like that, girls?"

"We want Stephenson!" my sister and I shouted, jumping up and down. "We want Stephenson!"

Pauline shook her head and went into the kitchen to make dinner. Maybe she could finish before everyone got too drunk to eat. "I still don't understand why ending the war in Korea would be a bad thing," she said.

"Because most of the tungsten deposits in the world are in China and Korea," Warren said. "But America has become the number-one consumer of petroleum and mineral products in the world."

"Just as Warren predicted," Evelyn said.

"And that puts us at risk if we can't find domestic sources for some of these resources. We certainly can't depend on communist countries for them. Truman put together the Paley Commission so that companies like ours can get funds to search for oil and mineral deposits right here in our own country. But if the war ends, *pffft*, tungsten is in surplus again, prices fall, the government stops paying for domestic exploration—and we lose everything." He raised his glass. "So . . . here's to Adlai Stephenson for president!"

In June of the following year, Nana and Warren appeared again, this time for my sixth birthday. Again they came bearing gifts, and while I opened them, Nana spent the time talking about the Korean War, which was at a stalemate.

"Well, we were right," she said. "Now that Eisenhower is president, the government is planning to send all the tungsten contracts to South Korea as soon as the war is over. Soon we'll have nothing left but our oil wells."

She pulled the hair out of my eyes and placed the cowgirl hat she had just given me on my head, gave it a critical look and adjusted its angle. I sat through this silently. Nana would never let me change anything once she got it the way she wanted it, even if the garment was supposedly mine and even if I felt uncomfortable in it. *Beauty hurts, dear.*

After the singing of "Happy Birthday," my mom bathed my sister Donna and me and prepared us for bed. Donna and I kissed everyone goodnight and tried to warm up to the plastic "Walkie Talkie" dolls Nana and Warren had brought us from Las Vegas.

I fell asleep sucking on a hard candy from Nana. Despite her gloomy predictions about mines and minerals, she whispered me to sleep with candy-coated promises for the future. "If things don't work out as planned, darling, there will always be Maybelline."

As the end of 1953 approached, Maybelline's print ads appeared in international magazines all over the world, with models presenting an air of fashion, intelligence, and sophistication. Gone was the all-American girl next door look. Instead, models wore strapless gowns, elegant pearl and diamond earrings, gloves, and lots of mascara; they had mysterious, half-smiling, inscrutable expressions. On television, Maybelline before-and-after demonstrations ranged from thirty seconds to a full minute in length, reaching an ever-expanding and increasingly diverse audience. America was growing up and so were American girls.

At age fifty-two, Evelyn still carried the torch for her generation. Although she loved her granddaughters, she preferred the company of men. While the homemaker types with their aprons and children had their place, Evelyn would rather be seen in a pair of slacks, a starched shirt with cufflinks, a rawhide coat with fringe, and a pair of boots—her current incarnation as hardboiled, yet stylishly smart and worldly. She lived in a man's world, yet was independent, a power to be reckoned with. For her, being a grandmother didn't mean cooking comfort food; it meant being tough and teaching "her girls" how to act like ladies, with their pinky fingers in the air, or how to properly twist a curl in place with one hand while pinning it securely with the other. (From experience, I can tell you that this is an art that takes a six-year-old girl many hours of practice in front of the mirror to master.)

But this could not last forever, and she knew it. Unlike Dorian Gray, Nana could not project the accumulating years elsewhere; she could not remove them from her life. Inexorably, beneath the expertly applied Maybelline and determined attitude, she was aging.

Forty-Six
Searching
for a Niche

*I*n late December, my father got a call from Nana, who sounded more distraught than he had heard her in years. While in her car at a stop sign, she had been hit from behind by a drunk driver going forty miles an hour. She was in the hospital having a neck brace fitted, and begged my father to bring his family to stay with her and Warren in Bakersfield for Christmas.

Almost as an afterthought, she added that all her worst fears about the international tungsten trade and domestic oil and gas exploration had come true: she and Warren were broke.

When we arrived in Bakersfield on Christmas Eve, Warren, already half-soused, escorted us into their house. I found it disorienting to see Nana with her hair in a turban and her neck in a brace, unable to get up from her chair to greet us. All she managed to do was stretch out her arms for half a second before dropping them back in her lap and whispering, "Darlings, come here and kiss your Nana."

But kids have the ability to rise above upsetting situations, and Nana herself had taught me to transcend disappointment and carry on with the show at all costs. So I dressed my little sister and myself in costumes made of towels and prepared to act out the Christmas story for the family.

Before I stepped out "on stage," I noticed Warren in the background, reading the newspaper with a cocktail in his hand. I refused to continue my performance until he paid full attention. I was a first-grader, and this was a very serious performance about the Wise Men and Baby Jesus.

He raised his eyebrows. "How do you think the Wise Men got so wise if they didn't read the headlines?"

Everyone laughed—except me. Nana took the paper away from him and told me to continue. After the performance and my final bow, she yelled "Bravo!" while everyone, including Warren, applauded raucously. I forgave Warren then for the newspaper incident.

From that moment on, Nana would be my stage mother and biggest fan. "Isn't she darling?" she would say. "Doesn't she remind you of me?"

The next call from Evelyn came on New Year's Eve. This time she wasn't just crying, she was hysterical. There had been yet another automobile accident, she said. This time, Warren was the victim. He and a business partner had been hit head-on by a drunk driver—and killed.

My parents immediately departed for Bakersfield again, leaving Donna and me with our maternal grandparents. They tried to explain to us the meaning of dying and going to heaven, but all I knew was that Warren was never coming back, and Nana would be moving in with us.

A pivotal point for us all came in 1954. Nana became our nanny—or rather, I became hers. She cried day and night as I tried to soothe her with half-cooked potatoes and runny chocolate pudding. I did all I could to make her smile, but all she wanted to do was listen to "I'll Never Smile Again," "The Falling Leaves," and Liberace's theme song, "I'll Be Seeing You." When I asked why she was so sad, she told me that I was too young to understand.

But being Nana, she did begin to recover, taking my sister and me on the bus to visit Chinatown, or Olvera Street in downtown Los Angles, or the famous Farmers Market. She told us she felt sorry for us. "It's a pity you don't have a real mother who stays home with you," she said. She said we reminded her of Topsy, a poor little black girl from the book *Uncle Tom's Cabin,* and we "just growed."

That was the first derogatory comment I heard from Nana on how my mother was raising us—but it would be far from the last. It confused me. From my point of view, my mother was the best mom in the whole world. Of course, she was busy a lot at the cleaners and might not have been home baking cakes and letting us lick the frosting off a wooden spoon, but she liked to have us with her at the cleaners, where she simultaneously worked and chatted with us. I remember sitting on a pile of clothes and talking her ear off as she ironed blouses and skirts, wiping her brow and responding to my every question. She told me I was smart and had good ideas, and she expanded my imagination by asking questions that made me think creatively and want to write stories.

But whenever we were with Nana rather than Mommy, Nana kept making cutting remarks about our mother. This hurt my feelings, but I didn't show it. As Nana herself had taught me, feelings were to be hidden, and a smile should be my umbrella.

Another thing I was becoming increasingly aware of was Maybelline. Although I didn't understand what the big deal was about television commercials, I remember hearing how important it was that over half of American households now had TVs, because that meant more women would buy makeup. I remember hearing that Maybelline was no longer a little Chicago-based company as it had been when my dad was my age, but was now an international institution. It seemed that all this was very important.

Frighteningly important.

Although I was just learning to count and spell, I already knew the meaning of the word "kidnap." Nana constantly drilled it into my head: I must never, ever tell strangers about Unk Ile or Maybelline, because if I did, Donna and I might be snatched up by strangers and held in some terrible place in exchange for money. Apparently, this danger lurked everywhere, though Nana had a specific fear as well: creditors were looking for her, seeking compensation for the debts she and Warren had run up while living beyond their means. She taught me to always look out the window before answering a knock at the door and to say "I don't know" if a stranger ever asked me anything about anything.

In retrospect, I understand that at that point in her life, Nana was not only broke, she was almost broken—a remarkable situation for the strongest-willed woman on the planet.

But once again, she bounced back. As time healed her sprained neck and her broken heart, she began dating her lawyer. He would pick her up in a Cadillac and sometimes not bring her back home for a day or two. This put Donna and me back into the care of our grandmother Elna—until the lawyer took off, at which point Evelyn went right back to crying and dumping her disappointments on me. I sat patiently listening to her sobbing that she should have known. After Warren died, she had tried to step in and run his company, but his partners had sent attorneys rushing in from all directions; they had even entered her home in Bakersfield, where they had stolen all the important business papers. She couldn't possibly fight them all and simultaneously operate a business. Lawyers were responsible for wiping her out financially—and now one had wiped out her heart as well.

And they still weren't done with her, she said. Nana believed the attorneys responsible for handling Warren's business holdings were now working behind the scenes with his enemies' attorneys to swindle her out of her rightful property. She even suspected her own attorney of being in cahoots with the others.

Then there was the matter of sex. At the time, I didn't understand this any more than I understood Nana's laments about contracts and debts and mineral rights, but later I came to understand that she believed that she was being taken advantage of sexually as well. And she probably was. It was understandable that a fifty-three-year-old woman who was still extremely attractive might think her sex appeal and power over men remained intact, but as time went on, her old ways of using that power backfired more and more often, leaving her broken-hearted and bereft time and again.

This pattern extended beyond our little house in Culver City. Each time Evelyn cycled through another man, Tom Lyle would let it be known to the family that Evelyn had just visited him. "She could make coffee nervous," he would laugh. But he generally gave her whatever she wanted, including, once, a new Buick.

She claimed she needed a car to look for a job, but instead, with a few bucks of Tom Lyle's money in her purse, she was off to Frederick's of Hollywood. "My neck pain will not allow me to wear straps on my shoulders," was how she explained the new corsets she bought to hold in her stomach and lift her breasts.

Of course, my grandmother wasn't the only person in the United States infatuated with appearances. At the same time, Maybelline had become the number-one sponsor of the Miss America Pageant, an extravaganza of beauty watched by every American female anywhere near a television set. Maybelline's first million-dollar before-and-after commercial hit the air. A full minute in length, it not only described what Maybelline products could do, it demonstrated application techniques in real time.

This was another first for the team of Tom Lyle, Emery, and Arnold, but they didn't stop there. They continued to develop innovative methods of advertising through nearly every form of mass media—movie magazines, fashion magazines, radio, television, even the comics section of newspapers—to top the efforts of all their competitors combined. As Tom Lyle's time became more and more valuable, he increasingly turned responsibility for family phone calls over to Milford, whose soft voice and sweet manner helped lift the burden of family problems (and requests for money) off Tom Lyle's back.

Except when it came to Evelyn. When Evelyn needed something important to her—a check, a few minutes of personal time with Tom Lyle—she somehow found a way to get it.

Still, things had changed between her and Tom Lyle. She could feel it, if not understand it. But to Tom Lyle, the difference was obvious: she was no longer

Evelyn Williams. After marrying Warren, she had become Evelyn Deuel. So, although Tom Lyle still loved her, she was no longer family—and to him, family was everything.

Forty-Seven

Taking Stock

In 1954, when my father approached Unk Ile about getting a loan to help launch a new and improved Hill Top Cleaners with its own dry cleaning machine—which would make it unnecessary to have clothing trucked miles away to a processing plant—Tom Lyle gave my father both the money and a word of encouragement: "Bug, I'm proud as hell of you and Pauline for what you've done with your life. I want you to know that no matter what happens with the cleaners, I'm cooking up a plan that will ensure you and your whole family have a good future."

"What do you mean?"

Tom Lyle smiled. "Just wait until this fall. Then you'll find out."

As the time for the unveiling of Tom Lyle's big surprise drew closer, my uncle Allen called Bill and announced that he, Jean, and their two children were finally leaving Chicago and moving to California. "I don't want to go through another winter here, and I'm sick and tired of my mother giving Jean a hard time," he said.

"I know exactly what you're going through," Bill sighed. "My problem is I can't run away from my mother—she lives with us."

Allen laughed. "You've got my sympathy. You can cry on my shoulder when we get there."

Before long, Allen and Jean had settled into a little house just down the street from Hill Top Cleaners.

The big surprise was unveiled in November, when our families received letters on Maybelline stationery. The notes announced Tom Lyle's "great satisfaction" in giving each family member preferred cumulative stock in the Maybelline Company.

The news sent shockwaves through the family. Not even Bill had expected so much from his uncle's surprise. Although the annual dividend they could all expect to receive was not initially overwhelming, it would almost certainly go up.

My father and Allen agreed: when their stock started paying at the rate of twelve thousand dollars a year, they would both retire.

Tom Lyle had incorporated the Maybelline Company in Delaware on October 21. Apart from the shares he provided to a few important employees who had been with Maybelline, in some cases from the very beginning, the stock would remain privately owned by him and his relatives, guaranteeing a secure future for no fewer than twenty-six families.

This was where Allen's decision not to join the business had unexpected consequences—especially for Rags Ragland. Rags had always been far more than an employee to Tom Lyle; apart from being the sole member of the sales and sales promotion department, he had played so many other roles in the company that Tom Lyle referred to him as "my bandleader" in reference to Rags's early experience as a jazz musician. During Rags's tenure, sales at Maybelline had increased a hundred times over, and he had resisted all efforts from other companies to lure him away. Tom Lyle genuinely considered him family.

And that was the problem. After Allen turned down the offer to work for the company, Tom Lyle took a good look at Maybelline's organizational structure and saw a potential difficulty. Rags had three college-age sons. Although Tom Lyle respected them, he feared that if they entered the company, the balance of power would eventually shift from the Williamses to the Raglands, and that would never do. So Tom Lyle exercised his right as CEO to prevent any future family members—his or anyone else's—from entering the business. Though Rags did ask if his youngest son, Alan, a marketing major, might be invited to join, Alan turned his father down so as to not make his two older brothers jealous.

In the end, there was only one exception to the no-family rule: Mabel and Chet's son Tommy, who had a different last name, would go to work for his father at Deluxe Mascara.

I remember a day in early 1955 when we drove through the wrought-iron gate of Tom Lyle's estate to find parked there cars belonging to all the families. Milford met each of us, taking our coats and purses and ushering us into the living room where the adults were served refreshments. I had never before met Auntie Mabel, Auntie Eva, Auntie Frances, or Uncle Chess and Uncle Chet, but I was excited to see my cousins Chuck and Nancy. Their mother, Allen's wife Jean, kept them as disciplined as soldiers, which was why she didn't particularly care for me coming over to visit—my spontaneously playful ways tended to get Chuck in trouble. She also didn't look too impressed with the collected Maybelline heirs; she just stood there smoking and keeping Nancy and Chuck in line so that their father could mingle.

The hierarchy of adults in the room was obvious, even to me. The men seemed comfortable in their skins and secure in their places. Of the women, Auntie Frances was icy and proper; Mabel warm and sweet; and Eva full of fun—she gravitated to Nana as if they were sisters.

Still, an air of feminine competition filled the room, growing especially strong between Frances, Jean, Evelyn, and my mother. Some clash of the titans there. My mother had become a master at hiding her feelings, so as always, she was cordial to Evelyn—although later, behind Nana's back, my mother would almost certainly get into a fight with my dad about Nana. To me, my mom was the prettiest of all the mothers. She wore an off-the-shoulder peasant blouse, cinched tight with a wide belt around her still remarkably small waistline. A long circle skirt grazed her ankles. Her facial scars had disappeared by now, and, with her carefully applied makeup and sparkling eyes, she was a knockout. My dad seemed just as proud of my mother at age thirty as he had been when they were teenagers.

But of course, Evelyn was determined to steal the show. This was the first time most of these people had seen her since she left Chicago in 1936, and I overheard Jean say to Frances, "My God, isn't she beautiful?"

"You should have seen her when she was young," Frances replied.

Tom Lyle took Nana's hands and remarked that she had gotten more beautiful with the years. "How do you do it, Ev?"

"Oh, you know, darling—a good paint job covers a lot of sins."

He threw his head back and laughed. "Well, my dear, if you live long enough, you may well become the most beautiful woman alive."

Looking around the room, I could tell that there was something special about this Williams family. Although I didn't understand a lot of the dynamic, I was proud to be part of it.

Unlike my parents' parties, Tom Lyle's gatherings didn't last late into the night. Soon he settled into his favorite chair, surrounded by the piles of magazines he usually studied throughout the night, checking on the competition and studying Maybelline's position, style, and impact on readers. The rest of us also settled down, Donna and I sitting on the floor cross-legged, watching our cousins Nancy and Chuck perch properly on their parents' laps.

That night, Unk Ile did not touch the magazines. Instead, he began to speak—and everyone else, including the children, fell silent.

After describing in detail the corporation he had created, he told everybody what they could expect during the years to come. He gave all the adults the name of a financial advisor and recommended that they consult him. "And be sure to keep your certificates in a secure place, like a safe-deposit box."

As he spoke, Emery walked around handing out envelopes containing A- and B-grade stock certificates. Nana watched all this without expression, uncertain of where she fit in. She had not received her own copy of the incorporation announcement—but then, she was no longer a member of the Williams family. She hadn't even been personally invited to this party; she was here as a guest of her son. Still, always the actress, she held her head high, even after Emery's hands were empty—and so were hers.

Then Tom Lyle stood up and walked to her with an envelope. He smiled. "Welcome back, Ev."

Forty-Eight
Jockeying
for Position

After being blessed by Tom Lyle with a secure financial future, my grandmother left our little world again, this time to live with a friend in Long Beach. She said she needed time to think about what she wanted to do now that she was no longer married. Her friend Mrs. Cole was a widow in her seventies, and brilliant when it came to mining and oil rights. She also had valuable contacts who might help Nana regain some of Warren's contract rights.

We didn't see my grandmother for months after that, but, when she finally did call, she told us she was putting together a plan that would make good on her promises about ponies and swimming pools. "My word is my bond," she said. "And Nana never gives up."

Given that, I expected my pool to be built by summer. When it wasn't, Plan B consisted of going swimming with Sparkie, Unk Ile's cocker spaniel, in Unk Ile's pool. This was always exciting, because Unk promised five dollars to anyone who could stand up on the pool float. After many tries and much laughter, the only winner was Sparkie, comfortably balanced on his four feet as he floated around us.

At the end of such a day, Milford would escort Donna and me into the kitchen for ice cream and Cokes while he prepared Unk Ile's dinner. This usually consisted of a hamburger doused in Tabasco sauce, with Campbell's tomato soup on the side and a dish of ice cream for dessert—not something to be served to guests, but it was all Unk Ile wanted to eat lately. He had a chronic overabundance of iron in his blood, which among other things had destroyed his taste buds and stolen away the pleasure of food.

On one of these pool dates, Tom Lyle mentioned to my parents that Rags Ragland had gotten yet another offer to leave the Maybelline Company. Although Rags had shown no sign that he intended to go, Tom Lyle was concerned. He owed a lot to Rags. Therefore, he had decided to not only raise Rags's commission to 1.5 percent, but also give him 3 percent of Maybelline's stock and make him the official executive vice president in charge of sales. This positioned him as an equal with Tom Lyle and Tom Lyle Jr.—in other words, it essentially made him family.

Now, with Rags securely placed as a jewel in Maybelline's crown, Tom Lyle was ready to make his next marketing move. Although he continued to target both the sophisticated, intelligent woman in her thirties and the more mature woman, a new brand of female was beginning to emerge in America. This girl differed from both the World War II pinup girl and Rosie the Riveter. Thanks to movies like *East of Eden,* starring James Dean, and *Blackboard Jungle,* featuring the song "Rock around the Clock" by Bill Haley and the Comets, the rebel had become the latest cultural icon. Maybelline sales soared as heavy makeup appeared in every teenage girl's purse. The era of teen marketing was fully born that year in Jacksonville, Florida, when young girls jumped out of their seats to dance at an Elvis Presley concert—the first musical riot on record.

Along with "Rock around the Clock" and "I Hear You Knocking," another song skyrocketed to number one on the charts that year—"Maybellene," by Chuck Berry. Berry had asked Tom Lyle for permission to use the name Maybelline, with a slight spelling change, in the song. Before Unk Ile could even take a breath, Emery, who was involved with the Pasadena Playhouse and kept on the cutting edge of youth culture, said yes. Tom Lyle knew better than to disagree.

Even my father, who still believed that Frank Sinatra was the last word in music, admitted that he liked "Maybellene;" he said it made him move. He was sure the song would prove to be a brilliant advertising tool for reaching a new youth market through the power of music.

He was right.

My sister Billee Rae Williams—so named because she was supposed to be a boy—was born on the last day of November 1955 and named after both my father and my mother's uncle Ray. My parents immediately started looking for a bigger home in a more prestigious neighborhood. Nana returned briefly to help out but soon grew tired of sharing a room with a baby who cried all night, so she resumed her excursions with Mrs. Cole to the oil fields and mines.

On one of these trips, my grandmother met up with another respected geologist, a friend of Warren's named John Olsen. When John came to visit us, he brought rocks that glowed in the dark and a box of minerals that were all labeled and described in detail. I liked John, who wore plaid shirts and jeans, smoked cigarettes, and talked in a soft, low-key drawl. When we asked Nana if she was going to marry him, she insisted that as much as she loved his brilliant mind, she would never marry an "old hayseed." She preferred the bad boys of her era—God forbid she might hook up with a kind, old-fashioned grandfatherly type.

In April 1956, perhaps the greatest single marketing opportunity in Maybelline's history presented itself: Grace Kelly—already a familiar Maybelline face—and Prince Rainier III of Monaco were getting married in what was being hailed as the wedding of the year. The movie star and the prince had captured the imaginations of people around the world, and for the first time in history, the royal nuptials would be broadcast on live television, with over thirty million viewers expected to tune in.

Of course, Tom Lyle wanted Maybelline to sponsor the most romantic event ever publicly seen—in fact, he wanted Maybelline to be the exclusive sponsor. But many other companies sought the same prize. So when Maybelline won the contract against fierce competition, Tom Lyle basked in the excitement, glamour, and glory of every event leading up to the ceremony.

Once again he had judged wisely. The proof came even before the great event, when Rags Ragland called and said it was finally time to hire an assistant to help handle Maybelline's marketing responsibilities.

That summer, my parents got a letter from Maybelline announcing that all stockholders' percentages were going up to one percent—which meant, of course, that the amount on the dividend checks would also be increasing.

Prosperity was is the air, and my mother felt its impact as much as anyone else. Still looking to find the perfect new home for her family, she finally located a beautiful ranch house in a little pocket community called Blair Hills on the outskirts of Culver City. Not even the upgraded Maybelline stock income could place a twenty-eight-thousand-dollar house within my parents' price range, but nothing was going to stop my mother from nesting in an upscale neighborhood.

My parents could have asked Tom Lyle for the extra money, but they chose not to; they wanted him to see how well they were doing on their own. Instead, my dad made a deal with the builder: if he would cut his price for the house by five thousand dollars, my father would do all the painting, staining, and finish work himself, as well as help finish other houses in the neighborhood.

Of course, with a bigger and more beautiful home came a bigger and more expensive lifestyle. From various departments at MGM, my grandfather selected fabrics that my grandmother Elna handcrafted into drapes and curtains. This, along with the furniture Unk Ile had given us from the Villa Valentino, made the house look like a glamorous movie set.

On the outside, my father once again added cosmetic changes, such as a walkway and steps of old brick, diamond-shaped amber glass inset in a country-style wooden door, and old brick planters overflowing with tropical foliage. The result was a rich, finished feel for very little money. When Nana came for a visit, she was so impressed with the place that she made sure to mention it to everyone she saw afterward. She somehow managed to slip Bill's pricey house into almost every conversation. It was embarrassing for us, but the waitresses, shop girls, and the lady at the bank were—or at least pretended to be—thrilled for Nana. To think that her only child could afford a house like that! Of course she didn't add that Pauline had cashed in her $5,000 life insurance policy to swing the deal.

Everyone who knew Evelyn was aware that she had something to do with Maybelline, and with her charm and beauty still intact at age fifty-five—a "senior citizen," according to her—she wielded quite a bit of influence in her little world. Wherever she went, women asked for her secret to looking youthful, and she always had the same answer: "A lot of pain and suffering."

My mother had heard this routine so many times that whenever the subject came up, she would sniff and leave the room, rolling her eyes. Her relationship with Nana had only continued to deteriorate as the years went by. The only time they seemed to get along was at parties, which might explain why parties became regular and rather extravagant affairs at our house.

In 1956, the long-awaited first grandson of Tom Lyle, named Tommy Lyle Williams III in the patriarch's honor, came into the world. Tom Lyle called this birth the high point of his life.

The following January produced another boy for the Williams clan: James Noel Williams, the third child of Allen and Jean. At the same time, Evelyn finally gave up trying to continue Warren's work. Thanks to my grandfather Andy's connections and Evelyn's perfect grammar, she went to work as a proofreader for a new animation studio called Hanna-Barbera Productions. This job made her feel as if she were part of the Biz in Hollywood—so, being Evelyn, she decided she needed a nicer car in which to be seen driving into and out of the studio parking lot. She chose a white Rambler with hound's-tooth seat covers.

Thus Nana became a career woman, one of the few women her age to have a promising future.

My other grandmother, Elna, was also interested in a career: mine. She wanted to help me develop the talent she and my mother believed I had. I began taking twice-weekly voice lessons. Elna, who came to our house almost every day to look after us while our parents worked, helped me practice my scales. I remember how frustrating it was when Nana showed up, her powerful voice drowning out mine as she also ran scales.

Despite Evelyn's constant lecturing on the subject, at this point I still had no idea how important Maybelline really was in our lives. In fact, it wasn't until I was at the market with a friend and her mother that the magic began. As Nana always did, I was spinning the Maybelline rotating display to make sure it had been refilled when my friend asked me what I was doing. Without hesitation, I broke the cardinal rule of How Not to Get Kidnapped: "One of my uncles owns the Maybelline Company. So I—"

"Oh, no, dear," my friend's mother said. "You mean your uncle works for Maybelline."

I not only insisted that he owned the company, I explained how it had gotten its name.

That convinced them—and I discovered I possessed the magical key to success and popularity: all I had to do was mention being part of the Maybelline family. Nana, of course, warned me this tactic could be dangerous. She also said that if I planned to represent the Maybelline name, I had better work on myself.

So began my career of trying to live up to Nana's vision of beauty. Which, of course, involved a lot of pain and suffering.

Suffering was making its rounds. By 1958, Arnold Anderson's drinking had become so bad that his outbursts made not only living with him but also working with him difficult. Then he married a woman, and Tom Lyle asked him to leave the house—although he simultaneously secured Arnold's future by giving him stock in the Maybelline Company.

Fortunately, by that time, Arnold's skills as an artist were no longer essential. Most print ads were now handled by Rory Kirkland and Maybelline's ad agency, Post Keys Gardner.

"That might have been the real reason for Arnold's decline," my grandmother later told me. "Men identify with their work, and there was no longer any real work for him at Maybelline." The positive side of all this was that Emery and Tom Lyle drew closer to one another. In fact, as the two men moved into their middle sixties, they stopped looking for intimacy outside their relationship.

On the business front, Tom Lyle, always thinking ahead, wanted to repackage Maybelline to give it a more modern look. At the time, the product line included cake mascara in a beautiful gold-tone metal compact, a cream mascara in a leatherette case, a twenty-five-cent eyebrow pencil, and eye shadow in a clear plastic case. It was a limited selection—and more products were needed to catch the attention of women comparing cosmetics.

The company went to work. By the end of 1958, Maybelline's line included a red and gold plastic, self-sharpening eyebrow/eyeliner pencil with twin refills, a newly designed Jewel-Tone Eye-Shadow Stick that looked like a tube of lipstick, precision tweezers, a professional eyelash curler—and, most exciting of all, Maybelline's Magic Mascara, with a totally new spiral brush.

With this new line of products, Rags Ragland saw an opportunity for drugstore expansion. He conceived and produced the Permanent Eye Fashion Center, whereby the stores would install and maintain a permanent Maybelline display center where every type, size, and shade of Maybelline product would be kept available at all times. When these centers were unveiled, they promptly took their places in 45,000 out of 51,000 drugstores nationwide.

In a matter of three weeks, Maybelline had corrected an inadequate wholesale drugstore supply situation that had existed for all the years the company had been in business. Now Tom Lyle needed a new packaging slogan to go with it—and again Rags stepped in, suggesting that every piece of merchandise be placed on a card that featured instructions for use along with the slogan *Maybelline . . . dedicated exclusively to the Art of Eye Beauty!*

Beauty hurts.

My mother became pregnant again that year, and her doctor warned her that having another child would be dangerous to her health. After three daughters, she prayed for a son to make the experience worth the threat—but she had another fear as well: gaining weight. It wouldn't do for her to look less slim and glamorous than the other Maybelline wives.

Her doctor had a simple solution: Dexedrine diet pills.

That holiday season, my mother—still slim at thirty-six years old and seven months pregnant but with a white streak running through her hair—decided to orchestrate the best Christmas ever. For starters, she found the perfect gift for my dad: a street bicycle he could ride alongside Donna and me on our two new bikes. She also found another wheeled toy that four-year-old Billee could peddle after the baby was born. That year, the entire house was filled with presents—a Christmas no child could ever forget.

To make things even better, Unk Ile had developed the tradition of spending every Christmas day with us, arriving at five in the evening, staying up all night, and then leaving at five the following morning. That year when he got there, we took goofy pictures of him while he wore googly eyes and played his signature version of "Turkey in the Straw." Because Unk Ile didn't eat turkey or any other kind of fowl, my mother always made him an Italian feast that he claimed he waited for all year.

My mother was so happy that Christmas. Who would have believed what the future held for her only a few months down the road?

William Preston Williams III was born on March 5, 1960. Our family finally had its boy. In fact, it seemed as if everything in our lives was perfect, especially after my mother's brother Robert was nominated for an Academy Award for special effects on MGM's *Ben Hur*—a remake of the movie my grandfather had created special effects for in 1925.

But things were not perfect. Even after baby Preston's birth, my mother continued taking diet pills. In a month, she lost forty pounds and something else as well: her happiness. Nowadays, she would have been diagnosed with postpartum depression and, very likely, early-onset menopause. She would have been prescribed the appropriate drugs and given counseling. But back then, there were no such diagnoses and no appropriate medications. My mother had no support, and she plunged into a terrible downward spiral of depression.

When the Academy Awards aired and my uncle won, Pauline began to talk about killing herself. In retrospect, it seems obvious that she was comparing her brother's achievements to her own and seeing nothing but the unfairness of it all. She could have been a dancer at MGM! It wasn't her fault a drunken sailor had destroyed her body and her career. Now what was she? Not even a housewife, not really. She had four children, but her mother had to watch them so their mother could work twelve hours a day cleaning other people's clothing.

Unfortunately, at the same time this was happening, another emotional storm blew in—Evelyn, who had given up working for Hanna-Barbera to live with us and as she put it, to "help out at the cleaners and take care of the children." For reasons I have never understood, she did something else instead. She told my mother the secret that she had kept to herself for thirty-seven years: that her own son, Pauline's husband, had been born out of wedlock.

This news exploded in my mother's dark psyche like the Hiroshima bomb, and when the debris settled, Pauline had reached a conclusion that made absolute sense to her: if the father of her children had been born illegitimately, then her children were illegitimate as well.

She stopped having sex with her husband or even sharing his bed. She stopped taking care of her new baby. She stopped functioning as any kind of parent or spouse. After a psychiatrist examined her, he insisted she be sent to

Camarillo State Mental Hospital before she hurt herself or Preston III. At the time, it seemed a wise and beneficial choice. Camarillo was on the cutting edge of psychological diagnosis and therapy, a leader in innovative treatments.

At Camarillo, the doctors diagnosed my mother as a manic-depressive and a paranoid schizophrenic. Shortly after that, they began administering electro-shock treatments.

When she returned home, she seemed like a robot; her normally effervescent personality was flat; her words terse. She developed odd, compulsive habits, such as wearing the same white skirt and blouse every day and washing and ironing them each night, as if they were a uniform.

She also converted to Catholicism and told my father that the only way they could make their union legitimate in God's eyes was to remarry in the Catho-lic church. My father went along with this strange obsession, saying his vows for the second time to an emaciated woman whose hair was now entirely gray where it wasn't falling out. Even though she was still only thirty-six, my mother felt old and unattractive—and on top of that had to endure Evelyn's constant criticisms and comments, all intended to make her feel like a failure as both a wife and a mother.

Distraught by the situation, my father sought advice from the one man he respected above all others: Tom Lyle. His godfather's response was short and blunt: "Bug, get your mother out of that house as fast as possible."

Forty-Nine
Cracks in the Dam

I'm not sure how he did it, but my father did convince Nana to leave. This time she moved in with a lady who was going through a divorce. Beverly had three kids, and, remarkably, my grandmother—who had never cared much for children apart from my siblings and me—became devoted to them. Perhaps this was because they didn't take it personally when Evelyn suggested ways they might improve themselves—under her expert guidance, of course.

I, on the other hand, took all my grandmother's criticisms to heart. And there were a lot of suggestions, starting with Nana's frequent comment that I was fat and should do something about it. After hearing that remark one time too many, I asked my mother to get me some diet pills, too.

Although it had been drummed into me that being thin and beautiful was the best answer to almost any challenge a woman might have, including finding the right man and the right home, I could tell my mother was missing something even more important: pride in herself, in the things she had done in her life. I didn't want to ever feel that way, so I expanded my singing lessons to include Italian opera. One day I would become a singing star at MGM, just as my mother had tried to become a dancer there.

But of course being beautiful was still important, a part of attaining my goals—and as I had been told many times, beauty hurts. So in that summer of 1960, I lost a lot of weight by essentially eating nothing except diet pills. When

I contracted the Asian flu, I lost even more weight—which was good! Now I could buy a new pair of jeans. Surely, as soon as I added a nice tan to show off my new, slender shape, all my problems would be solved.

I would be guaranteed to live happily ever after.

Every year, a big box of Maybelline products would be shipped by the company to my mother and grandmother's addresses—but that year I too received my very own mascara, eyebrow pencil, and eye shadow. Evelyn showed me how to do my hair and apply just the right amount of eye makeup and lipstick. Then she helped me pick out songs from *South Pacific* to sing for Unk Ile when he came for his annual Christmas visit.

As always, Unk Ile pulled up in front of our house at exactly 5:00 p.m., bearing all kinds of goodies. His infrequent appearances were always a cause for joy in our home; even my mother perked up. She actually came up with a great gag gift for him: an old tin of Maybelline in a tiny gift box, which was placed in a larger box, which was placed in a still-larger box, and so on up to a huge carton that he had to open first. He got a big kick out of working his way down through the nested packages to the little joke at the end; I remember him slapping his knee and throwing his head back to laugh.

Later, he held baby Preston and kissed him gently on the forehead. After the baby was put to bed, Donna and I entertained Unk Ile by singing and dancing in costumes, for which he rewarded us with Christmas cards and crisp ten-dollar bills, one for each of us: always the highlight of our Christmases.

By the early hours of the morning, only my grandmother and father were still awake, sitting close to Tom Lyle's chair and listening to every word from the man they had worshiped all their lives. As it turned out, he had a special Christmas present for them: the news that they would be receiving more Maybelline stock in the coming year. The company was about to introduce a brand-new product called Fluid Eye Liner, which Tom Lyle was sure would be a big success.

Always attuned to the social issues reflected in the movies, when Joanne Woodward won an Academy Award for her role in *The Three Faces of Eve*—a movie about multiple personalities—Tom Lyle released an arresting two-page, full-color magazine ad depicting a dual-faced woman:

FOR THE MANY FACES OF EVERY EVE

YOU ARE EVE . . . The eternal woman, with a hundred faces
to beguile and fascinate. Which face do you wear this hour,
Eve? . . . Your eyes speak for you . . . so make the most of
their subtle beauty . . . always . . . with Maybelline.

Had this striking, cutting-edge idea been inspired by my mother's recent breakdown? No one asked, but every grownup in my family wondered.

Later that year, Maybelline faced its biggest business crisis since the monopoly accusations: F. W. Woolworth, one of the company's largest customers, threatened to take down all existing Maybelline displays and reduce the company to obscurity for placing its products in the stores of competitors who offered such deep discounts that Woolworth's could not hope to compete.

Rags Ragland leaped into the conflict. A master strategist, he suggested to Woolworth that they simply needed to change their long-established method of measuring profit. Rather than judging all merchandise on the basis of its percentage of total profit, Rags pointed out that the true revenue of a product is better judged on the basis of rate of return on total investment—that is, how much sales volume the product produced compared to how much it cost to sell and how many times the inventory turned over each year.

Woolworth and Company saw Rags's point. As a result, rather than reducing Maybelline's visibility in their stores, they expanded the company's displays and featured its products more prominently than ever before. They also met cut-price competition where it existed—and their Maybelline volume alone grew to account for 75 percent of all cosmetics sales industry wide.

That near-calamity had a happy ending, but as the year drew to a close, another threat arose to face Tom Lyle personally: he was almost certain to lose another house. In early November 1961, hot, dry Santa Ana winds howled west out of the desert, sparking the worst fire in Los Angeles's history. A wall of flame swept through the most expensive brush-shrouded real estate in the world, igniting shingle-and-shake rooftops by the dozens and launching sparks that whirled off to start more fires in areas that included the slopes of Bel Air.

As the flames climbed toward the summit of Airole Way, Tom Lyle and Emery were ordered to evacuate. They filled their cars with priceless Maybelline documents, pictures, and whatever else would fit. Then they threw all their patio furniture into the pool, sprayed water on the windows and roof, and sped off to safety.

Not until three days after the winds died and the fire was finally contained were Tom Lyle and Emery allowed to view their property again. They drove slowly up the hill, passing through a blackened landscape marked by chimneys standing like sentinels above the smoldering debris of once-magnificent estates. With every passing mile they braced themselves for what they would find at 900 Airole Way, but as their property swung into view, they gaped in astonishment: their house was still standing, though all others around it were gone.

Only after the final reports on the disaster were completed did the two men learn that their home had survived because its all-stucco, flat-roofed, steel-and-glass structure had given the flames nothing to ignite.

Even the furniture in the pool was undamaged.

By 1962, Maybelline sales had reached $12,960,189, and Tom Lyle spent $4,373,816 on advertising that year. After operating costs, the company yielded a net profit of over half a million dollars—three and a half million dollars in today's economy. As Maybelline grew—and stock dividends along with it—my mother and father decided to sell Hill Top Cleaners. They had devoted twelve years of hard labor to the business and considered it a success, but it had also almost destroyed their health and sanity. My mother could now stay home and care for her children. This was especially important because Elna had recently undergone the removal of a cancerous tumor and couldn't continue taking care of us.

Still, the transition was difficult for my mother. She had never relished the prospect of being a full-time, stay-at-home mom, and now she didn't even have my father around to talk to during the day—he had gotten a job at MGM. Not that this was a picnic for him either: the studio operated under strict rules and regulations, and being Andy's son-in-law made him the object of scrutiny much more intense than that his co-workers experienced.

Soon Pauline began suffering bouts of depression that kept her in her bed for days at a time, periods during which the weight of responsibility fell on me. I would come home from school, and have to clean the house, wash the clothes, and feed my sisters and brother. This was so taxing it left me little time for homework or anything else.

The situation worsened when my dad came down with what seemed to be a flu that wouldn't go away. Nana feared he had tuberculosis—and once again moved in with us so that she could take care of him. In practice, that meant she barked out orders like a drill sergeant, refusing to lift a finger while instructing me and my siblings on the importance of having a strong work ethic. "I'm only here to supervise," she would say. "I'm sixty now and I just want to be loved and respected."

When my father's condition did not improve, he was finally diagnosed with endocarditis, an inflammation of the heart valve, and he checked into a veteran's hospital for two months. His condition was serious. The doctors warned him that even with an around-the-clock penicillin drip, there was a chance that he would die. Fear kept him company at his bedside. Was he, like his own father, destined to die at far too early an age?

The hospital was some distance away, and my grandmother insisted that we all move so we could be closer to my father. Luckily, Bill showed signs of recovery before the house sold, and Evelyn, with Tom Lyle's financial assistance, found her own apartment. Her place was close enough to our house that she could check up on her "work crew" every day and make sure we got down on our knees and prayed for Dad to live.

She was sure our prayers worked—because little by little, my father began to get better.

On the day that my father returned home—thin, gaunt, and pale—Nana was waiting for him with her famous homemade beef and vegetable soup. My grandmother did have the ability to take care of ill people, nursing them back to health by insisting on rest, nutritious food, and positive thinking. Under her ministrations, my father soon got strong enough to consider taking on a different job—one he would really enjoy. He gained weight, became stronger, and went to work for the public school system in the maintenance department.

After the stress of working at MGM, he now woke up whistling each morning and came home in good spirits every evening. Working for the school was simple and fun for him. Soon my parents resumed their old pattern of throwing a party every weekend and going out several nights a week, with one difference. They now had a full-time babysitter: me.

When I turned fifteen in 1963, I decided to forget about my five years of opera lessons and instead become a model for Maybelline. Donna and I enrolled in the Patricia Stevens Modeling School, where we learned how to walk, talk, and sit like ladies. Some people said I came across as conceited and too sophisticated for my age, but I loved the way I felt and moved, and I decided that I also wanted to be an actress someday. There was only one problem with this plan: after two years of living on diet pills, I had developed the family stomach problem and was often sick in bed, swallowing painkillers and then throwing them back up.

Every time I got sick, Evelyn insisted that I stay at her apartment so that she could take care of me. As a result, I missed a lot of school, numbed out on a combination of Valium, sleeping pills, and Nana's pain medication.

My mother had her own issues with drugs. To stay thin and have enough energy to raise four kids and still throw parties, she continued to take diet pills, which contributed to terrifying bouts of rage. She hated that Nana had so much influence over me and once practically kicked down Nana's door demanding that I come home. But I refused. I preferred being at Nana's apartment with its soft music, low lighting, and drugs. Why would I want to return to a house full of kids screaming day and night?

That was the year my grandmother began to open up to me about her life. I loved these stories and began fishing for details about how things had been back before I was born.

For a speech in class, I described how my Auntie Mabel had burned some cork to fix her eyes, thus giving Unk Ile the idea for Maybelline. I presented this story with perfect diction, posture, and gestures, earning an "A" for my presentation and instant popularity in school.

By 1963, Maybelline was even being sold behind the Iron Curtain, where it became the first cosmetics company permitted to advertise and sell products. This international coming out was celebrated in the ads themselves:

> **The most beautiful eyes in the world are by Maybelline,**
> **and in the entire world, nothing does so much**
> **to make eyes beautiful as Maybelline . . .**

Although my family's quarterly dividends had by this time grown from ten thousand to twenty thousand dollars, my dad did not keep the agreement he had made with Allen; he did not retire. My father needed the structure of regular work in his life. So did my mother, but she continued to be relegated to the role of full-time housewife and mother. It wore her down. When she began to look older than her mother-in-law, she growled, "Evelyn must have made a pact with the devil."

Then her mother died of cancer. With her closest confidante gone, my mother soon ended up back in the psychiatric unit of the hospital. This time, when she came home, she wept constantly. My father was unsympathetic, and she couldn't understand it. All she wanted him to do was hold and comfort her—and all he wanted to do was run away. "Use your rosary, why don't you?" he would snap. She didn't comprehend that he had never been able to properly mourn his father's death, so could not bear her mourning now.

The marriage deteriorated to the point that my father moved in with Allen and Jean. I continued to cope in my chosen manner—by taking even more diet pills during the day, then pain pills at night to knock me out. When my parents filed for divorce, the judge asked me which parent I wanted to live with. I replied that I would rather go to a foster home than live with either one of them. This seemed to shock Bill and Pauline into a reconciliation of sorts, although I later discovered that both my father and Evelyn were unhappy that I had thrown a monkey wrench into the delicate machinery of their plan to get rid of "crazy Pauline."

This time Tom Lyle really put his foot down as far as my grandmother was concerned. "Stop trying to live your life through your son, Evelyn," he said. "Leave him and Pauline alone."

But of course she didn't.

Fifty
A Model
Family Member

That year when Unk Ile came to the house for Christmas, he brought along a new Maybelline product called Ultra-Lash, which he planned to launch in a month or two. He asked me to go put some on so he could see how it looked.

Ten minutes later I came out of the bathroom and told him I loved the new mascara and accompanying duo-tapered brush. He beamed. "Would you be willing to survey your girlfriends about it for me? Get their opinions?"

"I'd love to," I said. He gave me several tubes of Ultra-Lash and asked me to call him with the results of my survey.

After I conducted the poll and gave away the free mascara, I was asked to join an exclusive girls' club called "Saffrons." I received two club names: "the Maybelline Girl" and "Barbie," because I had a long ponytail and always dressed like a Barbie doll in coordinated outfits. Once again, my Maybelline connections had boosted my popularity.

Things got even better for me on my seventeenth birthday, when my mother gave me the blue and white 1957 Chevy that her mother had owned. Dad had it repainted, and I promptly hung a pair of fuzzy dice from the rearview mirror and started scooting around town in my new vehicle. I was really on my way to being somebody! I was still going to modeling school and had auditioned at MGM for a new TV show called *Room 222.*

When the phone rang, I flew to answer it, my hair in curlers, hoping to hear the results of my audition.

But it wasn't MGM, it was Unk Ile—sobbing.

I ran to get my father, and we all gathered around as he pressed the receiver to his ear. I could hear Tom Lyle's voice, small and choked with tears. "We'd just gotten back from a vacation in Hawaii. Of course he was tired, but we'd had the most wonderful time, and he was so excited about Ultra-Lash."

Emery Shaver had suffered a massive heart attack and died at sixty-eight years of age.

Tom Lyle slipped into such a depression that Tom Jr. and Rags Ragland had to take over every aspect of the business, including advertising. Tom Lyle said he couldn't go on without Emery. His own health began to decline. He rarely left the house except for twice-weekly trips to the doctor to have blood removed as a result of liver disease. Nothing seemed to matter to him anymore—not even his beloved Maybelline.

Ironically, Ultra-Lash pushed Maybelline's sales from $14,789,868 in late 1963 to $21,517,776 by 1965. Despite this, Tom Lyle began to look for a buyer for the company. After fifty years, he wanted to get rid of his demanding mistress, his jealous concubine, his ultimate love.

But he was still Unk Ile, gracious to a fault. To celebrate the success of Ultra-Lash, he invited me and my best girlfriends up to his estate for a day by the pool. When the gates of the estate opened and we pulled into the driveway, Unk Ile stepped out to greet us personally, as always. To my distress, he seemed to have aged ten years since the last time I had seen him—but he still had the same loving smile and courtly manner as he ushered us into the living room.

He asked my friends questions about Maybelline, just as he had done with my grandmother and mother when they were young, and endured their nervous laughter as they gushed over him and the house. As we prepared to leave, he surprised us with a giant box of Maybelline products.

We planned to give the box away as a door prize at our Saffron Dance the following week—but somehow, after we got home and divided up the loot, all that remained for the door-prize winner was one unit of each product.

One day in 1965, my parents received their latest Maybelline dividend check, looked at the amount, and were shocked to see the number $50,000. My dad promptly redesigned and rebuilt the old bomb shelter downstairs into an extravagant party room, complete with a mirrored bar, pool table, stereo, recessed lighting, and modern furniture. Every once in a while, I would see my parents dancing down there and feel sure that our new prosperity had injected romance and excitement back into their marriage.

My father also finally built the swimming pool Nana had promised years before—and to go along with it, installed an outdoor kitchen and barbeque, including a refrigerator with a beer keg that was always full.

Surely we were seeing the beginnings of the good life. We had extra money, my parents were back together, and my mother finally seemed stable and well.

Then she received a letter from her father. He was writing from New York, where he was honeymooning with his new bride, seventy-year-old Mary Washburn.

When my mother saw the name, the truth crashed in on her. Now she understood why her mother used to cry all the time. Now she understood the strange silences that had hovered over the dining room table. For more than thirty-five years, her father had been carrying on with another woman. Lying, cheating . . . having an affair.

In time, we would all come to accept Mary, at least to her face. But one member of the family, apart from my grandfather, found the situation truly gratifying: Evelyn. "I knew the old bastard had a woman on the side," she sneered.

Not one to maintain a decorous silence for five minutes, let alone thirty-five years, my mother chose the evening of my high-school senior play to inform me that her father wasn't the only man in her life to be having an affair: so was my own father. Of course, I couldn't keep my lines straight that night. Through the stage lights, I could see my parents sitting together in the audience as if everything was fine, but I knew this probably meant curtains for life as I knew it.

My mother was devastated, of course, even though my father eventually gave up his mistress. It was too late. He had developed a wandering eye, and with four kids to think about, my mother knew she couldn't keep up with him in terms of enjoying the nightlife. Even if she could have, Bill was still quite handsome at the age of forty-one, while Pauline . . . well, how excruciating it must have been for her to look old and worn out in a world that so prized youth and beauty.

The reverse was also true: if you were young and awkward, it was imperative to look and act older to appeal to the adults who had the power to grant your wishes. At home, I had learned to pass this test even by my grandmother's standards, but when I graduated from high school and turned eighteen, my real rite of passage still lay ahead.

One day, I called Unk Ile and asked if I could come visit him, and with his usual grace, he invited me up for lunch. While driving up the hill, I mentally reviewed my personal accomplishments to date: I had just been accepted into the London Shakespeare Company; I was still awaiting the results of my audition at MGM; I had earned one of the lead parts in my high-school senior play; I had fulfilled my role as Evelyn's little protégé, learning grace and balance while managing to stay thin and pretty at all times. I was proud of all I had done so far, but this was only the beginning. I had aspirations and also a plan—if only Unk Ile would grant me one little wish.

He listened intently to my spiel. He agreed that I had the looks, the eyes, the personality, and even the talent. "But," he said, "Sharrie dear, if I let you have a position modeling for Maybelline commercials, the rest of the women in the family will be jealous."

I blinked. Had he just turned me down? "Is it because I'm not pretty enough?"

"You couldn't be prettier; that isn't the reason."

"But . . . I don't know what to say. I've trained for this minute my whole life; this was always supposed to be my future."

He leaned toward me and said the same thing he had said to my father all those years ago. "Look, honey. If you go to college and get a degree in advertising and marketing, I can open every door for you."

College? I thought. But that means four or five more years of school! I'll be twenty-three; I can't wait that long, I want it all now!

He saw the anguish in my eyes. Reaching out for my hand, he said, "I'm making a pact with you right now, Sharrie. You get that degree, and you'll have my full support."

As if that dreadful letdown weren't enough, I soon learned that I had also failed my audition for *Room 222*. Why? Because I looked too mature and sophisticated to play the part of a high-school girl.

So I gave it all up: the singing, the acting, the modeling. I canceled my trip to London and the Shakespeare opportunity—a decision I would regret for the rest of my life—and remained in Los Angeles to be with my boyfriend, Jon, and feel sorry for myself.

Meanwhile, Tom Lyle continued to search for potential buyers for Maybelline. Among the leading candidates were Gillette, American Cyanamid, Revlon, and Kimberly-Clark, but none of the offers met Unk Ile's requirements in terms of cash and stock options. He wasn't going to sell his company cheaply. By 1966, Maybelline's yearly sales had reached nearly $25,000,000. The company had pioneered many firsts in the cosmetics industry, not only in the development of actual products but also in merchandising and advertising. Maybelline had introduced carded merchandise and improved self-service racks. It had invented four-step makeup, including both Ultra-Lash Mascara and the brand-new Ultra-Brow, Ultra-Line, and Ultra-Shadow. The "Ultra" line of products sent sales soaring even higher by offering women a sensibly priced, complete, superior quality system of related beauty aids—mascaras, shadows, and liners, even false eyelashes, brow brushes, and other accessories.

In other words, Maybelline had attained the position of undisputed world leader in its field, with an advertising budget that topped the combined efforts of all its leading competitors. Among industry insiders, it was said, "There will never be another company like Maybelline." It was only a matter of time before someone snapped it up.

Even as the company's value rose, Tom Lyle's health declined. More and more, he relied on his son to handle the responsibilities of running the mega-company. Even the effort to sell Maybelline fell on Tom Jr. and, of course, Rags. They were the ones to actively engage potential buyers, sending only the most qualified on to Tom Lyle for approval. Even so, the strain on Tom Lyle, at age seventy—especially without Emery at his side—was so great that he sometimes couldn't get out of bed. Or didn't bother to.

In the summer of 1966, when I turned nineteen, my grandmother arranged for me to spend the summer in Chicago with my great-aunts and great-uncles. I was thrilled, since the trip would give me an opportunity to gather notes for Nana's life story, which I was encouraging her to write—as well as providing one more chance for me to see my boyfriend before he shipped out to Vietnam.

During the flight, I sat next to a glamorous older lady. She reminded me of Nana, with her blond bouffant hair, perfectly applied makeup, marvelous clothes, and ebullient personality. She introduced herself as Mrs. Phil Harris and spent most of the trip telling me how wonderful it was to be married to that man. Although she never mentioned her own name, by the time we landed, I knew all about her husband. She also told me I could be a Las Vegas showgirl if I wanted to. She gave me her card and asked me to come visit her.

When Verona and Charlie picked me up at the airport, I told them all about Mrs. Phil Harris. Verona's eyebrows shot up. "You don't know who she is?"

"No."

"It's Alice Faye—Tom Lyle's old flame."

She went on to tell me the story of Alice Faye and Tom Lyle—the first time I had heard it. I was stunned. To think I'd sat that close to her! If there had been a lull in the conversation, I might have mentioned Unk Ile or Maybelline as filler—but Alice's stories about the cute guys she knew and wanted to fix me up with had been much more exciting. In fact, I realized that for the first time in my life, I had been so absorbed in someone else's conversation, I had forgotten who I was.

Fifty-One
Reliving the Past

*V*erona and Charlie introduced me to Chicago-area fine dining, country clubs, and young men my age who took me to the dog races, theater, and lavish parties at lovely homes. Verona told me I should set my sights higher than a boy in the military; I should only consider marrying a professional man.

I spent much of that summer gathering stories and old pictures of the family, and finally got to visit the Maybelline Company itself. Tom Jr. and Rags Ragland met me there and presented me with a big box of Maybelline products. On the tour, I saw pictures of the actresses who had modeled for Maybelline dating back to the 1920s, and, for a second, my heart ached. How I wished my picture might one day have joined the Maybelline models of old.

When I got back home, I wrote Unk Ile a letter, describing every detail of my trip, including my chance encounter with Alice Faye. He was surprised, of course, and regretful that I hadn't mentioned him. Although I kept her business card for many years, I never did call her. And that's something else I regret to this day.

My boyfriend broke up with me before he left for Vietnam. He wanted to be a Green Beret, and he said I wasn't military wife material. When I asked why not, he said, "You'd make the other wives jealous."

That Christmas, I was still so heartbroken that I spent most of the time in my room crying, even when Unk Ile made his annual appearance. But I do remember one highlight of that holiday: Tom Lyle and Nana engaging in a piano-playing contest. Watching them go at it, you would never have dreamt that the man was a cosmetics king, a millionaire who knew the most famous people in the world—because when he sat down to play "Turkey In The Straw," he became a simple country boy with an infectious laugh and a magical smile. Nana, on the other hand, in her bouffant blonde wig and designer dress, missed every other chord while banging out "Some Enchanted Evening." After they had both performed, we in the audience applauded, whistled, and howled with delight.

"I think I won," Nana said, tears of laughter streaming down her face.

Unk Ile spoke quietly. "I still think I'm the best."

In 1967, even while up for sale, Maybelline introduced yet another product to its line: Natural Hair Lashes. They came in a little box with easy-to-apply adhesive and easy-to-follow illustrated directions, all for $2.50. Unk Ile had brought samples for all of us at Christmas, and, after I tried them on and saw the difference they made, I felt naked without them. I wore not one, not two, but three pairs of those lashes—two on my top lids and one on the bottom— when I appeared on a TV show called *Dream Girl.* Produced by Gene Banks and Chuck Barris, who also did *The Gong Show* and *The Dating Game, Dream Girl* was a beauty pageant that took place over five consecutive days. I had been in beauty pageants before and was pleased to be selected as one of the five weekly contestants who would be judged on beauty and poise, fashion, talent, and the results of a personal interview.

My episode aired on July 3, 1967, with William Shatner, Abbe Lane, and Richard Prine as the judges. After the fifth day, Dick Stewart, the host, announced the winner—and it wasn't me. I came home with a Samsonite over-night bag instead of a crown. I used the bag for storing makeup and prescription drugs.

Once again I had been disappointed—and once again the letdown pushed my aspiration level still lower. I decided I wanted to be an airline stewardess, find a new boyfriend, and get a tan lying by our pool.

That year Evelyn turned sixty-six, so even as I continued to bloom into a young woman, she worried about fading away. The more I tried to break free from her control, the more she expected me to be her best friend. She enjoyed having me spend the night with her so that she could drink wine, take Valium, and relive her life over and over again.

But she often broke down in tears, something I hadn't seen her do since Warren was killed. She had so many things left to do, she said, and so little time. "I had talent. If things had been different, I might have been a star."

I could relate.

Shortly before Christmas, all the stockholders received a letter from Tom Lyle informing them that the sale of Maybelline to Revlon was going through. He was concerned about how the stockholders would handle the large sum of money they would receive. He wrote, "You should take some steps to work out an estate plan through gifts, trusts, wills, etc. It is foolhardy and costly not to do this."

Prophetic words.

When Unk Ile came to our house for Christmas that year, he told us he had turned down Revlon's bid after all and was now considering an offer by Schick Razor Company. What he didn't tell us, and we wouldn't learn until years later when Rags Ragland's son Alan spelled out the details, was this: during these negotiations, Rags Ragland also recommended Plough, Inc., as a buyer. His reasoning was that Plough was in a far better-leveraged condition than other candidates, in that it had many fewer shares of its stock outstanding.

Tom Jr. disagreed. "Rags, they don't have the money."

"Yes they do. I know their circumstances. I've been a stockholder for years, and they're cash heavy."

Tom Jr. knew better than to doubt Rags's wisdom, and Plough was chosen as the primary suitor. The company offered a minimum of $100 million, well above any other bid. Following a period of grace where the stock "floated," on February 28, 1968, the Plough, Inc., stock was "pegged" for the official exchange. On that day, the price of Plough rallied so dramatically that the effective buyout of the Maybelline Company was $132.3 million. This stock breakout was the direct result of leverage: high demand plus fewer outstanding shares.

During these negotiations, Tom Jr. worked to the point of exhaustion but did not include Rags at the meetings. Though deeply hurt, Rags remained quiet about it; Tom Lyle never knew about the crucial role he had played in the success of the sale.

Still, Tom Lyle wrote Rags a letter dated December 24, 1967—Christmas Eve—apologizing for not contacting him during the long, drawn-out negotiations. He admitted to having been so run-down that he couldn't think straight.

The old liver and iron condition I have had for many years has brought on a bad state of nervous exhaustion, and the slightest little thing just about knocks me out. And you can imagine what the problems and emotional strain I have gone through the past several months have done to me.

A few days after the beginning of the new year, I went to the mailbox and found an enveloped from the Maybelline Company. I brought it in to my dad, who opened it and stared at its contents for quite a while before realizing it wasn't a check for the usual sum of fifty thousand dollars. It was for *two million* dollars.

My mother and siblings gathered around him, studied all the zeros, then began to scream, "Oh my God!"

Just then, my grandmother called on the phone: "I'm a millionaire!"

On January 29, Tom Lyle sent another letter.

My only concern now is that you and the other stockholders will invest the proceeds from the sale of one-half of your common stock in a conservative manner and will not lose it through poor investments. If you wish to spend some of it for a new house or on traveling or otherwise, that is of course up to you. But when it comes to investing it, maybe you would like to have me give you some advice on how to go about it. I would be the last person to advise you what you should or should not buy, but I think I can tell you how to find the right people to give you that advice.

He went on to suggest that all the stockholders invest with an established company and recommended that everyone not allow friends in the brokerage business or otherwise to offer investment advice.

This is the place where friends should not enter into the picture in the slightest. The stock market is a very risky thing, and even those who spend their lifetime working with it are seldom able to beat it . . .

I hope you do not mind my passing this advice on to you, you know that I am pleased beyond words that you will be receiving this substantial increase in your estate and that I am deeply interested in your holding on to it.

Lots of Love, Sincerely, UNK

Finally, after years of fantasizing about it, my parents were in a position to build their dream home on the water in Newport Beach. Working with an architect, my dad was able to incorporate all his creativity into a showplace.

Several of his cousins made similar choices. Very few followed Tom Lyle's advice to remain conservative—although those who did are very wealthy today. Almost none of them stayed in their current homes or continued to live quiet, peaceful lives. Existence for the Maybelline heirs became a consumer free-for-all, a feeding frenzy.

As my parents started building their big house on the bay, with a fifty-foot yacht already parked at the dock, my sister Donna and I struggled with the suggestion of Tom Lyle's lawyer, Mr. Spindell, that we stay conservative "like the Nixon girls." Apparently, this meant we should get rid of our going-nowhere boyfriends. Mr. Spindell said we needed to bring professionals into the family; finding a doctor, lawyer, or businessman was the only way to go.

In 1968, there were many significant events in the world, including the assassinations of Martin Luther King Jr. and Robert Kennedy. The Vietnam War played out on TV every night, and riots erupted across the nation. Just as Mr. Spindell had predicted, Nixon was elected president, and a new era of Republican conservatism bloomed behind the so-called Orange Curtain of Newport Beach—the Southern California Riviera for the rich and famous. I floated through the turbulence of the period, rousing myself only to help my grandmother move into a penthouse in Marina Del Rey—then promptly move her down to the first floor so she could sit on her deck and watch the people walk by.

Amid all this excitement, I began to buy beautiful clothes using Nana's credit cards. I shared my clothes with her, and she shared her drugs with me.

I spent a lot of time with Nana while my parents were busy building their house on Lido Isle. My sister Donna struggled a bit more, torn between wanting to be a free-spirited, flower-child hippie and trying to live up to the sophisticated Maybelline image Nana demanded we maintain. I was more conservative than Donna, and though I had a boyfriend in a rock-and-roll band, I kept my eyes open for a professional man who would please my family. Nana was brutal to anyone I brought home who did not live up to her expectations, so to keep her credit card in my purse, I became more of a clone of her than I remained myself.

Life became increasingly complicated. How could I be the dutiful daughter and granddaughter while so many in my generation were rebelling against the establishment and dancing to a new beat? After all, the Beatles promised strawberry fields forever, The Doors wanted to light my fire, and Timothy Leary wanted me to turn on and tune out. Psychedelic head shops were popping up everywhere. When the mod musical *Hair* opened in L.A., I was lucky enough to find work there as an usher and be able to dress up like a rich hippie. But I had a day job, too: keeping Nana happy so that the money would continue to flow from her to me.

When Tom Lyle came to see our house in 1968, he could tell that much more than our location had changed. He knew the money had ignited a firestorm that would wind up being both a blessing and a curse. I could see the combination of sadness and joy in Unk Ile's eyes as he played "Turkey in the Straw" for us—for what would prove to be the last time.

My parents moved into their new mansion on the water in 1969 and anticipated a new life that would bring happiness to us all. It did, for a while—until my dad was diagnosed with polyposis of the colon, possibly cancerous. He dealt with the news that his life might be cut short by instantly adopting a new philosophy: "From now on I'm going to live life my way."

For him, this meant regularly hitting the hot spots in Newport Beach and checking out the local gold diggers for a little action, while my mother stayed at home and grew more outraged every day. My father took on new women to stroke his ego, while Mom spent his money to the tune of twenty thousand dollars a month. She swore to break him if he didn't stop catting around.

My grandmother bought a house five spots down from us so that she would be nearby in case she was needed. My dad dropped by her place frequently to share stories about how his wife was going crazy again. In the most recent installment, Pauline had decided to have all her teeth removed and replaced with implants so that she would look beautiful for her twenty-fifth wedding anniversary. In fact, she was planning a full mock wedding to be held in her new home, and she intended to invite one hundred guests and wear the wedding dress that her mother had made for her original wedding during World War II.

Every time my mother had a tooth extracted, her pain was exacerbated by the phone calls she would hear taking place between Bill and his girlfriend, Linda, who was twelve years her junior. My mother would cry and beg my father not to go see that woman, but off he would drive, leaving my mother alone to take drugs and alcohol until she passed out.

Poor little Preston. Poor little Billee. I wasn't there to help with them during this traumatic time because by then Donna and I were staying at our old house in Culver City so that we could be near our boyfriends and have parties without any parents around.

Even as this played out, the outside world tried to pierce our protected bubble. The first draft lottery since World War II had gone into effect, shortening the list of potential husbands. Although I was still with the boyfriend Spindell disapproved of, I also stayed on the lookout for a man who fit my other criteria: he wasn't being drafted, he came from a rich family, and he was cool.

That summer I moved out of L.A., renting an apartment with my friend Cheryl. But I soon realized that what I really wanted to do was live in my family's new house and hang out on the fifty-foot yacht, getting a tan between shopping trips to Fashion Island.

In July, when Neil Armstrong became the first man to walk on the moon, I watched the event on a TV on the yacht as I sipped a Coke and adjusted my new bikini. The bikini seemed far more important than the biggest event in history.

Our lives had rapidly become superficial. All we cared about was money, property, and prestige; we forgot about joy and family bonds. I felt heartsick at the changes happening around me; I had the feeling that all this money was going to destroy us—yet I couldn't seem to break away from it myself.

My mother bought cases of booze for the upcoming mock wedding, even though Dad told her she was crazy for demanding that he marry her for the third time. Perhaps this was why, when my father went into surgery to have his colon removed, my mother never bothered to come to the hospital. My grandmother was there, though, and vowed to destroy my mother for this apparent lack of concern.

Despite needing his heart restarted at one point on the operating table, my dad pulled through his operation and recovered rapidly. In fact, only six weeks later—one week before his upcoming mock wedding—he flew off to Acapulco with his girlfriend.

When my mother found out about this, she all but lost her mind. She had spent untold dollars and hours preparing for her big day. The bridesmaid's dresses my sisters and I would wear had been handmade in the style of the 1940s. My ten-year-old brother had a new suit and tie to show off in as ring bearer. My mother had arranged for catering, flowers, tables, entertainment. The ceremony would be conducted by the same pastor who had married them the first time.

Yet on the day of the mock wedding itself, she sat in her luxurious bedroom overlooking the patio with its table and chairs all set up for guests. She seemed to be in a drug-induced trance. Her gorgeous trousseau was all packed for a trip to Rome, where she hoped to have her marriage blessed by the pope.

No one knew if Dad would even show up for the ceremony.

All of a sudden, the crowd screamed in excitement. Bill Williams stood at the door, tan, devastatingly handsome, and thoroughly hung over. He didn't even remove his gold aviator sunglasses until his mother insisted that he do so, so that she could "see his beautiful blue eyes." They proved to be rather red.

Still, the "Wedding March" began to play, and my mother, high on drugs and wine, sauntered down the stairs looking more beautiful than I could remember her ever being before. Even my father took a breath as she descended behind their three girls.

Then my father took his wife's hand, and for a second you could see in both their faces the love they had once had for each other. Not an eye was dry as they walked toward the minister.

The magic lasted until after the ceremony, cake-cutting, and toast were over. Then my father started gulping down drinks, and, shortly after that, my mother left with some of her friends to take a sunset cruise—without her groom.

That night, after all the guests were gone, the fighting began. And escalated. Pauline threw her wedding band into the street. Bill hurled her new mink coat into the bay.

The next morning, my father moved out of the house, and my mother filed for divorce.

Part 5

Miss Maybelline Reborn
(1970–1979)

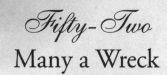

Fifty-Two
Many a Wreck

The divorce battle was vicious, and, in the end, my mother lost everything. This was actually Tom Lyle's doing, once again utterly protective of blood ties. He stated that all Maybelline money was to be given to his nephew as his sole trust, which meant that the court granted Pauline only a small settlement for her years of working at the cleaners. Once again, she was swept into the dark waters of depression and disconnection.

By then, Donna and I were of legal age, but my father got full custody of Billee and Preston. He sold the waterfront home, married Linda—who had three kids of her own—and moved to Palm Springs, next door to Liberace, an old friend of Tom Lyle's. Although my grandmother was delighted to finally be rid of Pauline and to take her place as the matriarch of her son's family, she continued to live on the bay.

In the midst of this storm of devastation, I met my future husband, Gene Dorney. He was exactly what Robert Spindell had urged me to look for in a man: a law-school student from a rich, successful family. Even better, he was what I was looking for as well: tall, dark, and handsome.

Between stints in psychiatric hospitals, my mother also made a new connection: she met a free-spirited hippie who smoked pot and called her "Gypsy Mama." He accepted her for who she was and recognized and appreciated her kind soul.

He introduced her to his friends, all of them just kids, part of the flower-child movement of the '60s. This was a breakthrough for my mother, who had virtually never had any kind of freedom in her life. She had never been able to live up to Evelyn's standards nor to the expectations—of others or herself—that went with being a member of the Maybelline family. To now be around people who encouraged her to develop in her own way and to be herself at all times was a liberation.

At the time, though, I didn't understand this. I was appalled by my mother's transformation into Gypsy Mama and disgusted with her story of helping to midwife a baby at a love-in at the beach. The more of a hippie she became, the more I turned to my grandmother for support. Of course, Nana reinforced this tendency by warning me that if I ever chose to throw my lot in with my mother, I would lose Gene in a minute.

"I know what's best for you," she said. "Always remember, I'm your best friend."

To make sure I kept my head in the right place—that is, on being a good conservative Republican in Newport Beach, with a rich desert-living father and a devoted grandmother—Evelyn spoiled me ten times more than before the divorce. I couldn't resist her offer of a trip to Europe, or a white convertible Shelby Cobra Mustang, or the freedom to shop at Fashion Island every day with her credit cards and cash. With Nana's money and blessing, I also purchased expensive clothes and jewelry for Gene, until he, too, fell under her spell. It helped that he was also crazy about my dad, who had reinvented himself with his young new wife and glamorous lifestyle.

After graduating from UCLA and Loyola Law School at the top of his class, Gene took the bar exam and, at the age of twenty-four, passed it on the first try. At the time, I was on vacation in Europe with his sister, studying architecture, art, and furnishings to expand on the knowledge I had gained during my first year at Brooks College for Women. I was majoring in interior design and aspired to be president of the school—but when I returned to the United States, I got an even better offer: Gene asked me to be his wife.

My grandmother decided to throw me not one but two engagement parties during the Newport Beach Boat Parade, scheduled for a week before Christmas. The day of the first party, she called at eight-thirty in the morning. "Sharrie, honey, come over and help me decide what to wear tonight."

"I'll come after my appointment at the beauty salon," I said. I had a hundred things to do before the party, starting with getting the red roots of my hair bleached to an acceptably glamorous blonde.

Nana called four more times that morning and afternoon, for various reasons, before I finally arrived at her place. The December day was warm and sunny, and Nana's old but ritzy beach house had a balcony and a fifty-foot dock to allow full appreciation of the blue sky and bluer water. Inside, Christmas trees, lights, Santa's reindeer, garland and tinsel glowed and sparkled from every nook, shelf, and corner. This would be a perfect night for the perfect party for the perfect couple and their perfect families. Nana, the perfect hostess, was having both parties catered with roasted turkey and all the trimmings, as well as prime rib, Yorkshire pudding, and candied ham. Gleaming silver dishes would soon be filled with See's candy, M&Ms, and, of course, my dad's favorite orange and chocolate squares and chocolate-covered cherries.

Evelyn had spent a fortune setting the stage to impress my fiancé and her future in-laws—and she expected me to show the proper appreciation.

Nana had a full-time seamstress who was literally on call day and night to take in or let out her corsets and designer clothes. The woman was there when I arrived, on her knees with pins in her mouth, rehemming a dress—the dress I was to wear at *my* engagement party.

The long, empire-waisted, cranberry, velvet gown belonged on a Juliet, celebrating love with her Romeo. It wasn't even Nana's style. The dress cried out for a young woman with long, romantic hair. *Not* a platinum bouffant wig.

My heart was pounding, but I kept my voice even. "Nana, I'm wearing that tonight. I bought it specifically to wear at my engagement party. You know that. You can*not* wear it."

She gazed approvingly at her reflection in her full-length mirror, bordered Hollywood-style in clear round bulbs, lighting her reflection with several thousand watts. "You have so much in your closets, I'm sure your can figure out something else to wear."

"No, I *can't*," I blurted. "It's *my night!* Why do you have to upstage me?"

Well that's all I had to say to light her fuse.

"*Me* upstage *you?* All I do is give, give, give to you! Have you any idea how much money you spend from my accounts?"

She jerked away from the seamstress, flung open her dresser drawer, and pulled out stacks of rubber-banded credit card receipts. When she threw them on the sofa where I had slumped, I kept my mouth shut, seething. Only later did it occur to me that those receipts had been awfully well-prepared and conveniently located for just such a moment.

As soon as the seamstress left, I shot to my feet. "How dare you embarrass me in front of her? You know I'm always available to you, at your beck and call every day! How can you act like I'm on a payroll? I'm your granddaughter, for God's sake!"

Nobody had a more caustic tongue than Nana. "Just how do you think Gene is going to afford to keep you in the lifestyle I've allowed you to become accustomed to?" Then she let me have it with both barrels: "Remember, Sharrie, I made you who you are. You'd be a complete nothing without me."

Fluffing her perfectly coiffed silver Ava Gabor wig in the mirror, she looked at my reflection behind her and waited for my response.

I unclenched my jaws. "Believe whatever you want, Nana, because it doesn't matter anymore. Gene loves me for myself, not for the perfect little mannequin you think you created."

She raised an eyebrow. "If you don't like how I treat you, maybe I'll just take you out of my will."

"Again? Well, go ahead. I don't need your money anymore."

She laughed. "You couldn't make it without me."

"I'm not going to take your goddamned shit anymore!" I lunged at her, tore the wig off her head, and ran out the door, screaming, "I hate you!"

Racing onto the balcony, I threw the wig as far as I could into the bay. On the way back through the house, I slammed every door behind me, and in my white Shelby Mustang, I roared off the island with enough noise to make sure the whole neighborhood heard. Most likely Nana didn't blink an eye at any of it. Most likely she smiled. She knew I didn't have the guts to miss my own party.

Parties.

At the summit of Bel Air, Tom Lyle stood watching the sun go down behind the purple mountains twinkling with lit windows and Christmas bulbs. He had not bothered to decorate his own house that year. Without Emery to help supervise the placement of lights and wreaths, without the added laughter and warmth, it just didn't seem worth the trouble.

Going out wasn't worth the trouble, either. Dressing presentably, grooming properly, driving off somewhere only to know all eyes were on you, forcing you to act a certain way—it just wasn't worth it. Especially since he was no longer the dapper young man of years gone by. Somehow age had caught up with him. He had known it would one day, of course, on an intellectual level. Everyone knew that. Still, he had fought it off through exercise, self-denial, artifice, and above all, the creative mental exercise of building and protecting his beloved Maybelline. But now Maybelline was gone, sold; it would continue under someone else's care. His body was weakening, his health failing. What was left for Tom Lyle?

Family, of course. Yet now even the thought of family made him feel old. Tonight Evelyn was throwing a party for her granddaughter Sharrie. An engagement party. Wasn't it only yesterday that Sharrie had been a roly-poly little redheaded delight, scrambling out of her father's car and running to greet her Unk Ile?

He had been invited to the party, of course. To both the parties; Evelyn couldn't throw just one. But what would he find there? Extravagance, shattered relationships, posing and posturing. Worse, merely by showing up, he would draw attention to himself, away from his dear Sharrie. That would never do.

He might not even go to her wedding.

When Gene and I arrived that evening, the party room was filled with all the people I had grown up with. Stacks of gifts covered the floor, and the stereo was playing Frank Sinatra singing "Have Yourself a Merry Little Christmas." My father wore his traditional red-and-black Christmas smoking jacket. He looked handsome and happy, as if he had never threatened to boycott the party when I had told him that I wanted to invite my mother. As if he hadn't told me he wouldn't even let me hold the Wedding of the Year at his home in Palm Springs, even though I had already sent out four hundred invitations for the event. So my father was there, with his new wife, but my mother was not.

Still, I smiled when my father introduced Gene and me to the crowd as a "future Mr. and Mrs. Beautiful." I wore a smart red suede jacket with a collar and cuffs of white lambs wool and a pair of black slacks. Mrs. Beautiful.

Nana caught my glance, gave me a quick once-over, and called out a toast of her own to my future husband and me. As usual, everyone gazed at her in admiration.

I walked over and kissed her. Hugged her. What else could I do? It was show time. Besides, I was floating on a lake of Valium.

Nana raised her glass—and her voice. "Isn't my granddaughter beautiful? Just like her Nana!"

The party the following night went smoother. Nana looked amazing in the Eva Gabor wig that had been fetched from the bay and reworked by her stylist, Danie King. Nana seemed crazy over this handsome young man, who played the piano while Nana entertained another fifty people with a catered midnight dinner overlooking the yachts. Danie was terrific on the keyboard, too, having once performed with none other than Tom Lyle's old friend and favorite pianist, Liberace.

My grandmother's infatuation with Danie might have stemmed from the way he was able to make her look almost as young as me, even though Nana was now almost seventy-three. Nothing made her happier than having people mistake her for being my sister.

Still, she hadn't forgotten our argument from the previous day. When no one was looking or listening, she muttered insults at me or gave me the cold shoulder. I couldn't stand it. In the kitchen, I broke down and apologized, begged for her forgiveness, hugged her with tears in my eyes.

She accepted my apology, and together we mustered up the emotional strength to carry on. Both of us were drugged half out of our minds, but we looked good to the crowd, and nobody, not even Gene, knew what it cost me to get through that night.

Shortly after 1973 began, Plough, the company that had bought Maybelline, merged with Schering, then the second-largest pharmaceutical company in the world. Each stockholder received 1.32 shares of Schering stock for every share of Plough they owned. Dad wound up with 90,000 shares. His and Nana's wealth doubled overnight.

It was intoxicating. Now that Dad was sure my mother wouldn't be attending my wedding, he offered me the moon in terms of what he would spend on the occasion. But I felt simultaneously guilty and justified. On the one hand, by not inviting my own mother to my wedding, I felt as if I had sold her out for glitz and glamour. On the other hand, how would Gypsy Mama fit in at the Wedding of the Year? I could imagine the rest of the family staring at her with her untamed gray hair, her loose earthy skirts, her sandals or bare feet. And how would she feel in such company? Everything would be ruined for everybody. Besides, which of my mothers would show up—the giddy, dancing, baby-delivering one or the one stumbling in black despair? She was again riding up and down on manic-depressive tsunamis. So, although it broke my heart to hurt my mother so deeply, I simply refused to have her ruin my wedding.

In the middle of all this hoopla, Auntie Mabel, Uncle Chet, Auntie Eva, and Uncle Chess came to town. Unk Ile invited everyone up to his house; this, he said, was probably the last time the Chicago clan would come to California.

Of course, the reunion couldn't be free from drama. When my father said he wanted to bring his new wife, Linda, along to meet Unk Ile, Nana threw a fit. By this time she had turned against Linda, who she felt paid her no respect. However, Nana privately granted me permission to bring my future husband to meet the great man, even though Gene was not yet technically part of the family. "Don't tell anyone," Nana whispered. "We'll just sneak him in at the last minute."

So we did. The recriminations began the moment Gene climbed out of the car in the parking area outside Tom Lyle's house. Dad asked Evelyn why she had been so terrible about his bringing his wife to the meeting if it was okay for me to haul my fiancé along. Before she could respond—and I'm sure she had the perfect answer fully rehearsed—the front door opened and Tom Lyle stood smiling out at us. I was shocked at how much he had declined, how withered he looked. Compared to him, the rest of us were overfed cows.

After we had all hugged and kissed and had our photo snapped by Milford, we went inside and took our usual positions around the room. Donna and I sat on the ottomans in front of the fireplace, just as we had when we were little, while the "big guns," as Nana called the older members of the family, sat around on a white sofa facing Unk Ile in his chair. Milford brought drinks on a silver tray, and we spent the afternoon talking about the old days. It must have been a bittersweet experience for Unk Ile, seeing his nephew, his Bug, looking like a swinger in his midlife crisis, wearing striped pants, a shirt open halfway to his waist, a gold chain around his neck, and sunglasses indoors, no doubt to hide his bloodshot eyes.

Evelyn insisted on taking a picture of Tom Lyle and Bill in front of "Blooming Colors," a Maybelline display designed by the new owners, Schering-Plough. Unk Ile leaned against the counter as if he needed it to hold himself up, while Nana capered around, trying to be the life-of-the-party Evelyn that everyone remembered.

I waited for a lull in the activities to introduce Gene to my uncle. Later, Gene told me he would never forget the honor of talking to such a great man. I snapped a picture of the two of them, sitting with their long legs crossed, looking like a pair of moguls having a light conversation.

But all along, I had a feeling that this would be the last time we would see Unk Ile. Before we left, he told me he hated to say it, but he was too weak to drive down to Palm Springs for my wedding.

Nana was standing nearby and told him that she was in poor health, too.

He smiled. "Ev, you'd never know by looking at you."

"Many a wreck is hid under a good paint job," she said.

Overall, the visit was somber, the voices quiet, the mood subdued. All that was left to us of our lighter spirited days past were memories . . . and, of course, lots of money.

Fifty-Three
The Wedding(s)
of the Year

We held our wedding rehearsal at four o'clock on a warm, slightly breezy evening in April. There was a glorious feeling in the air as the sun set over the San Jacinto Mountains behind my dad's Palm Springs estate. Dad was so proud of the way the place looked. He had worked on renovations and improvements up to the last second, in his torn shorts and tennis shoes, adding the finishing touches to the bar in his courtyard where the hors d'oeuvres and drinks were served. He and Linda had strung dozens of orange, yellow, and green paper flowers over the Mediterranean brick arches beneath which Gene and I were to be married.

The bell tower on top of Liberace's villa next door gave an old mission feel to the already romantic atmosphere, and though the great pianist wasn't in town to play the "Wedding March" for us, we did play a recording of his as we headed up the steps to the flower-covered arches.

Nana arrived at the rehearsal dinner wearing a custom-designed mother of the bride gown and had the photographer arrange us so that we surrounded her as she sat on a red throne, the matriarch of her dynasty.

Later, my dad took me aside and said, "This is the last night you're going to be a Williams," and I cried on his shoulder.

That following evening, after a ceremony worthy of royalty, Gene and I made our entrance into the courtyard for the reception, where two hundred and fifty people were getting drunk while waiting to be seated for dinner. The smell of honeysuckle and orange blossoms was intoxicating. The entire yard was alive with white oleander, red and pink bougainvillea, and twenty-foot palm trees; the full moon overhead illuminated the smiling faces of our friends and families.

I felt like an American princess in my designer wedding gown and simple jade and gold necklace, which my dad had given my mother during the war. I clutched the jade stone as I heard Nana whisper in my ear, "Oh, darling, your future is so secure." I believed her, but still, things were not perfect. I missed my mother. I missed Unk Ile. I also missed my grandfather Andy, and Mary, and my mother's brother Fred—all of whom had boycotted the wedding to protest my mother's exclusion. The pressure to bury my feelings and look radiantly happy would have killed Superman, but I pulled it off.

My dad and Linda divorced shortly after Gene and I returned from our honeymoon in Acapulco. They had been married only eighteen months. Although I was stunned, I also harbored the dream that my parents might get back together. My dad's response to this was blunt: "No way."

As for me, I just wanted to be a newlywed—which meant, among other things, spending less time with Nana. I also sought to reestablish a relationship with my mother. Fortunately, Gene was more than willing to accept Pauline into our lives, as crazy as she was.

Of course, this meant that Gene and Nana soon began fighting over who would control my life. Things came to a head as my sister Donna's birthday approached. I had invited everyone to our house for a party and gotten everything prepared, when Nana suddenly announced that the party would be held at her house instead. When Gene found out about this unilateral switch, World War III began.

The problem was that Gene was unprepared for a Williams family fight. I, on the other hand, was pumped and ready to go into the ring with Nana.

I stormed into her house with Gene behind me.

Nana, my dad, and Donna were in the kitchen. Dad was making something involving vodka, although he already looked hung over. Nana was pleading for him to take off his sunglasses: "Look at me, darling. It's your mother, who loves you so much."

Dad kissed her on the cheek, but refused to remove his shades. Instead, he stared out the window toward the bay, as if studying the scenery.

Nana turned to me as if just realizing I was there. "Sharrie, dear, would you put the vegetables on the stove for me?"

"No, I won't." I crossed my arms over my chest. "I'm sick and tired of being your slave."

"My slave? My slave?" Nana flung open a drawer and pulled out a stack of canceled checks made out to me. "Is this how slaves are treated?"

As the battle commenced, Donna walked into the other room and closed the door. Gene ducked for cover while my dad stood in the background, drink in hand.

I grabbed the checks and threw them across the room. "I earned every dime, catering to your every whim all my life!"

Nana turned to my father. "Bill, do something."

He sipped his drink and spoke in an even voice. "We all earned every god-damned dime we've got, putting up with your crap."

In an instant, Nana's expression transformed from shocked to enraged. "I've given and given to everyone and asked nothing in return but love and respect!"

"Bullshit," Dad said. "There's a price tag on everything you do for us, and we've all paid with our guts."

Nana paused long enough to reclaim her dignity. "I fought hard to put you all where you are." Then she turned to me. "Sharrie, if it weren't for me, Gene wouldn't have even married you. I financed that whole goddamned romance, right from the start."

"You bitch," I said. "You broke up my parents' marriage because you couldn't bear to let your son have a life of his own, and now you're trying to fuck up mine."

Dad waved his drink in her face. "You interfered with my first marriage and then my second marriage, and now I'm done, Mother. Done with your shit." He marched toward the bathroom.

Nana followed, screaming, "I don't deserve this!"

He slammed the door in her face. She hammered on it. "Come out of there! Come out right now!"

I rushed up behind her. "Do you have to hold his dick for him, too?"

The door swung open, and Dad glowered over his mother. "The only reason you have the things you have today is because of me. I'm the Williams. I'm the reason you got any money at all." He tore of his sunglasses, revealing red, blood-shot eyes. "My uncle loved me so much that he took pity on you after Daddy died. That's all there is to it." He stepped forward, backing her up against the wall. "And you? You were nothing but a goddamned gold digger when you left the family to take off with that asshole Warren Deuel."

She gasped and clutched her heart. "You deny me a little happiness?"

"You didn't need to marry the drunk and take on his debts as well as his name. It ruined your life—all our lives—for the years you were hiding from debt collectors."

Tears began to well up in Nana's eyes, but Dad threw the final dagger squarely into her heart. "Blood is thicker than water, and I'm the real thing."

She sobbed like a little child as Dad grabbed his coat. He turned his red eyes on her one more time. "I never want to see you again."

Gene and I followed him to the door, but before we stepped out, I got in the last word for once: "You can leave your money to the milkman, for all I care!"

I slammed the door behind me.

In the wake of this abandonment, Nana turned her attention to Danie King, her stylist, who took on the role of a son. Like me, he was infatuated with Nana's Maybelline history and suggested she write a book about it. I was furious, since that had been my goal forever. He sucked up to me, asking me questions about my life, my relationship with Nana, my father, Gene, my mom, my siblings. At the time, I assumed he was just a hairdresser who liked to talk with his clients. I had no clue he might have ulterior motives.

Nana and I hadn't spoken in weeks when Donna called to report that Nana had a new boyfriend. No alarm bells went off when I heard that Danie King had been the one to introduce Nana to this man. In fact, neither Donna nor I took the situation too seriously, but still, I called my dad to let him know what was going on.

He promptly called Nana. She told him yes, the boyfriend was twelve years younger than she, and yes, she was serious about him.

Dad responded with the usual tact he showed around Evelyn: "Mother, can't you see that Danie is a goddamned fag and that this fortune hunter is probably a fag, too, trying to take advantage of a rich old lady?"

She told him he was wrong. Her boyfriend, Charles Harrison Dimmick, who went by the name of Harry, was a man of stature. He was loving and kind and trustworthy. Besides, she was tired of being alone and making decisions by herself, especially since her family had made it very clear they weren't interested in her anymore.

Since Evelyn's only connection with her family now seemed to be Donna, it was Donna she called with the big news: her wedding to Harry would take place on November 24, two days before Dad's fifty-first birthday. The rest of us received written invitations prepared by a woman named Melinda.

We were flabbergasted, to say the least. When Dad heard that his mother was so in love with Harry—after a five-week courtship—that she was not even going to ask Harry to sign a prenuptial agreement, he insisted that his children boycott the wedding. He had never met Harry, but Dad was certain the man was after Nana's money.

He considered calling Tom Lyle about it but feared the news would kill his uncle on the spot. Evelyn might have thought the same thing, because she didn't call or invite Tom Lyle to the wedding.

On the day of the wedding, I told my father that we had all decided to go to the big event anyway. Already drunk, he shook his head and bellowed, "Tell my mother I'm dead set against it, and she'll be sorry!" This time, I was sure he really did intend to cut his mother out of his life—just as he believed she had cut him out of hers.

Gene and I walked into the Balboa Bay Club just as Nana swept toward us, wearing a silver-sequined blazer over a floor-length silver silk skirt, a platinum wig, and diamond earrings. She seemed thrilled that we were there and introduced us to Harry for the first time. He was a handsome man with a medium build and a full head of silver hair. I was amazed at how perfect he looked with Nana and how radiant Nana was. But when she asked if my dad was coming, too, I replied honestly and within earshot of Harry: "No, he doesn't trust this man."

She was hurt and, of course, embarrassed. I knew I shouldn't have spoken so bluntly, but this looked suspiciously like my wedding. Same guests, same elegance.

Would she never stop competing with her own granddaughter?

A couple of weeks later, Donna called with another announcement from Nana: she had put her beautiful waterfront home up for sale and was going to move with Harry and his stepdaughter, Melinda, to a place called Hot Springs, Arkansas.

This sounded so preposterous that we wondered if Nana had lost her mind or if—just as Dad had predicted—her new husband was taking advantage of her. But moving halfway across the country wasn't the worst of it. Evelyn had also arranged to have her trust removed from the Security Bank on Lido Isle, and her six million dollars' worth of Maybelline stock, bonds, and cash transferred to the Arkansas Bank and Trust Company in Hot Springs. She had also had a new Will created—by Melinda's attorney—wherein in the event of Evelyn's death, her entire estate would go to Harry, thereby disinheriting her son and grandchildren. In the event that Harry died before his wife, all of Evelyn's Maybelline money would go to Melinda upon Evelyn's death; if Melinda should die, the money would go to her son, Jake, a boy about the same age as Preston III.

Here, then, was Nana's revenge on her own family: after getting rid of Pauline so she could, as she always put it, "make our future secure," she had signed the control of her estate over to a couple of people she had known for only a few months.

When my dad heard the news, he clutched his chest and was rushed to the emergency room. Although he was told he was only having a panic attack, he now despised his mother completely. He considered her dead. He cursed her for tying his life in knots and continuing to do so even after he had washed his hands of her. He knew that's what her latest stunts were about. Of course she was free to do whatever she wanted with her money and her life—but why had she chosen precisely the course of action most certain to hurt her family? Why had she waited until we were all feeling emotionally stable before dropping this bomb on us?

When my father got wind that Evelyn had sold her Lido Isle home for a measly $150,000, he said he wanted to kill her.

Instead, he turned his anger inward. His drinking worsened, and he started making ill-considered business investments. It was as if his love-hate relationship with his mother had developed into an incestuous *War of the Roses,* with him and Evelyn destined to destroy everything Unk Ile had worked so hard to create for them.

The disturbing news kept rolling in. Great-Aunt Verona reported that Harry and Melinda had asked Evelyn to use the income from the sale of her home to purchase a business for Harry in Hot Springs. According to Verona, even Evelyn had been surprised by this request. Why did Harry need a business? They had more than enough money for cruises and travel, more than enough to do whatever they wanted. Why would she want to start a business at almost seventy-four years of age?

Harry insisted that he had to have something constructive to do for a few hours a day. When he traveled, he said, Melinda would run the business.

Melinda was another problem. She was around all the time; she had even gone along with Harry and Nana on their honeymoon. Evelyn was baffled and hurt by this. She had willingly given up her own family to start over with Harry in what might as well have been a foreign land—why couldn't he do the same for her?

In the end, Verona said, Evelyn gave Harry the money he asked for. She feared that if she didn't, he might leave her—and this time, if that happened, she wouldn't be able to run back to her son for help.

Once again she had made her bed, just as she had with Preston, and then with Warren. Only this time, she was going to have to lie in it for the long haul.

This was the insider report. On the outside, Evelyn claimed that all was well. She sent cards to my father, telling him how happy she was and that she felt loved and accepted by Harry's family in Arkansas. They were living in an apartment in Hot Springs while they looked for their own home.

But in reality, she bowed to Harry's every demand. She didn't even have her own telephone. She began to wonder if Harry was purposely isolating her from her family, but then she decided there was nothing left to isolate her from. She had disinherited everyone, after all. Her own son never replied to the cards and letters she sent. On the one occasion when she and Harry returned to California, she tried to visit my father and me. Bill refused to see her, and Gene forbade me to see her.

So she decided to simply move on with her life and dedicate herself fully to her new family. The newlyweds purchased an old estate on a lake outside Hot Springs. To Evelyn's dismay, Melinda and her son moved in with them. Nana coped by consuming more and more Valium and alcohol. Melinda helped out by mixing sleeping pills and tranquilizers into Evelyn's daily vitamins. So it was while in this drugged stupor, Evelyn signed papers that made Harry the trustee of her trust account she had transferred from the bank on Lido Isle.

One night not long after this, only half-conscious, Evelyn heard Melinda speaking in another room: "Harry, something has to be done with Evelyn—soon."

Or that's what she thought she heard. She was so groggy it was hard to be sure. Still, she thought perhaps she should call someone and ask for help. But who? Nobody from her old life wanted to talk to her.

Besides, there was another problem. All the phones in the house were kept out of her reach.

When Auntie Mabel died that year, my father broke down and sobbed. In his grief, he was suddenly willing to speak to his mother again—but he had no way to get in touch with her. He called Verona to see if she had heard from Evelyn lately. Verona said no—but she did have some thoughts about Harry and Melinda, based on information her sister had given her earlier.

"From the beginning," Verona said, "Melinda was impressed that your mother lived on the bay on Lido Isle. You know your mother, always bragging about herself and never imagining that anyone might be out to take advantage of her."

When I heard this, I had to laugh. How often had Nana warned me and Donna not to trust anyone for fear of being kidnapped?

Verona described the way events had unfolded. It had been Melinda, not Danie the hairdresser, who had actually introduced Evelyn to Harry.

"Your mother is easily impressed, as you know," Verona said, "and an easy mark as well. So Melinda mentioned that her stepfather, Harry Dimmick, a handsome and successful man, was interested in meeting someone."

"I should have hired a P.I. the second I heard about this," Bill said.

"How could you have known? Evelyn didn't want to meet him at first. But then Danie got into the act, saying 'You don't want to be alone anymore, do you?'"

According to Verona, when Evelyn met Harry, she thought he was just her type: a conservative Texan with a Southern drawl. His modesty intrigued her.

He admitted that he was a simple man with no money. But he liked her, and she believed he had great potential.

"Sounds familiar," Bill snorted. "She said exactly the same thing about my father and Warren."

In Hot Springs, Harry shifted money from Evelyn's Maybelline trust account to his new business—building a recreational park with a roller-skating rink and a miniature golf course. This supposedly simple, humble Texan spent money lavishly on himself, his stepdaughter, and her son, while back in the house by Lake Hamilton, Evelyn slept the sleep of the drugged.

Even Harry's own brothers were troubled by his behavior. One of them told Evelyn, "You'd better hire an attorney and a private investigator."

Despite everything, she refused to do it. She refused to believe it was necessary. Instead, she called her son and told him that he ought to send Billee and Preston out for the grand opening of Harry's new fun park. Bill agreed. At least that way, he could get a report on what was really happening out there in Arkansas.

When Billee and Preston arrived in Hot Springs, they were treated like celebrities. Harry took fifteen-year-old Preston to his new recreational park— so new it hadn't officially opened yet—and showed him a great time on the bumper cars and in the skating and roller rinks. When the children returned to California, they recited stories about how well Nana was doing out there in the Arkansas hills, just as they had been coached to do.

But in reality, Evelyn was reaching the end of her rope. Three days before the official opening of the roller rink, she begged Harry to send Melinda back to California. He refused. In fact, after that, he devoted even more time to his stepdaughter while avoiding his wife. Desperate, Evelyn suggested that Harry give Melinda $100,000 and then send her back to California.

Harry's response was hard to misinterpret: "Shut up, or I'll shut you up."

Evelyn was too proud to let her son know that he had been right about Harry all along. When she tried to regain control of her finances, the bank told her that her checking account balance had dropped from half a million dollars to less than fifty thousand.

When she confronted Harry with this, he looked her in the eye and said, "You're going to go along and do exactly as Melinda and I say, or you're going to be sorry."

Fifty-Four
Deeds and
Misdeeds

$\mathcal{E}$velyn knew she was in real trouble, but she still would not contact her son for help. Instead, from a public telephone, she called Harold Pointer, an attorney who had done some work for her in California. Pointer had, coincidentally, also moved to Hot Springs, and although he was retired, Evelyn hoped he could recommend a new attorney for her. She told him she knew Harry and Melinda were up to something: "They've gone through nearly half a million dollars in a couple of months, and they won't let me into the roller rink to see my own files," she said. On one occasion, Harry and Melinda had even physically thrown her out of the rink, bruising her arm so badly she could hardly use it. And of course there were Harry's increasing verbal threats. She told Pointer, "I've got to get a restraining order against them. They try to keep me sedated all the time and I'm terrified of what they might decide to do to me next."

"Is Harry co-owner of the house?"

"Yes."

"How about the roller rink?"

"I'm afraid so."

"And your Maybelline Stock?"

"Yes, again."

"Then you'd better have other grounds on which to base your complaint, because if you don't, there is no case."

"There is something," she said. "Harry can't get an erection. He took pills but it didn't work. We haven't had sex in all the time we've been married."

"Well, then the marriage was never consummated," Pointer said. "So you have a case for fraud and conspiracy—enough to file for divorce in the state of Arkansas."

Pointer recommended two attorneys: a local man named Peter Petrouski, and a California lawyer named Barry Winters. She decided to go with Petrouski, and invited him out to her estate on a day she knew Harry and Melinda would not be there.

After she gave Petrouski a tour of the house and grounds, the two sat down to discuss her situation. Petrouski promised to file for divorce on her behalf, and suggested that she get out of Arkansas as soon as the divorce was finalized. He also said that in lieu of his usual fees, he would accept her estate on Lake Hamilton as payment. This, he told her, would be the easiest way to liquidate the property and satisfy his legal bills, which could easily exceed $100,000.

When Evelyn balked, Petrouski got testy. "The only way I'll come into this case is if I receive the house as my fee—end of story." Feeling that her hands were tied, Evelyn agreed to this arrangement, on the condition that the house would be turned over to Petrouski only if she got back all the property and money that Harry had embezzled from her during their brief marriage.

"Fair enough," Petrouski said. The next day, he filed for divorce on behalf of Evelyn Dimmick and had a judge slap a restraining order against Harry Dimmick and Melinda to prevent them from returning to the estate or the roller rink.

Now Evelyn felt better, although not necessarily safe. Who knew what Harry and Melinda might do to retaliate? When she expressed these fears to Petrouski, he suggested that she get some personal protection, and hired a bodyguard for her named Simon Valli. Evelyn paid Valli one hundred dollars a day, with fifteen hundred up front to cover the first two weeks. He immediately moved into her estate and began escorting her everywhere.

Although at first Evelyn felt relieved, as time went by, Valli began to alarm her. He made vague comments about hit men and said that he could imagine Harry and Melinda wanting to get rid of her at any cost. Evelyn needed more protection. Perhaps, Valli said, she should hire his brother as well. Terrified, she handed Valli a check for five thousand dollars made out to Rocky Valli. On the note line of the check, he had her write: "To pay off gambling debts." And Rocky Valli's name was never mentioned again.

More unsettled than ever, Evelyn decided to fly to California to meet with the other attorney Pointer had recommended, Barry Winters. While there, she received a call from Petrouski, who tried to convince her to come back to Arkansas and settle the divorce out of court. When she refused, he informed her that he had arranged for her deposition to be taken in California by Harry's attorney, Bob Wilson . . . who happened to be a friend of his.

Her suspicions growing, Evelyn stayed in L.A. and gave her deposition. But back in Hot Springs, Petrouski told her she had looked bad during the proceeding—scattered and a bit paranoid. He strongly suggested she simply settle the divorce before, as he put it, "Harry's attorney rakes you over the coals and takes you for every last dime." He was bargaining with Harry's attorney for a simple $100,000 settlement, which was acceptable to Evelyn—until she learned that the agreement included no stipulation regarding the return of the half million dollars Harry had already stolen from her, nor the status of the roller rink that had been built with her money.

Next Petrouski demanded she write him a check for $100,000, a sort of belated retainer that he would hold in a trust account until the divorce was final. Feeling trapped, Evelyn called Pointer's wife, Lea, with whom she had become friends, and confided that she feared Petrouski and Valli were in cahoots. "Yesterday they took me to the bank. Petrouski cut coupons from my savings bonds and had me deposit eight thousand dollars from there into his personal bank account at the bank—where he just happens to be vice president."

"That sounds all wrong, Evelyn. But what about Valli?"

"That's what really frightens me. He told me his uncle is in the Mafia. He walks around the house dressed in a black shirt, with handcuffs hanging from his belt and a gun in plain view. When I told him that I felt that was a little extreme, he said, 'Actually I think you need even more protection. If you just put your name down here on this check, I'll fill in the amount.'"

"You didn't do it, did you?" Lea asked.

"Yes, I did. And he filled in twenty-five thousand dollars."

"Oh, Evelyn."

"After he left, I called Petrouski and told him not to allow Valli to cash the check because it had been written under duress. But I'm worried they're in this together."

Lea suggested that she and Evelyn go to the bank together to see if Petrouski had followed her instructions. When they arrived, they learned that Petrouski had not only cashed the check to Valli, he had also released the $100,000 check he was supposed to have put in trust for her—to Harry.

Lea told Evelyn she needed to be extremely careful, because if the press got wind of the story, it would, she predicted, "blow the top off of Hot Springs." Despite its remote location in the Arkansas hills, Hot Springs, she said, was a mob town to the core; organized crime was involved in all the banks and every kind of business deal. It controlled the lawyers, the judges, the police force. Lea had another piece of advice as well: Evelyn should make Barry Winters her chief counsel. "Go back to California," she instructed. "Bring Barry up to speed, then see what he thinks you should do next."

Evelyn agreed that this was a good idea. But before she could act on it, Petrouski showed up at her home with an entourage of rough-looking men. He asked her to step into the study, then closed the door and took the deed to her estate out of his briefcase. He handed her a pen. "Sign it over. Now."

With a flash of her old gumption, she picked up the phone and called Pointer, who told her to go ahead and sign it. "It's okay; it will be held in trust until the divorce is settled anyway."

Feeling this would give her the time to make her move to California and get Winters working on the divorce—and allow her to escape from Petrouski and his thugs—she signed her name:

"Evelyn F. Williams."

Barry Winters's expression went from neutral to concerned as Evelyn sat in his office and related her troubles, then turned outright grim when she told him that she had signed the deed to her estate over to Petrouski.

"Was anyone else present when you signed?" he asked.

"No, but right before he left, Lea Pointer did stop by to say hello."

"Did you authorize Petrouski to release the $100,000 to your husband?"

"No. Absolutely not!"

Winters shook his head. "This whole thing is a disaster. You're in a world of trouble and going to court is the only way to get out of it."

Evelyn left his office in tears. She called me—the first time we had spoken since she had married Harry—and said she would love to see me. She said Winters had gotten her a hotel room in Huntington Beach, so I suggested we meet for lunch there the next day. I dressed carefully for the reunion, choosing an outfit I knew would please my grandmother, in the Maybelline colors of red and black: a full-length red suede coat with white fur trim, black pants, a black sweater and black turban, and black suede gloves. I also wore dangling earrings, very high platform shoes, and my new Neiman-Marcus sunglasses—so that I could spot my grandmother before she noticed me.

I arrived at the hotel expecting to find the glamorous, confident powerhouse of a grandmother I had always known—and was shocked to see a tiny, frail-looking woman waiting in the lobby. When I held out my arms to my grandmother, she fell crying into my embrace, and I comforted her as if she were a child. "I never realized how tiny you are, Nana," I said; she had always seemed larger than life to me. But now I saw an exhausted and unkempt woman, devoid of her usual impeccable style. Tufts of her gray hair were even slipping out from under her lopsided wig.

"Darling," she said, "I want to see your beautiful new home and possibly stay a day or so."

"I'd so love that," I said, "but we don't have a guest room set up yet." Although this was true, it wasn't the whole truth. The real reason she couldn't stay with us was that my husband refused to allow her through the door. He felt that our lives were going pretty well with Evelyn hundreds of miles away in Arkansas, and he didn't want her to establish a new toehold.

I could tell that my grandmother was disappointed, but she tried to hide it. She held me at arm's length and looked me over. "You're wearing too many accessories, dear. You remind me of myself when I was young, all that gobbledy-gook. It's overpowering and covers up your natural beauty."

I couldn't believe it. This was coming from Evelyn? Miss Maybelline was accusing me of being overdone? What had become of my wonderfully cocky, arrogant Nana?

She must have seen something of my amazement, because all she said next was, "Let's go eat."

When Evelyn returned to Winters's office, the lawyer had a stunning piece of news: If Evelyn didn't get back to Arkansas immediately, Harry's attorney would have the case thrown out of court because she was no longer an Arkansas resident.

"How can he do that?" Evelyn asked.

"It's a new law. That's probably why Petrouski was so anxious to get you out of the state. If he's in cahoots with your husband and his attorney, they wanted you back here so they could divide up your property. That property's extremely valuable. There's talk of a Disneyland-type park opening up just a mile from the roller rink. Evelyn, Hot Springs is about to explode into a boomtown. Get back there, and we'll fight for what's rightfully yours. I'll be your sole attorney. I've already started an investigation into Harry and Melinda, and the facts are astounding. Trust me, we can beat them."

Evelyn did one more thing before she left L.A. Swallowing—or maybe choking on—her pride, she called my father. If she hoped he would step in to offer support, however, she was destined to be disappointed.

"I can't deal with your problems, Mother," he said. "I've got too many of my own, and besides, I'm not feeling well. My stomach has been acting up again ever since you sold your house for nothing and ran off with that gigolo."

"Darling—"

"And what about cutting your whole family out of your will?" Bill was on a roll. "How do you excuse that one? You can't. You got yourself into this mess, Mother, so go back to Arkansas and get yourself out. Until you do, I'm keeping my distance. We all are; we agreed on it."

Stung and humiliated, Evelyn drove to Newport Beach to visit her former hairdresser, Danie King. After she spilled her story, he poured her a shot of whiskey. "This is terrible. I feel responsible, since I introduced you to Melinda. You would never have met Harry otherwise."

Evelyn sipped her drink. "Danie, I have to ask. Did you know anything about their plan to get my money?"

"Evelyn, God no."

He poured her another shot.

"You know what you should do? Go back to Arkansas, win your case, take over Harry's roller rink, and recoup all your losses. Get even."

"I'd love to," Evelyn said, "But the last business I tried to run was my second husband's mining operation, and I lost it all to lawyers."

Danie straightened her wig. "This is different. Do this your way, dear. Build a business promoting yourself as Miss Maybelline, the Last of the Red Hot Mamas. Make a million bucks, then come back to California with your head up, and gloat. And get a facelift and look like a million bucks, too."

"Oh, what a wonderful idea!" She hesitated, looking into his eyes. "Danie. Come with me to Hot Springs. Help me put myself together so I'll make a good showing in court."

"Looking good is the best defense, huh?" He reached out and took her hands. "I'll do it. Together, we'll not only beat Harry and Melinda, we'll take over the whole town!"

For some reason, Danie the hairdresser's pledge gave Evelyn more confidence than did Winters the lawyer's. She flew back to Arkansas filled with a new resolve not only to get her money back, but to fight for what she now realized should have been her first priority all along—re-knotting her family ties.

In Evelyn's absence, big changes had taken place at the estate on Lake Hamilton. Petrouski met her at the door. "Please come in," he said, leading her into her own living room, which was now filled with his furniture. "Have a seat."

She did not sit. Controlling her fury, she said, "What did you think you were doing when you released the check for $100,000 to Harry?"

He shrugged. "By law, he owns half your estate."

"That's impossible. The estate is in my trust."

"Evelyn, perhaps you don't remember, but while you weren't feeling well, you signed a paper releasing your estate from the trust. That made it community property and therefore half Harry's."

She glowered. "Understand this. They drugged me to make me sign that paper, and I will fight for my rights if it takes every last dime I have." She turned and marched out, climbed into her car and roared back to town. From a hotel room, she called Winters in Los Angeles. He had good news: he had gotten her nonresident status dismissed.

"Good," she said. "Because I'm more than ready to go to court and fight for what's mine."

A few days later, Winters flew to Hot Springs, and he and Evelyn met with Harry's attorney. They gave permission for Harry to keep whatever he had already spent of the $100,000, provided he return the rest. He gave back forty-six thousand.

Next, Evelyn had Petrouski legally ordered out of her home, and to his surprise, he had no choice but to leave. It turned out that the deed to the property Evelyn had signed before going to California had been invalid because she had signed it "Evelyn F. Williams" when she was still officially "Mrs. Charles Harrison Dimmick." From a legal standpoint, Evelyn F. Williams had no legal capacity to sign over the deed to her home. Also, without the signature of her husband, the document was automatically null and void. So not only did Petrouski have to return the home, he stood to receive no fees at all, because he had failed to fulfill all the conditions of his alleged agreement to represent Evelyn.

Round one to Nana.

Fifty-Five
Trials

anie King arrived in Hot Springs and worked his magic on my grandmother. Looking in the mirror, she exclaimed, "Miss Maybelline is back!" Then she called her son and told him she would be going to court to finalize her divorce and get everything else straightened out.

"Damn good to hear it, Mother," he said. "If anyone can do it, you can."

She relished the praise but realized it would go no further than that; Bill would not be riding into Hot Springs on a white charger to battle on her behalf.

The trial, which began on May 23, 1976, turned out to be one of the nastiest Hot Springs had seen in a long time.

The day was hot and humid—inside the courtroom as well as outside. Barry Winters had uncovered the fact that Harry had been married a total of seven times. Furthermore, Melinda was both his stepdaughter and wife number six. Her mother had been wife number five. That woman, who had once shot Harry in the shoulder, had disappeared years before and had not been seen since. She was presumed dead. Melinda, who had at various times claimed to be an accountant, a public relations expert, a journalist, and a nurse, turned out to be none of these things—although she had once been married to a doctor. Melinda and Harry had married on February 8, 1970, and separated less than a year later; Melinda's son, Jake, testified that despite this, Harry had lived with his mother and him until marrying Evelyn in 1974.

This was lurid stuff, but the real bombshell was the revelation that Charles Harrison Dimmick had been convicted of, and served time in the Arkansas State Penitentiary for, multiple felonies including armed robbery and trafficking in stolen goods.

That night, when Evelyn's phone rang, she answered it with the strong, confident voice of someone who had been vindicated at every turn. She expected her caller to be a reporter or perhaps her son.

Instead, a man murmured, "Old lady . . . you're making powerful enemies in Arkansas."

Dial tone.

But Evelyn recognized the voice. She was probably supposed to: Simon Valli.

Winters hired a bodyguard to protect Evelyn during the remainder of the trial. This time, the precaution actually seemed necessary. Peter had already painted Evelyn's car with obscenities, and Harry and Melinda had been seen driving slowly past the roller rink on more than one occasion. Evelyn also put iron bars on the windows of her home, and had an alarm system installed.

Harry and Melinda refused to go down without a fight; the trial continued with the defendants countersuing for half of Evelyn's estate. One of their main arguments was that when Harry married Evelyn, he hadn't even known she was wealthy. He claimed that Evelyn had arranged the wedding and the sale of her home in California just to get Harry to marry her, and she had promised him money in return.

Danie King's testimony disproved this. He pointed out that the response cards in the wedding invitations had Melinda's home address and telephone number printed on them, as well as the phone number of Danie's business in Newport Beach—and that Melinda was part owner of Danie's business. As for Harry not knowing Evelyn was wealthy, Danie testified that during Harry and Evelyn's brief courtship, Evelyn had put five thousand dollars into her boyfriend's personal bank account so that he could afford to take her out to the places she was accustomed to patronizing.

During the long, hot three days the trial required, Evelyn always came to court looking like a million bucks thanks to Danie's talents with hair and makeup and his positive reinforcement. "Crush your enemies!" he told her each morning. "You are Miss Maybelline—an heiress, a queen!"

As Evelyn grew more confident, Harry and Melinda began to wilt under the barrage of damaging facts lobbed at them during Barry Winters's cross-examination. At one point, Harry refused to answer a question at all. The judge warned him that he was in contempt of court. Melinda crumbled when her past drinking problems and marital status were brought out.

In the end, Evelyn was awarded both her divorce and the return of her property. Everything that had happened to her was judged a conspiracy that started in Newport Beach, California, and ended in Hot Springs, Arkansas. The conspiracy charge was based on two main points. First, Harry and Melinda had drawn a circle around the number in a federal estate tax rates table that showed how much Evelyn's estate would be worth upon her demise. Second, they wrote down estimates of the attorney fees that would be allowed in the probate of such an estate. What made these estimates especially significant was that they had apparently been calculated and copied in the offices of a California attorney well before Evelyn and Harry's wedding.

The court recommended that if Harry and Melinda wanted to avoid jail, they should leave town as soon as possible.

Only hours after the end of the trial, Gary Gaines, the private detective whom Barry Winters had hired to protect Evelyn, warned her that Danie King was not the pal she thought he was. He suspected that Danie, like Harry, was after her money.

Evelyn was outraged—at Gary Gaines. She pointed out that Danie had been one of her greatest allies during the trial. His testimony had been devastating to the conspirators, and his emotional support and artistic skills were crucial to her in her time of need. Clearly the bodyguard was just looking for excuses to stay on her payroll.

Then Evelyn told Danie what Gaines had said about him.

And Danie was outraged, too.

"Danie King said what?" Gaines shouted into the phone.

Barry Winters's voice was measured and precise. "His exact words were, 'Evelyn's got another crooked bodyguard on her hands.'"

"Crooked? *Me?* King's the crooked one! Listen, Mr. Winters. Danie King is up to no good. I'm telling you. One of the things you wanted me to do was keep an eye on the old lady, make sure she took her medication, ate decent, got enough sleep, laid low. Well, you want to know what she's doing? She's going to the races, staying out all night, and throwing her family name around to get customers into that damned rink—all because King suggests it."

Winters remained unruffled. "If King can help her earn back the half-million she lost during the divorce, she'll be happy to get out of Hot Springs and return to California. That's all she wants."

"Great. But what is it that King wants?"

One thing King wanted, which Evelyn agreed to, was to be named general manager of the newly renamed Spa City Roller Rink. As such, he displayed a spirit of entrepreneurship worthy of Rags Ragland and Tom Lyle. It began with a full-page picture in the local papers depicting Miss Maybelline, looking fabulous of course. The accompanying article informed people of Evelyn's plan to create a safe, wholesome recreational environment for the youth of Hot Springs. It also introduced her new business manager: her nephew, Danie King of California. The people of Hot Strings welcomed them both, especially Evelyn. They were thrilled to have such a celebrity in their town.

Evelyn and Danie—"Aunt" and "Nephew"—lived extravagantly, showing off Evelyn's wealth with flashy cars and expensive clothes. Winters, who had convinced Evelyn to put her Maybelline trust in his hands for safekeeping, became concerned. With their flamboyant public personas, she and Danie might draw the wrong kind of attention. He advised them to buy a gun and keep it nearby at all times, and suggested that before Evelyn or Danie drive anywhere, they double-check under the hood of the car, then start the engine and walk away for a while. *I'm not trying to frighten you,* Winters wrote Evelyn, *but, as you recall, Gary Gaines did the same thing every morning.* They should maintain this ritual at least until Melinda, Harry, and Peter had left the area.

Winters also asked for another twenty-five thousand dollars for his work on the divorce, a sum Evelyn paid gladly; in fact, she was happy to turn all her legal worries over to him. He reclaimed the name Evelyn Williams for her, and recovered more than fifteen thousand shares of the Schering-Plough stock that Harry and Melinda had swindled from her.

Things were finally going my grandmother's way.

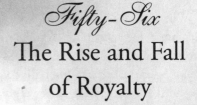

Fifty-Six
The Rise and Fall
of Royalty

Even as Evelyn and Danie's popularity rose among the citizens and businesspeople of Hot Springs, private investigator Gaines smoldered at the way he had been treated. He began sending letters to Danie, admonishing the hairdresser for telling Evelyn that Gaines was "another Simon Valli."

In response, Danie wrote to Gaines and insisted that he really was Evelyn's blood nephew—the son of her sister Bunny. He said he had come to Hot Springs to help his aunt out of her troubles and redeem himself with his cousin Bill.

Gaines replied to Danie's letter, stating that he had conducted an investigation and uncovered substantial proof that King was not Evelyn's blood relative.

Danie wrote back again, trying to patch the holes in his first story. According to the new embellished version, Bunny had married a young man in Vancouver, British Columbia, in 1943. This man already had a child from a previous marriage. The marriage had ended after two years, and the child, Danie, stayed with his father until he was old enough to leave home. Then he made his way to California, found Bunny, and met her sisters Evelyn and Verona.

Despite the fact that Evelyn had fired him, Gaines felt sick to see her being taken in by such a slimebag—but the lady wouldn't listen to him. Neither would anyone else.

Finally, aware that my father also disliked King, Gaines wrote to Bill, suggesting that Danie be investigated before it was too late and providing a persuasive list of reasons why. Danie both used and sold illegal drugs, which he stored at Evelyn's house. Danie was an obvious homosexual who was probably using the roller rink as a way to meet and seduce young men—a fact that, if ever disclosed to the public in a Bible Belt state like Arkansas, would certainly hurt both Evelyn's business and her reputation. Without Evelyn's knowledge, Danie had used Evelyn's money to establish his own personal slush fund at the bank, a fund that had grown to twenty-four thousand dollars. And he was forging Evelyn's signature on checks.

The last thing Bill wanted to do was get involved in a big investigation or even spend any money on one. Still, something had to be done, so he, his girlfriend, Gloria, and sixteen-year-old Preston III packed up his new 1976 Cadillac Seville and drove out to Arkansas to try to get to the bottom of things.

When Bill and his family drove up the last stretch of road approaching Evelyn's house, they encountered an enormous iron gate with "Maybelline Manor" scrolled across it. Bill looked at Gloria and shook his head in bemusement, then pressed the buzzer. When the gate opened, they cruised down the winding tree-lined lane, admiring the sweeping lawn and giant pine trees. Beyond the house, at the water's edge, they could see boathouses and swimming docks. The mansion itself was a low, sprawling structure punctuated at intervals by high-ceilinged A-framed sections, in which twenty-foot tall windows glittered.

As the Cadillac drew up to the house, the front door burst open, and Evelyn ran down the steps and across the lawn to greet them. Bill had barely emerged from the car before she had enfolded him in a fierce hug, eyes streaming with tears of joy. Preston was next, submitting good-naturedly to Nana's embraces, and even Gloria, whom Nana had never before met, received a peck on the cheek.

Behind her, slouching in the doorway, stood Danie King in all his glory: black mustache and swept-back hair, skintight jeans and a shirt unbuttoned nearly to the waist, and just the slightest hint of a smirk.

"You have quite a place here, Mud," Bill said.

"Isn't it wonderful?" Evelyn replied. "Come in, come in! Are you hungry? I hope so, because I've got dinner just about ready for you."

Evelyn had barely finished giving the visitors a tour of her house when Barry Winters, who had flown out for the occasion, arrived in a taxi. At a table extravagantly set with flowers and candles, the group sat down to Bill's favorite meal, not unlike the one Tom Lyle had preferred back before his blood disease killed his appetite: pepper steak smothered in onions and tomatoes; mashed potatoes;

sweet-and-sour purple cabbage; mashed rutabagas with lots of butter and salt; thinly sliced sweet-and-sour cucumbers, onions, and tomatoes; and pineapple upside-down cake.

Evelyn could hardly contain her joy. Looking around the table at her guests, she kept repeating, "I'm so happy you're here!"

After dinner, Evelyn, Bill, and Winters sat on the deck overlooking the boathouse, and Winters brought up the subject of Evelyn's will. He had mentioned it during the meal, but Bill had changed the subject because Danie King had been listening avidly at the time. "Your mother wants to leave everything she has to you," Winters said, "and make you the executor of her estate."

Bill turned his face away so the other two could not see his grimace. Typical Evelyn, trying to buy her way back into his good graces. "Thanks, Mud," he said, "but I don't need any more money. Leave it to the kids. I'd prefer to just be executor."

"Are you sure about that, darling?" she said.

"Yes," he said. "And there's something I want you to know. Look at this." He handed her a copy of the letter Gary Gaines had sent him. "Read this."

Evelyn obeyed, then handed the letter back. "That troublemaker. That's just jealousy, you know. That's all that is."

"Jealousy? Over what?"

"Oh, during the trial I mentioned to Gaines that I needed to find a manager for the roller rink. I thought about hiring him for the job, but then I realized that Danie would be a much better choice. Gaines has been trying to cause trouble for Danie ever since."

Bill grimaced again. Gaines was right: Evelyn would simply not believe anything negative about Danie King.

The next day, Evelyn held an old-fashioned barbecue, to which she invited all her friends and neighbors so they could meet Bill, Gloria, and Preston, III. The trio received a big dose of Southern hospitality; as Miss Maybelline's kin they were treated as celebrities and asked over and over what it was like to live in Southern California, home of Hollywood and movie stars, Disneyland and film studios.

That night, the family and Danie King took Evelyn's party boat—named *Miss Maybelline,* of course—to the Hamilton House, a fancy restaurant on the water, for dinner. As they sat at their table overlooking the lake, in walked a man wearing a black cape over a black suit, with a black hat. To Bill, he looked like a stereotypical sinister character straight of a comic book. The man took one look at Evelyn and her party, then turned and walked out as quickly as he had entered.

"Who the hell was that weirdo?" Bill asked.

Evelyn shook her head. "Pete Petrouski, my crooked attorney."

"You're kidding. He looks like some old vaudeville actor. How could you have ever taken him seriously?"

Evelyn had no answer. Bill found this frightening: if she had been gullible enough to take that guy seriously, who else might be able to manipulate her—and with what results?

Later, after Danie had navigated *Miss Maybelline* past the lakeside homes and back to Maybelline Manor, the adults sat up late talking and having drinks. Danie had everyone laughing with his hilarious impressions of Harry and Melinda's faces during the trial as he again and again refuted their testimony with his own. He fetched refills for everyone, and even Bill found him imminently likeable. Still, Bill's suspicions were not allayed, and when he was alone with his mother, he reminded her of the allegations in Gaines's letter. Once again, she simply brushed the accusations off, but her reaction was stronger when Bill muttered that Danie was an "obvious fag."

"He has several girlfriends," Evelyn contradicted angrily. "All the girls at the rink throw themselves at him!"

Bill stared at her incredulously. Could she really believe that?

"He has terrific ideas for the business," she went on, "and he's a marvelous manager. He's single-handedly turning the roller rink into a money-making machine."

"Look, Mother, I agree he's a lot of fun, and I understand why you enjoy his company, but for God's sake, don't you worry about what people think about you living alone with a young man?"

"Why, of course. That's why I tell people he's my nephew."

"Your what?"

"It's just a cover, dear, to keep tongues from wagging. Although I do feel that Danie's become one of the family."

Bill rubbed his forehead. He could feel his stomach churning.

"It was Danie who named my estate Maybelline Manor," Evelyn said.

"What the hell difference does that make?"

Evelyn's brows tightened. "It shows that Danie's been here for me. Our arrangement may not be to your liking, but it is to mine. He came out here from California to help me, and appeared as a witness in my defense. Without him, I might have lost everything to those terrible people! I owe him."

"Can't you see that he's one reason you got into this mess in the first place? Encouraging you to marry Harry so you wouldn't be alone?"

"He had no idea what Harry and Melinda were really like. You don't seem to see that unlike you, Danie understands me, appreciates my talents. Why else would he be working so hard to make me successful?"

"For his own gain, what else? He's using you for your money, like most of the men you've been involved with."

Evelyn raised her chin. "Thanks to Danie, I have come to represent glamour and dignity in this town. People greet me on the street. Bank executives and local dignitaries ask me for advice. In fact, Danie and I have been approached about putting together a huge spa, like the Golden Door or La Costa, in conjunction with the baths here. It would be the first in Hot Springs."

Bill drummed his fingers on the table. "That sounds great, okay? But even if it happens, I don't understand why you would want to begin such a giant undertaking at your age."

"Because I'm still Miss Maybelline! Danie knows this and he's using that to get publicity for us and our business. In fact, he's arranging a grand tour for me at the Maybelline factory in Little Rock."

"Mother, our family doesn't run Maybelline anymore."

Her eyes misted. "We'll always be part of Maybelline, Bill honey, and Maybelline will always be part of us. What I'm saying is that for the first time in years, I feel important, alive. My roller-skating rink is one of the largest in Arkansas thanks to Danie putting in every new innovation. We're building Hot Springs's first go-cart speedway, a trampoline field, an archery court, a miniature golf course, and a picnicking and barbecue area. This will be on the main route into Hot Springs, so it will attract tourists as well as locals. Pretty soon we'll recoup the money that was stolen from me. But best of all, until I came to Hot Springs, there was nothing for the kids around here to do—now we're helping put this town on the map for something besides gambling and the mob."

Bill could only listen. He had to admit, he hadn't seen his mother this enthusiastic over something in years. "I hope for your sake you're right and I'm wrong about Danie," he said. "Because God knows, Mother, if anyone can pull this off, it will be you."

Still, the churning in his stomach did not let up.

Soon after her son's family returned to California, Evelyn wrote Tom Lyle a long letter describing their wonderful visit and laying out her plans in Arkansas. She told him about Danie and her reclaimed title as Miss Maybelline, and advised him to expect a letter from a public-relations man at the Maybelline factory in Little Rock, who would ask him to confirm that she actually was who she claimed she was. She hoped Tom Lyle would approve of her touring the factory as Miss Maybelline—she knew she didn't need his blessing, but it would be so wonderful to have it.

She signed her name, put a lipstick kiss over her signature, and mailed the letter.

She never received a reply.

Tom Lyle died the very day she mailed it.

Tom Lyle Williams, our beloved Unk Ile, died September 26, 1976, at the age of eighty.

It was unbelievable news.

Tom Lyle had been quite sick for many years; still, nothing could have prepared us for his passing. The doctors said that he died of a heart condition compounded by the blood disease that he'd had for so many years. Be that as it may, I felt that it was in part from a broken heart—our Unk Ile had never gotten over selling Maybelline, the company that had been his life since he was nineteen years old.

Milford said that the week before Tom Lyle died, he anguished for death to take him, and though weak and frail, on his last day, he sat down at his Steinway piano and played "Turkey in Straw" one last time. This memory sustains me; though I have to say, I still pine that I didn't spend more time with him in those last couple of years—even though he isolated himself from the outside world and quite objected to anyone "disturbing" him in those last years. Mostly, we had honored this and given him the space he asked for. But I think that clapping and cheering at his playing "Turkey in the Straw" would have given his heart joy. It sure would have mine.

It has been difficult to reconcile my feelings, given the dream I had on the eve of his death. In it, I saw Unk Ile looking vibrant and healthy, wearing a light-blue and gold plaid suit. He was walking out a door, then halfway through, he turned to me and saluted, whispering, "It's your turn now." Startled, I woke up in a sweat. The next day, I called my mother and told her about it. She said that she had heard that once a person dies, his spirit remains for three days on earth before moving on. And then came dad's call, telling me that Unk Ile had died.

Thus, the kind, gentle, compassionate, gracious, and generous Tom Lyle was gone. The man who founded Maybelline and honored those who were loyal to him, sharing his wealth. He left a million dollars each to the butler and house-keeper, millions to family, and earmarked millions and millions for charity.

He was cremated and buried at Forest Lawn in Hollywood, California.

Fifty-Seven
Glory

Even without Tom Lyle's blessing, Evelyn had her grand tour of the Maybelline factory in Little Rock. As Danie had predicted, the media lapped up the story. Scores of people who had read about the tour journeyed to the roller rink to look at the Maybelline pictures adorning the entrance and, they hoped, to meet the Last of the Red Hot Mamas. The lucky ones got to see Miss Maybelline wearing the flamboyant costumes that Danie designed for her. She especially loved her red and white Mae West gown, with its big satin hoopskirt, red satin heart-shaped bodice, and enormous red satin hat covered in sparkling stones, feathers, lace, and plumes, which she wore tilted at a flirty angle.

The next few months were among the happiest of Evelyn's life. With the help of Danie's tireless promotion, she felt like she was living in a Hollywood movie. Every day was show time, full of the recognition and glamour that went with being a celebrity. Danie arranged for her to speak at dinners, meetings, and clubs throughout Hot Springs, and she made quite an impression telling her story. Every time she spoke of Tom Lyle, her eyes welled with tears of grief for the loss of the man she had loved for more than fifty-five years—and hers were not the only damp eyes in the house. Afterward, people gathered around to shake her hand, give her a hug, or ask for her autograph.

Throughout it all, Danie was by her side. When her physical energy flagged, he gave her the morale boost she needed to keep going. And his own energy seemed boundless. Apart from running the business, he had his own radio show called *Silver Ghost Rides Again,* during which he played disco music and aired commercials for the roller rink. He also wrote a column for the local paper, discussing health, beauty, and spirituality and Miss Maybelline's life.

In Hot Springs, Danie King and Miss Maybelline were becoming household names.

But despite Evelyn's illusions, Hot Springs was not a Hollywood set. As the fame and success of the "aunt" and "nephew" grew, in the background things began to take an ominous turn. It might be true that nothing breeds success like success, but nothing breeds jealousy like success, either.

Lines to get into the roller rink went around the block, which meant it was serious competition for night clubs, featuring bars and restaurants whose owners were quite unhappy at the resulting drop in their profits. On top of that, none of the other establishments could boast an attraction like Miss Maybelline; Danie had set up a system whereby people could make reservations just to meet her, and she was always booked.

At the same time Evelyn was arousing envy among her competitors, rumors about Danie's sexual orientation began to circulate around town. Worse, just as Gary Gaines had warned, so did stories about Danie seducing young boys and selling drugs to kids at the roller rink. When these rumors reached Evelyn, she dismissed them as coming from old-biddy church fanatics who had nothing better to do than slander innocent people, not unlike the old-maid aunts who had made her life miserable back in Chicago so long ago.

As for Danie, he believed that with Evelyn's support and the Maybelline name behind him, he was invincible. His ideas grew ever more grandiose; he encouraged Evelyn to establish a spa where people from around the world would come to get the "total look" of everlasting beauty that Miss Maybelline promised. Shrewd Danie recognized that because Evelyn was still unusually youthful-looking for her age, it would be easy to imply that she possessed cosmetic secrets that could keep other people forever beautiful, too—secrets that would be shared only with spa guests.

That Christmas, in 1976, Evelyn wrote to her family in California:

> I will miss you all terribly, as I know your hearts tell you. The memories of our precious Christmases with Unk Ile fill me with much sadness.

She pleaded with her son and grandchildren to start communicating with her again. She acknowledged that Danie was the reason for their current estrangement, but asked them to at least try to accept him for helping her and making her happy.

Then she said that although she had no money for extravagant Christmas gifts, she was sending a box of presents and a promise for a big future. She added,

> I'm sure, dears, you are all confident, in case anything ever happened to me, that all of you are taken care of with all the care that you know I have for you forever and ever. This to me is the supreme gift of Christmas, more important than commercial scrambling everyone everywhere suffers through every year.

Finally, she said that she and Danie were heading to Las Vegas and wanted to know if Bill's neighbor, Liberace, was in Palm Springs or if he was performing in Vegas; if the latter, could he get them a table in front of the stage?

Nothing too extraordinary, for Evelyn; after all, we had plenty of money to buy presents for each other, so it made little difference to us if she chose to buy inexpensive gifts for the family so she could afford a trip to Las Vegas for herself. Our nonchalance was shattered, however, when her box of presents was opened: it was full of cheap Arkansas souvenirs.

She would have done better to have sent nothing at all.

I had far more important things to worry about than Christmas presents, however, because shortly after the holidays, I called Nana with some big news: I was pregnant—she was going to be a great-grandmother! She sounded excited for a minute or so, then turned the conversation to her situation in Hot Springs.

It seemed that despite her newfound success and influence, Evelyn was not satisfied. She missed her family, and set out a plan to bring them to her that summer. Donna's bait was that Danie could arrange to have her photographed by his friend Harry Langdon, a world-famous photographer who specialized in capturing images of Hollywood celebrities, especially gorgeous women. Through the lens of his camera, Langdon could make Donna a star. She also promised Billee a chance at stardom thanks to Danie's connections.

Preston III was the easiest mark. He already loved Hot Springs, where the kids had treated him like a prince because he was the grandson of Miss Maybelline. He told his dad he wanted to go back that summer, see Nana, and make some money working at the roller rink. Bill not only agreed, he decided to return for a while himself—once again to check up on what was really going on.

When the five of them—Bill, my three siblings, and Gloria—arrived in Hot Springs, they were surprised to find that the Spa City Roller Rink had undergone a complete renovation and was now called the Palace Dinner Theater, although it was still known as the home of Miss Maybelline.

Evelyn's plan to lure her family to Hot Springs had mixed results. Billee, at age twenty-two, plunged straight into the limelight. Billed as a professional disco dancer, she drew crowds to watch her gyrate in a cage suspended above the rink, where strobe lights accentuated her moves. She soon became a local celebrity in her own right, and was confident that her newfound fame would follow her back to California. In that she was disappointed. Hot Springs might have been the entertainment capital of Arkansas, but among fiercer competition in California, Billee was just another pretty, talented girl.

Donna had none of Billee's expectations; she simply wanted to get a new pair of white roller skates and then head back to Venice Beach to make the scene on the boardwalk. Which she did as quickly as possible.

It was Preston III who proved to be Evelyn's most loyal ally, so on him she lavished the most. She revised her will again, giving Preston her home and 75 percent of the business; the cash, stocks, and bonds would go to Donna, Billee, and me. In this version of the Will, she also awarded Danie forty-five thousand dollars and the remaining 25 percent of the Palace.

That same summer, Evelyn announced that she and Danie had big plans for the 1978 tourist season: they were also going to get a liquor license for the Palace Dinner Theater. Dubious, Bill asked how much this transformation would cost.

"Danie figures it will take a quarter of a million dollars, but it will make millions when we sell it and open our Total Look Beauty Spa."

Bill scowled. Gloria raised another concern: "What about the local families? I thought you had the goodwill of the community because you provide a wholesome environment for their children. Won't this new plan hurt that?"

"Nonsense," Evelyn scoffed. "People will be more than willing to find other things for their kids to do when they learn how many jobs the Palace will create. Not to mention the overall economic impact on the community." She smiled. "My dream is to turn the Palace into a modern-day Grand Ole Opry—but instead of Minnie Pearl as mistress of ceremonies, it will be me, Miss Maybelline."

"Dammit, Mother," Bill said, "why don't you ever think about slowing down? You're not thirty-five anymore."

"Now you're hitting below the belt," she said with indignation. "Besides, I can't quit now; construction on the Palace is already scheduled to begin. It's got its own life. Also, I had a dream that Elvis Presley told me to do it."

"Elvis? Mother, Elvis is dead. He died a couple of days ago."

"I know that, thank you very much, and that's why my dream was so significant. He told me that if I helped develop young talent, I would be remembered long after my death."

"Mother!"

"Bill, darling, I don't want to talk about this anymore. You know I've always believed in past lives and spirit guides. I'm on a mission. I want to be remembered for doing something special."

Bill snorted, and added in what had become an oft-repeated refrain: "I just hope you haven't made a pact with the devil. Danie's like every other moocher, looking for a way to expand his world. He's out for everything he can get, and you're an easy mark, Mother. Why don't you wake up?"

In California, far removed from Evelyn's grand plans and schemes, I gave birth to a baby girl on September 21, 1977. We named her Georgia after Gene's father; five weeks premature, she had to stay in the hospital in an incubator for eight days.

In all the turmoil, time got away from me and before I realized it almost a month had passed without me sending out birth announcements. I decided to wait until Georgia was a full month old, then get some professional pictures taken and send those to everyone in the family.

But Nana took the lack of a formal announcement as a personal insult. She wrote a disapproving letter to my father, complaining about being the forgotten member of the family and asking for a picture of my baby. *I'm sure she looks just like her great-grandmother and is a great beauty,* she wrote.

In my exhaustion, this infuriated me. How dare Nana claim to be the source of my child's beauty? And how dare she try to make me feel guilty for neglecting her?

After all, she had been the one who left us.

Fifty-Eight
Finishing Touches

By January 1978, Evelyn and Danie were busy putting the finishing touches on the Palace, even as Bill continued to warn her that Danie was not only going to ruin her reputation but worse, embarrass the family.

Danie had had enough of this. He told Evelyn, "It's about time you realized it's me who's making your dreams come true, not your precious son or your spoiled brat grandchildren. I'm the one who's made you a household name in Hot Springs." Evelyn knew there was no disputing what he said. And besides, she told herself, she had no proof that any of the rumors about him were true.

But then came an evening while Evelyn was at the Palace checking on the ongoing construction, and her gaze fell on a letter she found in the office. As Evelyn read it, shock deepened to horror. It had been written by Danie to a boy she knew from the roller rink, and it left no doubt: Danie was substantially involved in the gay underworld of Hot Springs. In fact, he appeared to want to turn her business into a gay bar. This was nothing like the secret life that Tom Lyle had led in an effort to protect his company and his legacy. If this were made public, the Maybelline name and Evelyn's good reputation would be tarnished forever.

Once again Bill had been right—but Evelyn couldn't confront Danie with her discovery. Not now. She could not risk sabotaging everything she had worked for on the Palace.

And so Evelyn put on her game face and carried on. Some weeks later, she was a judge at the Miss Henderson University Pageant. She showed up as Miss Maybelline, looking more like a contestant than a seventy-seven-year-old woman. Afterward, she called me to tell me how much she had loved the attention from the audience. She added that she and Danie had then gone to Kansas City, where she had had a facelift and breast implants. The results were remarkable, she reported. "Why," she said, "I don't look a day over forty-five!"

While I was still assimilating this, she returned to the subject of the Palace Dinner Theater. Conway Twitty would be performing on opening night. "Someday," she said, "all you kids will be worth a lot of money because of the hard work Danie and I have done in the last two years."

"Nana," I said, "I'm amazed at everything you've done. You are an incredible woman, and I love you for it." And I meant it.

"I love you too, dear," she said, sounding happy and contented. She meant it, too.

That was the last time I ever heard her voice.

A few days later, a package arrived from Hot Springs. It contained a beautiful sterling silver baby cup, spoon, and fork, and the biggest, most impressive congratulations card imaginable. When I read the letter inside the card, I almost broke down in tears. It was full of wonderful little endearments to my baby about how her Nana loved her and wanted to give her the world on a string. Nana looked forward to her little princess arriving at her great-grandmother's Palace, where Georgia would be celebrated as a Southern belle.

Though Nana and I had made peace with one another, things were getting ugly in Hot Springs. The rumors about Danie were growing ever more rampant, and now there were even worse stories circulating—stories that organized crime wanted to harm her and sabotage her new nightclub.

Evelyn found herself in an uncomfortable position—the sad truth was although she had finally accepted that Danie had his own agenda, he was all she had in Arkansas. She had little choice but to trust that he was ultimately on her side. Above all, she must stay focused on the grand opening of the Palace. After construction costs of $500,000—double what Danie had predicted—opening day was finally on the horizon.

As the weeks flew past, Danie stepped up the promotion of Miss Maybelline and the upcoming opening of the dinner theater, telling the local papers about their future plans to create the Evdan Corporation (a name coined by combining "Evelyn" and "Danie"). "After the dinner theater opens, Miss Maybelline plans to open the Total Look Beauty Spa, where people from around the world can come to rejuvenate themselves," he told the community. "Evelyn F. Williams's imagination is boundless, and the time for a Hollywood-style dinner theater in Hot Springs has come."

Evelyn prayed that he was right. And that he could keep out of trouble, at least until the Palace was successful and she could cut him loose and be done with him.

One evening, Evelyn was awakened in the middle of the night by loud music coming from Danie's quarters downstairs. It wasn't the first time this had happened. Pulling on a robe, she went down to tell him that this nonsense had to end.

The door to his room was unlocked. She pushed it open—and stood frozen in shock. Unfolding before her eyes in glistening flesh was an orgy worthy of ancient Rome: naked young men drinking, doing drugs, taking pictures of one another.

At first, none of them noticed her, then Danie finally looked up. She looked him straight in the eye. "Tomorrow," she said with as much of her old haughtiness as she could muster, "I'm taking you out of the will, the partnership in the Palace, and the partnership in Evdan Corporation." Then she turned and walked out.

The next day, she wrote a letter to my father.

Dear Son,

Honey, I want you to know how sorry I am for not following your advice about getting rid of Danie sooner. I know now what you were talking about as far as him having motives opposite mine concerning the Palace. I have found out some things about him that would make your hair stand on end, and because of that, I plan to cut him out of my will as soon as the Palace opens and dissolve my partnership with him in the Evdan Corporation. I hope this makes you happy because all I care about is your happiness.

Also, darling, as you requested, I have authorized Barry Winters to make you the sole executor of my estate when I die, which I hope won't be for a very long time, and with that, I pray you will make sure all the kids are provided for and taken care of, as that was Tom Lyle's wish.

These are the times we realize we love someone. Thank God. That's all I can say.

All my love,
Mud

The night of the grand opening of the Palace Dinner Theater—March 1, 1978—Danie was his usual charming self. He and Evelyn hadn't spoken about what she had seen, but he doubted she would actually follow through on the threats she had made. She still needed him.

Like right now, for example.

As curtain time approached, Danie worked his special magic with Evelyn's makeup and wig. When he was finished, he looked at his creation in the mirror and gushed, "Miss Maybelline, you've still got it!"

And Miss Maybelline looked at her reflection and smiled.

After Danie left the dressing room, Evelyn squeezed her torso into a corset, slipped her smooth white legs into a pair of silk stockings that attached to satin garters, wriggled into her black silk pants, buttoned up her sequined blazer, and placed a black-and-silver-sequined cowboy hat over her perfectly coiffed wig. Finally, she put on silver gloves, diamond earrings, and a necklace.

She looked like a million bucks.

Show time.

Fifty-Nine
Show Time

*N*ever had an affair been more glamorous.

Danie and Evelyn swept up to the canopy of the Palace Dinner Theater in her white El Dorado Biarritz. The valet said, "Welcome, Mrs. Williams, Mr. King," as he opened their doors. But they were not prepared for the crowds that met them. They had expected to make a big entrance, but they were swallowed up by the mob in the lobby, surrounded by hands thrust out to congratulate them. When they finally got on stage, Danie leaned close to Evelyn and said, "Miss Maybelline, you have never looked so beautiful."

And she saw in his eyes that he meant it.

She introduced Conway Twitty, who brought down the house down by singing, "Maybellene, why can't you be true?" Three hundred people cheered as Evelyn danced on stage, her silver sequins sparkling under the spotlight as Danie stood grinning beside her. She basked in the applause, all for her. This was it. This was the moment she had dreamt of all her life.

After taking their bows, Evelyn and Danie descended the stage together. Evelyn's arms overflowed with roses, and surrounding her was a crowd of Arkansas's most prominent citizens, expressing congratulations and goodwill. The Arkansas elite cheering her on, just as she had hoped.

At the end of the magical evening, back at the Maybelline Manor, Evelyn poured herself a vodka, swallowed a Valium, and changed out of her costume into a silk kimono. She sat down in her favorite chair and closed her eyes.

She thought about the important friendships she had made over the last year, and also the enemies. Those enemies included some of the finest townspeople, who resented her taking money away from their businesses, and worse, the business owners rumored to be connected to organized crime. Then there were those whose resentment stemmed from her association with Danie, who they had felt brought evil elements into their lives. In the end, Hot Springs, Arkansas, was a very small town.

But there were other things on her mind, too. Being on stage, standing in the bright hot lights with applause rising around her had been wonderful, yet now here she sat, all by herself. Fame and glory seemed awfully empty without the companionship of her beloved family.

It was three in the morning, and she heard Danie moving around in the living room. It sounded as if he was making a drink and talking with the houseboy, Pax. Another drink might help her sleep. She decided to join them, stopping to admire the many photos on the wall capturing her family history: a portrait of herself as a young girl with her parents, violin in hand; a picture of herself age twenty-two, arm in arm with her devilishly handsome husband Preston. Several shots of her as a beautiful young wife in Chicago; a glamorous widow in Hollywood; an extravagant grandmother in her bay-front home on Lido Isle. More shots of Bill and his children; and the largest photo of all, occupying a place of prominence in its embossed silver ornate frame: Evelyn as a beautiful young lady posing on the steps of Villa Valentino, gazing adoringly at Tom Lyle, still a handsome, elegant man with the pencil-line mustache she always remembered.

Pax excused himself when she appeared. Danie poured her a nightcap.

"Here's to the greatest night of our lives," he said.

She clinked glasses with him.

"I told you we'd create a showplace," he said. "I told you we'd be invincible together. And I was right, wasn't I?"

He went on trying to affirm his importance in her life, the success of the evening, and his role in it. But she could no longer brush off all the rumors, nor forget the personal letter, nor the obscenity she had witnessed firsthand. She knew she must make a choice: sever their relationship now or allow him to, sooner or later, destroy everything she had worked so hard for. "Danie," she said, interrupting his monologue.

"Yes, Evelyn?"

"I'd like you to move out of the house. As soon as possible."

"But . . . why? You can't do that to me. You invited me here. I've worked so hard for you. Where would I go?"

She sighed, too exhausted to think about it further. "All right, we'll discuss it in the morning, after I've read the reviews of the opening in the paper."

"They'll be incredible," Danie gushed. "You'll see." And he hurried off to bed.

Evelyn retreated to her own suite, climbing into her Queen Anne bed of red silk and satin. She lay there, tossing, but still wasn't tired. Finally, she gave up at four, arose, and checked all the doors to make sure they were locked. Outside, dark rain clouds moved across the stars. She closed the drapes and went into the guest bedroom, where she kept important papers, letters, and family pictures. She rummaged around until she found a favorite old letter from Tom Lyle, the only man who had been a good, true, constant presence in her life.

"You are an incredible force, my dear Evelyn," he had written. *"You always were, and you always will be. I've always believed in you."*

She read the letter, then held it to her heart. "I've always believed in you," she repeated to herself. "You'd be proud of me, Tom Lyle," she whispered. "I wish you were here. If only you knew how I missed you, and how hollow success feels without you."

Then she went back to bed.

At around one thirty in the afternoon the next day, two men stepped out of a stand of swamp pines and onto a winding, paved road near the shore of Lake Hamilton, Arkansas. Each man carried a five-gallon tin of gasoline, and headed toward Maybelline Manor. . . .

Sixty

Ashes, Ashes

*L*ate in the afternoon of March 2, I got a call from my dad. His voice was choked with rage. "Honey, they got her."

"Who got who?" I asked.

"Nana."

"Nana? What are you saying?"

"The bastards burned her house down."

"Well, she can rebuild it, can't she?"

"No, she was in it. She's dead; the bastards killed her."

"What?" I sat down on the bed.

"It was that bastard Danie King," my father said. "I know it was."

"Dead?" I said. "Nana? That can't be right."

I sat in the little chapel at Pacific View in Newport Beach, looking around at the family members who had gathered for Nana's memorial service. Somehow, I kept expecting to see Tom Lyle. If anyone should have been there, it was he.

My gaze kept returning to the two photos of Nana on display. Her body had been cremated—twice, really; first in the foyer of her home on Lake Hamilton, and then again at the crematorium. Soon her ashes would be placed in a mausoleum.

But for now, she stood among us in a pair of photographs. In my favorite, the one that really made me think of Miss Maybelline, she wore a black pantsuit with a red blouse and black hat with red plumes, and she had a foot propped up on a chair.

My father had had to fly to Arkansas to identify her. Gloria, Allen, and Jean had gone along, which was a good thing; in the end, Bill just couldn't go to the morgue, so Allen had had to handle that grim duty. Still, Bill remained in Hot Springs for a while to give the police whatever assistance they needed and to check into the status of his mother's estate.

Everything turned out to be as bad as he had feared.

"The house was a disaster," he told me when he got back to California. "That beautiful place, just gutted. The police say that Mother was found right by the front door. And you know what else? The doorknob came off in her hand. She had tried to get out, and the goddamned knob had been loosened. That's what the detectives say."

"So it was murder?" I shuddered.

"Of course it was. You know what I saw on the front lawn? Thirteen of Mother's wigs, still on their stands, strung out in a line. Smoke-damaged but not burned. Creepy. Set out there like some kind of a message. And that doorknob? Danie King says it was always loose. Everything else in the house is in perfect repair, but the front doorknob is ready to fall off? I don't believe it."

"You think it was Danie?"

"Or someone he hired. But the detectives, they say they can't even prove it was arson. There were two fires, they say, but one of them might have started in a pot of chicken left on the stove in the kitchen. Okay, fine, what about the other fire?"

"But what makes you think it was Danie?"

"I got sick in Hot Springs. For a while I was too sick to do anything, so Gloria took Mother's Eldorado and drove around to take care of some things. Well, one night these two cops pull her over and make her get out of the car, then search the whole interior for a gun."

"Why would they think Gloria had a gun?"

"Because Danie King told them she did—and was threatening to kill him. Gloria, for God's sake! Can you believe that? This scumbag murders my mother, then acts the victim. And that's not all."

"What else?"

"When I saw that the police weren't doing anything, I put ads in the local papers offering a reward. Next thing I know, King calls me and says that if I don't back off, he'll tell the newspapers that Nana was not only involved in his sex parties, she took pictures—and he's got proof."

"How can he get away with this? Will they investigate it as a homicide?"

Bill's laugh was bitter. "Probably not. I spoke with the mayor, a senator and the Secretary of State. They were all friends of my mother's, and they all agreed to help, and do you know what happened? Nothing. Except the senator invited me to watch Bill Clinton play the saxophone up at the governor's mansion and smoke a joint."

"So we're just going to let this go?"

"Allen and I talked about it, and yeah, that's all we can do. I could spend a fortune on private detectives, and it wouldn't make a damned bit of difference. No one is going to tell us the truth. We've got to pick our battles, and right now we have another one to fight out there."

"What's that?"

"Barry Winters submitted a Will that names him executor of her estate. I've got to go back out there and fight it in probate court. Not that I think it will do any good."

Although my father channeled his grief into anger at the authorities' refusal to investigate Nana's death, I was numb, in shock at my shattering, unexpected loss.

There was so much speculation about the fire and Evelyn's death that I tried to piece it together, going through her last moments time and time again. I've imagined it so often that I can almost see it as a movie, playing in my head. . . .

Evelyn wasn't sure what time it was when she woke up. The middle of the day, judging by the quality of the light and how terribly groggy she felt. What had awakened her? Shotguns blasts? Hunters in March? Not the best thing about Arkansas.

Before going to bed in the wee hours of the morning she had taken a sleeping pill—well, at least one sleeping pill—but it was clearly not enough. She really needed her sleep before preparing for tonight, her second night at the Palace. The second of what promised to be many exciting nights to come. Danie had been right: the entertainment critic in the paper had called the Palace Dinner Theater an "extraordinary success."

As she was lying back again, she heard the unmistakable, shivering crash of crystal breaking. Oh, God, was Danie having one of his infernal parties in the middle of the day now?

Sitting up again, she saw what looked like gray shadows flickering into the room through the crack above the door. She blinked, looked closer. Could that be . . . smoke?

Then she smelled it, that unmistakable biting stench, and alarm rose up in her. She fumbled her way out of bed and pulled on her satin robe. Above the door, the smoke flowed in, faster and blacker.

Although her room was only slightly elevated above the ground, it didn't occur to her to break the window and jump out onto the cushion of lawn outside. The tranquilizers sloshing in her blood took the edge off her concentration; all she could think was "Get out of here!"—and a door is, of course, the way out of a room.

She reached the door, pulled it open, and peered into Hell.

The majestic, cathedral-ceilinged living room at the far end of the hall was engulfed in flames.

"Danie?" she cried into the roar. No response. Smoke had filled the enormous space of the living room and was now creeping down the walls of the hallway. Inhaling smoke was what killed people in fires, she knew. Not the flames or the heat—the smoke.

Hunching over, her heart pounding with terror, she inched into the hall. She cringed as flames soared to the ceiling in the living room. Again she called out for Danie; again there was no answer. He was not there. The houseboy was not there. No one was coming to rescue her.

The smoke drifted lower, blocking out the light and seeping into her lungs. She plunged forward, coughing, clutching her gown closed. Where was the door? Flames erupted here, there, then she saw a five-foot gap in the lake of blazing gasoline; a walkway, a lifeline. She bolted down it, the heat singing her gown and her skin, and abruptly found herself in front of the door. Coughing, gagging, she grabbed the crystal doorknob and turned it.

The knob came off in her hand . . . the inferno closing in on her.

At the memorial service, tears running down my cheeks, I talked about a grandmother who, for all her caprices, wanted only the best of everything for herself and for everyone she loved. A grandmother who fought fiercely for her dreams, a woman who lived with gusto, who lived life on her own terms to the extent that she could.

Despite all the conflicts between Nana and me during my youth, I knew with the wisdom that comes with maturity that she had genuinely tried to create a world where her grandchildren could flourish, and live up to our aspirations. She did know us. She did listen to our dreams. She knew my brother Preston loved to play the drums, so she made sure that the very best instruments and equipment were provided for him at the Palace. She knew I loved the stage, so she dreamed I would someday follow in her footsteps as mistress of ceremonies at the club. Donna was the artist, so Nana imagined she would be in charge of all publicity and advertising, designing the stage and decorating the theater. And Billee the dancer, well, for her what could be more wonderful than a place filled with music, laughter, and fun, where she could show off her natural talent?

In my gratitude, I spoke to her directly. *"Nana, thank you for loving us as fiercely as you did, and especially for all the years of showing us your guts and gumption. You have set the bar pretty high for us, being ageless, timeless, and one of a kind. Our beloved Tom Lyle called you the real Miss Maybelline, and in our hearts and minds, that you will always be. Oh, we will miss you. We will miss you dearly."*

Back in Arkansas, it turned out my father was right about the probate court. Barry Winters had submitted a signed Will from Evelyn that named him her official executor, and my father's claims that the Will had been tampered with, or that Winters had never made the corrections in the Will that Evelyn had requested, were ignored.

Things could have been worse, though. The Will still bequeathed the Palace and all the property inside it to Preston. He also received the land on which Evelyn had planned to build her spa, as well as the six-acre estate on Lake Hamilton. Thanks to Evelyn, Preston would be one wealthy eighteen-year-old.

Danie King received forty-five thousand dollars and 25 percent of the Palace.

We girls were less fortunate. Evelyn had bequeathed us cash and stock, but under Arkansas law, before these assets could be dispersed, all outstanding debts had to be paid out of the available working capital. By the time all the creditors had submitted their bills—sometimes more than once—our inheritance was effectively wiped out.

No one was ever arrested for the arson at Maybelline Manor or the murder of Evelyn Francis Boecher Williams.

A few months after the memorial service, Nana's ashes were stolen from her mausoleum. My father was told that a Satanist who lived in the area was to blame, but of course Dad had his own suspect: Danie King, who had recently returned to Newport Beach and would soon disappear altogether.

Epilogue
(1980–Present)

*O*range County, Wednesday, October 27, 1993. At 11:15 a.m., a man parked at the entrance to Laguna Canyon stuffed rags into bottles filled with gasoline, ignited them, and tossed them into a stack of dry mesquite bushes. At 11:56 a.m., the first fire trucks arrived; by 12:08, a full ninety fire engines had been ordered to Laguna Beach as the blaze devoured acreage faster than the firemen could beat it back.

Acrid smoke turned the sun blood red. Hot dry Santa Ana winds shrieked at the Laguna Beach community, eclectic home of mega-millionaires, hippies, artists, and middle-class families. The onrushing flames terrified the residents, who had never dreamed the fire could muscle its way through the ravines and climb up to strike from hilltop to hilltop and roof to roof. People desperately scurried to save pets, documents, family pictures, heirlooms—and finally their own lives. Only the Pacific Ocean would stop this monster. News choppers captured hellish images that would tax Dante's imagination. Cauldrons of flame devoured homes; tornadoes of fire whirled in the twilight.

My little Spanish hacienda with its decades-old adobe bricks and roof of Moroccan tiles rested in what I thought of as a safe harbor. I had raised my daughter in this home and treasured it as my own special fortress—not to mention a museum of priceless family artifacts. In custom-built cases lay letters and personal mementos from my family's history at Maybelline on one side and MGM on the other: four generations' worth of memorabilia.

I hurriedly gathered up as much as I could. Within an hour, an eighty-foot wall of flame would build up such tremendous pressure and heat that my little house would explode into flames.

Fire gave, and fire took.

Day after day, I returned to the charred rubble that had been my home and dug around, searching for anything I could salvage from my life before the fire. Now and then, a remnant turned up, and I cried over the memories it generated: My daughter's baby soap dish, which had been in our bathroom since we had moved in twelve years before. A broken cup with the word "Lawyer" printed on it—my gift to Gene after he passed the bar, back when we were newly engaged. Another cup, still in perfect condition, from my wedding china. The broken china head of a doll from MGM that my grandfather MacDonald had given my mother when she was a girl. By the time I finished excavating, everything I could save fit comfortably into a little red shoe box. I held it to my chest.

Then I opened the safe.

It was buried in the floor of the garage, where I hoped it had escaped the worst of the fire. But when its door fell open, out poured a slurry of black watery ash and lumps of metal—all that remained of valuable coins and my most important private documents. But as a new wave of despair swelled over me, I saw a speck of pure white in the muck. Reaching down, I pulled out a tiny diamond ring in an art deco setting—the baby ring Unk Ile had given me at my birth. I held it up to the light, astonished. It was in perfect condition.

I cried. And cried. Then, gazing at it, I realized that like the ring, I, too, could survive. Events may seem to crush me, but I could arise anew, sparkling like a diamond. I could rebuild.

It was then that I finally felt strong. Resolved. Tenacity and courage flooded through me, for the first time in my life in fact. Suddenly I was free from a family steeped in history—one that had ruthlessly demanded conformity to its ways, ways that were so often destructive.

For decades I had struggled with issues of self-esteem and appearance, the result of my grandmother's indoctrination. And just like her—and my own mother for that matter—I had sought to tame those demons with prescription drugs. Burning inside me was an inferno of rage as powerful as the fire that had destroyed my home: rage at the childhood that was stolen from me; at the super-ficiality of the intense expectations heaped upon me; at the unnecessary suffering that I had endured, that my father had endured, and most especially, my mother had endured. And so with nothing else to do, with nothing left, I dug deep into my own being and vowed from then on to determine my own goals and needs and desires and responsibilities, and make a plan to achieve them.

The list was long. There were nutrition and fitness goals, and I wanted to go back to college to complete my degree—even if it meant graduating at age fifty-four. I wanted to be the best mother in the world to my beloved daughter. I wanted to rebuild my home. I wanted to reclaim my mother and make up for lost time. I wanted to find and place a headstone on Tony's unmarked grave. And I wanted to step out into the real world and find new friends and create a community with likeminded people. I wanted to reclaim the Spirit within me and commune with that Spirit. I wanted to become charitable and give back. And I wanted to share with others the wisdom I had gained from living primarily through the dreams of others. I had lived a lifetime of observation and reflection. Now I wanted to be a doer.

Finally, I have done all those things.

It's magnificent, yet painful, to look back. Certainly I am blessed with a legacy that is interesting and profound, even though the money we had come into all too suddenly from Tom Lyle's simple product called Maybelline unintentionally produced a disastrous effect on the family he loved so much.

One of my greatest heartaches is the result that living in our family had on my mother. It's safe to say that she was a long-term casualty of the Maybelline empire and dynasty. Thankfully, she is still alive, but she has lived in nursing homes for the last thirty years, ever since falling and breaking her knee at age sixty. I'll always think of her as the talented young woman who was forced to relinquish her aspirations in exchange for a long, cloistered life of slow loss. On the other hand, our years together since the destruction of my home have been nourishing and healing for her. For this, I am so grateful.

After Evelyn died, my father lived a charmed life. He married Gloria on New Year's Eve 1979, and she gave him stability and peace for more than twenty-five years, until his death in 2006. He was my confidant and a best friend for all my life. I still miss him immensely.

As for Nana herself, she was a woman ahead of her time; a woman of drive and determination, born in an era that associated femininity solely with physical beauty and domesticity. It was easy for me to rail at her when I was young, and resent her controlling ways. But with maturity, I understand her. I admire her. She was a woman who insisted on having it all—and almost did.

There is a lot of Nana in me. I'm a product of charm and grace, but there is a steely side, too. Like her, when I say I'm going to do something, it will get done. I survived a divorce, got healthy after twenty years of being constantly sick, and am now a grandmother myself. It's exactly the kind of thing she would have done.

My brother and two sisters have also strived to heal, each in their own way and in their own time. Their lives are sane and focused on things that matter.

As odd as it sounds, I am grateful for not only what was given to me, but what was taken away. I was finally forced to become a mature, independent individual, willing to carve out my own identity, to find my own path and calling.

Above all, I am grateful for the time I had with the elegant and gracious Tom Lyle Williams and to this wonderful cast of family characters for the journey that was mine to take. For all the ups and downs, for all the burdens and joys, for all the memories—good and bad—I am grateful for my legacy.

And it has been exciting to watch the Maybelline brand endure, and thrive. Tom Lyle sold his Maybelline in 1967 to Plough Inc. And in 1990 Maybelline was acquired by the investor group Wasserstein Perella & Co. Then, in 1996 L'Oréal USA, Inc. acquired Maybelline. In 2000 Maybelline became the number one cosmetic brand in the United States, and by 2002 Maybelline had become the number one cosmetic brand in the world!

Maybelline officially became Maybelline New York in 2001, and today, Maybelline New York is the number one cosmetic brand globally—and is in over 129 countries worldwide. Maybelline products are carried in virtually every major U.S. mass-market retailer including drugstores, discount stores, supermarkets and cosmetics specialty stores.

Surely Tom Lyle is smiling.

Book Club Discussion Questions

- Tom Lyle Williams, the founder of Maybelline, was an exemplar of the American virtues of thrift, determination, and hard work. But later, most members of his family became wealthy only because they were members of his family. How were they affected by turning into overnight millionaires? What is the significance of the fact that Tom Lyle himself tried to guide his family toward conservative financial planning? Have you ever come into money, and, if so, how did it affect you?

- As a young man, Tom Lyle was rejected by his community and, for a while, by his own family. How did this shape his determination and entrepreneurial spirit? How did it drive him to Chicago? If he had been accepted by the people of Morganfield, Kentucky—including the parents of his first love, Bennie Gibbs—what sort of man would he likely have become? How would you react to being ostracized by your peers?

- More than once, Tom Lyle lost everything. He lost out on living with his child and young bride. He lost his investment in his first business and, later, everything he had invested in Maybelline. How and why did he battle his way back to the top? What qualities drove him to persist, no matter what? Have you ever been knocked down and had to fight your way back up? Could you do it as many times as Tom Lyle did?

- From an early age, Tom Lyle worshipped beauty and perfection, standards that permeated the fabric of his business and his family. While the desire for beauty brought in a fortune, it came with a price. How did the philosophy "beauty hurts" play out in the lives of various generations of Maybelline women—Evelyn, Pauline, and Sharrie? How did seeking to become and remain beautiful affect their interactions with family, friends, and themselves? Do you agree with that philosophy, or do you believe that beauty is only skin deep?

- Despite pressure from all sides, Tom Lyle's brother Preston was the only member of the immediate family reluctant to become part of the business. What prompted his resistance? How did it play out as the years went by? If you were in a similar situation, would you join the business? Why or why not?

- In many important respects, Tom Lyle Williams's personal code of conduct came down to two words: family first. It led him to dispense and withhold power and protection based on blood ties. How did this affect the behavior of his brother Preston and his sister-in-law Evelyn? How did it affect the way he structured and ran the Maybelline Company? Were any nonrelatives ever treated like family? If so, why them? Do you believe that family is everything, or should other factors be taken into consideration?

- Preston and Evelyn's relationship was tempestuous, to say the least—yet, in the end, they both expressed love for one another. In what ways were they similar enough to be attracted to each other for all those years and through all that adversity, and in what ways did their differences pull them apart? How do you think you would react in a similar love/hate relationship?

- As she ages, Evelyn repeats several times that all she wants in return for the things she had done for her family members is their "love and respect," while her son disputes this, saying that the family has paid dearly for everything she has given them. Who do you think is correct? Might they both be? Have you ever questioned the motives of someone who has done something for you, and if so, why?

- Modern psychologists define someone suffering from narcissistic personality disorder as being extremely preoccupied with, and having an exaggerated sense of, oneself. Other symptoms include needing constant attention and admiration, disregarding the feelings of others, having trouble maintaining healthy relationships, taking advantage of others to achieve one's own goals, and expressing disdain for anyone seen as inferior. To what extent does Evelyn exhibit these traits? To what extent do any other members of the Williams clan? Have you ever been negatively affected by someone exhibiting these traits, and if so, how did you deal with it?

- How and why did Evelyn end up moving to Hot Springs? To what extent was the move a reaction against her own family and to what extent a genuine desire to start a new life on her own terms? What kind of life did she ultimately choose to create in Hot Springs, and why? Would you have done the same things? What would you do differently?

- In Hot Springs, Evelyn remade herself as Miss Maybelline. How much of this transformation was actually new, compared to how she had projected herself in Chicago and Los Angeles? To what extent do you believe she was promoting the beloved company that had given her riches and power, and how much to promoting herself at any cost?

- Evelyn's public persona in Hot Springs earned her the dislike of powerful people. Why? In what ways was Evelyn different from the many hustlers and entrepreneurs who came to that city in search of fame and fortune? Suppose you were warned to get out of town or else. Would you leave or stick it out?

- One of Evelyn's goals toward the end of her life was to bring her family to the new town that she seemed to rule. What were her motivations for trying to draw her grandchildren, in particular, to Hot Springs? Which of the kids were interested, and why? Would bribery work on you?

- The book proposes that Evelyn's death was the result of arson, which was one of the immediate conclusions of investigators. Later, the theory that the blaze began with an unattended pot in the kitchen became the dominant official explanation. Which theory seems more likely, given the circumstances? Why do you think the official explanation changed after state authorities stepped in? What reasons would authorities have to turn a murder into an accident?

About the Authors

SHARRIE LYNN WILLIAMS, heir to the Maybelline legacy and family steward of Maybelline's history, is the great-niece of Tom Lyle Williams—founder of the Maybelline Company—and granddaughter of his brother William Preston Williams and Preston's wife Evelyn Boecher Williams.

As a young woman, while pursuing a degree in theater arts, Sharrie acted in local theaters and appeared on the popular TV show *Dream Girl,* as well as in the film *Goodbye Norma Jean.* At the age of forty-five, she was divorced with a teenage daughter, and a wildfire razed her home, forcing her to realize that she needed to rebuild her life from the ground up. She returned to college to complete her degree in television production and screenwriting and produced a series of cable television shows. At age fifty-three she completed a degree in psychology.

A self-described avid health nut who practices yoga and meditation, today Ms. Williams's work centers on inspiring women to develop lifestyles that foster their talents so that they may pursue their dreams and live purpose-filled lives.

To contact Ms. Williams, visit www.MaybellineBook.com.

BETTIE B. YOUNGS, PHD, EdD, is the author of thirty-six books, which have been translated into twenty-eight languages. Her book *The House That Love Built: The Story of Millard and Linda Fuller, Founders of Habitat for Humanity* is an inspirational biography that was chosen as a "must read" by OprahSelects.com and has been acquired for film production. Dr. Youngs is a former Teacher-of-the-Year and a former professor of graduate studies at SDSU. Bettie has been a guest on television and radio talk shows, including *The Today Show, NBC Nightly News, CNN, Oprah,* and *Good Morning America.* Her work has been recognized in publications including *Time, U.S. News & World Report, USA Today,* the *Washington Post, Redbook,* and *Working Woman.* Currently, she is founder and CEO of Bettie Youngs Publishing Co., a house that specializes in publishing memoirs and bringing them to film.

To contact: www.BettieYoungsBooks.com or info@BettieYoungsBooks.com.

Other Books by Bettie Youngs Books Publishing Co.

Out of the Transylvania Night

Aura Imbarus

In an epic tale of identity and the indomitable human spirit, OUT OF THE TRANSYLVANIA NIGHT explores tyranny, freedom, love, success, and the price paid for misaligned dreams. An incredibly powerful memoir.

"I'd grown up in the land of TRANSYLVANIA, homeland to Dracula, Vlad the Impaler, and, worse, the Communist dictator, Nicolae Ceaușescu—who turned Romania into a land of gray-clad zombies who never dared to show their individuality, and where neighbors became informants, and the Securitate made people disappear. Daylight empowered the regime to encircle us like starved wolves, and so night had always been the time to steal a bit of freedom. As if bred into our Transylvanian blood, we were like vampires who came to life after sundown. I buried the family jewels, tucked the flag into my sweater and left my outpost to join the action . . . tonight Ceaușescu would die!"

Known for using stand-ins to pose for him, Aura doubts if it was even Ceaușescu himself who was killed that night. Nevertheless, when her country-men topple one of the most draconian regimes in the Soviet bloc, Aura Imbarus tells herself that life post-revolution will be different. But little in the country changes. With two pieces of luggage and a powerful dream, Aura and her new husband flee to America. Through sacrifice and hard work, the couple acquire a home, cars, and travel—but trying to be Americans is much more complicated than they expect. More difficulties set in; the stock market crash takes their savings, house, and cars; thieves steal three centuries' worth of heirloom jewels; and Aura's beloved mother dies.

Aura's marriage crumbles under the stress. Devastated, she asks herself, "How much of one's life is owed to others?" Tested even further by the vagaries of fate, Aura discovers a startling truth about striking a balance between one's dreams and the sacrifices and compromises that allow for serenity, selfhood, and lasting love. More resolution comes when in 2010, Ceaușescu's body is exhumed to answer questions of a cover-up, and Aura can fnally lay to rest the haunting mysteries of her past.

> Aura's courage shows the degree to which we are all willing to live lives centered on freedom, hope, and an authentic sense of self. Truly a love story!
> —**Nadia Comaneci, Olympic gold medalist**

> If you grew up hearing names like Tito, Mao, and Ceaușescu but really didn't understand their significance, read this book!
> —**Mark Skidmore, Paramount Pictures**

> This book is sure to find its place in memorial literature of the world.
> —**Beatrice Ungar, editor-in-chief, *Hermannstädter Zeitung***

ISBN: 978-0-9843081-2-5 • $14.95

In bookstores everywhere or from the publisher:
www.BettieYoungsBooks.com

On Toby's Terms

Charmaine Hammond

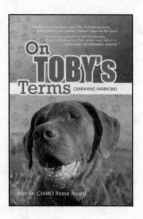

When Charmaine and her husband adopted Toby, a five-year-old Chesapeake Bay retriever, they figured he might need some adjusting time, but they certainly didn't count on what he'd do in the meantime. Soon after he entered their lives and home, Toby proved to be a holy terror who routinely opened and emptied the hall closet, turned on water taps, pulled and ate things from the bookshelves, sat for hours on end in the sink, and spent his days rampaging through the house. Oddest of all was his penchant for locking himself in the bathroom, and then pushing the lid of the toilet off the tank, smashing it to pieces. After a particularly disastrous encounter with the knife-block in the kitchen—and when the couple discovered Toby's bloody paw prints on the phone—they decided Toby needed professional help. Little did they know what they would discover about this dog. On Toby's Terms is an endearing story of a beguiling creature who teaches his owners that, despite their trying to teach him how to be the dog they want, he is the one to lay out the terms of being the dog he needs to be. This insight would change their lives forever.

Simply a beautiful book about life, love, and purpose.
—Jack Canfield, Co-author *Chicken Soup for the Soul*

A touching portrait of a remarkable dog. If you're looking for a feel-good story, this is it.
—Jamie Hall, *The Edmonton Journal*

In a perfect world, every dog would have a home and every home would have a dog—like Toby!
—Nina Siemaszko, actress, *The West Wing*

This is a captivating, heartwarming story and we are very excited about bringing it to film.
—Steve Hudis, Producer, IMPACT Motion Pictures

ISBN: 978-0-9843081-4-9 • $14.95

In bookstores everywhere or from the publisher:
www.BettieYoungsBooks.com

Diary of a Beverly Hills Matchmaker

Marla Martenson

The inside scoop from the Cupid of Beverly Hills, who has brought together countless couples who have gone on to live happily ever after. But for every success story there are ridiculously funny dating disasters with high-maintenance, out-of-touch, impossible to please, dim-witted clients!

Marla takes her readers for a hilarious romp through her days as an LA matchmaker and her daily struggles to keep her self-esteem from imploding in a town where looks are everything and money talks. From juggling the demands her out-of-touch clients, to trying her best to meet the capricious demands of an insensitive boss, to the ups and downs of her own marriage to a Latin husband who doesn't think that she is "domestic" enough, Marla writes with charm and self-effacement about the universal struggles all women face in their lives. Readers will laugh, cringe, and cry as they journey with her through outrageous stories about the indignities of dating in Los Angeles, dealing with overblown egos, vicariously hobnobbing with celebrities, and navigating the wannabe-land of Beverly Hills. In a city where perfection is almost a prerequisite, even Marla can't help but run for the Botox every once in a while.

Marla's quick wit will have you rolling on the floor.
—**Megan Castran, international YouTube Queen**

Sharper than a Louboutin stiletto, Martenson's book delivers!
—**Nadine Haobsh,** *Beauty Confidential*

Martenson's irresistible wit is not to be missed.
—**Kyra David,** *Lust, Loathing, and a Little Lip Gloss*

ISBN: 978-0-9843081-0-1 • $14.95

In bookstores everywhere or from the publisher:
www.BettieYoungsBooks.com

Bettie Youngs Books

We specialize in MEMOIRS
. . . books that celebrate
fascinating people and
remarkable journeys

VISIT OUR WEBSITE AT
www.BettieYoungsBooks.com
email: info@BettieYoungsBooks.com